W9-BSZ-206

Dreams in Steel
From a photograph by W. M. Rittase

CORRECT ENGLISH

Second Course

By

WILLIAM M. TANNER

Author of "Composition and Rhetoric"

GINN AND COMPANY

COPYRIGHT, 1931, BY WILLIAM M. TANNER

ALL RIGHTS RESERVED

PRINTED IN THE UNITED STATES OF AMERICA

436.4

GINN AND COMPANY

BOSTON · NEW YORK · CHICAGO · LONDON
ATLANTA · DALLAS · COLUMBUS · SAN FRANCISCO

This book is intended to follow *Correct English, First Course,* or a similar textbook. Though resembling in some respects the author's *Composition and Rhetoric,* this is essentially a new book, containing, for the most part, new text, new selections, and new exercises. The relatively small amount of material taken over from the earlier book has been thoroughly revised and rewritten.

It is assumed that the pupil has acquired through his previous study a sufficient mastery of the mechanics of composition to warrant placing primary emphasis in this book on the development of ability to speak and write effectively. Ample provision is made, however, for pupils who need review or require further instruction and drill in sentence structure, functional grammar, word study, punctuation, spelling, and the essentials of good form. The book provides equally for those pupils who will later enter college and for those whose study of English will end with their graduation from the high school.

Effective self-expression, the goal of all successful speaking and writing, demands that the pupil develop self-reliance and confidence through proper self-cultivation. Recognizing this fact, the author has given principal consideration to five points.

1. Interest. The book is written throughout from the pupil's point of view and is addressed directly to him. His personal interests, his ambitions, his experience, his practical needs, and his creative ability have governed the choice of specimens and illustrations, the making of the exercises, and the scope and variety of composition

iii

activities. Better English for immediate use is emphasized. The specimen compositions by other high-school pupils stimulate the pupil to do his best to equal, if not to surpass, the achievements of these young writers.

2. Motivation. In all speaking and writing, something to say and a definite purpose to be achieved in saying it constitute the natural motivation. The selections included in this book, most of which have been chosen from the writings of reputable modern authors or of high-school pupils, are intended to stimulate interested endeavor. To as great an extent as possible, the exercises are definitely motivated. A large number of them function directly in situations common in the home, school, and community life of the pupil. There are many assignments in which the pupil is encouraged and guided in writing for his school newspaper or magazine. At appropriate places exercises in writing verse have been provided. A chapter on the writing of the short story and another on dramatizing stories and writing short plays challenge the pupil's creative ability. For pupils who possess more than usual talent there are a number of "extra credit" exercises. Throughout the book pupils are encouraged to speak for an audience instead of merely giving talks, and to write for readers instead of merely writing compositions.

3. Clear thinking. Few pupils have learned to think clearly. The approach to planning and writing original compositions is made natural and easy through practice in speaking and in retelling in the pupil's own words what another person has said. The making of an outline as an aid to clear thinking is taught (1) by analyzing specimens to discover the author's plan, (2) by arranging lists of topics in the form of an orderly outline, and (3) by constructing original outlines. In planning his earlier compositions, the pupil is guided by specific questions and suggestions. Précis writing likewise develops in the pupil the ability to think more clearly.

4. Mastery of the mechanics of composition. Until a pupil has mastered the mechanics of composition, he is seriously handicapped in his efforts to speak and write effectively. The oral and written activities of Part One and Part Two will help him to discover his deficiencies and will provide him with the means of overcoming them. The intelligent use of Part Four for reference will give him a fair mastery of the mechanics of speaking and writing.

5. Critical ability. Much attention is devoted to developing in the pupil the ability to criticize his own work. Many exercises contain questions and other specific directions to guide him in detecting and correcting errors in his compositions and those of his classmates. Analysis of specimens and group discussions of the oral and written work of the class train him in giving fair and accurate criticisms.

The devices by means of which the pupil gains instruction are varied and economical. Textbook explanation has been limited to the essentials. Every important point is illustrated by one or more examples. Through the study of specimens, through practice exercises, and through accurately directed group discussion the pupil learns much. Preliminary discussions preceding certain chapters afford him a preview of the subject to be taken up. Test exercises enable him to diagnose his needs and help him to direct his efforts properly in supplying them. Through achievement tests he is able to estimate how much he has actually learned. Most important of all, the numerous and varied exercises in creative speaking and writing develop in him greater power of expression.

The book may be easily adapted to a wide variety of courses of study. The organization provides for the utmost flexibility in use, and a wealth of exercises affords the teacher unusual latitude in choice of material.

⬛⬛⬛⬛⬛◄ ACKNOWLEDGMENTS ►⬛⬛⬛⬛⬛

Grateful acknowledgment is made to D. Appleton & Company, for selection from Jordan and Kellogg's "Animal Life"; Brandt and Brandt, for "The Pear Tree," copyright, 1919, by Edna St. Vincent Millay; The Century Co., for selections from Collingwood's "Life and Letters of Lewis Carroll," Fulcher's "Descriptive Passages," Gorky's "In the World," all copyrighted by The Century Co.; Chatto and Windus, for selections from Stevenson's "Walking Tours," "Essays," "An Inland Voyage," and "El Dorado"; Dodd, Mead & Company, Inc., for "The Convent Free from Care" from Bosschere's "Christmas Tales of Flanders," used by permission of Dodd, Mead & Company, Inc.; Doubleday, Doran and Company, for selections from Bennett's "The Old Wives' Tale," Conrad's "Lord Jim," Ferber's "Cheerful by Request," Morley's "The Romany Strain," Norris's "The Octopus," Ollivant's "Bob, Son of Battle," Helen Keller's "The Story of My Life"; Funk and Wagnalls Company, for selection from Bruce's "Self-Development"; Ginn and Company, for selections from "The Herford Æsop," Stickney's "Æsop's Fables," Gowin, Wheatley, and Brewer's "Occupations," Hill's "Community and Vocational Civics," Gruenberg's "Biology and Human Life," Carver and Carmichael's "Elementary Economics"; Harper & Brothers, for "Etiquette" from Guiterman's "The Laughing Muse"; Harr Wagner Publishing Company, for Bashford's "Morning in Camp"; Houghton Mifflin Company, for selections from Bates's "Talks on Writing English," Forbes's "The Romance of Business," Hawthorne's "The Great Stone Face," Husband's "America at Work," Mills's "The Spell of the Rockies," Repplier's "Essays in Idleness," poems by Longfellow and Lowell, used by permission of, and by arrangement with, Houghton Mifflin Company; Alfred A. Knopf, Inc., for selection from Cather's "Youth and the Bright Medusa"; Little, Brown & Company, for selections from Thurber's "The Value of Précis Writing," Merwin's "Dogs and Men" from "Atlantic Classics," Tanner's "Essays and Essay Writing" and "How I Teach Essays and Essay Writing"; The Macmillan Company, for selection from Zangwill's "The Red Mark"; The Macmillan Co. of Canada, Limited, for selection from London's "The Call of the Wild"; Mrs. Macy, for selection from Matthews's "Vignettes of Manhattan"; Hughes Mearns, for selections from "Creative Youth" published by Doubleday, Doran and Company; G. & C. Merriam Company, for précis of "Jack and the Beanstalk" adapted from Webster's Dictionary, Knott's "Carving Your Speech"; National Council for Prevention of War, for "Joan of Arc" from "Portfolio of World Heroes"; Lloyd Osbourne, for selections from "Treasure Island" and "Letters of Robert Louis Stevenson"; James B. Pinker and Son, for selections from Bennett's "The Old Wives' Tale" and Conrad's "Lord Jim"; Quill and Scroll, for selection from "Best Creative Work in American High Schools"; The Scholastic Publishing Co., for pupil theme "The Casein Industry"; Charles Scribner's Sons, for selections from Galsworthy's "The Consummation" and "The Forsyte Saga," Matthews's "Parts of Speech," Van Dyke's "Poems," and selections from the works of R. L. Stevenson; Frederick A. Stokes Company, for selection from Atherton's "The Splendid Idle Forties"; and Mrs. Zangwill, for selection from "The Red Mark."

To the following the author is indebted for selections from school papers: High School, Aberdeen, South Dakota; Walnut Hills High School, Cincinnati, Ohio; Classical High School, Lynn, Massachusetts; William Penn High School for Girls, Philadelphia, Pennsylvania; Girls' High School, Atlanta, Georgia; St. Joseph's Academy, St. Paul, Minnesota; Eastern High School, Baltimore, Maryland.

Acknowledgment is made also to the following: *The Boston Herald*; *The Boston Evening Transcript*; *The News and Courier*, Charleston, South Carolina; *American Boy*; *McClure's Magazine*; *Outlook and Independent*; also to the Curtis Publishing Company for the use of the picture on page 473, reproduced by special permission from the *Saturday Evening Post* of Philadelphia.

vi

................◀ CONTENTS ▶................

PART TWO. THE UNITS OF COMPOSITION: THE PARAGRAPH,
THE SENTENCE, AND THE WORD

PART THREE. TYPES OF SPEAKING AND WRITING

CORRECT ENGLISH · SECOND COURSE

The Whole Composition: a Gradual Approach to the Writing of Original Compositions

EFFECTIVE SPEAKING AND WRITING

THUS far in your life you have learned many facts. Through imitation of others, without much conscious effort, you learned to speak and to write and to do various other things. The most valuable part of your education has come, however, as it must continue to come, not through unconscious imitation, but through effort consciously directed to achieve a definite purpose. Your previous study of English has acquainted you with many of the fundamental principles that govern effective speaking and writing. To be most useful, your knowledge of English must be applied in all your communications with others, whether oral or written.

Your own attitude will determine your progress in the use of English. Unless you realize your need for better English and work to achieve it, you cannot hope to improve. To be content to "get by" is fatal to your progress; you must resolve and then labor to "get ahead." Effective speaking and writing cannot be "caught," unconsciously, through imitation, or "taught" in the English class; they must be "learned" through self-cultivation, daily practice, and intelligent self-criticism.

Part One of this book will help you to think more clearly, to choose and arrange the material for your compositions properly, and to express your thoughts effectively. It will show you how you may learn from more experienced speakers and writers. It will afford you abundant practice in applying what you learn. Most important of all, it may lead you to realize that the rules and principles of composition are nothing more than applied common sense.

CHAPTER I

Effective Speaking

1. Importance of Speaking Well

Most of us speak a hundred times more frequently than we write. Every day we engage in conversations with relatives and friends. We often take part in informal discussions at club and society meetings. In school we make recitations in our various subjects and give talks before our schoolmates. Speech is, in fact, our principal means of communication during both our school days and later life.

If we desire to speak well, we must watch our everyday conversation. In this most of us are careless. We are content to suggest a fraction of our meaning, and then, with some such pitiable acknowledgment of our laziness and inability as "Oh, you know what I mean," we leave the other person to guess the rest. The result is that when occasions arise on which we wish to speak well, we often fail to make ourselves understood or to get what we want, because we cannot say clearly what we mean. We make an unsatisfactory recitation in history, civics, science, mathematics, or literature, not because we have failed to prepare the assignment but because we cannot state accurately what we have learned. We apply for a desirable position, but we are unsuccessful for the reason that we use slovenly English and consequently are unable to set forth our qualifications adequately or to impress an employer favorably. It is only by daily practice in speaking well that we can effect any real improvement in our speech.

3

Ability to speak clearly, correctly, and effectively should be our goal. The mastery of English as a tool, the development of skill in the use of our language, comes chiefly through daily practice in oral expression. And good speech, we should realize, lays the foundation for good writing.

Exercise 1

A. Consider thoughtfully the following situations and discuss with regard to each the extent to which your ability to speak clearly, correctly, and effectively would determine your success:

1. Giving directions to someone.
2. Applying for a position.
3. Acting as chairman of your class.
4. Nominating a classmate for some office.
5. Petitioning the principal to let you change your schedule.

B. Make a list of at least five other situations in which your ability to speak well would help you to get what you wanted.

Exercise 2

Select for consideration some pupil who has won marked success of some kind because of his or her ability to speak well. Without mentioning any name, give the class your idea of just what qualities make the conversation of this pupil successful.

Exercise 3

What is your present choice of a business or professional career? Point out to the class the value that ability to speak well will be to you in this business or profession.

Exercise 4

Organize your class into a permanent "Better-Speech Club." Select each week a committee of three pupils, to whom the other members of the class may hand in, on slips of paper, errors in speech heard in the classroom, on the playground, on the street, or elsewhere. No names need be mentioned. At a class period once each week these errors may be read by members of the committee, and others in the class may be called on to explain the errors and correct them.

Exercise 5

After a member of the class has been appointed chairman, discuss for one class period the qualities of good conversation. Here are a few questions that may help to start the discussion:

Who is the most interesting talker in your group of friends? (No name need be mentioned.) What does he talk about? Are the subjects that he chooses unusual, or do they merely seem unusual because of the manner in which they are presented? Does this person talk most about his own affairs and interests, or about things that you enjoy and understand? Does he do all the talking himself, or does he encourage other persons to talk also? Is he a good listener? Do your friend's posture, facial expression, and manner of speaking add anything to the attractiveness of his conversation? What is the quality of his voice? What makes it pleasing? Does he use good English? Does he use slang at all? If so, to what extent and in what way? Is his conversation well adapted to the other person or persons? Does his conversation help to express his personality? If so, in what ways? What other qualities can you mention?

When several pupils have discussed these and other questions, the chairman or some other member of the class may summarize briefly the necessary qualities of a good conversationalist.

Exercise 6

With a classmate hold a conversation in class that will illustrate the qualities of a good conversation discussed in Exercise 5. It will be well for you and your classmate to decide in advance upon the topic that you will talk about and to practice your conversation at least once outside of class. Such topics as the following might be used :

1. Two girls discuss a novel or a play.
2. A boy and a girl discuss a recent social affair.
3. Two boys discuss some vacation experience.
4. Two girls discuss the new styles in dress.
5. Two boys sitting on the substitutes' bench discuss the game being played.

Exercise 7

Think of three persons with whom you frequently talk over the telephone. (No names need be given.) What telephone habits, good and bad, can you mention as characteristic of each one? With which one of them is it most difficult to carry on a conversation? Why? Is any one of them ever discourteous, either consciously or unconsciously? In what way?

Following this discussion, summarize briefly what you consider good telephone manners.

Exercise 8

With a classmate hold an imaginary conversation over the telephone. Begin by calling the operator, who may be impersonated by a third member of the class. Such topics as the following might be used :

1. Finding out a class assignment.
2. Inviting a friend to visit you.
3. Telling a friend a bit of good news.
4. Making an engagement for some social affair.
5. Apologizing for some act of thoughtlessness.

2. Essentials of Speaking Well

Informal speaking, such as conversation, requires little, if any, previous thought or preparation. When we speak more formally, however, as in giving a talk before the class or at the assembly, we find it necessary to choose in advance a specific subject, to plan carefully what we shall say, and to practice giving the talk until we can deliver it effectively. In the following sections we shall consider briefly the six essentials of speaking well.

3. The First Essential: Something to Say

How we dread to have to say something when we have nothing to say! How we suffer and how we bore others! Such suffering and boredom are unnecessary if we select our subject with proper care. The following suggestions should help us to make a wise and accurate choice:

1. The best subject is one that you fully understand. It should be thoroughly familiar to you from personal experience, observation, or reading, supplemented, if necessary and permissible, by well-governed imagination.
2. Your subject should be so limited that your information may be presented adequately in the time that is yours.
3. It should be one that interests you greatly and about which you have decided opinions or feel strongly.
4. It should be one that arouses in you a genuine enthusiasm to present it clearly and entertainingly to others.
5. It should be one that will interest your hearers or readers.
6. It should be not merely a good subject but the *best* subject.

4. Limiting the Subject

Suppose that we have the following list of topics from which to select a subject for a short talk before the class:

1. Outdoor Sports.
2. Motion Pictures.
3. Insect Pests.
4. Costume Designing.
5. Manual Training.
6. George Washington.

As we look over these topics, we may discover that we know something about each of them, but not enough about any one of them to deal with it satisfactorily. Each topic in its present form is too large and general to be discussed in a brief talk, even if we had adequate information about it. By a little ingenuity we may derive from each topic, however, several *limited* subjects, such as the following:

1. How to Throw Curves.
2. Why I Like Basket Ball.
3. The Power of an Umpire.
4. Motion Pictures in the Study of Geography.
5. Advertising by Means of Motion Pictures.
6. Recording Vacation Pleasures in Motion Pictures.
7. How the Mosquito Carries Malaria.
8. The House Fly as an Enemy of Good Health.
9. The Use of Sprays in the Growing of Apples.
10. Why I Wish to Be a Costume Designer.
11. How I Made my Last Party Dress.
12. An Interesting Project in My Sewing Class.
13. How to Make a Bookrack.
14. An Amusing Toy That I Made.
15. How to Make Animal Silhouettes of Wood.
16. George Washington's Smile.
17. The Trait That I Most Admire in Washington.
18. An Unusual Washington's Birthday Party.

Exercise 9

In accord with the suggestions given in section 3 and the illustrations provided in section 4, derive from each of the following general subjects at least one limited subject that you could treat satisfactorily in a short talk:

1. School Games.
2. Vacation Camps.
3. Training Animals.
4. Photography.
5. Electricity.
6. Salesmanship.
7. Boy Scouts.
8. Domestic Science.
9. Great Inventions.

Exercise 10

Guided by the suggestions given in section 3 and the illustrations provided in section 4, derive from each of the following sources two limited subjects that you could treat adequately in a short talk:

1. Personal experience and observation.
2. Subjects studied in school.
3. School athletics and contests of various kinds.
4. Occupations, interests, and amusements of your family.
5. Individual interests, ambitions, and hobbies.
6. Economic and social life of your town or community.
7. Radio talks and public lectures.
8. Newspapers, magazines, and books.
9. Nature and outdoor life.
10. Science and invention.

5. The Second Essential: a Definite Purpose

Whenever we speak, we do so to inform, to convince or persuade, or to entertain others. In addition to such general purposes as these, effective expression demands that we have an immediate valid reason for speaking, a definite end to be achieved by what we say. In every talk we should have clearly in mind just what it is we are trying to accomplish; otherwise, we shall fail to get the results that we desire.

A proper consideration of our hearers will aid us greatly in attaining our purpose. In our choice of a subject and in the preparation of our talk we should be governed by their point of view, the extent of their information about our subject, and their interests. Unless we arouse their interest and make it easy and pleasant for them to get our precise meaning, we shall fall short of accomplishing our purpose.

Exercise 11

Consider carefully each of the subjects listed below and state which one of the following purposes would guide you in giving a talk on each subject: Would you seek to inform your hearers? Would you try to convince or persuade them? Would you endeavor to entertain them?

1. Why Our School Should Have a Glee Club.
2. How Our School Bank Is Conducted.
3. My Favorite Outdoor Sport.
4. A Memorable Masquerade Party.
5. Getting Advertisements for the School Paper.

Exercise 12

Make a list of ten good limited subjects and state after each which one of the purposes given in Exercise 11 would guide you in making a talk on it.

6. The Third Essential: Clearness of Thought

Our success in speaking depends largely on the clearness of our thinking. If we are inexperienced, we are likely to fail to make ourselves clear for one or more of five reasons: (1) we do not give our audience a clear, concise statement at the beginning as to what our talk is to be about; (2) we fail to follow a natural or logical order in taking up the details or incidents of our talk; (3) we use too many vague, general terms instead of specific words; (4) we bring in unimportant, if not irrelevant, details; and (5) we omit entirely some important details.

Exercise 13

In the following groups of sentences, which of the five errors given in section 6 are responsible for the lack of clearness in the first paragraph? What definite changes have been made in the second paragraph?

How to Reach My Home from the Station

1. I live about five or six blocks from the station. To get to my home you go down the street until you come to a street that goes over a bridge. This bridge was rebuilt a few years ago to take the place of an old wooden one that used to be there. This one is of concrete. My grandfather helped build the first bridge. Then go along the right side of the street till you come to a street with an old brick house on the corner. I live just about halfway up the block from the corner. The house has just been painted.

2. I live six blocks from the station. When you come out of the front door of the station, you will find yourself on Main Street. Walk up Main Street one block to Magnolia Avenue. Here turn to your right and walk three blocks to a cross street marked "Sycamore." Then turn to your left on Sycamore Street and walk two blocks to the corner of Linden Avenue. The second house from this corner, on the right side of Linden Avenue, is my home.

Exercise 14

For which of the reasons given in section 6 does the following answer of Mrs. Brown's lack clearness? What changes would you make in the order? How much of Mrs. Brown's reply is necessary to answer the lawyer's question? Reword Mrs. Brown's answer in good form.

LAWYER. Are you sure that the house was robbed on Wednesday?

MRS. BROWN. Yes, sir, I'd just stepped over to Mrs. Davis's a minute to borrow a bit of yeast for my baking. Her husband won't eat a bite o' bread that's baked with store yeast. You know, all the Davises are queer. His father was the one who wouldn't ever paint his house, though I'm not sure but that he was right, for an old building like his was hardly worth painting. Our woodshed is just about as bad as his house, if you come right down to it. Well, before I started baking I went into the shed to get Mr. Brown's old coat; he is always so absent-minded, leaving his things around everywhere. I 'most always bake bread on a Wednesday, you know. Yes, I'm sure it was Wednesday.

Exercise 15

Come to class prepared to give some of the following directions. Do not write them out, but think over carefully what you will say.

1. Direct a friend from your school to your home.
2. Direct a stranger from your school to the railroad station.
3. Direct a visitor that you have met outside the schoolhouse to the principal's office.
4. Direct a stranger to the nearest tourist camp.
5. Tell a friend how to reach a certain place where you will meet him.

The following questions will help other members of the class to estimate the effectiveness of your talk: Did the speaker state clearly in the first sentence what he was going to talk about? Did he take up details in their proper order? Did he use specific words throughout? Did he introduce any unnecessary or unrelated details? Did he omit any necessary details? What was the speaker's purpose in giving the talk? Did he make this purpose clear? Were the directions so clear that you could easily follow them yourself? What other criticism of the talk can you offer?

Exercise 16

Explain in a short talk how some simple game is played. The class will estimate your success by answering the questions given in Exercise 15.

Exercise 17

Tell the class how to train some pet animal to perform a trick, or give a recipe for preparing some article of food. The questions given in Exercise 15 will aid the class in estimating your success.

Exercise 18. Extra Credit

A. Bring to class a copy of a road map showing the route of an automobile trip you have taken recently. If possible, copy the map on the blackboard. Be ready to explain in class each step in the trip and to explain the meaning of each symbol on the map. You will be judged on the talk according to your success in meeting the requirements set down in Exercise 15 and in section 6.

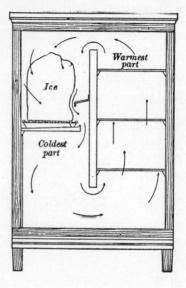

B. Here is a drawing [1] which shows the movement of air currents in a refrigerator. Explain the meaning of the arrows and the principle of air movements they illustrate.

Exercise 19

Read aloud each of the short talks printed below. Is the subject of each talk, as stated in the title, properly limited? What is the purpose of each talk? Which talk has the better beginning and ending? Which do you consider the better talk? Explain your answer.

How to Throw Curves

In throwing the outcurve the pitcher usually grasps the ball with the first two fingers and the thumb. The third finger is sometimes used to steady the ball. The hand is turned downward,

[1] From Caldwell and Eikenberry's "Elements of General Science, with Experiments."

and the ball is allowed to pass between the thumb and the first finger. This imparts a rotary motion which causes the curve. The arm must be swung around the side of the body, a movement which is known as the side, or underhand, delivery. If the arm is swung over the body at about halfway between horizontal and vertical, the result will be an outdrop. If the arm is swung directly over the body, the result will be a drop. In throwing the incurve the pitcher grasps the ball in exactly the same manner as in throwing the outcurve, but the ball is allowed to roll off the ends of the fingers instead of passing between the thumb and the first finger. The incurve may be thrown either with the side delivery or with the overhand delivery. A "spit ball" is a ball moistened on one side with saliva. It is thrown by gripping the ball and swinging the arm in the same manner as would be used for any of the curves just explained. Because of the moistened side the ball moves with greater speed, and the resulting curve is more uncertain.

George Washington's Smile

Many people have noticed and commented on the peculiar smile in numerous pictures and busts of George Washington. This smile has an interesting story back of it. After the Revolution, a sculptor went to Mount Vernon to make a plaster of Paris bust of Washington. The sculptor stretched him out on a cot, daubed his features with oil, and applied the plaster of Paris. A few moments later, when the plaster was beginning to harden, Martha Washington entered the room. Seeing her husband lying on the cot and noting the deathlike pallor of his face, she screamed with fright. Her scream caused Washington to smile, and when the plaster was removed, the impression of the smile had been recorded in it. Today many of the lithographed pictures of Washington. which are copies of this bust, bear this peculiar smile.

Exercise 20

Prepare a short talk on the *best* limited subject that you devised in Exercise 9 or 10. Plan your talk carefully. If necessary, make a few brief notes to aid you, but do not write out what you intend to say.

7. The Value of an Outline in Planning a Talk

In our efforts to think clearly and to present our subject in an orderly manner, we shall find that the first step is the making of an outline. The plan of the short talks that we have given thus far we have been able to carry in our minds. For our longer oral and written compositions, however, it will be necessary for us to write out our plan in the form of a brief outline.

If we have chosen a familiar subject and have limited it properly, we should have little difficulty in choosing the necessary material and in discovering a natural or logical order of grouping the details. Since every composition should be a complete treatment of the subject selected, we should use care in choosing the points at which to begin and end. Few, if any, of our compositions will require a formal introductory paragraph. Usually a sentence or two stating what our talk is to be about will furnish sufficient introduction. Likewise, we shall rarely need a formal concluding paragraph, though a sentence or two rounding out and completing our talk is often felt to be necessary.

The three suggestions that follow will guide us in planning our compositions:

1. Select only material that belongs to the subject, but do not omit anything that is important.
2. Arrange this material according to its proper time, space, or logical relationship, so that your composition will be orderly and clear.
3. Begin directly, but naturally and clearly, and stop as soon as you have presented your subject.

When we have devised a satisfactory outline, we have completed more than half of the preparation for our talk; by this planning, we shall save time and insure better results.

Study closely the simple outlines printed below. Notice that each numbered topic is a division of the subject stated in the title. Try to discover from a study of these outlines the principles governing the orderly arrangement of material. You may refer to these outlines as models of correct form in planning your own compositions. The making of such outlines will be studied in Chapter III.

An Unusual Pet

1. How I acquired him
   a. Place
   b. Time
   c. Circumstances
2. His intelligence
3. His unusual habits
4. His one bad habit
5. Tricks that I have taught him
6. His devotion to me
7. His place in our family

Getting a Vacation Job

1. Introduction
   a. My desire to earn some money
   b. My friend's advice
   c. Father's advice
2. My letters of application
   a. Favorable replies
   b. Unfavorable replies
3. My personal applications
   a. Reasons for my failure at first
   b. Improvement of my method
4. Securing the job
5. The value of the experience to me

How We Earned Our Car

1. Why we had not bought a car earlier
   - *a.* Heavy family expenses
   - *b.* Father's small increase in salary
   - *c.* Our disappointment
   - *d.* The compensating feature
2. Our New Year's resolution to earn a car
   - *a.* Mother's plan
   - *b.* Mother's duties as treasurer
   - *c.* Our weekly reports
3. How mother earned her part
   - *a.* A dollar a week as treasurer
   - *b.* Selling home products
   - *c.* Knitting sweaters and mufflers
   - *d.* Her needlework prize
4. How father saved and made his share
   - *a.* Tobacco money and carfare
   - *b.* Extra work at night
5. How Mary earned her share
   - *a.* Clerking in vacation
   - *b.* Selling homemade candy and jelly
   - *c.* Knitting silk neckties
6. How Tom obtained his part
   - *a.* Clerking on Saturdays
   - *b.* Mowing lawns and caring for flower beds
   - *c.* Keeping time for a construction company
7. How I made my part
   - *a.* Fattening my pig
   - *b.* Picking fruit and helping mother
   - *c.* Selling my pig
8. Mother's report in December
   - *a.* Our total earnings and savings
   - *b.* Mother's success
   - *c.* Grandfather's unexpected check
9. Buying our car last Christmas
   - *a.* The selection of the car by the entire family
   - *b.* More than enough money
   - *c.* Father's remark as we rode home

Exercise 22

Read the composition printed below. Then, referring to the last outline given in Exercise 21, notice how the pupil followed his plan in composing his talk. Observe the direct, natural beginning and the brief, appropriate ending. Be prepared to discuss in class each step in the development of this composition from the outline given.

How We Earned Our Car

Christmas before last we were all greatly disappointed when father could not buy a car for us, as he had planned. Mother's long illness and the repairs on our house that the fire of the previous summer necessitated had left very little of the money that father had been saving. Besides, father got only a small increase in salary at the end of the year. For these reasons he and mother decided that we had better wait to buy a car until we could pay cash. Mother sympathized with Mary and Tom and me in our disappointment, which seemed particularly hard to bear, because all our neighbors had cars. But when we thought how fortunate we were in having mother still with us, we felt compensated for doing without a car.

On New Year's morning mother proposed that we make a resolution to earn a car during the coming year. We were not to touch father's salary, but were to get the money by doing extra work and by saving all we could. We readily agreed. Tom, Mary, and I decided at once that we would try to find jobs on Saturdays, and that we would stay in town and work during vacation instead of going to grandfather's, out in the country, as we usually did in summer. We elected mother treasurer at a dollar a week. Every Saturday night we were to report to her and turn over our earnings, which she would deposit in the savings bank. No one but mother was to know until December how much we had.

When we agreed to pay mother a dollar a week as treasurer, we thought that would be all she could earn; but we did not know mother. She hired Mary and me on commission, and paid us half of all we helped her make out of the garden, the orchard, the cow, and the chickens. She and Mary also made preserves, pickles, jelly, and candy to sell. At odd times mother knitted sweaters and mufflers, and Miss Cartwright sold them in her shop. Besides, mother had the good fortune to win a needlework prize of twenty-five dollars.

In order to earn his part, in addition to his salary, father gave up smoking and walked home from work every day. Three evenings a week he taught bookkeeping in the night school. On the other three evenings he audited accounts for some of the stores. He was always telling mother that he believed she was getting ahead of him.

Of course Mary could not make as much as the rest of us. During vacation she clerked in Miss Cartwright's shop. Miss Cartwright let her sell the candies and jellies that she and mother had made. Mary sold some silk neckties, too, that she had knitted. But she had to spend part of her money for clothes.

Tom was sure that he was making more than any of the rest of us. On Saturdays he clerked for Mr. Morse, and in the evenings he mowed lawns, took care of flower beds, and did other odd jobs for several old ladies. In the summer he struck it rich and got a job keeping time for a construction company at five dollars a day. How I envied Tom!

At first it seemed as if all the money that I could earn would be what mother paid me for helping her. But, in March, Uncle Frank surprised me by sending me a pig to fatten. How proud I was of that pig, and how I did feed him! I kept the garden weeded and the cabbages almost stripped of leaves getting green stuff for him. Two of the neighbors saved all their garbage for me to give him. In the summer I earned several dollars picking berries and peaches. Almost every day mother paid me something for delivering milk, butter, eggs, and vegetables to the neighbors. When I sold my pig in December, I received forty-six dollars and eighty cents for him. Mary was terribly jealous of me, and so was Tom, though he would not admit it.

At breakfast on the day after I had sold my pig, mother made her report. We held our breath in eager expectation. During the year we had earned and saved a thousand and forty dollars. Mother had made more than any of the rest of us, and Tom came second. I was fourth. But that was not our only surprise. Grandfather had written mother that he wanted a share in our car and had sent her a check for a hundred dollars. The shouts of joy that we gave as mother finished her report must have been heard by all our neighbors.

Three days before Christmas all of us accompanied father to purchase the car. Though we each at first had wanted a different make, mother finally persuaded us all to agree to her choice. After paying cash for the car, we each had fifty dollars left as a savings account in the bank to begin the new year with. As Tom drove us home, father remarked, "Well, ours is a real family car."

Exercise 23

Prepare a talk on one of the other subjects outlined in Exercise 21. You may modify the printed outline to fit your particular material if you find any change necessary. Try to make your opening and closing sentences particularly direct and natural in expression.

Exercise 24

Make a brief outline of some fable or folk tale that you know. Come to class prepared to relate the fable or tale orally. Before beginning the talk, place your outline on the blackboard or hand it to the teacher or class chairman. Your talk will be judged by the care and accuracy with which you follow the outline.

Exercise 25

Make an outline for a talk on one of the subjects listed below. Select your subject in accordance with the suggestions given in section 3.

1. My Recipe for Devil's Food Cake.
2. Why I Joined the School Band (Orchestra, Glee Club).
3. My Personal Budget System.
4. When I Do Not Know My Lesson.
5. The Joys of Being the Tallest in the Class (Family).
6. My Most Interesting Experience Last Vacation.
7. A limited subject of your own choice.

Exercise 26

Your class will be divided into groups of three or four pupils, with one pupil in each group designated as chairman. Each group will then take up in turn for discussion, criticism, and revision the outline that each member of the group prepared in Exercise 25. The following questions will help in criticizing and revising each outline : Are the principal topics clearly indicated? Are the topics arranged in the proper order? Are any unnecessary topics included? Are any essential details omitted? Does the outline as a whole give a clear preliminary idea of what the talk will contain? Are the beginning and the ending indicated? What other improvement can you suggest?

Exercise 27

Come to class prepared to place on the blackboard the outline that you made in Exercise 25 and revised in Exercise 26. As you give your talk, the class can see whether your talk and your outline agree. The following questions will guide them in their criticism of your talk : (1) Did the speaker discuss his subject so that you thoroughly understand its main points? (2) Was his beginning clear and direct? (3) Should any topics have been arranged in a different order? (4) Should any topics have been omitted? (5) Were any topics mentioned in the talk that are not in the outline? (6) Was the ending natural and satisfactory? (7) Did the speaker omit entirely any necessary points? (8) Did he use and fail to explain any words or terms not familiar to you?

Exercise 28. Extra Credit

Make notes on some lecture or discussion that you have recently heard. Arrange these notes in the form of an outline, and prepare an oral report.

Exercise 29. Extra Credit

Make an outline of the chief points in a short newspaper article, and come to class prepared to retell it in your own words.

Exercise 30. Extra Credit

Outline some incident recorded in your history textbook, and come to class prepared to retell it clearly and interestingly.

8. The Fourth Essential: Effectiveness of Speech

Though something to say, a definite purpose, and clearness of thought are all highly important in effective speaking, there are other qualities that we should consider. All of us are influenced, consciously or unconsciously, by the manner in which a talk is given. One lecturer interests us, another bores us, although their subjects may be the same. One speaker easily holds our attention; another puts us to sleep. The voice of one pleases us; that of another irritates us. Sometimes the subject matter and the voice may be sufficiently pleasing if we can close our eyes to the incorrect posture or the useless movements of the speaker. However carefully a subject may be chosen and a talk planned, therefore, it will not impress the audience favorably unless it is delivered well.

By following the suggestions given below we may do much to increase the effectiveness of our talks.

1. Stand at the front of the room, facing your audience.
2. Do not begin speaking before you have taken your position.
3. Assume an erect, though natural, posture, which you may alter slightly now and then, but do not fidget.
4. Do not slump or lean against a wall, a desk, or a chair.
5. Use your hands naturally, but do not toy with a pencil or other object.

6. Keep your head up, look at the members of your audience, and speak directly to them.
7. Speak in a clear, deliberate, pleasant tone of voice.
8. Enunciate your words distinctly.
9. Pronounce your words correctly.
10. Do not slur letters and syllables that should be sounded.
11. Avoid blurring the latter part of a sentence because of haste to complete it.
12. Pitch your voice so that it will reach every member of your audience.
13. Try to speak with force and proper expression.
14. If you must pause in the midst of a sentence or between sentences for an idea or a word, do not fill in the pause with "er," "uh," or "and-uh."
15. Avoid distracting the attention of your audience by mistakes in grammar, errors in diction, and violations of idiom.
16. Do not memorize what you intend to say, but be so familiar with your subject that you can speak readily.
17. Overcome timidity and self-consciousness by careful preparation, enthusiasm for your subject, earnestness of purpose, and force in your manner of speaking.

Exercise 31

Read the following selection aloud several times. If you are called upon to read it to the class, try to make your reading a good example of effective speaking. The other members of the class will estimate your success by applying the suggestions given in section 8 that are pertinent.

Carving Your Speech

Once more: Speak clearly, if you speak at all;
Carve every word before you let it fall.   Holmes

Human speech has two purposes — expressing and conveying. Often, when you are angry or disappointed, you speak only to express your feelings. Your language is a safety valve. This is a useful function of speech.

But the most important task of speech is conveying your thoughts to someone else, or someone else's thoughts to you. Every day, every minute, millions of persons are asking, demanding, ordering, instructing, buying or selling, in the home, the church, the school, in shop and store, in street car, motor bus, or garage. In every personal contact between human beings, speech is used to communicate their thoughts.

The most important element in a human being is his thought. The next is the manner in which he communicates his thought. And the most important thing in conveying thought, more important even than exact wording or a pleasing intonation, is correct pronunciation and a clear, distinct enunciation. You may choose precisely the right word, but unless you pronounce it correctly and distinctly you are likely to be misunderstood.

I remember the principal of my boyhood high school and many of the talks he gave us to help us grow up. One reason so many of his talks have stayed with me was his beautiful, clean-cut articulation. He rarely raised his voice, but every word that issued from his mouth made a sharp, permanent stamp on our minds, and his clear thinking was made clearer to us by the precision of his words. They were like cut gems, or Greek statues.

We do not pronounce every letter in our words, it is true, but we should pronounce every sound with a carved precision like a beautiful engraving, or a page from a fine old book. The carving will lend distinction, as well as distinctness, to our thought.— THOMAS A. KNOTT, in " Word Study," April, 1927

Exercise 32. Extra Credit

Memorize a short poem (10 to 25 lines) of which you are fond. Be prepared to recite it to the class. They will estimate your success by applying the suggestions given in section 8.

Exercise 33

Read the sentences on page 26 aloud. Enunciate the italicized words so distinctly that your hearers can easily distinguish them.

© Wide World Photos

A Boy Scout Pyramid

1. In the *picture* was a *pitcher*.
2. He rose from his *chair* and gave a *cheer*.
3. We saw a *fire* not *far* away.
4. The *council* gives *counsel* to the mayor.
5. I bought this *bird* from Mr. *Boyd*.
6. *Where* shall I *wear* these flowers?
7. My sister *Mary* is always *merry*.
8. James *Watt* observed *what* steam could do.
9. "*I'll* bring you some *oil*," said *Earl*.
10. The *statue* represents a man of heroic *stature*.

Exercise 34

Give yourself further practice in enunciating distinctly by using the following words in original oral sentences. You may make a sentence for each word if you cannot use both words in the same sentence.

and, end	pen, pin	then, den
costume, custom	pillow, pillar	there, dare
illusion, allusion	poor, pore	ten, tin
finally, finely	place, plays	those, doze
find, fine	rice, rise	ton, turn
just, jest	since, sense	which, witch
like, lack	till, tell	your, yore

Exercise 35

In hasty or careless speech many persons slur or omit the final letter or letters of certain words. Make short oral sentences in which you use the following words. Be careful to enunciate distinctly the final letter or letters of each word.

attempt	extra	myself	potato	slept
banana	fellow	nothing	problem	something
doing	going	object	program	subject
except	insect	piano	saying	tomorrow
expect	kept	pillow	shelf	worrying

Exercise 36

Certain words are often indistinctly enunciated because the speaker carelessly slurs or drops a letter or a syllable within the word. Make short oral sentences in which you use the following words. Enunciate distinctly each letter and syllable that should be sounded.

accurate	February	interesting	probably
American	foreigner	laboratory	quantity
arctic	general	library	recognize
because	gentleman	memory	regular
candidate	geography	mystery	salary
children	governor	original	separate
chocolate	government	particular	several
different	handkerchief	perhaps	similar
distinctly	hesitate	poetry	strength
factory	history	positively	visitor

Exercise 37

The correct pronunciation of a word may be found in the dictionary. The sound of each syllable is indicated by certain signs placed above, called diacritical marks. These sounds and marks are illustrated in the explanatory key printed at the top or the bottom of the page. The stressed syllable in a word is indicated by an accent sign ('). Intelligent use of the dictionary as a guide to pronunciation requires that the user understand the marking of each syllable of a word.

The following examples will show you how words are diacritically marked and accented to indicate the pronunciation. Find in your dictionary the sound that each mark designates and pronounce each word aloud. Notice that two words given below have a primary accent (heavy stress) on one syllable and a secondary accent (light stress) on another syllable.

accent	ac'cent	ăk'sĕnt
consonant	con'so-nant	kŏn'sŏ-nănt
diacritical	di'a-crit'i-cal	dī'ȧ-krĭt'ĭ-kăl
dictionary	dic'tion-a-ry	dĭk'shŭn-ȧ-rĭ
effectiveness	ef-fec'tive-ness	ĕ-fĕk'tĭv-nĕs
enunciate	e-nun'ci-ate	ē-nŭn'shĭ-āt *or* ē-nŭn'sĭ-āt
pronounce	pro-nounce'	prō-nouns'
recitation	rec'i-ta'tion	rĕs'ĭ-tā'shŭn
syllable	syl'la-ble	sĭl'ȧ-b'l
vocabulary	vo-cab'u-la-ry	vȯ-kăb'û-lȧ-rĭ

Exercise 38

In the words listed below the accent is frequently misplaced. Copy each word and place the accent mark where it belongs. Practice this exercise until you can pronounce the entire list without an error.

abdomen	discipline	indisputable	recourse
acclimated	discourse	inexplicable	research
address	express	insurance	resource
adult	exquisite	interesting	respite
advertisement	finance	lamentable	romance
automobile	formidable	mamma	sonorous
contrary	horizon	mischievous	superfluous
decade	hospitable	precedence	theater
dessert	idea	prestige	vagary
detail	impious	pretense	vehement
detour	incomparable	recess	vehicle

Exercise 39

Copy the words in one of the columns of Exercise 38. Separate each word correctly into syllables, and by the aid of your dictionary write each word diacritically marked.

Exercise 40

Make short oral sentences in which you use and pronounce correctly each of the words in Exercise 38.

Exercise 41

Make a list of ten words that you have formerly mispronounced and hand it to the secretary of your "Better-Speech Club." The secretary will prepare from all the lists submitted a class list, which will be written on the blackboard and used for drill.

Exercise 42

Make an outline for a talk on one of the following subjects. Come prepared to place your outline on the blackboard and to discuss your subject before the class. In giving your talk, pay particular attention to effectiveness of speech. (See section 8.)

1. An Experiment in Science.
2. How to Print a Kodak Picture.
3. How to Make a Butterfly Tray.
4. How Coke is Made.
5. How to Fill a Silo.
6. A Fashion (Custom) That I Detest.
7. The Importance of Good Manners.
8. An Incident in the Early History of Our Town.
9. An Ideal Camping Place.
10. How I Earned My First Money.
11. A limited subject of your own choice.

9. The Fifth Essential: Correctness of Speech

It is a mistake to think that we can talk in an ungrammatical, slangy, or careless way most of the time during our school days and then easily and permanently assume correct speech when we need it. Although slang is often more vivid at the time it is uttered than accepted language, it is to be avoided, because it is seldom permanent or universal. The slang used by the English people of Queen Elizabeth's time is in many instances without meaning to the Englishman of today. Even much modern slang which is clear, let us say, to a person living in New York conveys little or no meaning to a resident of Wyoming, Oregon, or Alabama. A still stronger argument against slang is that those who use it are not likely to learn good English words with which to express their ideas. Such people can talk only with those who understand slang; when they associate with others, they are at a loss how to express themselves. In our efforts to speak effectively, we should make it a practice, therefore, to use reputable English. In our efforts to speak correctly we shall find Chapters X, XIX, and XXII of this book helpful.

Exercise 43

List ten or more sentences containing errors in grammar that careless or illiterate speakers make. After each sentence write a correct version.

Exercise 44

Write ten or more sentences containing slang words and expressions that you and your associates use. After each sentence express the same thought in reputable English. What gain in clearness do you note in each rewritten sentence?

Exercise 45

Prepare by means of an outline a talk on one of the following subjects or on a subject suggested by your teacher. Be sure that your plan is clear. If you give your talk in class, see that your manner of speaking is effective and that the words chosen are grammatically correct and in good repute.

 1. The Protection of Bird Friends.
 2. A Defense of the Motion-Picture Theater.
 3. The School Building as a Social Center.
 4. The Influence of the Automobile on My Community.

5. My Favorite Winter (Summer) Sport.
6. A Plan for Improving My Use of English.
7. Why I Desire to Go to College.
8. A Humorous Experience with the Telephone.
9. An Amusing Mistake and Its Result.
10. My First Experience Selling ——.
11. A limited subject of your own choice.

The following questions will guide the class in the criticism of each talk: Could you follow the main points that the speaker endeavored to discuss? If not, what point was obscure? Why? Was any topic introduced that did not relate to the subject? Was any important topic omitted? Was the speaker's delivery effective? (See suggestions 1–14 in section 8.) Where did the speaker through lack of earnestness fail to be effective? What words were pronounced poorly or incorrectly? Did the speaker make any mistakes in grammar or in the choice of words? What unpleasant mannerisms did you notice?

10. The Sixth Essential: Vividness of Speech

Even though we speak clearly and correctly, we may fail to interest our hearers because we do not express ourselves vividly. Vividness of speech is gained by choosing specific words that stimulate the imagination and by carefully selecting details that make a clear picture or result in an accurate explanation. (See Chapter XI, especially sections 135–139.)

Exercise 46

Read the selection on page 32. The italicized specific words are those in the original passage. Reread the selection, substituting the words in parentheses (which are general terms carelessly used by everybody), and notice the loss in vividness.

At the same moment, another pirate *grasped* (took) Hunter's musket by the muzzle, *wrenched* (took) it from his hands, *plucked* (pulled) it through the loophole, and, with one *stunning* (hard) blow, laid the poor fellow senseless on the floor. Meanwhile a third, running unharmed all round the house, appeared suddenly in the doorway, and *fell with his cutlass on* (attacked) the doctor. . . .

I *snatched* (took) a cutlass from the pile, and someone, at the same time *snatching* (taking) another, gave me a cut *across the knuckles* (on the hand) which I hardly felt. I *dashed* (went) out of the door into the *clear sunlight* (air). Someone was close behind, I knew not whom. Right in front, the doctor was pursuing his assailant down the hill, and, just as my eyes fell upon him, *beat down his guard* (attacked), and sent him *sprawling* (flat) on his back, with a great *slash* (cut) across the face. . . .

Mechanically I obeyed, turned eastwards, and, with my cutlass raised, ran round the corner of the house. Next moment I was *face to face with* (opposite) Anderson. He *roared* (cried) aloud, and his *hanger* (sword) went up above his head, flashing in the sunlight. I had not time to be afraid, but, *as the blow still hung impending* (before the blow fell), leaped *in a trice* (quickly) upon one side, and missing my foot in the soft sand, *rolled headlong* (fell) down the slope. — STEVENSON, "Treasure Island"

Exercise 47

The verb *say* is a general verb. People *say* something in a great many different ways. They may *shout, whisper, murmur, stammer, lisp*, etc.

1. For the verb *say* list as many other specific verbs as you can.

2. For each of the following general verbs list as many specific verbs as you can : *tell, do, move, look, make.*

3. For each of the following general nouns list as many specific nouns as you can : *person, building, animal, machine, clothing.*

4. Rewrite each of the following phrases in as many different ways as possible, substituting more specific adjectives or adverbs for those in italics : a *good* book, a *very nice* dinner, *awful* weather, *terribly* glad to see you, a *fine* parade, a *grand* party.

Exercise 48

Prepare a talk on one of the following subjects or on a subject of your own selection. Choose details and use specific words that will make your talk vivid. Make the class see and feel what you formerly experienced.

1. A Spectacular Play.
2. The Bravest Deed I Ever Witnessed.
3. My Worst Scare.
4. An Exciting Ride.
5. The Last Five Minutes of the Game.
6. Our Burglar.
7. A Humorous Blunder.
8. My First Experience with an "Automat" Lunch.
9. My First Experience as an Actor.
10. Alone in the House.

The following questions will guide the class in their criticism of each talk: Did the speaker succeed in his attempt to make you see the picture or feel the excitement of what he was telling? What nouns, adjectives, or verbs can you mention that were particularly good? Explain in what way each of these words was unusually clear and effective. Where can you suggest better words?

11. Two Devices for Keeping Attention

Even though we plan carefully what we have to say and say it well, our talk may not be entirely successful unless we use some device to render it more effective, to make our audience see the thing we are talking about. One helpful means is the use of objects, or small models of them, to illustrate our talk.

A second device for making a talk before our class more effective is the use of a rough blackboard sketch. It may be made before the recitation begins or while the talk is being given. A perfect drawing is not necessary; the important things are that the sketch shall give some idea of the subject, shall have its parts properly lettered, and shall not contain too many details. (See Exercise 18.)

Exercise 49

Bring to class an object, a group of objects, or a model to illustrate a talk which you will prepare on one of the following subjects or on a subject of your own choice:

1. The Artistic Arrangement of Flowers.
2. The Root System of a Plant.
3. The Mechanics of an Electric Bell.
4. The Making of a Batik Scarf.
5. How to Group Objects for a Still-Life Picture.
6. The Law of the Lever.
7. How to Select Seed Corn.
8. A Poultry-Feeding Device.
9. How to Tie Various Knots.
10. Something that you have recently made in the domestic-science or manual-training class.

Exercise 50

Come to class prepared to explain orally one of the following subjects. Before you begin your talk, place on the blackboard your outline and a drawing to illustrate your explanation.

1. How to Play Tennis.
2. How to Make a Parchment Lamp Shade.
3. Modeling a Hat Frame.
4. A Trap Nest.
5. An Attractive Bird House.
6. A Plan for a Flower Garden.
7. A Box Kite.
8. How to Use a Terracing Level.
9. How to Graft a Tree.
10. The Circulation of the Blood in the Human Body.

The following questions will guide the class in their criticism of each talk: Was the drawing complete and properly lettered? Did the speaker talk to the blackboard or to the class? Were there any details that you failed to understand? Was any part of the drawing unexplained? (The class will vote on the best talk. The speaker receiving the highest vote will be given extra credit.)

Exercise 51

Prepare a talk on one of the following subjects. If any subject seems too broad, limit it to fit your information and purpose.

1. How to Repair a Tire.
2. First-Aid Treatment in Cases of Drowning (Burning).
3. A Tastefully Furnished Sitting Room.
4. The Work of the Red Cross in My Community.
5. Ice Harvesting.
6. How a Lobster Pot is Used.
7. Blanket Weaving.
8. A Nature-Study Adventure.
9. Unusual Traits of a Pet.
10. What the Boy Scouts Did in the World War.
11. A Needed Improvement in Our Town.
12. How an Alien May Become a Citizen of the United States.
13. Cranberry (Rice) Growing. (See page 267.)
14. A Local Indian Legend.
15. How to Secure a Patent (Copyright).
16. The Uses of a Gasoline Engine on the Farm.
17. Salmon (Sardine) Packing.
18. A Process in a Cotton Mill.
19. What it Means to be a Camp Fire Girl (Girl Scout).
20. An Ideal Vacation.
21. Rope (Wire) Making.
22. Characteristics of a Good Salesman.
23. My Grandfather's Favorite Story.
24. The History of Some Interesting Invention.

25. How to Make Cider. (See page 381.)
26. The Mechanics of an Artesian Well.
27. How an Irrigation System Works.
28. The Latest Improvements in Dairying.
29. Fire Protection in Our Town (School).
30. How to Catch Woodchucks (Rabbits).
31. The Usefulness of Dogs in the World War.
32. Ice Boating.
33. How the Schools of My State are Supported.
34. Our Athletic Schedule for This Year.
35. A Good Joke.

Exercise 52. Group Assignment

Your class will hold an informal "At Home." The class will be divided into three divisions. One group, acting as hosts, will be responsible for all the conversation during the time that their visitors (another group) are present. The hosts should decide beforehand on the subjects to be introduced, and during the reception they should see that each visitor is drawn into the conversation. The third group will act as critics. They will take notes during the class period, and under the direction of a chairman appointed from their number prepare a definite criticism of the meeting. About two thirds of the class period should be devoted to the conversation, and the remaining third should be used for criticism. Five minutes should be allowed the critics for consultation after the conversation has ended. The chairman will then lead the discussion of the group. The critics should feel free to call attention to neglect of any of the rules and suggestions given in this chapter. Pupils will vote on the most successful host, the best visitor, and the keenest critic. To the three pupils receiving the highest vote extra credit will be given.

Exercise 53. Group Assignment

Your class will select some subject of local interest for investigation. Here are a few possible subjects:

1. The history of an old house in the neighborhood.
2. What our town did in the World War.
3. The most important industry in our town (city, community).
4. The history of our school (town) library.
5. The story of the most famous graduate of our school.
6. How our community (town, city) protects the health of its citizens.
7. How our city gets its food.
8. Some other subject of local interest that a pupil or your teacher may suggest.

When a satisfactory subject has been selected, discuss it at some length in class and then gather all possible information about it. Under the direction of a chairman chosen from the class, prepare a good outline and place it on the blackboard. Now divide the class into as many divisions as there are principal topics in the outline. Each pupil will prepare a talk on the topic assigned his division. At a later class meeting he will give his talk before the other members of his division. The best talk in each division will be given before the entire class at the next meeting. At this time the class may decide what is needed to make the various topics fit together properly to form a complete report on the subject. If possible, have some pupil take down in shorthand the talks on the individual topics and make a typewritten copy. From this the best speaker in the class will then prepare a talk, which he will give before the entire school at an assembly. (Extra credit will be given for this complete talk.)

CHAPTER II

Retelling Another Person's Thought
(including Précis Writing)

Preliminary Discussion

Discuss the truth of the statements made in the following paragraph as applied to your school work and the business or profession that you have chosen. Give definite illustrations if possible. What essentials of effective writing are mentioned here? What other qualities can you name as equally important?

Perhaps in other days a man who was too indolent to give attention to his writing might have avoided the necessity; crude expression might have served him. But today, under the influence of our quickened civilization, a man can scarcely hope to become an important factor in society unless he can express himself with some degree of adequacy. People will not stop to listen to him if he cannot explain his wants clearly and without unnecessary hesitation; and they will not do what he desires if he cannot convince them and move them to action. And if a man is unable to use his mother tongue accurately, he not only turns many away from him day by day because of his obvious habits of carelessness, but when the supreme opportunity comes, he is, through his lack of power, unable to reach a large part of his audience of readers. Unless he is content to be a third-rate lawyer, minister, business man, or scientist, and is willing to be forever classed as uneducated, he must be able to increase the value of his thoughts by expressing them skillfully.[1]

[1] From "The Art of Writing English." Copyright by R. W. Brown and N. W. Barnes. Used by permission of the American Book Company, publishers.

12. Effective Speaking as an Aid to Writing

Conversation develops in us natural and spontaneous expression. Speaking to an audience trains us in selecting and arranging our ideas for a definite purpose and in presenting them so that they will make the right appeal to our hearers. In writing we must usually plan and compose more deliberately, in order that the reader will get a clear and accurate understanding of our meaning without the help of vocal inflection, gestures, and other aids that we employ in speaking. Talking with our voice, however, makes talking with a pen a more natural process and serves as a helpful approach to written expression.

13. Learning from Other Speakers and Writers

Listening attentively to good speakers and reading with care selections from reputable writers will teach us much about effective speaking and writing. In listening and in reading we should notice both *what is said* and *how it is said*. We should hold in mind the speaker's or the writer's subject, notice his choice of material, and try to discover his plan of grouping details under appropriate topics. We should likewise observe his sentences and his choice of words.

Reproducing what another person has said or written will afford us valuable training in effective expression. The author whose thought we reproduce provides a subject and all necessary material, properly organized, to develop it. In writing our version of it we use his material and follow his plan of arrangement, but *we retell it in our own words*. From such practice in retelling we learn much about the way to build a good composition. If we later go one step further and emulate the author's style in expressing our own thoughts, we find our approach to the writing of original compositions made natural and easy.

Whenever we retell what we have heard or read, honesty demands that we give full credit to the speaker or the writer whose material we have used.

14. How Stevenson Taught Himself to Write

In the passage given below, Robert Louis Stevenson, one of the most versatile English writers of the nineteenth century, tells us how he taught himself to write by means of conscious imitation and emulation.

All through my boyhood and youth I was known and pointed out for the pattern of an idler; and yet I was always busy on my own private end, which was to learn to write. I kept always two books in my pocket, one to read, one to write in. As I walked, my mind was busy fitting what I saw with appropriate words; when I sat by the roadside, I would either read, or a pencil and a penny version-book would be in my hand, to note down the features of the scene or commemorate some halting stanzas. Thus I lived with words. And what I thus wrote was for no ulterior use; it was written consciously for practice. It was not so much that I wished to be an author (though I wished that too) as that I had vowed that I would learn to write. That was a proficiency that tempted me; and I practiced to acquire it, as men learn to whittle, in a wager with myself. Description was the principal field of my exercise; for to anyone with senses there is always something worth describing, and town and country are but one continuous subject. But I worked in other ways also; often accompanied my walks with dramatic dialogues, in which I played many parts; and often exercised myself in writing down conversations from memory.

·   ·   ·   ·   ·   ·   ·   ·   ·   ·   ·

Whenever I read a book or a passage that particularly pleased me, in which a thing was said or an effect rendered with propriety, in which there was either some conspicuous force or some happy distinction of style, I must sit down at once and set myself to ape that quality. I was unsuccessful, and I knew it; and tried again, and was again unsuccessful and always unsuccessful; but at least in these vain bouts, I got some practice in rhythm, in harmony, in construction and the coördination of parts. I have thus played the sedulous ape to Hazlitt, to Lamb, to Wordsworth, to Sir Thomas Browne, to Defoe, to Hawthorne, to Montaigne, to Baudelaire, and to Obermann. . . . Even at the age of thirteen I tried to do justice to the inhabitants of the famous city of Peebles in the style of the "Book of Snobs." . . .

That, like it or not, is the way to learn to write; whether I have profited or not, that is the way.

Exercise 54

Among other authors who trained themselves in clear thinking and effective expression by imitating successful writers may be mentioned Benjamin Franklin and Mary Antin. Like Stevenson, they were not content to remain mere imitators. They employed the skill that they had thus acquired as a means of more effectively expressing their own thoughts.

Your class will be divided into two groups. Using one of the references given below, the members of each group will prepare a report on the method of learning to write employed by the author assigned.

Group 1. Benjamin Franklin's "Autobiography," in the section in which he tells of his boyhood.

Group 2. Mary Antin's "The Promised Land," Chapters X and XI.

15. Importance of Good Form in Writing

To be effective, what we write must be easy to read and neat and attractive in appearance. Whether we are re-telling another person's thought or writing an original composition, we should prepare our manuscript in accord with the demands of good form. Unless the teacher or the school prescribes a special form for arranging all manuscripts, we should follow the directions given in Chapter XXIV of this book.

16. Retelling Another Person's Thought Closely

To retell closely what someone else has said or written means to reproduce as nearly as possible his thoughts in words of our own. If the passage to be retold is expressed in figurative rather than literal language, we shall often find that a paraphrase, or an amplified statement of the thought, will render our version of the original more clear. The value of retelling closely lies in the fact that in retelling we are forced to pay strict attention to the author's choice of material, the orderly arrangement of it, and the clear and effective expression of his thoughts. Furthermore, we must understand every word used in the original. To do this we must increase our vocabularies by looking up new words and discovering their exact meaning. Perhaps the greatest value of retelling closely is that it compels us to read more attentively. When we read hurriedly, we get only a general impression and therefore often miss important details.

In the following examples of retelling closely, if we compare each retold version with the original, we shall notice that the first four reproductions are literal, whereas the fifth is a paraphrase.

1. "To say nothing and saw wood" seems to me one of the most sagacious phrases passed down by our hard-working forbears.

RETOLD. I think that the expression "to say nothing and saw wood" is one of the wisest sayings handed down to us by our energetic ancestors.

2. It is not that the outside world is wearisome: the trouble is with the monotony of our own minds.

RETOLD. When we are bored, as we think, with life, it is not the world without that is uninteresting, but our own minds that are dull and commonplace.

3. There can be no doubt that for some people mathematics has flavor, even though for me it is as the apples of Sodom.

RETOLD. It is true that for some persons mathematics is a delight to their mental taste, but for me it is dry and insipid.

4. The world is so full of a number of things,
   I'm sure we should all be as happy as kings. — STEVENSON

RETOLD. There is such a variety of interesting things in our everyday lives that we should all be supremely happy.

5. "There is none like to me," says the cub,
   In the pride of his earliest kill.
   But the jungle is large, and the cub — he is small.
   Let him think, and be still. — KIPLING

RETOLD. After his first achievement a young person is apt to believe that he can accomplish more than anyone else. He must discover, however, that the affairs of the world are much more important than his own, and must learn to be modest.

17. General Directions for Retelling Closely What We Read

We shall usually find it easier to retell what we read than what we hear, for we can reread the passage we are considering as often as we wish. We shall need, however, to give careful attention to the work of reproducing closely what we have read. The following directions should be observed:

1. Read attentively the selection that is to be retold. Reread it until you understand clearly what the author has said. Make use of an unabridged dictionary to find the correct meaning of any words that are not familiar to you.

2. When you have become thoroughly familiar with the passage, reproduce as nearly as you can, in your own words, the exact meaning of the original. Use words and phrases that the writer has employed only when expression of the thought in your own words would result in a change in meaning.

3. Be careful *not* to make the process of retelling closely an exercise in the *mere substitution* of words. Get the author's thought and then interpret it in your own language.

4. It is not necessary to follow the original construction of a sentence. Variety may sometimes be secured by changing from indirect to direct discourse, or from a declarative sentence to an interrogative or an exclamatory sentence. There will be a greater number of changes of construction in retelling poetry than in retelling prose.

5. In giving a prose version of poetry avoid any suggestion of rime. Avoid also the use of poetic words, such as *morn, eve, oft, e'en, o'er, ere, methinks, forsooth, erstwhile.*

Exercise 55

Reproduce in your own words as accurately as you can the meaning expressed or implied in each of the following passages :

1. The face is the index of the mind.
2. Things not understood are admired.
3. A good name is rather to be chosen than great riches.
4. He that looks not before, finds himself behind.
5. One Today is worth two Tomorrows.
6. The fairest apple hangs on the highest bough.
7. He was like a cock who thought the sun had risen to hear him crow.
8. Praise makes good men better and bad men worse.
9. Falsehood, though it seems profitable, will hurt you; truth, though it seems hurtful, will profit you.
10. Evil, like a rolling stone upon a mountain top,
    A child may first impel, a giant cannot stop.
11. Lives of great men all remind us
       We can make our lives sublime,
    And, departing, leave behind us
       Footprints on the sands of time.
12. Who to himself is law no law doth need,
    Offends no law, and is a king indeed.
13. There is a tide in the affairs of men,
       Which, taken at the flood, leads on to fortune;
    Omitted, all the voyage of their life
    Is bound in shallows and in miseries.

14. So nigh is grandeur to our dust,
  So near is God to man,
  When Duty whispers low, *Thou must,*
  The Youth replies, *I can.*
15. The longer on this earth we live
  And weigh the various qualities of men,
  The more we feel the high, stern-featured beauty
  Of plain devotedness to duty,
  Steadfast and still, nor paid with mortal praise,
  But finding amplest recompense
  For life's ungarlanded expense
  In work done squarely and unwasted days. — LOWELL

Exercise 56

Reproduce in your own words a good anecdote or joke that you have recently read. Bring the original to class with you.

Exercise 57

Read a fable, a myth, or one of the parables in the New Testament, and retell it in your own words.

Exercise 58

Retell in your own words a brief news story that you have lately read. Bring the original to class with you.

Exercise 59

Write a good prose reproduction of the following fable told in verse. Try in your own version to preserve the pleasing qualities of the original.

Etiquette

The Gossips tell the story of the Sparrow and the Cat,
The Feline thin and hungry and the Bird exceeding fat.
With eager, famished energy and claws of gripping steel,
Puss pounced upon the Sparrow and prepared to make a meal.

The Sparrow never struggled when he found that he was caught
(If somewhat slow in action he was mighty quick of thought),
But chirped in simple dignity that seemed to fit the case,
"No Gentleman would ever eat before he'd washed his face!"

This hint about his Manners wounded Thomas like a knife
(For Cats are great observers of the Niceties of Life);
He paused to lick his paws, which seemed the Proper Thing
    to do,—
And, chirruping derisively, away the Sparrow flew!

In helpless, hopeless hunger at the Sparrow on the bough,
Poor Thomas glowered longingly, and vowed a Solemn Vow:
"Henceforth I'll eat my dinner first, *then* wash myself!" —
    And that's
The Universal Etiquette for Educated Cats.

ARTHUR GUITERMAN

Exercise 60

Read the following poem several times until you have
a vivid picture of the half-real, half-imagined scene, and
then reproduce it in prose, using as far as possible your
own words and phrasings.

Indian Summer

A soft veil dims the tender skies,
And half conceals from pensive eyes
    The bronzing tokens of the fall;
A calmness broods upon the hills.
And summer's parting dream distills
    A charm of silence over all.

The stacks of corn, in brown array,
Stand waiting through the placid day,
    Like tattered wigwams on the plain;
The tribes that find a shelter there
Are phantom peoples, forms of air,
    And ghosts of vanished joy and pain.

At evening, when the crimson crest
Of sunset passes down the west,
  I hear the whispering host returning;
On far-off fields, by elm and oak,
I see the lights, I smell the smoke —
  The camp fires of the past are burning.

HENRY VAN DYKE

Exercise 61

Read several times the following poem, which was written by a high-school pupil. When you are sure that you thoroughly understand it, write a prose reproduction of it in your own words.

Wind-Wolves

Do you hear the cry as the pack goes by
The wind wolves hunting across the sky?
Hear them tongue it, keen and clear,
Hot on the flanks of the flying deer?

Across the forest, mere, and plain,
Their hunting howl goes up again.
All night they'll follow the ghostly trail,
All night we'll hear the phantom wail.

For to-night the wind-wolf pack holds sway
From Pegasus Square to the Milky Way,
And the frightened bands of cloud deer flee
In scattered bands of two and three.

18. Translation a Valuable Means of Retelling Closely

Translation from a foreign language is one of the best exercises in reproducing closely the thought expressed by another. In order to translate a passage successfully, we must first understand the thought as it is expressed in the foreign language and then be able to reproduce this thought accurately in our own language.

It is sometimes desirable to translate *literally*, to give word by word, in the most exact manner, the English equivalent of each foreign construction. The chief value of such translation is that it enables us to understand the peculiarity, or *idiom*, of the foreign tongue. It is without value as a piece of English, however, unless the idiom is common to the two languages. "He went walking" is idiomatic in both German and English; but if we wish to say "I am better," and use the German idiom "It goes to me better," we are not speaking English at all.

We should never rest content, therefore, with merely translating words: we should translate idiomatic expressions into idiomatic English. In many cases, too, even if a literally translated passage is grammatically correct, it will gain much in clearness and force by a *free* translation.

If we compare the following literal translations with the idiomatic English versions, we see the superiority of the latter.

LITERAL TRANSLATION OF FOREIGN IDIOMS	IDIOMATIC ENGLISH EQUIVALENTS
LATIN	
A book is to me.	I have a book.
Clad in armor as to his head.	His head covered by a helmet.
The army having been put to flight, Cæsar went into winter quarters.	After routing the army, Cæsar went into winter quarters.
FRENCH	
At the house of you.	At your house.
What age has John?	How old is John?
How go you?	How are you?
I have sickness to the head.	I have a headache.
SPANISH	
I have hunger.	I am hungry.
The boy serves for nothing.	The boy is good for nothing.
Your coffee puts itself cold.	Your coffee is getting cold.
How well to her falls that dress!	How well that dress fits her!

GERMAN

How goes it?	How are you?
To house.	At home.
Where let you for yourself your clothes to make?	Where do you have your clothes made?

Exercise 62. Extra Credit

Select a passage in one of your foreign-language texts and make both a literal and a free idiomatic English translation of it. Arrange the two versions of your translation in parallel columns on the page. Come to class prepared to point out and explain each detail in which the idiomatic English translation is superior to the literal.

19. Retelling Another Person's Thought by Condensing It

Almost every day we summarize in conversation and in social letters what we have seen, done, and said on certain occasions. Often we retell briefly what we have heard or read. In making a recitation, in giving a report, and in writing an examination paper we condense what we have learned about a topic or a group of topics. Unless we have carefully trained ourselves in retelling in fewer words what another person has said or written, we very likely make summaries that are somewhat inaccurate, rambling, and wordy. The value of retelling by condensing is that, to produce a good summary, we must listen or read attentively, select the really important topics and ideas, and then reproduce them accurately, briefly, and clearly in our own words.

Exercise 63

Come to class prepared to give a brief and accurate oral summary of a news story that you have recently read. Include only essential topics, but do not omit any important details. Bring the original to class with you.

20. Taking Notes

Whether we are preparing an assignment or a report that involves condensing another person's thought or are collecting our ideas for an original composition, the ability to take notes and arrange them in proper form will aid us greatly. Unless we have had some training in the taking of notes, we shall find it profitable at this point to study sections 265 and 266 of Chapter XXIII.

21. Making Recitations and Giving Reports

In making recitations and in giving reports based on facts learned from books and other sources, we usually condense the original into an oral summary. By following the simple directions given below we may be able to improve our recitations and reports.

1. In reciting consider thoughtfully what the question means and what it demands as an adequate answer.
2. Stick closely to the question and make your answer clear and accurate.
3. In giving a report on something heard or read, follow the order of arrangement found in the original.
4. Include all important topics, but do not make your summary tedious by bringing in unnecessary details.
5. In reciting and in giving a report, use your own words. Do not memorize the original. Avoid such expressions as "the book said," "it said," and "he said."
6. Try to increase the effectiveness of your recitations and reports by applying the suggestions given in section 8.

Exercise 64

In each class in your various subjects pay particular attention to your own and your classmates' manner of reciting. Without mentioning any names, write a report of not more than a page in which you point out the faults that you observed and make specific suggestions for improvement.

Exercise 65

Come to class prepared to summarize in an oral report an experiment in science, a process in manual training or domestic science, a topic in history, or a biography in the history of literature.

22. Writing Examinations

In answering a question on an examination we summarize briefly the information asked for in the question. Success in writing an examination requires that we (1) think quickly and accurately, (2) plan our answers carefully, and (3) express them in clear, correct English. In developing greater skill in this important type of composition we shall find the following directions helpful:

1. As soon as all the questions are before you, read them over, and try to estimate the time that you will need to answer each question.
2. Read each question attentively. Think of what it means, and decide what a satisfactory answer will include.
3. Plan your answer carefully. Unless a question can be adequately answered in one or two sentences, take time to collect the necessary facts and ideas and to arrange them in the right order.
4. In beginning your answer repeat the words of the question in the first sentence or in the first part of the sentence.

Question. Enumerate the principal causes of the Hundred Years' War.

First sentence of your answer. The principal causes of the Hundred Years' War were the following:

---

5. If the answer to a question includes several subtopics, you may write it in the form of an enumerative paragraph. If no discussion is required, you may arrange the answer in the form of an outline.

6. Be sure to arrange the parts of each answer in the order demanded by the question.

7. See that you cover each question fully in your answer, but do not include any unnecessary facts or details.

8. Make your sentences brief, clear, and to the point. Long sentences are likely to become involved and vague.

9. Unless you are solving problems in mathematics or are answering a question in the form of an outline, express all your answers in complete sentences.

10. If you do not know the answer to a question, omit it. You can rarely guess correctly, and writing merely to fill up space wastes time and does not deceive the teacher.

11. Every examination paper in every subject is an English composition. Do your best, therefore, to write grammatically, spell correctly, and capitalize and punctuate intelligently. Legibility, proper arrangement of material on the page, and neatness in every detail count strongly in your favor.

12. Try to apportion your time so that you will have a few minutes left in which to read over and revise your examination paper. A carefully revised paper almost always wins a better mark.

Exercise 66

Below are five questions for a written examination in English. One class period (45 minutes to 1 hour) will be allowed for completing it. Follow the directions given in section 22.

1. Name and explain briefly but clearly the six essentials of oral composition.

2. What is meant by limiting a subject? Explain by giving two concrete illustrations.

3. How can you train yourself to be a better speaker? Name and discuss at least five practical ways of improvement. If possible relate briefly a personal experience in self-training.

4. What are the relations between oral and written composition? Point out the ways in which they differ and the ways in which one aids in the other.

5. Of what value is the study of English composition to the high-school boy or girl who is not going to college? Prove your answer by concrete illustrations.

23. Précis Writing

One of the most important types of retelling by condensing is the précis (pronounced *praysee'*). A précis is a brief statement of the essential thought of a paragraph or a longer passage. It is a short, concise summary or abstract containing only the most important points of the original. Usually it is not more than one fourth the length of the passage to be condensed. Often the précis of a paragraph consists of only a few sentences, and many times a single sentence is adequate.

A précis is not a paraphrase or a close reproduction of the original in other words. It is not, as a rule, the topic sentence of a paragraph or a quotation made up of a few selected sentences. It is not a group of running or topical notes, though notes taken in the form of summarizing sentences that include only the essence of the passage concisely and coherently stated may be a précis.

Exercise 67

Below is given a selection that will help to increase your understanding of what a précis is and how the making of précis will teach you to read, think, and write more effectively. Read the selection "comprehendingly and thoughtfully," and come to class prepared to take a part in a discussion of its meaning. You will probably meet a few words that are not wholly familiar to you. Look these up in an unabridged dictionary, so that you may get the author's meaning accurately.

The Value of Précis Writing [1]

The first and perhaps greatest value of précis writing is the demand it makes upon us to read comprehendingly and thoughtfully. Newspapers, magazines, books surround us and thrust themselves into our busy lives. So overwhelmed are we by this avalanche of reading matter that before we know it we become "mere skimmers of the printed page." We glance from headline to headline, from sporting column to cartoon. If a paragraph is long or dull, we skip it; if a sentence is a bit involved, we lose the thought — and let it go; if a word is unfamiliar, we dash on. Time is precious. A hundred other things wait to be done. Books — more books — offer their honey for us to sip.

Now this glancing into many pages, this flitting butterfly-fashion over print, is a debilitating process. It develops the habit of seeing and thinking superficially. Our thoughts remain continually fluttering on the surface of things. Worse still, our minds are trained to wander, to start and jump, to snatch a bit here and a bit there, to look at books as they look at pictures that glide by on a shimmering screen and make no lasting impression. But to write a précis we must look steadfastly at words, and carry sentences through to the end. We cannot skim. We must "read to digest," to distinguish between unimportant details and the central thought, to understand perfectly the very heart of the whole matter. In a word, we must think. Such reading, even if it be of only a few pages, is of profound educational value. The words of Ruskin are just as true today as they were seventy years ago when he wrote them: "If you read ten pages of a good book, letter by letter,— that is to say, with real accuracy,— you are forevermore in some measure an educated person."

Précis writing not only demands care and thought when we read; it requires discrimination when we write. We must express ourselves clearly, briefly, precisely. Into a few well-ordered sentences we must pack the essence of a paragraph, or even a whole page. To do this effectively we must explore our stock of words, arrange and rearrange them, hunting for the most concise, and,

---

[1] Adapted from "Précis Writing for American Schools," edited by Samuel Thurber.

© Ewing Galloway

An Archery Contest at Camp Akiwa

at the same time, the most exact terms. Prolixity, verbosity, repetition, looseness of style — these we must conquer, for they are the bitter foes of précis writing. Our words must "fit our thoughts like a glove and be neither too wide nor too tight." Thus the making of an abstract is an exercise of the highest value in vocabulary building, in sentence construction, and in clear, concise expression.

"Besides being an intellectual exercise of the highest order, the précis is also of great practical use. There are many occasions in the lives of ordinary citizens when they are required to grasp quickly the sense of a speech or document, to turn it round in their own minds, and either to give judgment on it themselves or to pass it on for the consideration of others." [1] If it is not a speech or a document, it may be a story, the plot of a play, a lecture, or a sermon which we wish to summarize. Hardly a day passes that we do not make an oral abstract of news. The person who cannot judiciously condense the story of what he has seen or heard is almost sure to be a bore; whereas he who speaks briefly, but straight to the heart of the matter, commands steadfast attention. Précis writing, more than any form of composition, as it encourages thrift and care in the use of words, offers a practical training in the most useful art of being clear, and brief, and therefore interesting.

"The précis cannot be called in itself a literary form. It stimulates primarily not the creative but the analytical powers. But since in its construction the relation of ideas must be ferreted out, since a deliberate choice must be made between what is essential and what is not, and since lucidity is of paramount importance, précis writing must be said to foster the qualities that underlie all composition of lasting value. By its demands are dissipated looseness, vagueness, and diffuseness, the recognized foes of good literary production. . . . The pupil who has worked out exercises in summarizing has surely sensed the force of brevity and point. Both his reading and his own writing must necessarily benefit from the clearer grasp of organization of material. Mussy thinking will have received a tremendous blow, so that the pupil through his précis writing may conceivably be a better citizen." [2]

[1] C. L. Thompson, "Précis Writing for Schools."
[2] From an article by L. Frances Tucker, printed in the *English Leaflet*, May, 1924.

24. Directions for Making a Précis

The following directions will aid in writing a précis:

1. Read slowly and attentively the paragraph or passage to be summarized. Focus your attention on getting the author's exact meaning.
2. Read the selection a second time. Try to pick out the really important points. Mental notes may be sufficient if you are dealing with a short, simple paragraph. But if you have difficulty in holding in mind the essentials, make brief, written notes.
3. From your notes, mental or written, formulate in your own words a sentence or a few sentences that will give, as concisely as clearness and accuracy will permit, the gist of the passage. Omit all subordinate details and illustrations.
4. With the first draft of your précis before you, read the passage again. If you have omitted any important points or included unnecessary details, revise your précis, and then make a final copy.
5. In writing a précis of a selection containing several paragraphs make a separate paragraph in your summary for each paragraph of the original. The abstract of a short poem may be written as one paragraph.
6. A précis should always be expressed in complete, well-constructed sentences, never in phrases or fragments of sentences. The sentences should be coherently grouped, and the summary should read smoothly and be easily comprehended.

Exercise 68

Read again the paragraph quoted in the preliminary exercise at the beginning of this chapter. Make brief notes of the thought in each sentence. Then read the précis given on page 58. Does it accurately summarize the thought of the paragraph? Is any important idea omitted? Can you improve it in any way?

Précis. Today, more than ever before, unless a man can use his mother tongue with accuracy and power, he cannot hope to be an important factor in society or to achieve the greatest success in his business or profession.

Exercise 69

Read the following sonnet. Then study the précis given below. Criticize and, if possible, improve the précis.

Nature

As a fond mother, when the day is o'er,
    Leads by the hand her little child to bed,
    Half willing, half reluctant to be led,
And leave his broken playthings on the floor,
Still gazing at them through the open door,
    Nor wholly reassured and comforted
    By promises of others in their stead,
Which, though more splendid, may not please him more;
So Nature deals with us, and takes away
    Our playthings one by one, and by the hand
Leads us to rest so gently that we go,
    Scarce knowing if we wish to go or stay,
    Being too full of sleep to understand
How far the unknown transcends the what we know.

HENRY W. LONGFELLOW

Précis. When in old age we approach the end of our life, Nature leads us so gently to our rest that we go less reluctantly than does a child who is led from his play by his mother and put to bed.

Exercise 70

The précis given below summarizes in about a hundred and fifty words the familiar story of "Jack and the Bean Stalk." Criticize and, if necessary, revise this précis to produce a condensed version of the narrative with all its essential points.

Once upon a time a boy named Jack was sent by his mother to sell a cow. He soon met a butcher, to whom he sold the animal for a few colored beans. His mother was very angry, and threw them away. Now, one of the beans fell in the garden, took root, and grew so rapidly in one night that in the morning the top reached into the heavens. Jack climbed up the vine, and came to an extensive country. After various adventures a fairy met him and directed him to the house of a giant, from whom he acquired great wealth. Several times he returned, and the last time he was pursued by the giant. Jack scrambled down the vine, and as the monster attempted to follow, he seized his hatchet and cut away the bean stalk, whereupon the giant fell and was killed. Jack and his mother lived afterward in comfort. — Adapted from Webster's New International Dictionary

Exercise 71

Study the following selection. How many paragraphs has it? What is the topic sentence of each? Refer to Exercises 512 and 513 of Chapter XXIII for notes on each of these paragraphs. Do these notes include all the important ideas of the original? Comment on the clearness of their arrangement.

Mental-Health Conditions

One of the most important factors in the poor health of workers is irregularity of employment. This produces very marked physical effects, because it is usually accompanied by low income, and therefore inadequate nourishment, unsuitable housing and clothing, lack of proper recreation, and so on. Moreover, irregularity of employment leads to *worry*, more often than any other one thing connected with work. This worry leads to bad mental habits, irritability, nervousness or mental strain, and loss of sleep. On the physical side it shows itself in indigestion and general weakening of the whole system. There are other sources of worry besides irregularity of employment; but whatever the reasons may be in any particular case, it is bad for the health of the body, and it may be considered in itself an unhealthy condition of the mind.

Closely related to worry, and in many ways similar in its effects, is *fear*. Such anxieties result not so much from the conditions in any particular occupation or establishment as from the general working and living conditions in a given industry or community. For example, in a factory town where people are often out of work, or where accidents are frequent, or where most people never have a chance to become skilled workers, we are likely to find a combination of poverty and this kind of anxiety.

A great deal of unhappiness at work, and consequently of bodily inefficiency and poor workmanship, comes from small annoyances of various kinds, such as the rudeness or boisterousness of fellow workers, the harshness or inconsiderateness of the foreman, irritating noises, the monotony of the work, offensive odors, bad lighting, and unsatisfactory toilet arrangements. The worker as a rule is unaware of what annoys him, or he dislikes to complain. It is therefore seldom that difficulties are discovered by those who could remedy them, and a worker remains until he can stand it no longer or until an outbreak of bad temper leads to a discharge.

A very important and frequent source of mental disturbance is the lack of harmony between the worker and the manager or between the worker and the character of the work. This is a serious matter both for production and for health and happiness. Yet it is very difficult to make suitable adjustments in every case, and sometimes it is not at all possible. Nor is it always possible to place the responsibility for the bad conditions, or rather bad relations. If a worker cannot get along with the foreman or with his fellow worker, it may not be the fault of either person; each one may be all right in his own way, but they simply do not belong together. The same thing may be said where a person is not getting along well with a particular kind of work. — BENJAMIN C. GRUENBERG, "Biology and Human Life."

Exercise 72

Compare each paragraph of the following précis with the original in Exercise 71 and with the notes given in Exercises 512 and 513 of Chapter XXIII. In what ways did the notes help in the making of the précis? Is the précis complete?

Paragraph 1. Irregularity of employment, one of the chief factors in the poor health of workers, results in lack of the necessities of life. It likewise causes worry, which injures both their mental and their physical well-being.

Paragraph 2. Like worry, fear arising from poor working and living conditions, from the possibility of unemployment and accidents, and from the lack of a chance to become skilled workers keeps the minds of workers disturbed and thus impairs their health.

Paragraph 3. The worker's environment and his association with other workers, as well as the character of his work, often give rise to small annoyances that result in unhappiness, bodily inefficiency, and poor workmanship. Usually neither the worker nor the manager is aware of the exact nature of such annoyances.

Paragraph 4. Good mental health demands harmony between workers, between the worker and the manager, and between the worker and his work. It is often difficult, sometimes impossible, to make adjustments that will bring about this harmony.

Exercise 73

Your teacher will divide your class into five groups. To each group will be assigned one of the five paragraphs of "The Value of Précis Writing" printed in Exercise 67. Following the directions given in section 24, write the best précis of your paragraph that you can prepare.

Exercise 74

Following the directions given in section 24, prepare and write a précis of the poem "Indian Summer," printed in Exercise 60, or of some other short poem that your teacher may assign or permit you to select.

Exercise 75

Come to class prepared to give an oral précis of a paragraph in this book that your teacher may assign or permit you to select. Do your best to make your summary as brief, accurate, and clear as a précis you would write.

Exercise 76

Following the directions given in section 24, prepare and write a précis of a fable, a myth, or a parable in the New Testament. Try to give a complete summary of the narrative in a hundred words or fewer.

Exercise 77

Following the directions given in section 24, prepare and write a précis of a story or other narrative that your teacher may assign or permit you to select.

25. Retelling Another Person's Thought by Expanding It

When we reproduce closely or condense what another person has said or written, we have all the material provided for our composition, and it has been carefully chosen, properly arranged, and effectively presented by the author. We have only to understand the meaning and then, using our own words, retell the original fully or reduce it to a summary of the most important points. In retelling by expanding, we have merely a part of the material needed, often nothing more than a few facts or other details, and sometimes only a single central idea. We are required to elaborate this scanty material into a composition by adding appropriate facts and ideas rightly chosen and arranged and clearly presented. We are called upon to make liberal use of our own knowledge, to exercise our selective judgment, and frequently to give free play to our creative imagination. The practice that we get in retelling by expanding serves as a most valuable final step in our approach to the writing of original compositions.

Exercise 78

Make a précis of a short passage that your teacher will assign or will permit you to select. Then with the précis before you, and without further reference to the original, rewrite the passage in your own words by carefully expanding the précis. This is a very important assignment.

26. Directions for Retelling by Expanding

Though our procedure in making a composition out of the material furnished us will vary somewhat in each case, the following general directions may prove helpful:

1. Concentrate your attention on the facts and ideas that you are called upon to expand into a composition.
2. If possible, formulate an appropriate title.
3. Jot down facts, ideas, and other details related to your subject as they come to you.
4. Revise this rough plan, adding, substituting, and omitting such details as seem advisable. Then prepare a good outline.
5. Write a first draft of your composition. Expand each principal topic into a paragraph.
6. Read over your first draft, to see whether you have said too much about some topics or not enough about others.
7. When you have improved your composition to the extent of your ability, write a final copy of it according to the directions given in Chapter XXIV.

Exercise 79

Read a fable or one of the parables in the New Testament, and state in a sentence or two the central thought illustrated by it. Show how the thought was made more emphatic and entertaining by being expanded.

Exercise 80

Following the directions given in section 26, expand one of the groups of facts given below into a composition of about a hundred and fifty words.

1. Low standards of achievement in youth usually prove a handicap throughout life. The pupil who is content with "getting by" in school rarely "gets ahead" after he leaves school.

2. Good teeth are essential to good health. Many persons are careless in matters of dental hygiene. Be true to your teeth now, else they may later be false to you.

3. School life affords many opportunities for developing good citizens. Pupils equip themselves for some useful life work. Many activities help in the formation of good character. Sports and contest provide valuable training.

4. An education should equip us to make a life, not merely to make a living. In addition to learning how to work efficiently, we should learn how to utilize leisure wisely and enjoyably. Pleasurable mental and social recreation is highly important in well-balanced living.

5. A balanced diet in reading is as important to our mental health as a balanced diet in eating is essential to our physical health. Too many of us read only the school paper, the newspapers, and sensational fiction. How can we choose a better balanced literary diet?

Exercise 81

Expand one of the following sentences into a composition of one paragraph about a hundred words in length:

1. It seemed that luck was against our team from the very start.

2. Never in all my life had I dreamed that such an opportunity as this would be mine.

3. Several times my uncontrollable curiosity has proved most embarrassing to me.

4. The view from my window is more beautiful in autumn than in spring.

5. Domestic animals play an important part in life on the farm.

6. In several respects our community (city, town, village) is a very desirable one in which to live.

7. If I win first prize in the title contest, I know exactly how I shall spend the money.

8. Modern styles of girls' clothing are much more sensible than those of a generation ago.

9. Many persons are wholly dependent upon others for their amusement.

10. Our school should provide one period a week for showing educational motion pictures.

27. Writing News Stories

Perhaps the most common example of retelling by expanding is to be found in the daily newspaper. News stories dealing with other than local events are usually based on brief telegraphic dispatches that contain nothing but a few bare facts. Until a writer on the newspaper staff expands these facts by adding amplifying details that will give them life and reality, they are colorless and only slightly interesting to the reading public. A comparison of the brief news dispatches on the bulletin board of a newspaper office and the complete news story printed in the issue of the paper that follows will show how much has been added in the expanding process.

Exercise 82

If your school publishes a newspaper, get a student reporter who has had a year or more of experience in writing for the paper to tell your class how he collects material and then expands it into an article or a news story. It would be even more helpful if you were able to persuade a reporter on one of the local newspapers to address your class.

Exercise 83

After reading the newspaper story printed below, write out a news brief of the story told here.

LINER BALTIC RESCUES 5 MEN OFF STORM–WRACKED SCHOONER

NORTHERN LIGHT, BLOWN TO SEA FROM ST. JOHN'S, N.F., FISHING FLEET, LEFT TO MERCY OF WAVES

Two Boats Out of 10 Still Missing

St. John's, N. F., Dec. 6 (AP) — Another of the 10 little fishing schooners blown far to sea in the storms which have swept the North Atlantic ocean since last Friday night was accounted for today with the rescue of the captain and crew of the Northern Light by the liner Baltic.

Only two members of the ill-fated fleet still are missing, the schooners Neptune and the Lloyd Jack.

Five seamen were taken off the Northern Light today by the Baltic and the schooner was abandoned. It was a daring rescue, made in heavy and dangerous seas, and it resulted in the death of one of the Northern Light's crew, Rex Parson, 20.

The big liner sighted the disabled schooner about 600 miles southeast of Cape Race, according to a radio message received from the Baltic's commander, J. Kearney. The deserted fishing vessel was left in a sinking condition, and the Baltic was forced to cast adrift the lifeboat in which the five men were rescued.

The Baltic's rescue follows that by the liner Republic yesterday, in which the captain and 10 seamen of the schooner Gander Deal were picked up nearly 1000 miles off Cape Race.

Both the Baltic and Republic are due to arrive in their New York docks Monday with the survivors of the two schooners.

The full gale and high seas sweeping over the Atlantic which have delayed all transoceanic liners also have hampered the rescue work of two other of the fishing fleet schooners, the Effie May Petite and the Merry Widow.

Both of the schooners broke loose from their tow lines, and the Effie May Petite was lost sight of by the government steamer Meigle, which was bringing her into port. The Meigle was forced to return for coal but will renew her search for the schooner later.

The Merry Widow broke away from the steamer Boethic during the gale, but the Boethic reported that she was keeping the schooner in sight and will attempt to take her in tow again when the storm dies down.

Only two of the 10 tiny vessels which disappeared in the storm a week ago have been able to make back to port. The Watersprite put back into here after four days of hard battling. The schooner Jean Blackwood, however, is believed to be making its way along the northwest coast of Newfoundland, the home of the fishing fleet.

Four of the vessels have been abandoned in a battered condition after their crews were rescued. The other two still missing carried crews of six and eight men. — *Boston Herald*

Exercise 84

Bring to class a list of news briefs copied from the bulletin board of a local newspaper, and with your list bring a printed news story in which one of these briefs has been expanded. Be prepared to point out just how much was added by the newspaper writer in expanding the brief.

Exercise 85

Suppose that you are a newspaper writer. Using the scant details given in one of the following groups, expand them into a news story of about two hundred words.

Our team won meet by seven points. Allston Academy second place. Brighton High School third. Hanson won eleven points. Carder broke two-twenty record. Our boys lords of the town. Home Sunday evening.

Train hits automobile at Lewiston crossing. Hiram Dodge, wife, and nephew killed. Mrs. Dodge's sister fatally injured. Baby and dog unhurt. Family on the way to county high-school meet. Nephew a contestant.

Couple eloping in stolen car caught by girl's father and her jilted suitor. Girl refuses to return home with her father. Begs officers to give her cell in jail, as they had given her lover. Car being held for owner.

Cyclone hits Amesbury. Ten known dead. Thirteen missing. More than a hundred injured. Many families homeless. Property loss over five million. River reached maximum at six this morning. Dam safe if no more rain falls. City without lights and water. Mayor calls for aid.

Miss Isabel Hightower dead at age of eighty-seven. Leaves house to historical society. Large collection of interesting family relics. House built in 1760. Lover killed in Civil War. Miss Hightower active in Red Cross work during World War. Gordon Bryce, nephew, senior in medical college, sole heir.

Planning an Original Composition

28. Approach to Original Composition

The study of effective speaking has prepared us in three ways for writing original compositions. First, we have learned something about choosing a subject that we are capable of making clear and interesting to others. Secondly, we have had practice in selecting necessary material and in arranging it by means of a simple outline. Lastly, we have acquired some skill in presenting our subjects effectively in talks before our classmates.

In retelling another person's thought we have observed how experienced writers develop their subjects through the skillful arrangement of material that is carefully chosen. In expanding another person's thought we have had some practice in selecting additional material and arranging it according to our own plan. If we have thus far made good use of our training in speaking and writing, we shall find the planning and writing of original compositions comparatively easy and natural.

29. Writing the First Original Composition

Let us suppose that we have been asked to write our first wholly original composition. Too often it happens that in such a case we forget the instruction that we have received and go about the work in some such time-wasting manner as this. Because we are told that we may choose our own subject, we decide, perhaps, after considering a great many subjects, to write on "School Papers." Since we are slightly familiar with our own school paper or magazine, we feel, doubtless, that we know so much about our subject and the material that should go into our composition that we need not make an outline. Giving little, if any, thought to what topics we should discuss and how we should arrange them, we begin at once to write. After many false starts we produce an opening sentence that satisfies us. We are so proud of it that we set it off by itself as the first paragraph. With much more effort than we had anticipated, and after wasting a great deal of time, energy, and good theme paper, we write several other sentences. These we arrange singly or in groups of two, three, or more, and indicate by indenting the first line of each group that it is a paragraph. We hastily copy what we have written and submit to our teacher the faulty composition that follows.

School Papers

Not many boys and girls in this or any school probaly realise it takes a great deal of hard work to get out a school paper.

As soon as they get the paper the average pupil looks through the personals and jokes to see if their name is mentioned and looks at the ads and then leaves the rest of the paper until they get home and have more time.

If you ask any member of the staff how the school paper is got out they will tell you they have to do a lot of hard work to put out the paper for even one month — and they print eight copies every year.

Before a school paper can be started they have to get a lot of ads so they will have enough money to pay for it. It takes a great deal of time and hard work to get enough ads. The business manager and his helpers have to get them and every month they have to get some new ones.

The stories, jokes and poems that are printed in a school paper mean a great deal of hard work by the pupils that write them and the teachers that read them and turn them in to the editor — but the staff members have to work hardest for they have to select the best stuff turned in and get it ready for the printer. And they have to decide how many pages it will take and what part of the paper it is going to appear in. They also have to get pictures and make drawings if there are going to be any, and also a drawing or picture for the cover.

When the stuff is already they send it to the printer or turn it over to the printing class if the school has any and they send it back in linotype form. The staff and faculty adviser have to make a dummy copy to show the printer where to put what is going into the paper. Then they send it back to the printer and when the printing is done the paper is finished. The ads must be aranged in the right place too.

The work of getting out a school paper is divided between the Editorial staff and the business manager, and they both work with the Faculty adviser who advises them what should go in the paper and how to get enough money to pay for the printing.

The Editor in chief has several other editors to help him but he must plan the paper and look over everthing that goes in it. And he writes most all of the editorials too and sees that the Business manager is getting enough ads to pay all the expenses. He has to have good judgement and be able to write good english.

Each pupil in the school can help make their paper a success in three ways. First they ought to try and write something for the paper every month. Second they should try and secure at least one ad for the paper, and they should not only take the paper themselves but try and get other pupils and people outside of school to take it. They ought to trade at the stores also that put ads in the paper and show appreciation. By doing this pupils will help the school put out a paper they will be proud of.

Pupils don't get any extra credit in english for the work they do on the school paper but it helps them in there english for they try to write something that will be printed in the school paper and this helps them do better work. Drawing pictures for the paper also helps pupils. And getting ads trains them to be good salesmen and this will help them make a success in real life.

Exercise 86

Now that you have read the so-called composition on "School Papers," study it closely and criticize it by giving specific answers to the following questions:

1. Is the subject as stated in the title rightly chosen and properly limited? Does it fit the composition accurately? Has it been fully discussed?

2. How many principal topics can you find? Are they easy to discover? Why?

3. Try to make an outline of what has been written. Are there too many paragraphs?

4. Point out sentences that seem to you poorly constructed. Which are too long or overloaded?

5. What errors in grammar and idiom do you discover?

6. Indicate all mistakes that you find in capitalization and punctuation.

7. What words have been misspelled? Give the correct spelling of each word.

8. What improvements in the choice of words can you suggest? Point out words that are too frequently repeated.

9. Indicate any other errors that you discover.

10. How might the writer have avoided the mistakes that you have pointed out? Make your answers definite.

Exercise 87

Read again the composition on "How We Earned Our Car," in Exercise 22, and compare it with "School Papers," regarding each of the points indicated in Exercise 86.

30. Steps in Planning a Composition

To write a composition that will be clear, accurate, and complete, we must first of all think clearly and plan what we shall say. This we failed to do in preparing to write on "School Papers." As a result, we gave the reader only a confused idea of our subject. In all our assignments hereafter let us proceed by the following steps in thinking clearly and in planning our compositions: (1) select a familiar subject and limit it properly; (2) gather the necessary material; and (3) arrange the material in the right order by means of an outline. Such a procedure will save us both time and energy and will insure much better results.

31. Selecting and Limiting the Subject

In our criticism of the faulty composition on "School Papers" we discovered that one serious weakness is the poor choice of a title. The subject chosen is too broad. We cannot deal with it adequately in the time and space that are ours.

More important still, we lack the information and the ability to do it justice. Are we familiar with the papers of other schools? What do we know about college papers, which are included in our title? If we examine again what we wrote, we shall see that we drew entirely on our knowledge of *one high-school* publication, which is, apparently, our school magazine, for our discussion shows in several details that we are thinking of a magazine, not a newspaper. If we had gone one step further and limited our subject to "The Making of Our School Magazine," we should then have had a subject that accurately fitted our information.

Exercise 88

From each of the following general subjects derive a limited subject that would be suitable for a written composition of about five hundred words:

1. Transportation.	5. Education.
2. Athletics.	6. Famous Women.
3. Climate.	7. Fire Prevention.
4. Fashions.	8. National Holidays.

32. Gathering the Necessary Material

In writing on "School Papers" we obviously did not give enough time and thought to the gathering of material, for we omitted several important details. We made no mention, for example, of proofreading, which is an essential process in correcting any mistakes that the printer may have made and in improving in quality the contents of the paper. We also failed to tell how the paper is distributed among the readers or how subscribers are secured. In the last two paragraphs we included, on the other hand, certain details that seem not to be very closely related to the subject.

In gathering material for a composition we should concentrate our attention on the subject as stated in the title, which should be written out at the top of a sheet of paper and kept before us. We should likewise keep in mind our purpose and the understanding of our subject that readers are likely to have already. By doing this we shall help ourselves to think more clearly and accurately, and we shall find it much easier to decide what to include and what to omit in planning our composition. As we think through our subject, we should jot down our thoughts in the form of running notes. (See Exercise 512 in Chapter XXIII.) The details that we later select from our notes should be written in the form of a list of topics beneath the title.

Exercise 89

Holding in mind the subject as stated in the title, examine closely the topics that follow. Discuss the value of each in developing the subject.

The Making of Our School Magazine

1. The work of the editor in chief
2. Organizing his staff
3. Writing editorials and articles

4. Coöperating with the business manager
5. The work of the faculty supervisor
6. Making a contract with the printer
7. Securing advertisements
8. Distributing copies of the magazine
9. Value of the magazine in creating school spirit (×)
10. The work of the business manager and his assistants
11. The literary editor
12. The sports editor
13. The exchange editor
14. The jokes editor
15. Distribution of work among assistant editors
16. The work of the reporters (×)
17. Planning the contents of the magazine
18. Coöperating with teachers of English
19. Selecting material and reading proof
20. The social-life editor
21. The art editor
22. Importance of coöperation among members of the staff
23. Importance of coöperation between departments
24. Valuable training in English (×)
25. Work of the managing editor
26. Counseling the editorial department
27. Counseling the managerial department
28. The publication board
29. The editorial department
30. The managerial department
31. A visit to the printing plant (×)
32. Coöperation between departments and faculty supervisor
33. Coöperation between pupils and the staff
34. The book editor
35. The staff poet
36. Valuable training in salesmanship (×)
37. The importance of coöperation
38. Coöperation between the school and the advertisers
39. The work of the more important assistant editors
40. The work of other assistant editors
41. Suggestions for improving our magazine (×)

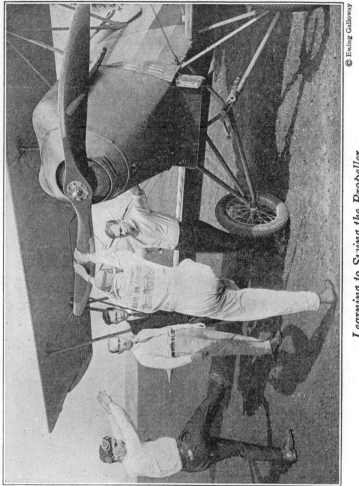

© Ewing Galloway

Learning to Swing the Propeller

Exercise 90

Following the suggestions given in section 3, choose with care one of the limited subjects that you have listed in Exercises 9, 12, and 88. Write at the top of a sheet of paper the title representing the limited subject. Make running notes on your subject and then prepare a list of such topics and details as you think are required to develop your subject adequately.

33. Arranging the Material by Means of an Outline

Though the list of topics that we made in Exercise 89 may contain all details related to our subject, it is not yet an outline. The topics are arranged in no definite order, and they all appear to be of the same importance. If we should write a composition from this list as it stands, readers would get only a very much confused idea of our subject. Before we attempt to write, therefore, we should construct an outline in which the principal topics are arranged in proper order with the necessary subordinate topics grouped under each.

34. The Form of an Outline

In making an outline we should indicate principal and subordinate topics by a definite system of numbering and lettering and by their arrangement on paper. Usually figures precede main topics, and letters stand before subordinate topics. Unless figures and letters are inclosed in parentheses, each should be followed by a period. If a topic is stated in the form of a sentence, a period should follow it. A topic expressed by a phrase requires no punctuation after it, though it is permissible to use a period. The subordination of topics is also shown by indenting them and placing them under their appropriate main topics. Usually each principal topic, with its subordinate topics, constitutes the material for a paragraph. It is advisable in all outlines, except a brief prepared for a formal argument, to express each topic in the form of a phrase instead of a sentence. We should always avoid using both sentences and phrases as topics in the same outline.

The simple form of outline explained in the preceding paragraph and illustrated in Chapter I and in this chapter will answer our present needs. In planning a longer and more complex composition we may require a more elaborate outline to show in greater detail the contents and the arrangement of topics. The form of such an outline is indicated below.

I. _____
   A. _____
      1. _____
         a. _____
         b. _____
      2. _____
         a. _____
         b. _____
   B. _____
      1. _____
         a. _____
         b. _____
      2. _____
         a. _____
         b. _____
II. _____

We should bear in mind that the form of the outline must be adapted to the demands of our subject. The subordination of each topic, we notice, is indicated by an appropriate letter or figure. In some cases the topic designated by the roman numeral, together with all the subtopics related to it, may be dealt with in a single paragraph. In others a paragraph may be required for each of the subordinate topics designated by capital letters. Usually the matter of paragraphing can be accurately decided by giving due consideration to the principle of unity.

Exercise 91

Examine again the form of the outlines given in Chapter I. Prove that they satisfy the requirements explained in the first paragraph of section 34.

35. Three Essentials of Composition-Building

In choosing and arranging the topics of a composition we should be guided by the following principles of composition-building.

Unity. Unity requires that all topics necessary to a clear and complete presentation of our subject be included and that all topics included be directly related to the subject. In other words, our composition should deal with the subject, the whole subject, and nothing but the subject. It must be a unit, a complete whole.

Coherence. Coherence demands that the main topics of a composition be arranged in the best natural or logical order and that all subordinate details relating to the same thought, the same period of time, or the same position in space be grouped together under the appropriate main topic. The three principal relations existing between topics of a composition are (1) succession in thought, or logical sequence, (2) succession in time, or natural chronological sequence, and (3) succession in space, or natural spatial sequence. By coherence in a composition we mean, therefore, the right arrangement of all principal topics and subordinate topics to afford the reader a clear and accurate understanding of our subject.

Emphasis. Emphasis requires that, so far as the natural or logical arrangement of material will permit, the most important topic be so placed that the reader will readily understand its greater importance and that each main topic be given space in the composition in proportion to its importance. We emphasize a topic both by the position that we give to it and by the amount of space that we devote to it. The most emphatic position in a composition is the end or the latter portion, and next in emphasis is the beginning. Of the three principles of composition-building emphasis is subordinate to the other two; but force, as well as completeness and clearness, is desirable in all compositions.

36. Testing and Revising the Outline

As we prepare our outline, we should apply the three principles of composition-building. Before we attempt to develop the outline into a composition, we should test it thoroughly to see if it satisfies in all respects these three principles, and revise it if necessary. Such questions as the following will help us in the process of testing and revising:

> *Testing for unity.* (1) Have I included all topics needed to develop my subject adequately? (2) Should I include other topics? (3) Should I omit certain topics in my list? (Note that topics 9, 16, 24, 31, 36, and 41 listed in Exercise 89 have been omitted from the outline given in Exercise 92 because they do not belong to the subject.)
>
> *Testing for coherence.* (1) Which of the topics listed are the principal topics? (2) In what order shall I arrange them? (3) Under which of the principal topics does each of the remaining topics belong?
>
> *Testing for emphasis.* (1) Which is the most important principal topic? (2) Without violating coherence, how can I emphasize this topic by position? (3) Will the amount of space that I shall devote to this topic help to emphasize it?

Exercise 92

Below is given the outline made by selecting and properly grouping the topics listed in Exercise 89. Observe that there are only seven principal topics. Compare the outline with the list of topics from which it is made.

The Making of Our School Magazine

1. The publication board
    a. The editorial department
    b. The managerial department
    c. The faculty supervisor
2. The work of the editor in chief
    a. Presiding at meetings of the staff
    b. Organizing the staff
    c. Distributing the work among his assistants
    d. Planning the magazine and selecting the contents
    e. Writing editorials and articles
    f. Attending to technical details
    g. Reading proof
    h. Keeping in touch with the business manager
    i. Giving talks before the school
3. The work of the more important assistant editors
    a. The literary editor
    b. The art editor
    c. The sports editor
    d. The social-life editor
4. The work of other assistant editors
    a. The jokes editor
    b. The exchange editor
    c. The book editor
    d. The staff poet
5. The work of the business manager
    a. Making the contract with the printer
    b. Securing advertisements
    c. Getting pupils to subscribe
    d. Distributing copies of the magazine
    e. Acting as treasurer of the publication board

6. The work of the faculty supervisor
   a. Managing editor
   b. Adviser of the editorial department
   c. Adviser of the managerial department
7. The importance of coöperation
   a. Between departments
   b. Between departments and the faculty supervisor
   c. Among the members of the staff
   d. Between other pupils and the staff
   e. Between the school and the advertisers

Exercise 93

Holding in mind what was said in section 35 regarding unity, coherence, and emphasis, compare the outline given in Exercise 92 with the list of topics given in Exercise 89 and explain how these principles have been followed in constructing the outline.

Exercise 94

Test for unity, coherence, and emphasis the outline of "How We Earned Our Car," given in Exercise 21. Use the questions in section 36, and try to give a definite answer for each one.

Exercise 95

Guided by the discussion and the questions given in sections 35 and 36, arrange in the form of an outline the topics that you listed for your original composition in Exercise 90. Revise your outline until it meets the requirements of the three principles of composition-building.

Exercise 96

Study the following outlines carefully. Do they satisfy the principles of unity, coherence, and emphasis? If not, point out violations of these principles and reconstruct the outlines so that they conform to them. Omit and add topics as you see fit. (Read again sections 35 and 36.)

My Home

1. The front of the house
   a. Old-fashioned
   b. Style of architecture
   c. Color
   d. The new roof
   e. The east side porch
   f. The vine-covered back porch
2. The front yard
   a. The street
   b. The gravel walk
   c. Flower beds
   d. The lawn
   e. The ornamental fence
   f. The trees
   g. The tennis court in the rear
3. The interior of the house
   a. My room upstairs
   b. The front hall
   c. The pictures I like best
   d. The living-room
   e. The library
   f. The kitchen and the dining-room
   g. The view from my window
   h. The attic
   i. Grandmother's old trunk
   j. Other rooms
   k. The basement
4. The garage
   a. Built of concrete
   b. Spanish style
   c. Our car
5. Other houses on our street
   a. The old red brick house
   b. The new bungalow
   c. The school building
   d. The vacant lot

My First Visit to My Uncle's Home

1. Introduction
   a. My age
   b. Companions
   c. Circumstances of my visit
2. Amusements
   a. Horseback riding
   b. Fishing
   c. Indoor games
   d. Tennis
   e. Old-fashioned barn dance
3. Our journey
   a. Preparations
   b. Means of conveyance
   c. Late start
   d. A blowout
   e. Interesting sights
   f. Our arrival
   g. Length of trip
4. My uncle's home
   a. Fine stock
   b. Stables
   c. Grounds
   d. Old-fashioned house
   e. Servants' quarters
   f. Tennis courts
5. My uncle's family
   a. Aunt Betty
   b. Jack, his dog
   c. My four cousins
   d. Grandmother Hayes
   e. Three servants
6. My return home
   a. Our accident
   b. The quaint old inn
   c. Greetings from my family
   d. My return to school

Exercise 97

Read attentively the selection on "School Spirit," in Chapter XXIV, and then construct a good outline of it. Find the principal topic for each paragraph and the subordinate topics. Prove by your outline whether this selection is a well-organized composition.

Exercise 98

According to the directions given in Chapter XXIII, make running notes on Chapter I of this book. From your notes construct an accurate outline of the chapter. (Your teacher may ask you to exchange papers and criticize one another's outlines.)

Exercise 99

According to the directions given in Chapter XXIII, make running notes on a chapter in some other textbook. Construct from your notes a good outline of the chapter.

Exercise 100

Choose one of the subjects given below and make a list of all the topics that you think should be included in a composition on the subject. From your list construct an outline. Test your outline by means of the questions in section 36 and improve it in any way that you can.

1. Our School Building.
2. How to Play Tennis.
3. An Interesting Industry.
4. How Our School Bank is Conducted.
5. An Unusual Halloween (Valentine) Party.

CHAPTER IV

Writing an Original Composition

37. Steps in Writing a Composition

An outline, as we are doubtless aware, is nothing more than the framework, or skeleton, of a composition. Nor can the expansion of each topic into a complete sentence and the grouping of these sentences in their respective paragraphs be regarded in any true sense as the *full development* of the outline. Though the subtopics represent the main ideas to be used in developing the principal topic under which they stand, they themselves often require additional ideas for their own development. Furthermore, the relationship between these subtopics must be shown by means of carefully constructed sentences. The connection between the principal topics, which are the subjects of their respective paragraphs, must likewise be made clear.

The writing, like the planning, of a satisfactory composition involves three distinct steps: (1) writing the first rough draft from the outline; (2) revising the composition; and (3) making the final copy to be submitted.

Our aim in all writing should be the discovery and use of the most effective means of expressing our thoughts. We can accomplish this aim only through numerous experiments and through painstaking revision and rewriting. From the very outset we should understand what every successful student of writing has learned from his own experience to be true: *Good compositions are not merely written; they are rewritten.*

38. Writing the First Rough Draft

Now that we have gathered the material for our composition on "The Making of Our School Magazine" and have prepared, tested, and revised our outline, we have thought out in general *what* we are going to say. Our outline is the map of the course that we shall follow in discussing our subject. Having this plan written out before us, we can concentrate our whole attention and energy on developing each topic as we come to it. The subordinate topics that we have set down remind us of what we intend to say in each paragraph. In writing the first draft we may be able, it is true, to improve our outline, and this we should by all means do if we can; but usually we shall find, if we have devised our plan carefully and revised it thoroughly, that there are few important changes to be made.

Our first rough draft represents our initial attempt to solve the problem of *how* to say what we have to say. Up to this point we have been trying to decide *what* to say. Though we should attempt to make the first draft represent our best knowledge of composition, we should think and write as rapidly as we can. Each principal topic should be developed into a paragraph, which, as we write it, we may consider a composition in itself. We should express each principal topic in a topic sentence as a means of giving the reader the central idea, or gist, of the paragraph and of aiding ourselves in writing a unified paragraph. We should stick close to the central idea as stated in the topic sentence, but we should develop it as fully as our readers and our purpose in writing may demand. When we have completed our first rough draft, there should be one paragraph for each main topic in our outline. In writing on "The Making of Our School Magazine," for example, we shall have seven paragraphs.

Exercise 101

With your revised outline that you prepared in Exercise 95 before you, write the first rough draft of your composition.

39. The Beginning of a Composition

The beginning, or introduction, of a composition should be clear, direct, and brief, and should be appropriate to the subject. It should acquaint the reader with our point of view and with what we intend to write about, and should arouse his interest in what is to follow. Though it is desirable to get to the actual discussion of our subject as quickly as possible, we should avoid beginning our composition so abruptly that the reader may find it difficult to get his bearings and understand our meaning. From the very first sentence we must take the reader with us and never forget that he depends on us to pilot him through our composition. Sometimes a sentence or two at the beginning of the first paragraph will serve as an adequate introduction; occasionally we may need to write a brief introductory paragraph. Whatever the length of the introduction, it should gain the reader's attention and, while making clear our general purpose, leave in his mind a pleasant sense of expectancy.

Exercise 102

Read again the first paragraph in the quotation from Stevenson on pages 40–41. This paragraph is found at the beginning of an essay called "A College Magazine," in which Stevenson tells of his first attempt to edit a paper. The magazine "ran four months in undisturbed obscurity, and died without a gasp," and Stevenson went back to the practice writing that he describes in this paragraph.

The first sentence serves as an introduction to the essay. Discuss its value in meeting the requirements named in section 39.

Exercise 103

Examine closely the following beginnings of compositions. Does each satisfy the requirements mentioned in section 39? Make your answers definite by mentioning the specific qualities of a good beginning that each specimen contains.

Mark Twain's Double

Not long ago I heard the following interesting anecdote about Mark Twain. The story was told by an old friend of his and illustrates well a prominent trait in the great American humorist's character.

The Great Stone Face

One afternoon, when the sun was going down, a mother and her little boy sat at the door of their cottage, talking about the Great Stone Face. They had but to lift their eyes, and there it was plainly to be seen, though miles away, with the sunshine brightening all its features.

The Limerick Gloves

It was Sunday morning, and a fine day in autumn; the bells of Hereford cathedral rang, and all the world smartly dressed were flocking to church.

The Outcasts of Poker Flat

As Mr. John Oakhurst, gambler, stepped into the main street of Poker Flat on the morning of the twenty-third of November, 1850, he was conscious of a change in its moral atmosphere since the preceding night. Two or three men, conversing earnestly together, ceased as he approached, and exchanged significant glances. There was a Sabbath lull in the air, which, in a settlement unused to Sabbath influences, looked ominous.

The Big Game

I had slipped away from the office early. Even if that meant that the boss would discharge me on Monday, I was not worried then; for I knew that I would much rather lose my job than miss the big Stanford-California game.

A Night in the Desert

One November day just at dusk five of us sat huddled over a fire in an isolated part of the New Mexico desert. It looked as if we should have to spend the night in this cold, uninhabited place, for our car had refused to carry us any nearer to our destination, Elephant Butte Dam.

Exercise 104

Examine and criticize in the same way the introduction to each of the following selections:

1. "How We Earned Our Car," in Exercise 22.
2. "Carving Your Speech," in Exercise 31.
3. "Mental-Health Conditions," in Exercise 71.

40. Showing the Connection between Paragraphs

In preparing our outline, if we have arranged the topics in their natural or logical order, we have indicated the general relation of one topic to another. When we develop these topics into paragraphs, we must be sure to make the connection between them clear to the reader. Each paragraph after the first should show its relation to the one that precedes it, and each paragraph except the last should prepare the reader for the one that is to follow. Unless the close association in thought, time, or space clearly shows the connection between successive paragraphs, we shall need to use reference words or other expressions to indicate the relationship. Such connecting words and expressions used at the beginning and at the end of paragraphs we call *transitional devices.*

Some of the most natural and useful transitional devices are the following: (1) repetition of a word or a group of words employed in the preceding paragraph; (2) beginning a new paragraph with a word or a group of words referring to something mentioned in the previous paragraph; (3) ending a paragraph with a sentence pointing forward to what is to be discussed in the next paragraph; and (4) transitional words and phrases, such as *however, therefore, moreover, furthermore, accordingly, notwithstanding, nevertheless, in addition to all this, in spite of this fact, for this reason, in this way, by such a method, on the contrary.*

In all our writing we should be careful to show clearly the connection between paragraphs; otherwise the reader may have difficulty in following the development of our subject.

Exercise 105

Explain the thought connection between paragraphs in the following selections. Make a list of the transitional devices that show the relation between the paragraphs.

1. "How We Earned Our Car," in Exercise 22.
2. "Carving Your Speech," in Exercise 31.
3. "Mental-Health Conditions," in Exercise 71.

41. The Ending of a Composition

Every composition should have a satisfactory ending. The final paragraph or the concluding sentence or sentences should complete our composition and satisfy the reader that we have appropriately finished what we intended to say. In the short compositions that we write we shall generally find that one or two sentences at the end of the final paragraph will serve adequately as a conclusion, but in a few instances a brief paragraph may be necessary. In such a paragraph we may give a concise summary of what we have said, or we may make appropriate inferences from what has preceded.

The ending should add strength and point to our discussion, but it should not introduce a new topic or idea. Though a good conclusion should not attract attention to itself, it should not be so mechanical that it seems commonplace and unemphatic. Nor should a composition simply stop. Writing the words "The end" should never be used as a conclusion.

Exercise 106

Test the suitability of each of the following endings. The title of each selection is given to help you.

A Friend of Mine

Of course Mike is only a dog, but somehow I can't help believing that dogs have souls and that our own are made better by our response to their honest love and faith.

Peace Meeting

They shook hands, screwing up their mouths with pain, for their fists were badly bruised, and parted, Rudstock going to the north, Wilderton to the west.

The Character of Queen Elizabeth

We must distinguish, therefore, between the private and the public character of Elizabeth. As a sovereign she was energetic, wise, and clever. As a woman she varied from grave to gay, wise to foolish, kind to cruel, and faithful to faithless. Elizabeth the queen was a strong and trustworthy ruler. Elizabeth the woman was often the creature of the hour.

The Matter of Idling

.·. . Idling, in the true sense, is a gracious, not an inane, thing. It is what Pliny did at his villa; it is what Wordsworth did when he came upon a crowd of golden daffodils; it is what *you* do when, with your pipe, you sit out a serene hour of leisure snatched from a dull day of labor; it is what I do when I pause between tasks to ponder upon imponderable things and breathe a spiritual ozone. Surely our spirits, happily unhampered for the moment, reap a harvest not measurable in dollars or bushels. Let us disabuse our minds of the thought that the man who leans a quarter-hour over one of June's fences to watch a daisy bud unbutton itself with rosy fingers is of necessity any more of a time-waster than he who frets the day from dawn to dusk with nagging busyness.

Exercise 107

Examine carefully the ending of each of the following selections. Point out the sentences that serve as the conclusion of each.

1. "How We Earned Our Car," in Exercise 22.
2. "Carving Your Speech," in Exercise 31.
3. "Mental-Health Conditions," in Exercise 71.

Exercise 108. Extra Credit

Below you will find the titles, opening paragraphs, and closing paragraphs of two short stories and an essay by three well-known authors. Study each quotation given here. What ideas does it suggest to you for an original short story or essay?

Select one of the three; use the title and opening and closing paragraphs given here; then call on your own imagination to supply the main story. Write four or five paragraphs of your own. The completed narrative or essay should be between 300 and 500 words.

After you have written your theme, perhaps you will be interested to read the original story or essay. Your teacher will tell you where it may be found.

1. The Consummation

[*Opening paragraph*] About 1889 there lived in London a man named Harrison, of an amiable and perverse disposition. One morning at Charing Cross Station, a lady in whom he was interested said to him:

"But Mr. Harrison, why don't you *write*? You are just the person!"

(Write four or five paragraphs showing how Mr. Harrison carried out the suggestion.)

[*Closing paragraph*] Returning to his cottage, he placed the manuscript in a drawer. He never wrote another word.

2. The Red Mark

[*Opening paragraph*] The curious episode in the London Ghetto the other winter, while the epidemic of smallpox was raging, escaped the attention of the reporters, though in the world of the Board-schools it is a vivid memory. But even the teachers and the committees, the inspectors and the Board members, have remained ignorant of the part little Bloomah Beckstein played in it.

(Notice the key words to a story given in these paragraphs. Use them in your story. Make Bloomah your heroine.)

[*Closing paragraph*] Next Monday morning saw Bloomah at her desk, happiest of a radiant sisterhood. On the wall shone the Banner.

3. Round Columbus Circle

[*Opening paragraph*] The other evening as I was walking along Fifty-ninth Street I noticed a man buying a copy of *Variety* at a news-stand. Obedient to my theory that life deserves all possible scrutiny, I thought it would be interesting to follow him and see exactly what he did.

(Write three or four paragraphs telling what he did.)

[*Closing paragraph*] At this point, fearing that my sleuthing might cause him to become self-conscious, I went thoughtfully away.

42. The Importance of Revising a Composition

Our chief aim in writing should be to communicate our thoughts, observations, and experience clearly, forcefully, and entertainingly to our readers. To do this, we must make easy the reading of what we have to say. Because of the complex nature of a composition and our lack of experience in composing, we cannot expect to give our thought its best expression in the first, or even the second, writing. Only by carefully revising, polishing, and rewriting our compositions until they honestly represent our best effort can we ultimately attain real skill in writing.

Since we desire that our readers give their whole attention to what we say, we should studiously avoid distracting their attention by violations of the fundamental principles of structure or of good form. When we have written the first rough draft of our composition, we have really taken only the initial step in adequately presenting our subject to the reader. If we have written the first copy in pencil and have left wide margins and considerable space between lines, we can do much in the way of revision by erasing, crossing out, and writing between the lines and in the margins. From the revised first draft we should make a neat second copy.

© Ewing Galloway

Camping in Yellowstone National Park

We should remember that a good composition is not merely written; it is rewritten. A subject has little chance of impressing others favorably until it has been well presented. Readers must be won by our skill in making our compositions clear, entertaining, and attractive.

43. Directions for Revising a Composition

In criticizing and revising a composition we shall find the questions given below helpful. We should take up the questions one at a time and answer each definitely by examining the composition and making whatever corrections and improvements we can.

1. *Testing for unity.* Have I omitted from my composition or my outline any topics that should be included? If so, where should they be brought in? Are there any unnecessary topics in my composition or my outline? After the necessary revision, do my outline and my composition agree in all details?

2. *Testing for coherence.* Have I so arranged the topics of my composition that their relation one to another is perfectly clear? If not, what changes are required?

3. *Testing for emphasis.* Does the most important topic of my composition occupy the most emphatic position? Have I given to the more important topics their proportionate amount of space?

4. Is the beginning of my composition clear, direct, brief, and appropriate? Do I need an introductory paragraph?

5. Have I one and only one paragraph for each principal topic? Should I make clearer the connection between any paragraphs by using other transitional devices?

6. Have I devised an appropriate ending for my composition, or does it merely stop? Do I need a concluding paragraph?

7. Are all of my sentences clear and correct? Have I overlooked any fragments of sentences, "period faults," or "comma faults"? (See sections 115, 116, and 117.)

8. Are any of my sentences too long or overloaded? Do my sentences, when read aloud, sound natural and easy?

9. What other mistakes in grammar have I made? Do all verbs agree with their subjects? Do all pronouns agree with their antecedents?

10. Have I used capital letters correctly, and have I punctuated my sentences intelligently?

11. Are the words that I have used correct and reputable? How can I improve my choice of words? (See sections 131 and 133.)

12. Are there any misspelled words that I have overlooked?

13. Does this composition honestly represent my best effort?

Exercise 109

Review section 29 and Exercise 86. Observe how careful planning and thorough revision would have enabled the writer of the unsatisfactory composition to produce a creditable piece of work. Make some specific suggestions for improvement in this composition.

Exercise 110

Following the directions given in section 43, criticize and revise carefully the first draft of the composition that you wrote in Exercise 101.

44. Making the Final Copy of a Composition

After we have thoroughly revised the first rough draft of our composition and have made a second copy, we shall probably find that we can improve it still further. *Not until it represents our best effort to write correctly and effectively are we ready to make the final copy.* In preparing our manuscript we should follow the instructions given in Chapter XXIV. When we have completed it, we should read it over attentively. If we discover that we have made any mistakes in copying, we should correct them, even if we have to rewrite an entire page. Every manuscript that we submit should be neat and correct in all details.

On a separate sheet of paper we should make an **ac-**curate copy of our outline. This should be placed in front of the first page of our composition.

Exercise 111

Below is printed the final copy of "The Making of Our School Magazine." In the column at the right of each page are given the topics of the outline, as a means of showing how the outline has been developed into a composition. After you have read the composition through and have compared it with the outline, note (1) the beginning, (2) the methods of showing the connection between paragraphs, and (3) the ending. Observe also the structure of the sentences and the choice of words throughout.

The Making of Our School Magazine

Not many readers of our school magazine understand the process by which it is made. As they look through their copy each month, they are aware that somebody is responsible for it, but they do not realize the great amount of detail work on the part of a large number of pupils that has been required to produce it. This work is distributed among the members of the publication board, which is composed of two departments. One department, the editorial, plans the magazine and selects and arranges the contents; the other, the managerial, has charge of finances and other business matters. Both of these departments work under the direction of the faculty supervisor.

(Introduction)

1. The publication board

    a. The editorial department

    b. The managerial department

    c. The faculty supervisor

At the head of the editorial department is the editor in chief, who is directly responsible for the efficient working of the whole system. His duties are many and varied. As chairman of the publication board, he presides at all meetings of the staff. At the beginning of the school year he organizes the staff and distributes the work among his assistants in each department. He plans the contents of each issue of the magazine, and when his assistants have gathered the necessary material, he selects and arranges it. He writes most of the editorials, and now and then contributes an article, a story, or a poem. He also attends to numerous technical details in preparing for the printer a dummy copy of the magazine showing the exact layout for each issue. Though his assistants read the proof of the material in their respective subdepartments, the editor in chief reads and criticizes all the proof at least once before it is returned to the printer. He keeps in close touch with the business manager and assists him in arranging the advertisements. At intervals he gives talks before the school to arouse greater interest in the magazine. To perform so many duties satisfactorily, the editor in chief has to be a capable and responsible person.

The editor in chief depends for most of the contents of the magazine on four important assistants, each of whom has two or more helpers. It is

2. The work of the editor in chief

   a. Presiding at meetings of the staff

   b. Organizing the staff
   c. Distributing the work among his assistants
   d. Planning the magazine and selecting the contents

   e. Writing editorials and articles

   f. Attending to technical details

   g. Reading proof

   h. Keeping in touch with the business manager

   i. Giving talks before the school

3. The work of the more important assistant editors

the business of the literary editor to secure from pupils stories, essays, articles, plays, and poems. If he cannot secure satisfactory material, he and his assistants write something themselves. The art editor, who is the staff artist, draws most of the cover designs as well as some of the illustrations, and he has general charge of selecting and placing the pictures and drawings. To many pupils the sports editor seems the most important member of the editorial staff. In our school, as in many other schools, a boy and a girl share this position, since both boys and girls constitute the athletic teams. These co-editors report athletic contests, discuss athletic prospects, and furnish pictures and drawings to illustrate their department. Accounts of social activities and other personal news of the school are written by the social-life editor and his assistants.

Besides these four assistant editors, there are four other helpers on whom the editor in chief relies. The most popular section of the entire magazine is the humorous page, which contains a collection of *bon mots* heard in classes and about school and a few amusing anecdotes and bits of humorous verse. The material for this page is provided by the jokes editor, who has unofficial assistants in every class. The exchange editor is of great service to the publication board. He sends out

a. The literary editor

b. The art editor

c. The sports editor

d. The social-life editor

4. The work of other assistant editors

a. The jokes editor

b. The exchange editor

copies of our magazine to other schools, receives copies of their publications in exchange, comments on the latter as he sees fit, and now and then quotes something from one or more of them. The book page is in charge of an editor, who either writes or secures from other pupils reviews of interesting books. Occasionally he prepares lists of books that he thinks pupils will enjoy reading. Last, but by no means least, is the staff poet, who gives much pleasing variety to our magazine by his verses on timely topics. He is also a helpful adviser to the editor in chief in making selection of other verse to be included.

c. The book editor

d. The staff poet

Though the members of the managerial department work behind the scenes, they provide the necessary financial support for our magazine and attend to various business details. At the head of this department is the business manager, who has several assistants. It is he who makes the contract with the printer. He and his assistants sell advertising space to business men. At the beginning of school he has charge of getting pupils to subscribe for the magazine. When each issue appears, the managerial department distributes copies to subscribers and advertisers. As treasurer of the publication board, the business manager receives all money and pays all bills.

5. The work of the business manager

a. Making the contract with the printer

b. Securing advertisements

c. Getting pupils to subscribe

d. Distributing copies of the magazine

e. Acting as treasurer of the publication board

Such is the mechanism required in producing our magazine. The publication board is a miniature government, with the editor in chief at its head. But there is someone higher in authority than the editor, and that person is the faculty supervisor. The latter is in a sense the managing editor. In conference with the editor in chief, he discusses various matters concerning the interests of the magazine. He helps the editor plan the publication, and he usually reads the material for each issue both before and after it is printed. He also advises the business manager in the making of the printing contract, the fixing of advertising rates, the best method of soliciting advertisements and subscriptions, and in all other important matters connected with the managerial department. He attends meetings of the staff and is accessible at all times for conferences with members of the publication board.

We can readily see that our magazine is the result of the combined efforts of many people working together in harmony. The editorial department depends upon the managerial department for the money necessary to pay expenses, and the latter looks to the former for suitable material. Under the guidance of the faculty supervisor all members of the staff work to produce an entertaining magazine. Each assistant editor, by willingly aiding his co-workers, helps to insure a better publication. By doing their best to

6. The work of the faculty supervisor

   a. Managing editor

   b. Adviser of the editorial department

   c. Adviser of the managerial department

7. The importance of coöperation

   a. Between departments

   b. Between departments and the faculty supervisor

   c. Among members of the staff

write something that may be published in the magazine, pupils make
it easier for the staff to select good
material. Business men, because of
their desire to assist in a worthy
undertaking, do much to support the
magazine by advertising in its pages.
For such support every member of
our school should show his appreciation by trading with our advertisers.
Through the coöperation of all persons, departments, and organizations
concerned, our school is enabled to
publish a magazine of which we are
all justly proud.

d. Between other pupils and
the staff

e. Between the school and
the advertisers

(Conclusion)

Exercise 112

Read again the composition that you revised in Exercise
110. Make any further corrections and improvements in it
that you can. When it represents your best effort, make a
good final copy of it to be submitted, with your outline,
at the next meeting of your class. (See Chapter XXIV.)

45. Rewriting a Corrected Composition

Since our teachers are more experienced writers than
we, they can usually give us valuable suggestions for the
improvement of our compositions. Special corrections are
indicated by means of symbols (see the inside of the back
cover of this book) placed in the margin of each page, and
general suggestions are often written on the outside of
the paper. These corrections and suggestions are of little
real value to us until we have revised and rewritten our
composition in accordance with them. Within a week,
therefore, after a corrected composition has been returned
to us we should carefully revise it and rewrite it. This
final version, together with the paper corrected by the

teacher, should be submitted to show that we have understood and profited by the corrections and suggestions.

Failure to rewrite our compositions after we have been shown how to improve them results in a waste of our own and our teacher's time and effort. We should preserve all our corrected compositions and read them over frequently throughout each course. Rereading them will show us to what extent we are becoming more skillful writers and will usually encourage us to take even greater interest in expressing ourselves well.

Exercise 113

Select one of the outlines given below for a composition. Make any changes in the outline that you find necessary. Omit and add topics as you see fit. Proceeding by the steps discussed in this chapter, write your composition. Hand in your outline with it.

How to Plan and Make a Dress

1. Introduction
   a. Dressmaking an enviable accomplishment
   b. Skill and judgment required
2. Planning the dress
   a. Purpose for which it is to be used
   b. Finding suitable materials
   c. Choosing an appropriate style
   d. Selecting a satisfactory pattern
3. Making the dress
   a. Laying out the pattern on the material
   b. Cutting
   c. Basting
   d. Fitting
   e. Sewing
   f. Finishing
4. Pride in the completed dress
   a. Economy
   b. The joy of creating something

How to Make a Tennis Court

1. Preliminary considerations
   a. Best time of the year
   b. Choosing a suitable location
2. Preparing the court
   a. Clearing the ground
   b. Leveling the ground
   c. Surfacing
   d. Rolling
3. Completing the court
   a. Laying off the court
   b. Putting in the net posts
   c. Constructing the backstops
4. The finished court

Exercise 114

Select one of the following subjects and prepare an outline for a composition. Limit your subject properly. Proceed by the three steps explained in Chapter III.

1. How to Install a Radio.
2. How to Prepare a Baseball Diamond.
3. A Visit to an Interesting Factory.
4. Why _ _ _ _ _ _ Is My Favorite Magazine.
5. A Project in Manual Training.
6. A Project in Domestic Science.
7. My Favorite Picture (Statue).
8. A Visit to the Public Market.
9. A subject suggested by your teacher.
10. A subject of your own, approved by your teacher.

Exercise 115

Proceeding by the three steps explained in this chapter, develop into a good composition the outline that you prepared in Exercise 114. Submit your outline with your composition.

Social Letters

Test Exercise

Using appropriate stationery, rewrite the social letter printed below. Divide it accurately into three paragraphs. Space it correctly, divide it into sentences, and supply the necessary capital letters and punctuation. Fold the letter properly and place it in an envelope of the right size and kind, correctly addressed but left unsealed.

This exercise gives you the opportunity to show how much you know about good form in social letters. It is also a test, to some extent, of your knowledge of paragraphing, sentence structure, capitalization, and punctuation. Do your best to prepare a perfect manuscript. If your letter is perfect in every detail, you may be excused from as many of the drill exercises in this chapter as your teacher thinks best.

167 lake street detroit michigan september 12 1931 mr h w draper central high school columbus ohio dear mr draper last week i entered the lincoln high school here in detroit how strange it seems not to be back in central this is a good high school but i fear that i shall never feel so much at home here as i felt there i am living with my aunt who provides me room and board for my services around the place the money for my other expenses i must earn by outside work as you will recall i was assistant manager of the lunch room last year i have applied for a similar position here i am sorry to bother you at this busy time of the year but i shall greatly appreciate your kindness if you will write a letter to mr frank g

norwood the business manager recommending me for the position you will find inclosed a stamped envelope addressed to mr norwood let me thank you again mr draper for your many kindnesses to me i wish for you and central a pleasant and successful year sincerely yours robert d chalmers

Preliminary Assignment

With the approval of the teacher, the entire class may be divided into three groups during the study of this chapter. Group I will be known as Readers, Group II as Editors, and Group III as Compilers. A chairman should be appointed for each group.

After the teacher has examined the letters written for each assignment, they will be turned over to the chairman of the Readers to be divided equally among the members of that group. Each Reader will mark with a pencil the errors he finds on the letters he has been given. He will attach to each letter a separate sheet of paper with brief suggestions for improving the letter. All letters should then be turned over to the chairman of the Editors for distribution in his group.

Concerning the suggestions made by the Reader each Editor will confer with the writer of each letter he has received. He will aid the writer in every way possible to make a revision of his letter, and he will be responsible for seeing that the writer makes his revised letter perfect in mechanical form.

The rewritten letters will then be given to the chairman of the Compilers. This group, working together, will then select the best letters. Each letter selected must be perfect in mechanical form, and above the average in subject matter. The Compilers will then assemble these letters in some permanent form to be used as a class exhibit. They may be mounted on cardboards or filed in a loose-leaf binder. After the class exhibit this material may be placed in the school library to serve as models for other classes studying the social letter.

46. Social Letters as Personal Compositions

For each of us the social letter constitutes an important part of our writing. Like conversation, it serves us as a useful means of personal communication with others. More than any other type of composition it affords us practice in the clear, natural, and entertaining expression of our thoughts and feelings. A letter expresses our individuality with great accuracy and vividness. By its subject matter, style, and form it impresses the reader either favorably or unfavorably with respect to our personality and education. A correspondent whom we have never met has no other means of estimating us. The growth of a friendship begun through personal acquaintance often depends on our ability to write a good letter.

Realizing the importance of letter writing, we should make the best use of our opportunities while we are in school. In no other type of composition are our chances of success better, for we have something to say, an immediate valid reason for saying it, and a definite person to whom we wish to say it. We have a strong natural incentive, too, in our desire to entertain our correspondents; but to accomplish our desire, we must put our best efforts into writing correctly and clearly and in accord with the demands of good form.

47. Requirements of Good Form in Social Letters

Though the general principles of composition govern the writing of letters, there are certain particular rules relating to form and arrangement that we should understand.

Correct usage and proper courtesy to our correspondents demand that we follow these established rules in all our letters.

1. Writing materials. Use regular four-page sheets of correspondence paper, unruled and preferably white. Notes and letters not more than a page in length may be written on single sheets of note paper or on correspondence cards. Write with a pen, never a pencil, and use black or blue-black ink.

2. Manuscript. Make your letter neat and attractive by spacing the various parts (see sections 48–53) correctly and arranging the contents symmetrically on the page. At the top of the page and on each side leave a margin in proportion to the size of the stationery. Make the indention of paragraphs uniform. See that the manuscript of your letter is free from finger prints, smudges, blots, and unsightly erasures. Do all you can in respect to the form and the arrangement of your letter to make the reading of it easy and pleasurable for your correspondent.

3. Order of pages. In a letter of more than two pages, use both sides of the sheet and write on the pages in regular book order. If your letter does not exceed two pages, write on pages one and three.

4. Legibility. Use a pen suited to your style of handwriting and write legibly. Avoid flourishes and the peculiar formation of letters. Keep the lines straight, and do not crowd lines so close together that the letters of one line run into those of the line above. Leave the proper amount of space between words, and avoid crowding the letters in a word. Capitalize and punctuate distinctly.

5. Revising. See that your letter is correct in form, grammar, sentence structure, paragraphing, choice of words, spelling, capitalization, punctuation, and other mechanical details. Rewrite it if necessary.

6. Folding. Fold your letter so that it will fit exactly the envelope designed for it. The four-page sheet should be folded once horizontally across the center. Note paper should be folded once or twice, according to the size of the envelope. Place the letter in the envelope in such a manner that when it is removed and unfolded it will be in the right position to be read.

Exercise 116

Examine carefully the letter on page 111. Observe the spacing, capitalization, and punctuation. Point out in detail how the letter satisfies the requirements of good form.

I. PARTS OF A LETTER
48. The Heading

The heading of a letter is usually placed in the upper right corner of the page, about an inch from the top. It should include the street (avenue, road, or rural route) and number, the town and state, and the date. In a letter to an intimate friend we may omit the address, although it is better to include it. The date should never be omitted.

The heading may be written in two, three, or even four lines, according to the length of the address, either with or without punctuation at the end of each line. Furthermore, the address may be written in block form, or each line after the first may be successively indented.

The style of arrangement and the punctuation adopted for the heading of the letter should be followed consistently in writing the inside address and the address on the envelope.

49. The Inside Address

In a letter to any person who is not a relative or an intimate friend, the correspondent's name and address should appear. The name should be written about two

212 Prairie Avenue
Middleton, Indiana
September 21, 1931

Dear Miss Erskine,

Why did you ever leave our school? Of course we are all glad that you secured the excellent position that you did in Denver, but we shall never cease to miss you. It seems strange to see Miss Anderson in your room. Every time that I go to my English class I still expect to find you there.

Last Friday the juniors held their class election. Bob Preston was chosen president, Edith Hart, vice-president, Helen Drury, secretary, and Dick Howard, treasurer. I was elected junior editor of The Chronicle. Next Wednesday the Girls' Debating Club will hold its first meeting. How we wish that you were again to be our adviser!

You should have been here last summer for the wedding of Miss Noyes and Mr. Johnson. They were married at the Country Club. It was a beautiful wedding. Miss Foster was maid of honor, and Mr. Trent was best man. Mr. and Mrs. Johnson received many lovely presents. The School Board presented them with a radio. Dorothy, mother, and I gave them a set of table linens. They spent their honeymoon in California. They are now living in Mrs. Bronson's little cottage, where you and Miss Spencer lived the first year you were here. Mrs. Johnson is again teaching domestic science.

Mr. Pratt is as devoted as ever to Miss Hoyt. Many predict that they are going to be married at Christmas time. Just think, you might have been Mrs. Pratt! Wouldn't that have been thrilling! No?

Mother says give you her love and tell you that we certainly do miss you at tea on Sunday afternoons. Dorothy joins me in wishing for you a happy and successful year in your new work.

Sincerely your friend,
Louise Ripley

Miss Frances Erskine
1647 Astoria Street
Denver, Colorado

line spaces below the line of the date, and should begin at the left side of the page, about half an inch from the edge of the paper. This half-inch margin at the left should be observed on every page of the letter.

The inside address may consist of three or four lines, according to its length. In semiformal letters it is often placed at the end, instead of at the beginning, on the left side of the page and a little below the line of the writer's name. In familiar letters it is permissible to omit it altogether.

50. The Salutation

The salutation, or greeting of affection or respect, should begin even with the left margin of the page and be placed one line space below the last line of the address. In semiformal social letters, where the address is written at the end, or in familiar letters, where it is omitted, the salutation should be placed two line spaces below the line of the date.

The wording of the salutation will vary according to our relation to our correspondent, but the first word and the name of the person or the word standing for his name should always be capitalized. If the tone of the letter is formal, a colon may be used after the salutation, but in a familiar letter a comma is preferable.

Exercise 117

The beginning of a letter includes the heading, the inside address, and the salutation.

Study the spacing, capitalization, and punctuation of the specimen beginnings of letters illustrated below. The inside address in the first illustration may be placed after the letter if it is semiformal. (See the letter in Exercise 116.)

In each of the other three illustrations the inside address may be omitted altogether. Why? Observe the capitalization and punctuation of each greeting. Be prepared to write without an error all four headings from dictation.

1. *Successive Indention without End Punctuation*

> 421 Huron Avenue
> Chicago, Illinois
> January 17, 1931
>
> Mr. Charles H. Sprague
> 78 West Sixth Street
> Portland, Oregon
>
> My dear Mr. Sprague:

2. *Successive Indention with End Punctuation*

> 187 Prospect Street,
> Montreal, Canada,
> March 27, 1931.
>
> Mrs. Louise Carrington,
> 37 Ellsworth Place,
> Hartford, Connecticut.
>
> Dear Grandmother,

3. *Block Form without End Punctuation*

> Rural Route 3
> Port Arthur, Texas
> February 21, 1931
>
> Dr. J. W. Earhart
> 140 Park Road
> Los Angeles, California
>
> Dear Uncle John,

4. *Block Form with End Punctuation*

167 Adams Street,
Louisville, Kentucky,
April 19, 1931.

Miss Eleanor Clifford,
1428 Lakeside Drive,
Gary, Indiana.

Dear Eleanor,

Exercise 118

Using the models given in Exercise 117, write the beginning of four letters to relatives and friends.

51. The Letter Proper

We should begin the letter itself one line space below the salutation and indent the first line. If the letter contains more than one principal topic, we should devote a paragraph to each topic. In a long letter we may find the use of a simple outline very helpful. We should make a practice of expressing our thoughts in complete sentences, though elliptical, or abbreviated, sentences that are instantly clear are permissible. In every respect our letter should be clear, correct, and entertaining.

52. The Conclusion

The conclusion of a letter is made up of two parts, the complimentary close and the signature.

By the complimentary close we mean the concluding words of respect or affection, such as the following:

Sincerely yours,   Cordially yours,
Yours sincerely,   Yours affectionately,
Your sincere friend,   Yours with love,
Gratefully yours,   Your loving daughter,
Faithfully yours,   Devotedly yours,

The complimentary close should be placed one line space below the last line of the letter proper. Only the first word should begin with a capital letter, and the last word should always be followed by a comma. The examples given below illustrate conclusions properly written.

1. My brother joins me in wishing you a happy vacation.

Your sincere friend,

Grant Moreland

2. Mother and I shall expect to see you in Denver next summer.

Sincerely yours,

Harriet Whilman

3. I hope to have the pleasure of seeing you this summer.

Cordially yours,

Gordon Maveriek

We must bear in mind that styles change in letter writing as well as in other things. The old-fashioned form of closing a letter with such an expression as

Hoping to hear from you soon,
I am
Sincerely yours,

is no longer considered permissible. The body of the letter should be complete in itself, and not joined to the complimentary close. The three forms given above are the best usage of the present day.

The signature is written one line space below the complimentary close. In letters to intimate friends or to relatives we may sign merely our first name, but in other cases we should write our name in full. When a woman is writing to a stranger or to anyone else who is not familiar with her position, it is customary for her to indicate whether or not she is married by inclosing her title in parentheses at the left of her name or by prefixing her title to her husband's name, in parentheses, immediately beneath her own. Below are given some examples of conclusions thus written.

1. *An Intimate Friend*

Affectionately yours,

Marion

2. *An Unmarried Woman*

Sincerely yours,

(Miss) Eleanor Marsden

3. *A Married Woman*

Very truly yours,

Louise Medford
(Mrs. Lawrence Medford)

4. *A Widow Who Prefers to Use Her Own Name*

Very truly yours,

(Mrs.) Louise Medford

53. The Superscription

The superscription, or the address of the person for whom the letter is intended, should be written symmetrically on the lower half of the envelope. In content, spacing, and punctuation it should be the same as the inside address.

In addition to the superscription, we should write our address in the upper left corner of the envelope. This insures the return of the letter if it cannot be delivered.

The two specimens given below illustrate envelopes correctly addressed.

1. *Indented Form with End Punctuation*

> David C. Kemp,
>   87 Lake Street,
>   Clinton, Oregon.
>
>
>   Mr. John H. Brennan,
>   115 Iroquois Avenue,
>   Madison, Wisconsin.
>
> Please forward.

2. *Block Form without End Punctuation*

> Helen C. Ives
> Hotel Wentworth
> Boulder, Colorado
>
>
>   Mr. Horace W. Patterson
>   Superintendent of Schools
>   1912 Wyandotte Avenue
>   Williamsport, Louisiana

Using appropriate stationery, write a social letter to one of your relatives or friends. Do your best to make it entertaining. See that it is correct in form and in all details of composition. Submit it in an envelope properly addressed.

II. TYPES OF SOCIAL LETTERS

54. Contents and Style of Social Letters

It is impossible to state definitely what a good social letter should contain. The subject matter will depend, obviously, upon our purpose in writing, our relation to our correspondent, and our recognition of his interest in our choice of topics. The style, or manner of expression, that we employ will be governed by our personality and that of the person to whom we are writing, and to some extent by our mood and purpose. The style should be that of good conversation, easy, natural, and animated, yet colloquially correct, courteous, and refined. Both by what we say and how we say it we should make our letter entertaining to the reader. He should experience pleasure while he is reading it; and when he has finished, he should feel that it was written for him and him alone. Proper courtesy demands that our letters be neat and attractive in manuscript and that they be correct in all details of good form.

In our study of the various types of social letters illustrated in the following exercises and in writing the letters assigned we should give attention to contents and style as well as to form and arrangement.

55. Personal News Letters

The most common type of social letter is that in which we tell others of ourselves and our affairs. Frequently we include also news of our relatives and friends. In contents a personal news letter should show that we have due regard for the interests of our correspondent, and in style it should be natural and entertaining.

Exercise 120

Read again, as an example of the personal news letter, the specimen given in Exercise 116.

Exercise 121

Study the specimen given below as an example of the personal news letter. Point out its good qualities, and explain its form.

> Royal Palace Hotel
> London, England
> August 16, 1931

Dear Bob,

Well, here I am in London. Uncle John and I arrived here last Monday by airplane from Brussels. How you would have enjoyed that trip! It was a perfect day for flying. What a thrill I got looking down four thousand feet at the English Channel and seeing the white cliffs of Dover! The English landscape was a perfect picture of bright green fields and darker green woods cut by a network of tiny streams that looked like silver ribbons. The little villages resembled groups of toy houses. All too quickly for me the trip came to an end.

London is a wonderfully interesting city. I like it much better than Paris, possibly because so many of the places seem more familiar to me from my study of English history and literature. I feel more at home here also because I can understand what people are saying. My one year of French did not help me very much in Paris.

Every day since our arrival Uncle John and I have been sight-seeing. I have been twice to Westminster Abbey. It seemed like a dream to be standing in the midst of the graves of so many of the kings, queens, statesmen, and poets that made English history and literature. We also went through the Houses of Parliament and many other places of historic and literary interest. Last night we ate at the quaint old Cheshire Cheese, where Dr. Johnson, Dickens, and many other great writers used to eat and talk. Tomorrow we leave for a three-day tour to Stratford-on-Avon, Warwick Castle, and Oxford.

We sail for home on September first. When I see you, I will try to give you a full account of my wonderful trip.

Sincerely yours,

Fred

Exercise 122

Write a good personal news letter suggested by one of the situations given below. Make your letter correct in form, interesting in subject matter, and natural in style.

1. Suppose that your father or mother is away from home. Tell him or her all the interesting home news.

2. Suppose that you are away from home. Give your family an account of what you are doing and of the persons whom you have met.

3. Write to a former teacher, giving an account of yourself and your school life at the present time.

4. Suppose that you are taking a vacation trip. Tell one of your friends at home of some of your most interesting experiences.

5. Write a letter to a chum, giving an account of a recent athletic contest in which your school took part.

56. Letters of Invitation

We often write brief letters and informal notes (see section 65) to extend an invitation to a relative or a friend to visit us or to join us in doing something enjoyable. Such notes and letters should be cordial and sincere. Sometimes, as in the letter given in Exercise 123, we may include an invitation in a personal news letter.

Exercise 123

Examine closely the following letter. Do you find the contents entertaining? Is the style natural and appropriate? Why is the letter divided into five paragraphs?

Greenacres Farm
Glencoe, N.H.
June 16, 1931

Dear Marjorie,

Here I am at Glencoe for the whole summer. It really seems too wonderful to be true — visiting this old house of grandmother's. You know, it's a Revolutionary farmhouse. Indeed, it certainly does not hide that distinction, for I don't believe a paintbrush has touched it for ever so many years. The wall papers inside are almost covered with stains; but this does not trouble grandmother. She says she wants Greenacres to look just as it was when she first came here with grandfather. The rooms downstairs are large and airy, but those upstairs are small and delightfully cozy. Grandmother has given me the one she used to have, and she couldn't have suited me better. It's furnished in dark walnut — just the things she used so long ago. And, Marjorie, I just wish you could see the view from the windows. I know you would be sketching it in no time.

But the most interesting thing about Greenacres is the secret room. As I know your fondness for such things, let me tell you a little about it. First, where is it? Where do you suppose? Why, behind a large portrait of the man it sheltered long ago — my great-great-great-grandfather. He seems a long way back, doesn't he? As it is behind a picture, it must naturally be high up on the wall. And so it is: you have to scale a stepladder before you can even see in.

It was in June, 1776, that, as my great-great-great-grandmother sat peeling apples by the kitchen window, a young soldier rushed up to the house. He said that some redcoats were on his trail, and that he must find a hiding-place. Grandmother jumped so that the apples rolled all over the floor; but the next minute she was over her surprise and had put the man in the secret room.

While he was in there he carved his initials on the wall, and as he was going that evening, he told grandmother — I can't write out all the *greats* — that sometime he would come back and thank her properly for sheltering him, and maybe sometime would add some initials to his own. He came back when the war was over and thanked her quite properly. Now, as you look into the room behind the picture, you can dimly see "B. M.," bracketed with "A. L." There is more to the story, but that must wait to be told.

And now, Marjorie, "the last the best of all the rest." I want you to come next week and see these sights with your very own eyes. Please, please come, Marjorie, and don't disappoint me.

Very lovingly your friend,

Estelle Wellwood

Exercise 124

Write a good letter of invitation to a relative or a friend. Make him feel, when he reads your letter, that he will be welcome and that you will be glad to do all you can to help him enjoy himself. If you wish, you may include in your letter appropriate personal news.

57. Letters Requesting Favors

Throughout life we shall have occasion now and then to write letters asking other persons to assist us in doing something or in getting something that we desire. We should always express our request courteously, and we should avoid asking our correspondent to do anything for us that would cause him embarrassment or serious inconvenience.

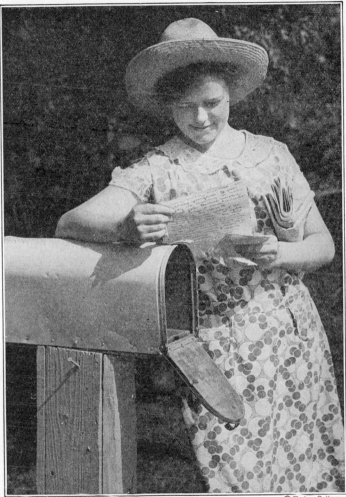

© Ewing Galloway

A Good Letter

Exercise 125

Read again, as an example of the letter requesting a favor, the one that you rewrote in the Test Exercise on page 106.

Exercise 126

Write one of the following letters requesting favors:

1. A letter asking a relative or a friend in another locality to purchase and have sent to you some article that you cannot obtain.

2. A letter requesting a man or a woman who is a friend of your school to speak at the next assembly or to write an article for your school paper.

3. A letter asking a competent relative or friend to advise you in choosing the college that you shall attend.

4. A letter requesting an influential friend of your family to assist you in obtaining a desirable position for vacation.

5. A letter based on a situation of your own choice.

58. Letters of Presentation

When we present a gift or other token of esteem to a person, we usually write an appropriate note or letter to accompany it. This is a social courtesy that adds to the recipient's enjoyment of the gift.

Exercise 127

Write a letter of presentation to accompany one of the following gifts:

1. A Christmas present.
2. A birthday present.
3. Flowers to a sick person.
4. A medal for heroism.

59. Letters of Appreciation

When we have been entertained as a guest, or when someone has presented us a gift or has done us a favor, we should express our appreciation in a letter of thanks. Such letters we should write promptly, and by our sincere personal style cause the reader to feel that we are truly grateful.

Exercise 128

Study the contents, style, and arrangement of the letter of appreciation given below. Discuss its good points.

Holmes Memorial Hospital
Buffalo, New York
November 16, 1931

Dear Louise,

How could I ever have endured the past ten days here in the hospital had it not been for your cheery letters and your most amusing class diary, "The Daily Doings of the Ten Bees!" I think Miss Newman should give you extra credit in English for this diary, though perhaps you'd hardly care to submit it to her to read. Your animated cartoons are splendid, especially those of Mr. Bleyer and Ira Kent.

Mother has perhaps told you that I am rapidly improving and that I expect to be back home by Thanksgiving. I hope to return to school early in December. It is surely dear of you, Agnes, and Thelma to offer to help me catch up in my studies. I shall perhaps be able to study some after I get home.

This is the first letter I've been allowed to write. It has been hard to wait so long, Louise, to thank you for all the fun you've given me. Now that I'm getting better, I'll write you often. I'm eagerly waiting for the next installment of the diary and the November number of *The Beacon* with your story in it. As soon as I return home, I want you to come to see me every day.

Please thank the class for the lovely flowers. I cried for happiness when the nurse brought them to me.

Lovingly yours,

Betty

Exercise 129

Write a letter of appreciation to the person who did you the favor requested in the letter that you wrote in Exercise 126.

Exercise 130

Impersonating the recipient of the gift and of the letter that you wrote in Exercise 127, write an appropriate letter of thanks.

Exercise 131

Suppose that you have recently been entertained as a guest in the home of one of your friends. Write an appropriate letter, thanking your hostess for her hospitality.

60. Letters of Congratulation and Commendation

When a relative or a friend has accomplished a difficult task, has gained recognition for his ability in some worthy undertaking, or has won success in spite of great difficulties, we prove our admiration for him by writing him a letter congratulating him on his achievement and commending him for his effort.

Exercise 132

Examine the following letter of congratulation:

127 Putnam Avenue
Tulsa, Oklahoma
May 31, 1931

Dear Allan,

Three cheers and heartiest congratulations! We knew that you'd pass the bar examination with flying colors. We are all delighted at your success, old man, and we are tremendously proud of you. You deserve to win, and we predict that you'll continue to win. May your future be as bright as the lamp that we used to see shining from your study window after your day's hard work was over and you had "earned a night's repose."

Your admiring friend,

Donald Clark

Exercise 133

Write a letter congratulating a relative or a friend upon his success in some worthy undertaking.

Exercise 134

You are doubtless familiar with the life story of Helen Keller. Though she could not see or hear, and in her early life was unable to talk, she learned to speak and write, gained an excellent education, and has achieved greater success as a lecturer and writer than most persons who are normally endowed.

Here is a letter of commendation that Oliver Wendell Holmes wrote to Helen Keller when she was ten years of age. Study the style and contents. Point out any details of form that are not in accordance with the best usage today.

> Beverly Farms, Massachusetts,
> August 1, 1890.

My dear little friend Helen,

It gratifies me very much to find that you remember me so kindly. Your letter is charming, and I am greatly pleased with it. I rejoice to know that you are well and happy. I am very much delighted to hear of your new acquisition — that "you talk with your mouth" as well as with your fingers. What a curious thing *speech* is! The tongue is so serviceable a member (taking all sorts of shapes, just as wanted), the teeth, lips, the roof of the mouth all ready to help, and so heap up the sound of the voice into the solid bits which we call consonants, and make room for the curiously shaped breathings which we call vowels. You have studied all this, I don't doubt, since you have practised vocal speaking.

I am surprised at the mastery of language which your letter shows. It almost makes me think the world would get along as well without seeing and hearing as with them. Perhaps people would be better in a great many ways, for they could not fight as they do now. Just think of an army of blind people, with guns and cannon! Think of the poor drummers! Of what use would they and their drumsticks be? You are spared the pain of many sights and sounds, which you are only too happy in escaping. Then, think of how much kindness you are assured of as long as you live. Everybody will feel an interest in dear little Helen; everybody will want to do something for her; and if she becomes an ancient, gray-haired woman, she is still sure of being thoughtfully cared for.

Your parents and friends must take great satisfaction in your progress. It does great credit, not only to you, but to your instructors, who have so broken down the walls that seemed to shut you in, that now your outlook seems more bright and cheerful than that of many seeing and hearing children.

Good-bye, dear little Helen. With every kind wish, I am

> Your friend,
>
> Oliver Wendell Holmes.

Exercise 135

Perhaps you have a relative or a friend who is struggling against some physical handicap or some unfavorable environment. Write a letter in which you encourage and commend him or her.

61. Letters of Sympathy

A relative or a friend who has suffered some bereavement or other misfortune greatly appreciates letters of kindly sympathy. In writing a letter of condolence we should try to put ourselves in the place of the unfortunate person, and by what we say and by the sincere, friendly manner in which we express our sympathy we should endeavor to show the genuineness of our feelings and help to divert the reader's thoughts from his troubles.

Exercise 136

Read the letter of condolence given below. Observe how simply and sincerely the writer has expressed her sympathy.

316 Linden Street
Asheville, North Carolina
October 18, 1931

Dear Marion,

I cannot put into words the deep sympathy that I feel for you in the loss of your mother. I wish that I might do more for you than assure you of my tenderest love. My life will always be richer and finer for having known your mother and for having had the privilege of being so often in your home. You were indeed fortunate to enjoy for so many years the comradeship of such a wonderful mother. And how happy you made her! The joy you gave her all your life by your jolly companionship and your loving care of her during her long illness should be a great comfort to you now.

Sincerely your friend,

Elizabeth Jordan

Exercise 137

Put your best effort into writing one of the following letters of sympathy:

1. A letter to a classmate who is in a hospital.
2. A letter to someone who has lost a pet that he loved.
3. A letter to a relative or a friend who has been crippled or who has been made blind by a recent accident.
4. A letter to a relative or a friend who has recently lost a member of his family.
5. A letter based on a situation of your own choice.

62. Letters of Apology

Occasionally we act thoughtlessly, speak rudely, or are otherwise discourteous to someone. We are later greatly embarrassed by our misconduct. Under such humiliating circumstances the best thing that we can do is to write to the person or persons whom we have mistreated, acknowledge our fault, make a sincere apology, and ask for forgiveness.

Exercise 138

Examine closely the contents and the style of the letter of apology printed below.

> 915 Forest Street
> Newark, New Jersey
> November 15, 1931

Dear Bob,

I am heartily ashamed of myself for allowing momentary jealousy to cause me to say to you what I said yesterday. I confess I was disappointed that my story was not awarded first prize, but I had no reason for saying that you were the judges' favorite. I know that their decision was fair and just. I sincerely congratulate you on your success. You won on merit. If you can forgive my rudeness, I will try to prove myself more worthy of your friendship.

> Yours sincerely,
>
> Joe Emory

Exercise 139

Suppose that your conduct on some recent occasion has been unbecoming and unworthy of you. Write the person or persons whom you have treated discourteously a sincere letter of apology.

63. Letters of Introduction and Recommendation

Now and then we write a letter introducing one friend of ours to another. In a letter recommending something that we have found profitable or enjoyable we may help a friend in making a wise choice. Such letters, as distinguished from business letters of this type, are primarily social in their purpose.

Exercise 140

Write a letter introducing one friend of yours to another. By mentioning some of the characteristics, tastes, achievements, and hobbies of the person whom you are introducing, try to interest the reader in knowing him or her personally.

Exercise 141

Write a letter to a relative or a friend in which you recommend one of the following:

1. A book.
2. A play.
3. An automobile.
4. A magazine.
5. A preparatory school.
6. A pleasure resort.

64. Occasional Letters

Such occasions in the lives of our friends and relatives as birthdays, wedding anniversaries, Christmas, Easter, and Thanksgiving we commemorate by writing appropriate letters. Letters of this type should always fit the occasion and be adapted to the age, personality, and interest of our correspondent.

Exercise 142

Write one of the following occasional letters:

1. A birthday letter to a little girl or boy.
2. A birthday letter to an aged relative or friend.
3. A letter congratulating relatives or friends on their wedding anniversary.
4. A letter of good cheer appropriate to Christmas, Easter, or Thanksgiving.
5. A letter in honor of an occasion of your own choice.

65. Informal Notes

Informal notes are brief social letters on any subject where friendly communication is desired. Because of their brevity they should usually be limited to one topic. They are always written in the *first* person, and should be simple, direct, and individual in expression.

For a note of more than a page we may use a regular four-page sheet of correspondence paper. A note of less than a page we may write on a single sheet of note paper, or on a correspondence card to be inclosed in an envelope, but good taste forbids our using a postal card for personal messages. In general, the arrangement is similar to that of a social letter, though the occasion and our relation to our correspondent must guide us in certain details of form.

Exercise 143

A. Study and discuss in class the contents, style, and form of the informal notes of invitation and acceptance given below.

1. *An Informal Invitation*

Dear Mr. Whitney,

I hope that you will give us the pleasure of dining with us next Friday, October twenty-first, at seven o'clock. Our friend Mr. Cranston, who has spent the past year in South America, will be our guest over the week-end, and I believe that you will enjoy meeting him and hearing an account of his travels.

Yours sincerely,
Margaret Chandler

286 Prospect Street
October nineteenth

2. *An Informal Reply*

> Dear Mrs. Chandler,
>
> It is kind of you to ask me to dinner. I shall be delighted to come, and shall enjoy hearing of Mr. Cranston's year in South America.
>
> Yours sincerely,
> James B. Whitney
>
> 17 Washington Street
> October twentieth

B. If Mr. Whitney had been unable to accept Mrs. Chandler's invitation, he would have followed the same general form in his reply but would have expressed his regret and given his reason for declining the invitation. Write his informal note of regret.

Exercise 144

A. Indicate the good points in each of the two informal notes given below.

1. *An Informal Note Accompanying a Gift*

> Christ Church, December 21, 1883.
>
> Dear Mrs. Hargreaves,
>
> Perhaps the shortest day in the year is not *quite* the most appropriate time for recalling the long dreamy summer afternoons of ancient times; but, anyhow, if this book gives you half as much pleasure to receive it as it does me to send, it will be a success indeed.
>
> Wishing you all happiness at this happy season, I am
>
> Sincerely yours,
>
> C. L. Dodgson.

2. *An Informal Note of Commendation*

> Valima, Samoa, December 3, 1893.
>
> Dear Johnnie, — Well, I must say you seem to be a tremendous fellow! Before I was eight I used to write stories — or dictate them at least — and I had produced an excellent history of Moses, for which I got £1 from an uncle; but I had never gone the length of a play, so you have beaten me fairly on my own ground. I hope you may continue to do so, and thanking you heartily for your nice letter, I shall beg you to believe me yours truly,
>
> Robert Louis Stevenson.

B. Write one or more of the informal notes suggested below. In contents, style, and form make each note appropriate to the occasion and to the person to whom you write.

1. An invitation to one of your teachers to dine at your home and meet a relative of yours who is also a teacher.

2. A note accepting an invitation.

3. A note declining an invitation.

4. A note to accompany a gift to a relative or a friend.

5. A note of thanks for a present that you have just received from an intimate friend or a relative.

6. A note explaining your absence from school.

7. A reply to a note of sympathy that you have just received from a classmate.

8. A note of congratulation.

9. A note inviting a chum of yours to a week-end party at your summer camp.

10. A note of apology.

11. A note for an occasion or purpose of your own choice, or one that your teacher may suggest.

12. A note expressing sympathy for a person who has been unfortunate.

66. Formal Notes

Formal notes usually pertain to the etiquette of social life. Such notes should be written in the *third* person. The month, the day of the week, and the hour of the event for which the invitation is intended should be mentioned, though the year, except in wedding and commencement invitations and announcements, is usually omitted. The date and the hour should always be spelled out. The place and time of writing are written below the body of the note and at the left side. Everything in these two lines except the street number should be spelled out.

Exercise 145

If the invitation and the reply given in Exercise 143 were expressed in formal style, they would be written in the form illustrated below. Study these examples closely.

1. *A Formal Invitation*

> Mr. and Mrs. Thomas Chandler request the pleasure of Mr. James B. Whitney's company at dinner on Friday evening, October the twenty-first, at seven o'clock.
>
> 286 Prospect Street
> October the nineteenth

2. *A Formal Reply, Accepting*

> Mr. Whitney accepts with pleasure Mr. and Mrs. Chandler's kind invitation to dinner on Friday evening, October the twenty-first, at seven o'clock.
>
> 17 Washington Street
> October the twentieth

3. A Formal Reply, Declining

> *Mr. Whitney regrets that he cannot accept Mr. and Mrs. Chandler's kind invitation to dinner on Friday evening, October the twenty-first.*
>
> *17 Washington Street*
> *October the twentieth*

Exercise 146

Write three or more of the formal notes suggested below.

1. A note, in the name of your father and mother, inviting the principal of your school to a reception at your home. Name the day and the hour.

2. A note, in the name of your class, inviting the superintendent of your school to attend a class dinner.

3. A note accepting an invitation to a birthday party.

4. A note declining an invitation to a dance.

5. A note accepting an invitation to the graduating exercises of a school.

67. Telegrams

A telegram is a communication as briefly expressed as clearness and courtesy will permit. In a telegram the salutation and the complimentary close, required in all letters and informal notes, are regularly omitted. In order that a message may be accurately transmitted by the operator, we should write legibly and use great care in phrasing, for the telegram read by our correspondent will not be punctuated or divided into sentences. We should give the complete address of the receiver, including, if possible, his telephone number. Unless we are communicating with a relative or an intimate friend, we should sign our full name. If we expect a reply, we should write at the end of the message our own telephone number and mail address.

Since the rate for transmitting a telegram is based on a ten-word limit, most persons try to condense their message to this limit, but there is no economy in restricting a telegram to fewer than ten words. As a rule, if we use only essential words, we can say clearly within this limit what we have to say, but we should never economize in words at the expense of clearness and courtesy. For messages of considerable length, day letters and night letters, each based on a fifty-word limit and sent at a reduced rate, are convenient, though they are not so promptly transmitted as a regular telegram. We should become familiar with the other kinds of telegraphic service, which are fully explained on the back of the sheet provided for the message.

Exercise 147

Examine closely the form and the contents of the following telegrams. Notice that careful phrasing makes each message clear without the aid of punctuation or division into sentences.

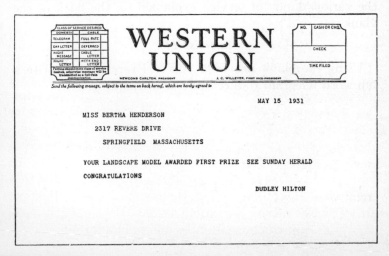

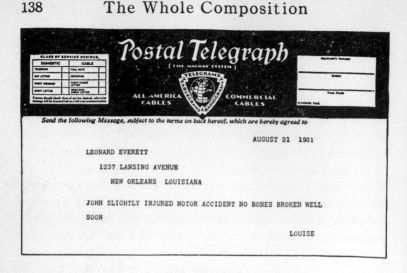

AUGUST 21 1931

LEONARD EVERETT

1237 LANSING AVENUE

NEW ORLEANS LOUISIANA

JOHN SLIGHTLY INJURED MOTOR ACCIDENT NO BONES BROKEN WELL
SOON

LOUISE

Exercise 148

Your teacher will provide you with a blank, secured from one of the local telegraph offices, for writing a telegram or a cablegram. Come to class prepared to discuss the various kinds of service explained on the back of the blank.

Exercise 149

Using the blank provided you in Exercise 148, write a ten-word telegram to a relative or a friend.

CHAPTER VI

Business Letters

Test Exercise

Using appropriate stationery, copy the business letter printed below. Divide it into two paragraphs. Space it properly on the page, divide it into sentences, and supply the necessary capital letters and punctuation. Fold the letter correctly and place it in an envelope of the right size and kind. Address the envelope but leave it unsealed. If you use a typewriter skillfully, you may type the letter.

This exercise affords you the opportunity to show how much you know about good form in business letters. It is likewise a test, to some extent, of your knowledge of paragraphing, sentence structure, capitalization, and punctuation. Do your best to prepare a perfect manuscript. If your letter is perfect in every detail, you may be excused from as many of the drill exercises in this chapter as your teacher thinks best.

127 magnolia road anniston alabama october 3 1931 roach typewriter exchange 618 commerce street atlanta georgia dear sirs through some error in your office you sent me a bill for $45 instead $35 when i bought the portable typewriter from you you agreed to allow me $10 for my old machine and to accept it and $5 as the first payment you must have received this first payment for the new machine was delivered to me early in september as soon as i receive the corrected bill crediting me with $10 for the old machine i will mail you a check for $5 the october installment very truly yours ruth c nugent

Preliminary Assignment

For the purpose of serving your school and community and of acquiring profitable experience, organize your class into a "Business-Letter Service Club." Select a chairman, who will later appoint such committees as may be needed to carry on the work of the Club.

During the time that skill in the writing of business letters is being developed by the study of this chapter, members of the Club may prepare a list of the persons, firms, and organizations that might be in need of such services as the Club can give. In such a list the following would probably be included:

1. Parents, other relatives, and friends.
2. The principal of the school.
3. Teachers of various subjects.
4. The school librarian.
5. The coach or the director of athletics.
6. The manager of the school bookstore or lunch room.
7. The editor of the school publication.
8. The chairman of the auditorium committee.
9. The school physician, dentist, or nurse.
10. The purchasing agent of the board of education.
11. The director of manual training, domestic science, or vocational studies.
12. Local firms suggested by the principal.

Before the Club seeks assignments in the writing of business letters, such questions as the following should be discussed:

1. What has the Club to offer in the way of service?
2. Can typewritten letters be supplied?
3. How soon after an assignment is secured can delivery be guaranteed?
4. What data will be needed from each person served?
5. In what form shall the data be recorded?

6. How can the data be made available to all members of the Club? (Posting a data sheet for each assignment on the room bulletin board is one good method.)

7. How shall the assignments be distributed?

8. How are the charges for materials used to be figured and paid? What use will be made of the money obtained?

When, in the opinion of your teacher, your Club has had sufficient training in the writing of business letters to render satisfactory service, the chairman may appoint one pupil, or a committee of not more than three pupils, to interview each of several of the persons chosen from the Club list.

During the actual preparation of the letters, the appointment of some members of the Club as Readers, Editors, and Compilers (see Preliminary Assignment, Chapter V) might prove helpful. In this case the Compilers would select the best letter, see that it reached the person making the assignment, and file a copy of it in a loose-leaf binder.

68. Importance of Business Letters

In spite of the use of the telephone and the telegraph as means of quick communication, letters are necessary in most business transactions. Millions of letters having a commercial purpose are written every week. Business men regard the letter as so true an index of the personality and education of the writer that they require applicants seeking responsible positions to make their application in writing. To write a good business letter we must satisfy the requirements of good form and set forth clearly, effectively, and briefly what we have to say. Such ability we should try to develop during our practice of composition in high school. If we will write whenever possible to real persons, firms, and organizations for the purpose of transacting actual personal business, we shall find the writing of business letters much more enjoyable and far more profitable.

69. Requirements of Good Form in Business Letters

Though in most respects the form of business letters is the same as that of social letters (see section 47), a few differences are to be noted in business letters.

Writing materials. Use unruled white paper approximately $8\frac{1}{2} \times 11$ inches, with envelopes to match. Write either with a pen and ink or on a typewriter.

Manuscript. Make your letter neat and attractive in appearance. If you use a pen and ink, keep your lines straight and the space between them uniform. Write legibly. If you use a typewriter, the body of the letter may be single-spaced or double-spaced, according to its length, but the lines composing the heading and the address should usually be single-spaced. In all typewritten letters leave double space between paragraphs or parts of the letter considered as paragraphs. In typing a line skip one space after each mark of punctuation within the line and two spaces between the end punctuation of one sentence and the beginning of the next. Leave a margin of at least an inch at each side of the page, and if the letter is very short, make the margins wider. The letter as a whole should be symmetrically spaced. If the letter exceeds one page, never write on the back, but use a new sheet.

Folding. Fold your letter neatly and accurately to fit the envelope and in such a manner that, when it is unfolded, it will be in the right position to be read. The ordinary commercial-size envelope (about $3\frac{1}{2} \times 6\frac{1}{2}$ inches) requires that the letter be folded as shown below.

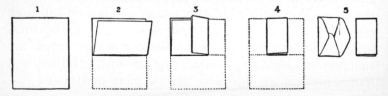

1   2   3   4   5

Exercise 150

Examine closely the form, spacing, capitalization, and punctuation in the letter given below. Point out the five parts. Are they the same as in a social letter?

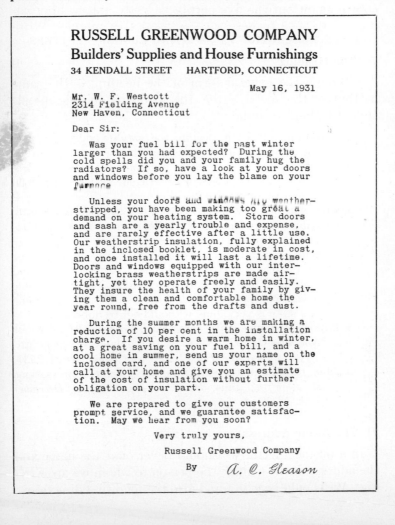

RUSSELL GREENWOOD COMPANY
Builders' Supplies and House Furnishings
34 KENDALL STREET   HARTFORD, CONNECTICUT

May 16, 1931

Mr. W. F. Westcott
2314 Fielding Avenue
New Haven, Connecticut

Dear Sir:

Was your fuel bill for the past winter larger than you had expected? During the cold spells did you and your family hug the radiators? If so, have a look at your doors and windows before you lay the blame on your furnace.

Unless your doors and windows are weather-stripped, you have been making too great a demand on your heating system. Storm doors and sash are a yearly trouble and expense, and are rarely effective after a little use. Our weatherstrip insulation, fully explained in the inclosed booklet, is moderate in cost, and once installed it will last a lifetime. Doors and windows equipped with our interlocking brass weatherstrips are made airtight, yet they operate freely and easily. They insure the health of your family by giving them a clean and comfortable home the year round, free from the drafts and dust.

During the summer months we are making a reduction of 10 per cent in the installation charge. If you desire a warm home in winter, at a great saving on your fuel bill, and a cool home in summer, send us your name on the inclosed card, and one of our experts will call at your home and give you an estimate of the cost of insulation without further obligation on your part.

We are prepared to give our customers prompt service, and we guarantee satisfaction. May we hear from you soon?

Very truly yours,

Russell Greenwood Company

By   *A. C. Gleason*

Exercise 151

Examine for form, spacing, capitalization, and punctuation the letter that you copied in the Test Exercise of this chapter. What improvements can you now make in your copy? Point out the five parts.

I. SPECIAL CAUTIONS IN WRITING BUSINESS LETTERS

70. The Heading

Although the general form of the heading is the same as that of the social letter, the following specific details should be kept in mind:

1. Always include in the heading the *complete* address. If you use paper bearing a letterhead that gives the address, write only the date in the position where the complete heading would otherwise be written. (See the specimen letter in Exercise 150.)
2. The name of a day of the week is not a sufficiently accurate date. Thus, *Tuesday* is not to be used for *October 13, 1931,* for example.
3. In general, avoid the use of abbreviations, especially for the names of streets, avenues, towns, cities, and months. The abbreviations *St.* and *Ave.* are permissible if lack of space demands their use. Unless the name of a state is very long, it should not be abbreviated.
4. Express all figures in the date; thus, *November 21, 1931,* not *November 21, '31.* Never write the date in "sales-slip" style; as, *11/21/31* or *11–21–31* for *November 21, 1931.*
5. After the day of the month do not use the abbreviations *st, d,* or *th*; thus, *December 12, 1931,* not *December 12th, 1931.*

71. The Inside Address

In a business letter we should never omit the name and the address of the firm or the person to whom we are writing. We should bear in mind also the following directions:

1. Write your correspondent's name as he writes it; for example, *Robert W. Sears*, not *R. W. Sears* or *Robt. W. Sears*.

2. Avoid abbreviations of Christian names, such as *Robt.*, *Edw.*, *Thos.*, *Geo.*, *Wm.*, *Chas.*, *Jno.*, *Jas.*

3. In writing to one person always use an appropriate title of courtesy before his name; thus, *Dr. Charles Magnuson*, *Mrs. Mary K. Donnelly*, *Miss Julia Randolph*, *Professor Allan H. Alexander*.

4. You may use the abbreviated form of the following titles of courtesy: *Mr.* (plural *Messrs.*), *Mrs.* (plural *Mesdames*), *Dr.* (plural *Drs.*), and *Esq.* (meaning *esquire*). *Esq.*, which is rarely used except in addressing lawyers and other professional men, is placed after a man's name and separated from it by a comma, thus, *Walter H. Trask*, *Esq.* Never use it after a name preceded by a title.

5. *Miss* (plural *Misses*), the title of an unmarried woman, is not considered an abbreviation and should not be followed by a period.

6. Proper courtesy demands that you write the following titles of respect or office as complete words: *Honorable, President, Governor, Senator, Superintendent, Principal, Professor, Secretary, General, Colonel, Major, Captain, Reverend.* *The* is usually placed before the title *Honorable* when it precedes the name of a high official; as, *The Honorable Charles Evans Hughes.* In addressing a clergyman the title *Reverend* should be preceded by *the*: thus, *The Reverend* Michael P. Doran.

72. The Salutation

The salutation, or greeting of courtesy, should be followed by a colon. The most common forms of salutation in business letters are the following:

1. *To one man:* Dear Sir, My dear Sir, *or* Sir.
2. *To one woman, either married or single:* Dear Madam *or* My dear Madam.
3. *To a man and a woman:* Dear Sir and Madam *or* My dear Sir and Madam.

4. *To a group or firm composed of men:* Dear Sirs, My dear Sirs, *or* Gentlemen.
5. *To a group or firm composed of women:* Ladies *or* Mesdames.
6. *To a friend (in semibusiness form):* Dear Mr. Loring, My dear Mrs. Irving, My dear Doctor Ames, Dear Professor Chase.

Exercise 152

Study the beginnings of the specimen business letters given in this chapter (see Exercises 150, 156, 159, and 162). Pay close attention to the spacing and the punctuation of the different parts. In what details does the beginning of a business letter differ from that of a friendly letter?

Exercise 153

Write the beginning of two business letters to different persons or firms. Illustrate the two ways of spacing and punctuating the heading and the inside address.

73. The Letter Proper

In writing a business letter we should satisfy the following requirements, which may be termed the "Five C's" of a good business letter:

1. It should be *complete* in contents.
2. It should be *clear* in expression.
3. It should be *courteous.*
4. It should be as *concise* as completeness, clearness, and courtesy will permit.
5. It should be *correct* in form and composition.

74. The Conclusion

The complimentary close includes such phrases of courtesy as the following:

1. *In a Formal Business Letter*

Yours truly,   Yours respectfully,
Yours very truly,   Respectfully yours,
Very truly yours,   Very respectfully yours,

2. *In a Semiformal or Friendly Business Letter*

Sincerely yours,   Very sincerely yours,
Yours sincerely,   Cordially yours,

In writing the complimentary close we should remember the following directions:

1. It should not be included in the last sentence of the letter proper.
2. It should begin far enough to the left to allow sufficient space to indent the signature beneath it.
3. Only the first word should be capitalized.
4. It should always be followed by a comma.
5. It should be in keeping with our relations to our correspondent.

The signature, or name that we sign to a letter, should be legibly written and be sufficiently full to identify us accurately. (See section 52.)

Exercise 154

Examine the conclusion of each of the specimen letters given in Exercises 150, 156, 159, and 162.

75. The Superscription

The address on the envelope should be the same in contents and form as the inside address and should be properly spaced. In the upper left corner of the envelope should be written, typed, or printed the writer's address, which will insure the return of the letter if it cannot be delivered.

The models given on page 148 illustrate the correct form and spacing of the material on the envelope.

Indented Form without End Punctuation

```
David H. Gregg
    Route 3
        Bastrop, Texas


                    Mr. Forest J. Cameron

                    University Y.M.C.A.

                        Austin, Texas
```

Block Form without End Punctuation

```
Ruth C. Nugent
127 Magnolia Road
Anniston, Alabama


            Roach Typewriter Exchange

            618 Commerce Street

            Atlanta, Georgia
```

Exercise 155

Address envelopes for the letter in Exercise 150 and for each of the letters for which you wrote the beginning in Exercise 153.

II. TYPES OF BUSINESS LETTERS

76. Letters of Request and Inquiry

Frequently we have occasion to write letters asking for information, soliciting aid, or requesting other favors.

Exercise 156

Examine the contents and the form of the following letter of request. Prove that it satisfies the five requirements mentioned in section 73.

Route 3
Bastrop, Texas
July 26, 1931

Mr. Forest J. Cameron
  University Y.M.C.A.
   Austin, Texas

Dear Mr. Cameron:

In June I was graduated from the Bastrop High School. I hope to enter the University of Texas in September, but in order to do so I must secure some kind of work that will enable me to earn a part of my expenses.

A friend of mine, Charles Downey, who is a junior at the University, said that you, as student-employment secretary, might be able to help me secure a job. Will you please send me a copy of "Opportunities for Self-supporting Students." If you will mail me an application blank, I will fill it out and return it to you.

This summer I am working as usual on my father's poultry farm. I shall have about $200 when I enter school. I am willing to do any kind of work to earn my college expenses. Whatever you can do in helping me to get a job I shall sincerely appreciate.

Very truly yours,

David H. Gregg

Exercise 157

Write one of the following letters of request or inquiry :

1. Ask a pupil in another school to tell you the plan that his school follows in obtaining support for its paper or magazine.

2. Inquire of the director of a boys' or a girls' camp the conditions of admission and the expenses for the summer.

3. Ask the registrar of a college or technical school to explain the admission requirements and to send you a catalogue giving information about a course in which you are interested.

4. Ask a manufacturer of novelties and specialties to allow you to represent him as salesman in your school.

5. A letter of request or inquiry on a subject of your own choice.

77. Informational Letters

When we reply to a letter of request and inquiry, we answer the writer's question or questions in what may be termed an informational letter. Courtesy demands that we answer promptly and give as full and accurate infor-mation as we can.

Exercise 158

Impersonating the receiver of the letter that you wrote in Exercise 157, write an informational letter that will answer adequately the question or questions that you asked.

78. Letters of Application

In a letter of application we introduce ourselves to a prospective employer and try to sell him our services. In it we should set forth accurately and completely all necessary information about ourselves. It should include the following details :

1. Reference to the way in which we heard of the position and mention of the fact that we desire to be considered an applicant.

2. A statement of our qualifications, such as age, health, education, training as an apprentice, practical working experience, and any other special qualifications that will show our fitness for the position sought.
3. The names and addresses of three persons who can vouch for our character and ability.
4. An expression of willingness to call in person for an interview should the prospective employer desire it.

Our chance of securing a position will depend almost wholly on our ability to write an effective letter. We should spare no pains, therefore, to make it correct, clear, and courteous in expression. By proper arrangement, neatness, legibility, and general attractiveness we should do our best to impress the reader favorably.

Exercise 159

Examine closely the letter of application that follows. Does it include the details listed in section 78? Point them out. Notice the contents of each paragraph. Prove that this letter satisfies the five requirements mentioned in section 73.

1764 Elmwood Avenue
Chicago, Illinois
May 17, 1931

Hanson, Fernald and Company
  37 Commercial Street
    Chicago, Illinois

Dear Sirs:

Yesterday Mr. Lucas of your sales department told my father that you need another office boy. Since I am anxious to secure a vacation job, I should like to apply for the position.

I have just completed the ninth grade in the Madison High School. I am fifteen years old, and my health is excellent. During the last two summers I have been employed in the law office of Boynton and Spencer.

They have offered me the job again, but I prefer, if possible, to work in a publishing house such as yours. I am energetic, and I believe that I could render you satisfactory service.

You may obtain further information as to my character and my fitness for this position by writing or telephoning Mr. Robert C. Dana, Principal of the Madison High School, 146 Garfield Street, Mr. J. H. Boynton, Ontario Trust Building, and Mr. George M. Sheldon, Secretary of the Y.M.C.A., 1242 Lake Street.

I shall be glad to call at your office if you wish to see me. My telephone is Regent 4321.

Very truly yours,

Clinton H. Moseley

Exercise 160

Clip from the Help Wanted column of a newspaper an advertisement of a position that you think you could fill acceptably. After studying the advertisement closely, write a letter applying for the position. See that your letter gives accurate information on every qualification mentioned in the advertisement. Do your best to secure the job. When you submit your letter, fasten the advertisement to it with a paper clip.

Exercise 161

Write one of the letters of application suggested below. Try to improve upon the letter that you wrote in Exercise 160.

1. Last summer your brother had a very satisfactory job. His employers have asked him to work for them again this summer, but he has other plans. He has given you the letter that they wrote him, and you decide that you would like the position for yourself. Write a letter in which you explain the situation and state your qualifications.

Which Team Will Win?

© Wide World Photos

2. Your best friend wishes to take a trip abroad next summer, but she must find someone to take her position temporarily. She feels sure that you, with the training that she can give you, could do the work satisfactorily. Write a letter to her employer, stating the circumstances and making application for the position.

3. Impersonating Robert D. Chalmers, author of the letter that you copied in the Test Exercise, Chapter V, write a letter to Mr. Frank G. Norwood applying for the position of assistant manager of the lunch room.

4. You have heard that a tea room in the town where your parents have recently bought a summer cottage needs another waitress for the season. Last summer you did similar work in an adjoining town, but you wish to live at home. Write the necessary letter of application.

5. Write a letter in which you apply for a position of your own choice or one suggested by your teacher or parents.

79. Buying Letters

Now and then we write a buying letter to a mail-order house, a publisher, or some other business firm. Clearness and completeness, upon which depend the prompt and accurate filling of our order, demand that we follow the directions given below in writing a buying letter.

1. Write legibly throughout.
2. Give your complete address.
3. Give the complete address of the person or firm to whom you send your order.
4. Identify accurately the merchandise that you are ordering and specify the quantity that you desire.
5. Give clear directions for the shipment of the merchandise.
6. Indicate how payment is being made or will be made.
7. In subscribing for a magazine or a newspaper, state the form and the amount of the remittance and give the name and the complete address of the person who is to receive the publication. When you ask a publisher to change an address, give the present address as well as the new one.

Exercise 162

Examine closely the buying letter given below. Show specifically how the writer followed directions 2, 3, 4, 5, and 6 mentioned in section 79.

```
                              R. F. D., Route 1
                              Camden, Arkansas
                              April 15, 1931
Grayson Seed Company
  149 Morton Avenue
    St. Louis, Missouri

Dear Sirs:

    You will find inclosed a post-office money order
for $10.80, for which please send me by express the
following items:

 1 "Sure Catch" Mole Trap . . . . . . . . . .   $2.50
 1 5-prong Norcross Hoe Cultivator. . . . . .    1.25
 1 Success Plant Box, Model A, 36 inches long    2.60
 1 pair of Brackets, Model D, No. 3 . . . . .     .80
 1 Brown Auto Sprayer, No. 26 . . . . . . . .    1.25
 4 pounds of Arsenate of Lead (Dry) . . . . .    1.15
25 pounds of Bone Meal. . . . . . . . . . . .    1.25
                                               $10.80
                  Very truly yours,

                            Walter C. Stone
```

Exercise 163

Following the directions given in section 79, write a buying letter in which you order merchandise that you desire.

Exercise 164

Write a letter to a publisher ordering a copy of a book that you have recently seen advertised.

Exercise 165

Write a letter renewing your subscription to a magazine and asking the publisher to send it to a new address.

80. Letters Requesting Adjustments

When a mistake for which we are not responsible has been made in filling an order, when goods reach us in a damaged condition, or when we are dissatisfied with service rendered us, we may present our claim to the dealer or the transportation company and ask that an adjustment be made. The letter that we write should state the facts accurately and clearly and be courteous in expression. (The letter that you copied in the Test Exercise of this chapter illustrates letters of this type.)

Exercise 166

Suppose that a mistake was made in filling the order that you wrote in Exercise 163. Write a letter to the dealer, stating definitely the nature of the error and asking him to make an adjustment.

Exercise 167

Choose one of the following situations and write an appropriate letter asking that an adjustment be made. See that your letter is accurate, clear, and courteous.

1. You asked a local department store to send a certain book as a gift from you to your aunt and to charge it to your account. The book was sent, but it was charged to your aunt's account.

2. In a parcel delivered to you from a store in another town there is included, along with the articles that you purchased, one article that does not belong to you.

3. Soon after you have alighted from the street car you discover that you have left your bag. Write to the "Lost and Found Department," and describe the bag. Tell when you lost it, and give the name of the car line.

4. The current number of a magazine to which you subscribe is two weeks overdue. If your subscription has not expired, write to the publishers.

5. Three days before you left for your summer camp you sent ahead by express three boxes to be delivered at the camp of your nearest neighbor. Two days have elapsed since your arrival, but the boxes have not been delivered. Write to the express company.

6. Write a letter asking for the adjustment of a situation of your own choice or one suggested by your teacher or parents.

81. Selling Letters

A good selling letter should arouse in the reader an interest in the commodity offered for sale, give him the necessary information about it, and lead him to want it so much that he will buy it. In writing a selling letter, we should bear in mind the following suggestions:

1. Understand fully the commodity that you are trying to sell and select its strongest selling point or points.
2. Consider very carefully the needs, the interests, the intelligence, the occupation, the taste, and the dominant characteristics of the person or persons whom you hope to interest in buying the commodity.
3. Plan your letter from the point of view of the prospective buyer.
4. In writing your letter, try to get the reader's interested attention by a striking personal appeal in the opening sentence or paragraph.
5. Set forth briefly and forcefully the merits of the commodity.
6. By showing that you have an intelligent understanding of his individual needs, lead him to see that the commodity would be useful to him — save him money, help him make more money, increase his comfort, aid him socially, or otherwise be profitable to him.
7. By inclosing an order blank and an addressed envelope, make it simple and easy for him to place his order while he is still under the influence of your letter.
8. See that your entire letter is attractive in contents and arrangement. Make it so clear and direct that the reader will understand it fully at one reading. Use relatively short sentences and brief paragraphs.

Exercise 168

Examine closely the selling letter printed as a specimen in Exercise 150. Does it satisfy the five requirements of a business letter given in section 73? Is it a good selling letter? Prove your answer by referring to section 81.

Exercise 169

Following the suggestions given in section 81, write a good selling letter in which you try to get a purchaser or purchasers for one of the following commodities:

1. A bicycle.
2. Cut flowers.
3. Pedigreed animals.
4. Home-cooked foods.
5. Model airplanes.

6. A used car.
7. Rustic furniture.
8. Bird houses.
9. A used motorboat.
10. A summer cottage.

Exercise 170

Acting in the capacity of secretary, write a good selling letter based on one of the following situations:

1. Sell to the citizens of your community season tickets to the football games.
2. Sell to the patrons of your school tickets to the school play.
3. Sell to some organization the services of the school band or orchestra.
4. Sell to the mothers of pupils the services of the sewing class or the cooking class.
5. Sell to the patrons of your school the services of boys who have proved their ability in manual training.
6. Sell patronage of the school lunch room to the members of the freshman class.

Exercise 171

In this exercise business letters of various types are provided for. Write two or more of the letters suggested, according to assignments that your teacher may give you.

Do your best to write letters that satisfy the five requirements mentioned in section 73. If you write letters of the types explained in sections 76–81, follow also the special instructions that apply to the types that you write.

1. Write a letter of application in answer to an advertisement for a clerk in a department store or a sporting-goods store.

2. Write a letter of request to some person of influence who knows you well, asking him to recommend you for a position that you desire. Be sure to make your letter complete.

3. Write a letter to the manager of an athletic team in another school, proposing a match game with your school team.

4. To a firm dealing in sporting goods write a letter in which you order certain athletic supplies. If possible, use a catalogue as a means of making your order accurate.

5. Write a letter accepting (or declining) a position that has been offered you.

6. Write a letter to a mail-order house calling attention to a mistake that was made in filling your order and asking for an adjustment.

7. Write a letter to the registrar of a college or a university, asking him to explain to you the entrance requirements and to send you a catalogue.

8. Write a letter, a copy of which will be sent to each pupil of your school, soliciting subscriptions for the school newspaper or magazine or asking each pupil to contribute to the Red Cross, the Salvation Army, or some other charitable organization.

9. Write a letter giving the necessary information to a pupil of another school who has asked you to explain how your school bank is conducted.

10. Write a letter of introduction and recommendation that will help the woman who cooks for your family to secure another position.

11. To a neighbor write a letter in which you try to sell him your services as caretaker of his place during the summer.

12. Write a letter to the proprietor of a community summer camp, asking about accommodations, conditions of admission, and expenses.

82. Other Types of Business Letters

In addition to the six types of business letters that we have thus far studied and written, there are four other types that we may at some time have occasion to write.

1. Letters of introduction. By writing for him a letter of introduction, we may be able to help a friend who wishes to ask a business favor of someone whom we know but with whom he is not acquainted. In our letter we should tell how long and in what capacity we have known him.

2. Letters of recommendation. When an acquaintance has applied for a position, he may ask us to write for him a letter of recommendation. Our letter should set forth truthfully what we know of the applicant's character, business ability, and general fitness for the position sought.

3. Letters of acknowledgment. A letter containing a request, an inquiry, an order, an application, an offer of a position, or a complaint — in fact, practically every type of business letter — requires a letter of acknowledgment. In such a letter the receiver states what action he has taken or intends to take in the matter which the original letter concerns.

4. Collection letters. When a purchaser abuses credit privileges granted him by a dealer, the latter usually writes the buyer a letter, courteously calling his attention to the overdue account, asking for an explanation of the delay, and requesting payment within a specified time.

Exercise 172

A friend of yours intends to apply to one of your acquaintances for a position. Write a letter introducing him or her.

Exercise 173

Write a letter of recommendation for someone who has been employed by your father or your mother. The person has given satisfactory service. State in your letter why the person is seeking a new position.

Exercise 174

Impersonating Mr. H. W. Draper (see the Test Exercise, Chapter V), write a letter recommending Robert D. Chalmers to Mr. Frank G. Norwood.

Exercise 175

You have been notified that you have obtained the position for which you applied in Exercise 160 or Exercise 161. Write an appropriate letter accepting the position.

Exercise 176

Impersonating the manager of the Roach Typewriter Exchange (see the Test Exercise at the beginning of this chapter), or impersonating the receiver of the letter that you wrote in Exercise 166 or Exercise 167, write an appropriate letter of acknowledgment.

Exercise 177

Write a courteous collection letter to someone (use a fictitious name and address) who owes you or some relative money for goods purchased three months ago.

Exercise 178

After reviewing section 67, write one of the following business telegrams in not more than ten words:

1. Ask a hotel proprietor to reserve a room for you.
2. Request an insurance company to send an appraiser to inspect some of your father's property that was damaged last night by fire.

3. Reply to the manager of another school team who has telegraphed you proposing a match game with your school team at an early date.

4. Order some commodity from a department store where your family has an account or have it sent C. O. D.

5. Write a telegram relating to business of your own choice.

Exercise 179. Extra Credit

Suppose that another pupil has written you a letter of inquiry in which he asks one of the following questions:

1. What are the essentials of a good business letter?

2. Will you please explain in detail what is meant by the "Five C's" of a good business letter?

3. What are the chief faults to be guarded against in writing business letters?

4. Will you please write for me a model letter of application?

5. What information regarding the education, habits, and personality of the writer do the form and the composition of a business letter give to the reader?

Plan and write a good informational business letter in which you answer one of these questions. If you have a relative or a friend who has had experience in writing business letters, interview him or her and get as much additional information as you can on the question that you select.

The amount of extra credit awarded you will depend upon the quality of your letter. If your letter is exceptionally good, you may be asked to read it to the class.

PART TWO

The Units of Composition: the Paragraph, the Sentence, and the Word

BUILDING A COMPOSITION

SUPPOSE that an architect draws for your father the plan for a house. Your father approves the plan and turns it over to a contractor. If the builder follows the plan accurately and uses the materials specified, he will produce a satisfactory house. If he disregards the plan, substitutes inferior materials, and works too hastily, the house will be a great disappointment to your father. A good plan results in a good house only when the builder is a skilled and conscientious workman.

Suppose that you, as a student of composition, carefully prepare an outline. Your teacher approves it and returns it to you to guide you in building a composition. As a builder, you must use the right materials — words, sentences, and paragraphs — and fit them together skillfully. If you conscientiously and painstakingly apply the knowledge of composition-building that you have acquired through study and practice, you will probably produce a satisfactory composition. But if you disregard your outline, use inferior materials, and work with too great haste, your composition will be a disappointment to your teacher and to you. A good outline results in a good composition only when the builder is a skilled and conscientious workman.

It is the purpose of Part Two to help you increase your skill in building a composition from an outline. It will aid you in choosing words that are correct and in using them effectively. It will help you to improve the structure of your sentences. It will also give you considerable training in the construction of paragraphs.

The Paragraph

83. What a Paragraph Is

A paragraph is not merely a group of sentences, but rather a group of properly related sentences that develop a single topic effectively. In its structure and the relationship of its parts, a paragraph resembles a tree. The trunk corresponds to the single topic, or central idea, of the paragraph; the branches and the roots, which are also essential parts of the tree, represent the subordinate details that are closely related to the topic and help to develop it. A paragraph is, then, an orderly composition on a small scale, which, like a longer composition, must be constructed according to definite principles.

A paragraph should be indicated by beginning the first line slightly farther to the right than the remaining lines. The space thus left is called the indention. Dividing a composition into paragraphs not only shows the topic units included in the discussion of the subject but also allows the reader a momentary rest of attention.

As to the length of a paragraph, no hard-and-fast rule can be given. Some topics may demand a paragraph of three hundred words or more for their proper development; others may be dealt with adequately in a hundred words; and some may require only a sentence or two. In general, we should avoid dividing our compositions into a series of short paragraphs. Such a practice is usually the result of hasty or careless planning.

Exercise 180

Study the composition of the paragraphs in "The Making of Our School Magazine," given in Exercise 111. Note in the outline the subtopics used to develop each principal topic into a paragraph. Be prepared to discuss their value.

Exercise 181

Read again the faulty composition on "School Papers," in section 29. What error in paragraphing do you discover? How might such an error have been avoided?

I. PRINCIPLES OF PARAGRAPH-BUILDING

84. Unity in the Paragraph

To be complete, a paragraph should (1) treat of a single topic, (2) include whatever is needed to develop the topic adequately, and (3) exclude everything that does not bear directly on the topic. In building a unified paragraph, we must therefore stick to the topic in thinking out what we are going to say and in writing and revising the paragraph.

85. The Topic Sentence

Let us examine closely the composition of the following paragraph:

The forest is a sanitary agent. It is constantly eliminating impurities from the earth and the air. Trees check, sweep, and filter from the air quantities of filthy, germ-laden dust. Their leaves absorb poisonous gases from the air. Roots assist in drainage, and absorb impurities from the soil. Roots give off acids, and these acids, together with the acids released by the fallen, decaying leaves, have a sterilizing effect upon the soil. Trees help to keep the earth sweet and clean, and water which comes from a forested watershed is likely to be pure. Many unsanitary areas have been redeemed and rendered healthy by tree-planting. — ENOS A. MILLS, "The Spell of the Rockies"

We notice that the author of the paragraph stated his topic in the first sentence. By so doing he found it easier to stick to his subject in writing the sentences that develop it. He likewise helped the reader to grasp quickly the central idea and hold it in mind as he read the paragraph. The sentence which states the central idea of a paragraph is called the *topic sentence*. It is most effective when short and striking.

86. Positions of the Topic Sentence in the Paragraph

1. At the beginning. In most explanatory and argumentative paragraphs the topic sentence is placed first. This is usually advisable when a statement is to be amplified, a principle is to be illustrated, or a general idea is to be presented. In learning to build good paragraphs we shall do well to begin with the topic sentence.

2. At the end. Sometimes it is desirable to place the topic sentence last. The sentences that precede it prepare the mind of the reader for a clearer understanding of the central idea than would be possible if it were stated first.

3. At the beginning and at the end. Now and then, especially in paragraphs of considerable length and complexity of thought, the topic sentence is stated at the beginning and is repeated, in different words, at the end. This repetition reminds the reader of the central idea and gives emphasis to the paragraph.

4. Within the paragraph. Occasionally a paragraph begins with a sentence or two referring, by way of transition, to the preceding paragraph, and the topic sentence follows or comes even later in the paragraph.

5. Topic not expressed. In most narrative paragraphs and in many paragraphs of other types, the topic is not actually stated but is implied. If the paragraph is unified, it is usually possible to state the topic in one sentence.

Exercise 182

In each of the following paragraphs select the sentence that states the topic and copy it. If you find the topic repeated in different words elsewhere, copy both sentences. If the topic is not definitely stated, make a sentence that will express this idea.

1. Dogs have the same sensitiveness that we associate with well-bred men and women. Their politeness is remarkable. Offer a dog water when he is not thirsty, and he will almost always take a lap or two, just out of civility, and to show his gratitude. I know a group of dogs that never forget to come and tell their mistress when they have had their dinner, feeling sure that she will sympathize with them; and if they have failed to get it, they will notify her immediately of the omission. If you happen to step on a dog's tail or paw, how eagerly — after one irrepressible yelp of pain — will he tell you by his caresses that he knows you did not mean to hurt him and forgives you.— HENRY C. MERWIN, "Dogs and Men"

2. At any given moment the different processes of the body are unified by the chief activity. If you are playing a game, like basket ball or tennis, the heart and the lungs and the perspiration glands and the liver and the kidneys are adjusting their activities to the body's needs. Your senses and your muscles also are "on the stretch" to see what your adversaries and partners are doing and to be ready to act according to the movements of the ball. You may become very much excited in the game, and everybody knows that excitement may work in two opposite ways. If you are not excited, or warmed up, enough, if you do not care enough, you will not hit hard enough; you will not see enough of what goes on to guide your movements; you will not be quick enough with your responses. On the other hand, if you are too much excited, if you begin to think about the score or about possible failure, if you begin to wonder whether certain eyes are watching you, you will spoil the game by playing too wildly. In any case the body works as a whole just as far as it is controlled by a single purpose or desire, and just in proportion to the strength of the purpose.— BENJAMIN C. GRUENBERG, "Biology and Human Life"

3. Just then a distant whistle sounded, and there was a shuffling of feet on the platform. A number of lanky boys, of all ages, appeared as suddenly and slimily as eels wakened by the crack of thunder; some came from the waiting room, where they had been warming themselves by the red stove, or half asleep on the slat benches; others uncoiled themselves from baggage trucks or slid out of express wagons. Two clambered down from the driver's seat of a hearse that stood backed up against the siding. They straightened their stooping shoulders and lifted their heads, and a flash of momentary animation kindled their dull eyes at that cold, vibrant scream, the world-wide call for men. It stirred them like the note of a trumpet. — WILLA CATHER, "The Sculptor's Funeral"

Exercise 183

Select from a textbook, a magazine, or the editorial page of a newspaper three or more separate paragraphs each of which is well unified. Point out the topic sentence, if it is expressed, or state the topic in your own words. Be prepared to show that in each paragraph the writer has kept strictly to the topic, avoiding all digressions.

Exercise 184

Using two of the topic sentences given below, write two paragraphs of from one hundred to two hundred words each. Place the topic sentence at the beginning, and see that each paragraph is unified.

1. Our car is always giving us a surprise.
2. Modern inventions have revolutionized home life.
3. The radio has become an important means of educating the general public.
4. What a change mother had made in the appearance of our back yard!
5. The training of a Boy (Girl) Scout is good preparation for citizenship.
6. We have planned a balanced diet of home reading.

7. Grandfather has an unusual summer camp.

8. First impressions are not always reliable.

9. Every pupil who is physically fit should take part in some kind of outdoor athletics.

10. One of the store windows contained an unusual display.

11. Attentive reading of good books is a great help in improving one's use of English.

12. Many boys would find a course in cooking helpful to them.

13. A lie once caused me great embarrassment.

14. Our cook told mother an amusing anecdote the other day.

15. My chum's room is tastefully furnished.

Exercise 185

Criticize and revise for unity each of the paragraphs that you wrote in Exercise 184. The following questions will help you:

1. Did I stick closely to the subject as stated in the topic sentence?

2. If not, what irrelevant details did I introduce?

3. Did I omit any necessary details?

4. Does my paragraph, as a whole, give a clear and complete presentation of the topic?

5. When read aloud, is my paragraph smooth and natural in expression?

Make a good corrected copy of each paragraph after you have revised it.

Exercise 186

Do the four sentences grouped together below make a real paragraph? Give a reason for your answer.

Rare things grow in gardens in the winter. Indeed, on that December morning no shape or surface looked familiar. I realized that not all the winter growths were hard and crisp. To find out how sensitive the bubble-flowers were, I tried to make them move by stepping on the ice above them.

Now study the four paragraphs that make up the selection that follows. In each paragraph you will find one of the sentences included in the group above. Prove that it is the topic sentence of the paragraph.

My Garden in Winter

Rare things grow in gardens in the winter. Instead of hibernating like a bear, a garden begins then to live a second life. Its summer self has been transformed by a winter change, which shows new flowerings and new contrasts. The strangeness of all gardens in winter I discovered in my garden when I looked at it for the first time after four months.

Snow with a glimmer of icy crust covered the whole garden. The pool in the center was hard and shining. Beyond it the little stone figure of a shepherd boy wore a shawl whiter than stone, and more surprising still, the boy had a white beard of snow, so long that Alexander the Great would surely have made him cut it off before permitting him to join the Macedonian army. Here, however, there was no enemy to seize him by the beard. He held his fuzzy pipes and played soundless music. At his feet a procession of candytuft lifted up blooms like lacquered ermine. Near these a race of glacial twigs and frosty leaves pricked through the snow. At the garden wall the waterspout where the toad had lived showed an icy threshold. The toad had retired into his ice palace, perhaps to practice skating unobserved. He would scarcely now have recognized the garden. Indeed, on that December morning no shape or surface looked familiar.

When I went nearer to the pool, I saw below the ice pearl-colored flowers, transparent and fragile. I realized that not all the winter growths were hard and crisp. These flowers were shaped like water-lilies, but looked softer and less substantial. I knew, of course, that they should look unsubstantial, for they were made of air. One of them was bent and narrowed like a three-quarters moon. All of them would have looked soft and translucent in any garden, among no matter what flowers. Here in this hard, fixed, wintry place they were like phantoms.

To find out how sensitive the bubble-flowers were, I tried to make them move by stepping on the ice above them. I pressed down first the ice at the edge of the moon-shaped flower. From three-quarters it changed to a full moon, and then wavered ahead of me as I walked forward. The flower nearest it began to move, also. A third I made join these two, and now all three were grouped in one place and were quivering slightly, like quicksilver. Seven or eight other flowers remained apart, but these, too, I collected by pressing hard upon the ice and walking with them as they moved. When all were together at the end of the pool nearest the shepherd boy, I stepped forward to admire this strange bouquet. The whole group moved with me. Suddenly an unseen hole in the ice sucked them all, fatally, into the outside air. Every one of them was gone, for this air was as hostile to them as it would have been to any summer flower. I moved back in dismay, and brushed against something behind me. When I turned, I saw that I had broken off the shepherd's beard.

87. Coherence in the Paragraph

The sentences of a paragraph should be so constructed and so arranged as to make the relation of one sentence to another unmistakably clear and to enable the reader to grasp easily the meaning of the whole paragraph. Coherence in the paragraph we may secure in two ways: (1) by arranging in their natural or logical order the sentences that develop the topic; (2) by using connecting words and phrases to indicate the proper relationship between sentences.

The principal methods of developing the topic sentence into a paragraph we shall find discussed and illustrated in sections 92–97 of this chapter.

88. Using Connectives to Improve Coherence

We may often gain added clearness in a paragraph by the use of reference words and connecting words and phrases to show more precisely the relation between our sentences and to indicate the direction in which the thought of our paragraph is moving. The most common devices for showing the connection between sentences within a paragraph are the following:

1. Repetition of the noun used in the preceding sentence or the use of one of its synonyms or of a related word.
2. The use of personal pronouns and pronominal adjectives, such as *I, we, he, she, it, they, my, mine, our, ours, his, hers, its, theirs.*
3. The use of demonstrative pronouns and adjectives, such as *this, that, these, those, such,* and *same.*
4. The use at the beginning of a sentence of demonstrative phrases with an adverbial function, such as *on this occasion, by such means, in the same manner, for this reason, under those circumstances, in former times, by these explanations, in that way.*
5. The use of conjunctional and adverbial words and phrases indicating the following relationships between sentences:
   a. Addition or continuation: *and, also, too, likewise, moreover, again, besides, in addition, further, furthermore, similarly, in the same way, in like manner.*
   b. Opposition or contrast: *but, yet, however, still, otherwise, nevertheless, notwithstanding, on the contrary, conversely, on the other hand.*
   c. Order or sequence: *first, secondly, next, thirdly, lastly, finally, in the first place, in the second place, in the next place, to begin with, in conclusion, first of all, last of all.*
   d. Time relation: *then, now, presently, thereupon, immediately afterward, thereafter, meanwhile, in the meantime, afterward, at the same time, after an interval, later, somewhat later, eventually, at last.*
   e. Space relation: *near at hand, in the distance, high above, on the right, at the left, in the center, immediately in front of, far behind, straight ahead, near the top, at the bottom.*
   f. Repetition of an idea: *indeed, in fact, in other words, that is to say, briefly stated, differently expressed.*
   g. Introducing illustrations: *for example, for instance, thus, as an example, by way of illustration.*

h. Introducing comparisons : *likewise, similarly, in the same way, in a similar manner.*

i. Conclusion or consequence : *therefore, hence, thus, so, consequently, accordingly, for this reason, as a result.*

NOTE. If the thought relationship between sentences is very close, connectives are unnecessary.

Exercise 187

In the following paragraph point out the connective words and phrases :

Devote some of your leisure, I repeat, to cultivating a love of reading good books. Fortunate indeed are those who contrive to make themselves genuine book-lovers. For book-lovers have some noteworthy advantages over other people. They need never know lonely hours so long as they have books around them, and the better the books the more delightful the company. From good books, moreover, they draw much besides entertainment. They gain mental food such as few companions can supply. Even while resting from their labors they are, through the books they read, equipping themselves to perform those labors more efficiently. This albeit they may not be deliberately reading to improve their mind. All unconsciously the ideas they derive from the printed page are stored up, to be worked over by the imagination for their future profit.— H. ADDINGTON BRUCE, "Self-Development"

Exercise 188

In the paragraphs quoted in section 85 and in Exercise 182, point out the connective words and phrases and tell what relationship they indicate between the sentences that they connect.

89. Showing the Connection between Paragraphs

When we write a composition consisting of several paragraphs, it is important that we show the reader the relation of one paragraph to another. Unless the thought relation between a paragraph and the one that precedes it is perfectly clear, we should use one or more of the connective devices listed in section 88. The use of such a device at the beginning of the new paragraph aids the reader in making the transition — that is, in passing mentally — from the topic just discussed to the one that is to be next considered.

Exercise 189

Read the student essay given below. Point out the means by which the writer has shown the relation of each paragraph after the first to the one that precedes it.

Point out also the connective devices used within each paragraph to show the relation of one sentence to another.

Personality and Pencils

There are a thousand schemes for entrapping the elusive myth personality — that strange part of us that is the sum of all that we are. They say that we betray it by the clothes we wear, by the rooms we live in, by the food we eat, by the way we walk, by the way we write, and, I would add to the grand total, by the pencils we write with! For in all other things but this we are influenced by public opinion. We wear what our friends and relatives tell us is becoming; we accept the hints of the *House Beautiful* and the *Ladies' Home Journal* in furnishing our homes; we eat what the advertisers tell us to; and we affect the postures and handwriting of our favorite movie actor. But no mother ever told her daughter that a green pencil went better with her pink dress than a yellow one. No advertiser boasts that Mary Pickford uses his Special Brass-Tipped No. 2 exclusively. The stern hand of law and the compelling one of fashion do not touch our pencils. By being below the notice, they are above the interference of outsiders; and on them we unconsciously record our personality.

To prove this, just lift up the desk-lids of your friends and look into their minds. Here is one girl, outwardly the incarnation of mild conservatism, who betrays an inward love of barbaric display by a copious collection of long pencils, red, green, and yellow, striped and shaded, and lettered in gold. Here is a girl whom you always thought calm and care-free; but these chewed and ugly stumps show her to possess a mind gnawed with care. Here is a dainty and feminine person, with a neat silver pencil. There is a thoughtless girl who has none at all. You have a feeling that she borrows from her friends and looks over their shoulders at what they are writing. And in this desk are three dark-red cylinders, sharpened to a hair's thickness. Here we have a fastidious person, pleased with herself, and a little too much interested in her tools to be greatly interested in her work.

And if the pencils themselves, factory made, are such telltales, how much more so are the movements we make in handling them! One girl will poise hers delicately between thumb and forefinger and, flourishing her little finger, write in an elaborate script. You may spot her as the owner of a vain and idle mind. The next girl will grasp hers near the point and scratch off her words in a violent concentration of energy and ability. Another will hold hers rather high up, with a light but firm touch. She is the artistic girl who can draw. The nervous girl will continually tap and fool with hers and leave her mark on whatever objects come within her reach. The careless girl you will usually see making a series of vague darts into her desk and books, to try to remember where on earth she left her pencil.

Then observe the points of the pencils of your friends, and you will be able to put the finishing touches to your estimate of their characters. The stingy girl shaves hers off with a bare quarter inch of wood showing and a nasty pin-prick of a point. The generous girl lays bare a long, free sweep of unvarnished wood and lead. The girl of a mechanical mind grinds hers in a pencil-sharpener. The precise person's knife-strokes form geometrical triangles in the cut wood, whereas those of the careless one wander toward the point in bumpy curves.

One and all doubtless think they hold in their hands a servile stick that must helplessly write out their thoughts; but all the time the pencil laughs and writes on itself their inmost secrets.

90. Emphasis in the Paragraph

A paragraph should be so constructed that the point or main idea will stand out prominently from the other details and thus impress the reader with its greater importance. We may secure emphasis in a paragraph in one or more of the following ways:

1. Emphasis by position. The final sentence of a paragraph, since it is the last read, is the most emphatic in position. The point of an anecdote gains emphasis, as we know, by being told at the end. By beginning a paragraph with the least important idea and arranging the other ideas in the order of their increasing importance, we make use of climax, which is itself an emphasizing device. The first sentence of a paragraph is also made forceful by position. Beginning with the topic sentence impresses the central idea on the attention and memory of the reader. Sometimes an author uses both the beginning and the end of his paragraph to enforce the point that he wishes to make.

2. Emphasis by proportion. A very natural and useful means of emphasizing the most important point in a paragraph is to devote to it more space than to other points included in the main topic.

3. Emphasis by repetition. Occasionally emphasis is gained by repeating certain key words, or by expressing the main idea in slightly different language the point of the paragraph may be presented more forcefully.

Exercise 190

Study closely the paragraph given below. Explain the methods by which coherence is secured. In which of the three ways mentioned in section 90 is emphasis secured?

Why should a foreigner become naturalized? Perhaps the chief reason is that in no other way can he cease to be a foreigner and become a member of the nation. A person who gets his living in a country and who is protected by its laws should be eager to defend it against enemies. Moreover, complete protection by the law and certain property rights are enjoyed only by citizens. In addition, a citizen is looked upon in a more kindly way by his neighbors than is a foreigner; he is more likely to be regarded as "one of us," as a member of the community rather than as an outsider. In the fifth place, an immigrant, as a citizen, will have less difficulty in getting a job when jobs are scarce; for some companies will not employ aliens, and other companies will discharge them first if they find it necessary to cut down the number of their employees. The right to vote and to hold public office are privileges that are also restricted to native-born or naturalized Americans. But the greatest value in naturalization, of course, is the satisfaction which comes from being an American — from belonging to the country of Washington, Lincoln, Roosevelt, and Wilson, and to a land founded on principles of justice, righteousness, and liberty. This desire has led many noble men and women to give up citizenship in the land of their birth and to become loyal citizens of the United States.— HOWARD COPELAND HILL, "Community and Vocational Civics"

Exercise 191

Tell in which of the three ways explained in section 90 emphasis is secured in the paragraphs of Exercises 182, 187, and 189.

Exercise 192

Discuss the following paragraph with reference to the beginning and the ending, the use of climax, and the use of proportion as means of securing emphasis:

In so far as Americanism is merely patriotism, it is a very good thing. The man who does not think his own country the finest in the world is either a pretty poor sort of man or else he has a pretty poor sort of country. If any people have not patriotism enough to make them willing to die that the nation may live, then that people will soon be pushed aside in the struggle of life, and that nation will be trampled upon and crushed; probably it will be conquered and absorbed by some race of a stronger fiber and of a sterner stock. Perhaps it is difficult to declare precisely which is the more pernicious citizen of a republic when there is danger of war with another nation; the man who wants to fight, right or wrong, the hot-headed fellow who would plunge the country into a deadly struggle without first exhausting every possible chance to obtain an honorable peace, or the cold-blooded person who would willingly give up anything and everything, including honor itself, sooner than risk the loss of money which every war surely entails. "My country, right or wrong," is a good motto only when we add to it, "and if she is in the wrong, I'll help to put her in the right." To shrink absolutely from a fight where honor is really at stake, this is the act of a coward. To rush violently into a quarrel when war can be avoided without the sacrifice of things dearer than life, this is the act of a fool. — BRANDER MATTHEWS, "Parts of Speech"

91. Paragraphing Conversation

A special rule for dividing conversation, or dialogue, into paragraphs should be observed. Each separate speech, together with the writer's explanation or comment (if any is included), should be placed in a separate paragraph. If an uninterrupted speech is very long, or if the writer wishes to give special emphasis to a part of it, he may divide it into paragraphs.

Exercise 193

In the two jokes given below, explain the division of the conversation into paragraphs. Notice also the punctuation, and give a reason for each mark.

Don't be Greedy

"Howard," asked the teacher, "do you remember the story of Daniel in the lions' den?"

"Yes, ma'am," said Howard.

"What lesson do you learn from it?" she inquired.

"Why, it teaches us that we shouldn't eat everything in sight," he replied. — *American Boy*.

Naturally

"What is a cannibal, Johnny?" asked the teacher.

"I don't know," he had to admit.

"Well, if you ate your father and your mother," she asked, "what would that make you?"

"An orphan," said Johnny. — *American Boy*

Exercise 194

Write a reproduction of a short but amusing conversation that you recently overheard, or relate an anecdote or a joke in the form of dialogue. Paragraph and punctuate it correctly.

II. METHODS OF DEVELOPING THE TOPIC SENTENCE

92. Development by Definition

To explain fully the meaning of a term we shall often require a paragraph of several sentences. After stating in the topic sentence the dictionary definition, we may proceed to limit further the application and use of the word or expression. We can sometimes define it more clearly by comparing or contrasting its meaning with that of another term, or we may state what is excluded from the definition as well as what is included in it. Development of a topic by defining it is most frequently used in formal exposition.

Exercise 195

Discuss as examples of topics developed by definition the paragraphs in section 23 and the first paragraph of section 83 of this book. Point out the connective words and phrases. Then find in another of your textbooks a paragraph that has the topic sentence developed by definition, and study it in the same way.

Exercise 196

Write a good paragraph in which you define one of the following terms. Begin with a brief definition as your topic sentence; then, by further limiting, explaining, and illustrating its meaning, make the definition clear and complete. Revise your paragraph carefully and rewrite it.

1. Recreation.
2. Oral hygiene.
3. Balanced diet.
4. Crop rotation.
5. Pasteurization.

6. Reciprocity.
7. Life insurance.
8. Domestic science.
9. Honor system.
10. Parliamentary procedure.

93. Development by Giving Details

One of the most common methods of building a paragraph consists in giving details that explain and illustrate the statement made in the topic sentence. This method is especially useful in exposition and description.

Exercise 197

Study and discuss as examples of topics developed by giving appropriate details the paragraph quoted in section 85 and the first paragraph quoted in Exercise 182. Point out the connective words and phrases.

Exercise 198

Write a good paragraph in which you develop by means of appropriate details one of the following topic sentences. Revise your paragraph carefully and rewrite it.

1. What a wonderful place we had found for a summer camp!
2. Our education should prepare us to live useful and happy lives.
3. My friend's room resembled a museum.
4. School life affords many opportunities for developing good citizenship.

5. There are several ways in which the quality of our school paper might be improved.

6. A topic sentence of your own choice.

94. Development by Citing Examples

Often a topic sentence that states a general fact may be effectively developed into a paragraph by the use of one or more examples. Sometimes the writer will illustrate his topic sentence by relating an incident or an anecdote.

Exercise 199

Study the following paragraph as an illustration of the development of a topic sentence by citing an example. Point out the connective words and phrases.

A puppy is the perfect waggler. Our Airedale, with the sad brown eyes and rough coat and comically pivoted tail, can hardly stir himself without waggling. He loves us vastly, and he loves to be full of bones and fresh air and implicit trust in all dogs and men. Life is one glorious, simple-minded, adventurous holiday for him. He is downcast only when all his arts fail to persuade us that he should accompany us to church or to a dinner-party. Then he cries and grieves and quivers; but even his grief has a naïveté and honesty that are akin to his joy. We know that when we come back and fumble at the latchkey, a happy urgent moaning and grunting will be heard behind the door, and Ben will leap out at us, pawing the air, tossing his ears, crimping his staunch black-saddled body into incredible patterns, skidding along the rug on the side of his funny face, — in short, waggling over us in an abandon of love and delight fit to melt the heart of the stoniest puppy-hater or cynic-at-large.— Anonymous

Exercise 200

Find, if you can, and bring to class a paragraph in which the topic sentence is illustrated by an incident or an anecdote. Be ready to explain its good points.

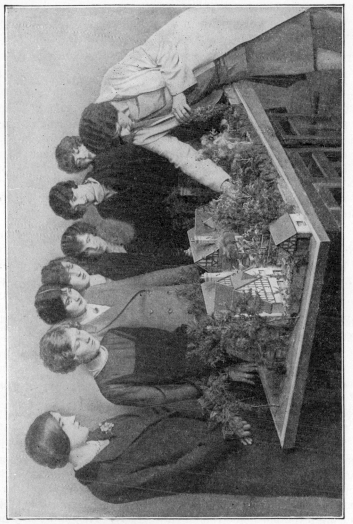

A Prize-Winning Architectural Model

Exercise 201

Write a good paragraph in which you develop by means of one or more examples one of the following topic sentences. Revise your paragraph carefully and rewrite it.

1. There seems to be no limit to my younger brother's (sister's) curiosity.

2. Idle gossip may make the best friends bitter enemies.

3. All that we know for certain about luck is that it is sure to change.

4. Great fortunes have been made from simple inventions.

5. Many men and women have achieved success in spite of poor health.

6. A topic sentence of your own choice which you develop by means of an incident from personal experience.

95. Development by Repetition

Repetition, when skillfully employed, is often an effective device for emphasizing the central idea of a paragraph and for driving the point home in the mind of the reader. By this method the principal thought is restated in other words or from a different point of view.

Exercise 202

Study the following paragraph as an example of the skillful use of repetition in developing the topic sentence. Point out the words that emphasize the main idea.

The Chinaman is probably the most frugal and least wasteful man on earth. He has to be. There are believed to be some four hundred million Chinamen in his corner of the earth, and they lack capital, machinery, and the means of communication and of international interchange of produce; so that their communities are too much self-contained and cannot earn largely. They must save or starve, and even with all their prudence and thrift they sometimes starve. At the hour of writing this paper, a fearful famine is going on in China and many people are dying of starvation. One never sees a Chinaman lose anything. China that he handles is never chipped or broken. When he supplies food, he has exactly enough, not too much or too little. With him thrift is an exact science. — W. CAMERON FORBES, "The Romance of Business"

Exercise 203

Write a good paragraph in which you develop one of the following topic sentences by repetition. Be careful not to overdo this method and thus make your paragraph unnecessarily wordy and unemphatic. Revise your paragraph and rewrite it.

1. Two wrongs never made a right.
2. Success is dangerous for some people.
3. Few of us truly appreciate good health until we are deprived of it.
4. Some athletic victories are won at too great a sacrifice of other school interests.
5. As citizens, it is our duty to discharge our obligations of citizenship.
6. A topic sentence of your own choice.

96. Development by Comparison or Contrast

Frequently the topic of a paragraph can be most effectively developed by comparing it with something similar to it or contrasting it with something unlike it. Occasionally both comparison and contrast may be used in the same paragraph.

Exercise 204

Explain the following paragraph as an example of a topic sentence developed by means of comparison. Point out the connective words and phrases.

The body of an animal may well be compared with some machine like a locomotive engine. Indeed, the animal body is a machine. It is a machine composed of many parts, each part doing some particular kind of work for which a particular kind of structure fits it; and all the parts are dependent on each other and work together for the accomplishment of the total business of the machine. The locomotive must be provided with fuel, such as coal or wood or other combustible substance, the consumption of which furnishes the force or energy of the machine. The animal body must be provided with fuel, which is called food, which furnishes similarly the energy of the animal. Oxygen must be provided for the combustion of the fuel in the locomotive and of the food in the body. The locomotive is composed of special parts: the fire box for the reception and combustion of fuel; the steam pipes for the carriage of steam; the wheels for locomotion; the smokestack for throwing off waste. The animal body is similarly composed of parts: the alimentary canal for the reception and assimilation of food; the excretory organs for the throwing off of waste matter; the arteries and veins for the carriage of oxygen and food-holding blood; the legs or wings for locomotion. — JORDAN and KELLOGG, "Animal Life"

Exercise 205

Explain in the following paragraph the use of contrast as a means of developing the topic sentence. Point out the connective words and phrases.

And, surely, of all smells in the world the smell of many trees is the sweetest and most fortifying. The sea has a rude pistoling sort of odor, and takes you in the nostrils like snuff, and carries with it a fine sentiment of open water and tall ships; but the smell of a forest, which comes nearest to this in tonic quality, surpasses it by many degrees in the quality of softness. Again, the smell of the sea has little variety, but the smell of a forest is infinitely changeful; it varies with the hour of the day, not in strength merely, but in character; and the different sorts of trees, as you go from one zone of the wood to another, seem to live among different kinds of atmosphere. Usually the rosin of the fir predominates. But some woods are more coquettish in their habits; and the breath of the forest Mormal, as it came aboard upon us that showery afternoon, was perfumed with nothing less delicate than sweetbrier. — R. L. STEVENSON, "An Inland Voyage"

Exercise 206

Write a good paragraph in which you develop one of the following topic sentences by comparison or by contrast. Revise your paragraph carefully and rewrite it.

1. Our nervous system resembles in many respects a telephone system.
2. Boys have more opportunities than girls to earn money during vacation.
3. I think living in the country is far more interesting than living in the city.
4. Four years in college had brought about many changes in my sister (brother).
5. My two dogs have few traits in common.
6. A topic sentence of your own choice.

97. Development by Giving Causes or Reasons

Some topic sentences raise in the mind of the reader the question *Why is this true?* In developing such a topic sentence into a paragraph, the writer explains the causes or gives certain reasons to support his statement.

Exercise 207

Study the following paragraph as an example of the development of a topic sentence by giving reasons to support the statement. Point out the connective words and phrases.

A doctor should have a strong and vigorous physique. If his practice is large, his work is especially trying. Calls may come at any hour of the day or night, rendering his hours for meals and sleep very irregular. It is only a sturdy physique that will enable him to stand this without his becoming nervous and irritable, two things which will lessen his success. The physician whose body supplies him with abounding vitality can, in spite of taxing demands, keep a clear mind and a strong personality. — GOWIN, WHEATLEY, and BREWER, "Occupations"

Exercise 208

Develop one of the following topic sentences in a paragraph that explains the causes or gives the reasons necessary to satisfy a reader that the statement is true.

1. Every week in the year should be a "Better-Speech Week."
2. There are several advantages (disadvantages) in being the youngest (oldest) child in a large family.
3. Teachers should be paid higher salaries.
4. The dog is man's best friend among the lower animals.
5. Newspapers should not be allowed to publish accounts of crime.

Exercise 209

Analyze each of the paragraphs given below according to the following directions:

1. Point out the topic sentence. If it is not expressed, formulate a topic sentence in your own words.
2. Explain by what method or methods the topic sentence was developed into a paragraph.
3. Indicate the relational words and connective words and phrases that the writer used to improve coherence.
4. Tell how the writer secured emphasis.
5. As means of showing that the paragraph is unified and coherent, write a précis of not more than three sentences in which you give an accurate summary of the main points in the paragraph. (See sections 23–24.)

1. Of course, the subway has its incidental charms — its gay fresco of advertisements, for instance, and its faint mysterious thunder when it runs near the surface of the street on which we stand. But its chief service to man — perhaps its reason for existence — is that it gives him adventure. In this adventure he meets the spirit of faith and the spirit of democracy, which is an aspect of charity. And by their influence he becomes, surely though but for a time, as a little child. — JOYCE KILMER, "The Great Nickel Adventure"

2. When I was a little boy, I used to get a great deal of satisfaction out of stroking a kitten or a puppy, or crushing a lilac

leaf-bud for its spring fragrance, or smelling newly turned soil, or tasting the sharp acid of a grape tendril, or feeling the green coolness of the skin of a frog. I could pore for long minutes over a lump of pudding-stone, a bean-seedling, a chrysalis, a knot in a joist in the attic. There was a curious contentment to be found in these things. My pockets were always full of shells and stones, twigs and bugs; my room in the attic, of Indian relics, fragments of ore, birds' eggs, oak-galls, dry seeds and sea-weeds, bottled spiders, butterflies on corks. All the lessons of the schoolroom seemed of no consequence compared with Things so full of intimacy, of friendliness. — ROBERT M. GAY, "The Flavor of Things"

3. "Bad weather" is mainly the fear of spoiling one's clothes. Fancy clothing is one of the greatest obstacles to a knowledge of nature : in this regard, the farm boy has an immense advantage. It is a misfortune not to have gone barefoot in one's youth. A man cannot be a naturalist in patent-leather shoes. The perfecting of the manufacture of elaborate and fragile fabrics correlates well with our growing habit of living indoors. Our clothing is made chiefly for fair weather; when it becomes worn we use it for stormy weather, although it may be in no respect stormy-weather clothing. I am always interested, when abroad with persons, in noting the various mental attitudes toward wind; and it is apparent that most of the displeasure from the wind arises from fear of disarranging the coiffure or from the difficulty of controlling a garment. — L. H. BAILEY, "The Outlook to Nature"[1]

4. Turn where you will, go where you will, today steel is always present, but it is not easy to realize how much steel has contributed to increasing the effectiveness of man's work. The part it has played, and still is playing, almost defies the imagination. Each steam shovel or steam hammer does the work of a small army. By moving levers a man whose greatest effort will not budge a weight of more than a few hundred pounds can put into motion and control absolutely mechanisms that handle with ease tons upon tons of stone or metal. There are cranes that handle masses of molten iron weighing as much as one hundred and fifty tons. There are hydraulic presses whose power is equivalent to seven thousand

[1] Used by permission of The Macmillan Company, publishers.

tons or more. In a power station of what was the Manhattan Street Railway Company there is a steam turbine of eight units, which produces *one hundred thousand horse power*. Skyscrapers, steamships, bridges — they all bear witness to the power that the mastery of steel has given to man.—W. CAMERON FORBES, "The Romance of Business"

5. When supper was over the sun was almost down and it was seven o'clock, yet there was still no decay in the brilliance of the light. She went to the window and looked out, and the sight drew her, in spite of herself, into the open. She was in the emerald heart of a world of coral-pink. Softer than scarlet, more glowing than pink, the earth lay suffused, tinted like the embers of a dying fire. Gradually the plains became one rose; deep purple lowered in the sky, orange and gold and pearl; yet still the marvel and the richness of the rose claimed them and won them all, won them into its heart. Dorothy watched it; and for long minutes there was no change, no diminution of its irresistible splendor; the beauty was flaunted unendurably, as if God would forgive the world no jot of abasement before his terrible glory. Then slowly a gray veil began to film the heavens; for a moment, as the rose faded, the bright colors gleamed and displayed themselves again in bands and streaks and burning, prismatic spots; then, suddenly, as if the fire were dead, the wind blew the embers black, and night fell. — JAMES WEBER LINN, "The Girl at Duke's"

6. Now, to be properly enjoyed, a walking tour should be gone upon alone. If you go in a company, or even in pairs, it is no longer a walking tour in anything but name; it is something else, and more in the nature of a picnic. A walking tour should be gone upon alone, because freedom is of the essence; because you should be able to stop and go on, and follow this way or that, as the freak takes you; and because you must have your own pace, and neither trot alongside a champion walker, nor mince in time with a girl. And then you must be open to all impressions and let your thoughts take color from what you see. You should be as a pipe for any wind to play upon. "I cannot see the wit," says Hazlitt, "of walking and talking at the same time. When I am in the country I wish to vegetate like the country,"— which is the gist of all that can be said upon the matter. There should be no cackle of

voices at your elbow, to jar on the meditative silence of the morning. And so long as a man is reasoning he cannot surrender himself to that fine intoxication that comes of much motion in the open air, that begins in a sort of dazzle and sluggishness of the brain, and ends in a peace that passes comprehension.— R. L. STEVENSON, "Walking Tours"

7. The question remains: How is skill in composition to be gained? The general principle is as simple as the details of the craft are complicated. The way to write is to write. Perhaps the most exact image of the process is that of piano-playing. Just as one acquires skill in the use of the piano by innumerable exercises and continual practice, so one attains to mastery in written language only by writing and writing and writing. It is necessary to compose and recompose; to write all sorts of things, to prune them, recast them, polish them; to elaborate and to simplify; to weigh each word and phrase; and when all is done to destroy the result as ruthlessly as we would destroy anything else which has become rubbish by outliving its usefulness.— ARLO BATES, "Talks on Writing English"

Exercise 210

Following the directions given in Exercise 209, analyze five paragraphs that your teacher may assign you in some other book that you are studying.

Exercise 211

Write a good paragraph in which you develop one of the following topic sentences. In securing coherence use any method or combination of methods that seems to you appropriate. When you have revised and rewritten your paragraph, analyze it according to the directions given in Exercise 209.

1. A county fair provides an interesting study of various types of people.

2. The entire barnyard population gave evidence that spring had come.

3. Those who live in glass houses should not throw stones.

4. There is one incident in my early childhood that I shall never forget.

5. What joy an aviator must experience in flying!

6. Nature is very economical.

7. Great literature has a refining influence on appreciative readers.

8. It is easy to understand why our team lost (won) the game.

9. A successful dairy requires skillful management.

10. Motion pictures are useful in teaching geography.

11. Our kitchen is equipped with many modern labor-saving devices.

12. Knowledge of a foreign language is a great aid in mastering English.

13. The best way to save time is to use it profitably.

14. What stamps a man as great is not freedom from faults but abundance of powers.

15. Last summer I had a very narrow escape.

Exercise 212

Choose one of the following groups of sentences, and write a composition of three or four paragraphs. Consider each sentence as a topic sentence of a paragraph, and place it where you think it will be most effective. See that each paragraph properly develops the topic and is unified. After your composition is thoroughly revised, analyze each paragraph by the directions in Exercise 209.

1. An old house in the country makes puzzling noises at night.
   The doors are much less peaceful than by day.
   In the walls are strange sounds.
   Other creakings and rustlings are less easily located.

2. Instead of going straight to my destination, I am frequently tempted to stop to talk with animals whom I meet.
   Another temptation is to look into shop windows.
   Most difficult of all is leaving an organ-grinder, his organ, and his monkey.

3. One way to make me angry is to ask me questions.
   It annoys me, also, to have people step on my feet.
   I am always irritable when I am awakened.
   However, with all my faults, I do not mind being laughed at.

4. It is sometimes embarrassing to be asked one's age.
   Even more annoying is it to be thought much younger than
      one is.
   On one occasion, however, I was glad to be thought older
      than my real age.

Achievement Test

The following assignment will test your knowledge of
the principles of paragraph-building and your ability to
write good paragraphs. Write the answer to each question
except the last in the form of a paragraph. Devise an
appropriate topic sentence, which you will underscore.
Underline also all connecting words and phrases that you
use. In writing this test do not refer to your book.

1. How does the use of a topic sentence aid the writer and the
reader of a paragraph?

2. Explain the methods of developing a topic sentence into a
paragraph.

3. In what ways may emphasis be secured in a paragraph?

4. Write a paragraph of about one hundred and fifty words on a
topic sentence of your own. (After the paragraph state the method
or methods that you used in developing the topic sentence.)

5. Retell a joke or an anecdote in which conversation is used.
See that the paragraphing and punctuation are correct.

CHAPTER VIII

The Sentence Grammatically Considered

Test Exercise I

Below are ten groups of words. Some are sentences and some are fragments of sentences.

A. At the left margin of your test paper write the numbers 1 to 10. Classify each group of words by writing after its number *S.* for a sentence and *F.* for a fragment of a sentence.

SCORE: 5 points for each classification

B. In the spaces marked "*S*" copy the corresponding sentences. Underline the subject once, the predicate twice. In the spaces marked "*F*" write original sentences in which you use the fragments given. Use each phrase in a simple sentence and each clause in a complex sentence. After each of your sentences write in parentheses either the word "simple" or the word "complex."

SCORE: 5 points for each sentence

1. Unless rain comes soon.
2. An experience never to be forgotten.
3. A sportsman whom everyone admires.
4. What answer should I have given?
5. What answer I should have given.
6. Having been injured in a practice game.
7. When the fire department arrived.
8. The cause of the fire was a mystery.
9. Before handing in my exercise.
10. The first pupil in the class to finish the test.

Test Exercise II

Below are ten sentences. Some are arranged in the natural order, some in the inverted order.

A. Copy each sentence. Underline the subject substantive (simple subject) once. Underline the predicate verb (simple predicate) twice. Indicate the order of arrangement of each sentence by writing after it in parentheses *N.* for the natural order and *I.* for the inverted order.

Score: 5 points for each sentence

B. Rewrite in the natural order each sentence now in the inverted order. Rewrite in the inverted order each sentence now in the natural order. Indicate the order of arrangement of each rewritten sentence according to the directions given in A, above.

Score: 5 points for each sentence

1. My mother stood in the doorway.
2. Down the street marched the parade.
3. Many were the hardships endured.
4. A dark cloud appeared on the horizon.
5. At intervals came the sound of fireworks.
6. A statue of Washington stands in the park.
7. Wonderful are the works of nature.
8. The flames mounted higher and higher.
9. Into the valley of Death rode the six hundred.
10. Here many centuries ago was fought a great battle.

Test Exercise III

Copy the sentences given below. Draw one line under each phrase and two lines under each subordinate clause.

Score: 5 points for each phrase or clause

1. During the winter we live in an apartment house.
2. As soon as the telephone rang, I answered it.

3. We were delayed because of an accident.

4. The officer arrested the other driver, because his car had defective brakes.

5. Anyone who returns the purse and its contents will receive a generous reward.

6. Unless we find the key, we cannot use the car to make the trip.

7. At five o'clock we returned to the garage where we had left our car.

8. The man entering the gate is our new postman.

9. If we can secure tickets, will you attend the play with us tonight?

10. The old gentleman greatly enjoyed going for long walks with his two grandchildren.

11. Do you not realize that you are taking a great risk?

12. With the money that I had saved I bought presents for my relatives and friends.

Test Exercise IV

Write simple sentences in which you use the phrases given below. After each sentence write the word "simple" in parentheses.

Write complex sentences in which you use the clauses given below. After each sentence write the word "complex" in parentheses.

SCORE: 10 points for each sentence

1. Before she could stop the car.
2. To win the game next Saturday.
3. Having prepared the assignment.
4. Who was once a good athlete.
5. Without telling us their destination.
6. That my chum gave me last Christmas.
7. Because I had a severe cold.
8. Instead of attending a summer camp.
9. If you had given me your address.
10. That you will enjoy reading this book.

Test Exercise V

Below are ten groups of words. Some are complete sentences; some contain the comma fault; some contain the period fault.

A. At the left margin of your test paper write the numbers 1 to 10. Classify each group of words by writing after its number *S.* for a sentence, *C. F.* for a comma fault, and *P. F.* for a period fault.

<small>SCORE: 5 points for each classification</small>

B. Copy in its proper space each correct sentence. In the proper space rewrite correctly in one or two sentences, as the construction demands, each group of words that is not now a correct sentence.

<small>SCORE: 5 points for each sentence</small>

1. Our school has two additional teachers this year. On account of the increased enrollment.

2. Jerry is a dependable player, last season he made at least one touchdown in each game.

3. My brother is a junior at college, he is studying to become an architect.

4. You will be benefited by entering the contest, even if you fail.

5. I slept very little last night. Because the radio next door kept me awake.

6. We became uneasy about mother. For a week had elapsed since we had heard from her.

7. I could not attend the game, I had already spent my allowance.

8. The dictionary is a storehouse of words. From which much valuable information may be gained.

9. This is a picture of my great-aunt, for whom I was named.

10. The cost of living will probably be higher this winter. Because the severe drought in many sections of the country has brought about a crop shortage.

98. Nature and Purpose of the Sentence

A sentence is the expression of a single complete thought in words. It is the unit of all expression, since words must be properly grouped into a sentence before they can express a thought. It is likewise the unit of study in grammar, inasmuch as words have constructions only because of their relation one to another in the sentence.

99. Essential Parts of the Sentence

A sentence requires a *subject* and a *predicate*. The subject of a sentence denotes the person, place, thing, or idea about which an assertion is made or a question is asked. The predicate of a sentence asserts something about the subject or asks a question concerning it.

1. Helen | laughed.   3. Who | called?
2. Vacation | has ended.   4. What | is wanted?

Each illustrative sentence is made up of a simple subject and a simple predicate. A *simple subject* (or *subject substantive*) consists of a noun or a pronoun. A *simple predicate* (or *predicate verb*) is composed of a verb or a verb phrase.

A *complete subject* is made up of the subject substantive and any word or words used to modify it or to complete its meaning. A *complete predicate* consists of the predicate verb and any word or words used to modify it or to complete its meaning. The following sentences illustrate the complete subject and the complete predicate:

1. The excited young puppy | barked at us loudly.
2. Several houses in our town | were damaged by the recent storm.

Exercise 213

Examine closely each of the following groups of words, and tell whether it is a sentence or less than a sentence. Write a sentence of your own in which you include each group of words that is not now a sentence.

1. The janitor seemed greatly amused about something.
2. Without waiting to receive permission from mother.
3. Not in the least impressed by the unusual scene.
4. Behind her walked a beautiful collie.
5. Being the youngest child in a large family.
6. What an interesting vase that is!
7. Upon learning the news, Marjorie smiled knowingly.
8. In which play is the quotation to be found?
9. Descending the stairs with both arms full of books.
10. Instead of consulting a dictionary to find a synonym.

100. Sentence Order

If the subject of a sentence precedes the predicate, the sentence is said to be arranged in the *natural* order.

1. The postman is late today.
2. You will be given a test in English soon.
3. (You) Please lend me your dictionary.
4. A large table stood in the center of the room.

If the subject of a sentence follows the predicate or is placed between parts of the predicate, the sentence is said to be arranged in the *inverted* order.

1. In the center of the room stood a large table.
2. Whom have you invited? (You have invited whom?)
3. What a pretty girl is Doris! (Doris is what a pretty girl!)

Exercise 214

A. Write five sentences arranged in the natural order. In each underscore the simple subject with one line and the simple predicate with two lines.

B. Write five sentences arranged in the inverted order. In each underscore the complete subject with one line and the complete predicate with two lines.

101. Kinds of Sentences

According to their use, sentences are *declarative, interrogative, imperative,* and *exclamatory.*

1. A *declarative* sentence makes an assertion or a statement.

　　a. Hot air rises.　　　　　*b.* We missed our train.

2. An *interrogative* sentence asks a question.

　　a. Who are you?　　　　　*b.* Has John returned?

3. An *imperative* sentence expresses a command, a request, or an entreaty.

　　a. Read the next paragraph.　　*b.* Look behind the door.

4. An *exclamatory* sentence is a declarative, interrogative, or imperative sentence uttered under the influence of strong feeling or emotion.

　　a. How could you make such a mistake!
　　b. What a beautiful garden this is!

According to their form, sentences are *simple, compound, complex,* and *compound-complex.*

102. The Simple Sentence

A simple sentence contains but one subject and one predicate, although either, or both of them, may be compound.

1. *John drove the car.* (Single subject and single predicate)
2. *Mrs. Houghton and her sister* live in Florida. (Compound subject)
3. Helen *missed the step and sprained her ankle.* (Compound predicate)
4. *Relatives and friends attended the wedding and gave the couple presents.* (Compound subject and compound predicate)

Exercise 215

Write five original sentences to illustrate each of the four types of simple sentences explained in section 102. Be prepared to point out the subject and the predicate of each sentence and to tell whether they are single or compound.

103. Phrases as Elements of the Sentence

A phrase is a group of closely related words that does not contain a subject and a predicate.

1. The children *in the park* play *with the squirrels*.
2. *On the table* I found a letter *from my mother*.
3. My friend, *accompanied by his sister*, came *to see me*.
4. It is a pleasure *to read good books*.
5. *Two days having elapsed*, we gave up hope *of finding them*.
6. The entire journey was, *in fact*, a dangerous one.

104. Kinds of Phrases According to Form

1. Prepositional phrases. A prepositional phrase consists of a preposition, the noun or pronoun that is its object, and the modifiers (if any) of the object.

a. A friend *from the city* returned home *with us.*
b. *In the summer* we live *at the seashore.*

2. Infinitive phrases. An infinitive phrase consists of an infinitive, its object (if any), and the modifiers (if any) of the infinitive or its object.

a. *To refuse his offer* required courage.
b. Will she never learn *to speak gently*?

3. Participial phrases. A participial phrase consists of a participle, its object (if any), and the modifiers (if any) of the participle or its object.

a. A man *reading a newspaper* was the only other passenger.
b. *Looking back*, he saw a large dog *following him.*

4. Gerund phrases. A gerund phrase consists of a gerund, its object (if any), and the modifiers (if any) of the gerund or its object.

> *a. Befriending the poor* made him happy.
> *b.* I remember *seeing him only once.*

5. Absolute phrases. An absolute phrase consists of a noun or a pronoun in the nominative case used with a participle and its object and modifiers (if any).

> *a. The day being cloudy,* we could take no pictures.
> *b. The price having risen,* he sold his cattle.

Sometimes the participle *being* or *having been* is omitted in an absolute phrase.

> *a. His mind relieved,* he returned to his work.
> *b. This done,* we climbed into the car and drove on.

105. Kinds of Phrases According to Use

According to their use, phrases perform five functions in sentences.

1. Noun phrases. A phrase that performs the function of a noun is called a noun phrase.

> *a. To return* was dangerous.   *c.* I dread *writing letters.*
> *b.* We decided *to take the risk.*   *d.* His duty is *to advise clients.*

2. Adjective phrases. A phrase that is used to modify a noun or a pronoun is called an adjective phrase.

> *a.* Here is a picture *of my mother.*
> *b.* A stranger *wearing a soft, black felt hat* entered the room.
> *c.* There was her name, *scrawled carelessly below.*

3. Adverbial phrases. A phrase that is used to modify a verb, an adjective, or an adverb is called an adverbial phrase.

    a. He made the trip *in his private car.*
    b. The story is too long *to be read at one sitting.*
    c. She has gone *to visit her mother.*
    d. Our finances permitting, we shall go abroad next year.

4. Verb phrases. A phrase that is used as a verb is called a verb phrase.

    a. We *will* gladly *help* you.
    b. The story *should* never *have been told.*
    c. The fortune-teller *may have guessed* correctly.

5. Independent phrases. A phrase introduced into the sentence parenthetically and usually serving as a transitional device is called an independent phrase.

    a. That woman, *by the way,* is making a name for herself as a scientist.
    b. You will, *in the first place,* be surprised to hear their decision.

Exercise 216

In the following sentences state (1) the form and (2) the use of each phrase. Give a reason for each classification.

    1. Toward evening we came to a quaint little village paved with broken shells.
    2. A boy, splashed with acid and badly frightened by the explosion, rushed out of the laboratory.
    3. Calling to his comrades, he led the way into the cave.
    4. At the blowing of the whistle every man returned to his work.
    5. Our plan to reach Los Angeles within three days had failed.
    6. Growing flowers for his friends is his avocation.
    7. He always has time to be courteous to everyone.
    8. With a steady income at last assured, he now had leisure for writing.
    9. In the summer I enjoy sleeping out of doors.
    10. Angela, strange to say, likes to study geometry.
    11. I regret being unable to accompany you on your trip.
    12. First of all, a dog wearing a silver collar attracted the attention of my friend.

13. In a small canoe we paddled up the river by moonlight.

14. Having several long assignments to prepare, I remained at home to complete my work.

15. For two hours we skated, the blood tingling in our veins.

Exercise 217

From your reading, copy and bring to class fifteen simple sentences containing phrases. Underscore each phrase and be prepared to classify it according to form and according to use.

Exercise 218

A. Write two original simple sentences to illustrate each of the five kinds of phrases explained in section 104. Underscore each phrase.

B. Write two original simple sentences to illustrate each of the five uses of phrases explained in section 105. Underscore each phrase.

Exercise 219

In Chapter XX study carefully the rules for the use of the comma in separating, or setting off, words and phrases in the sentence. Explain the use of all commas found in the sentences studied in the three preceding exercises.

Exercise 220

From each of the following groups form one simple sentence. Determine which sentence of the group contains the main thought. Convert the other sentences into phrases. In your completed sentences underscore each phrase and be prepared to classify it according to form and according to use. Punctuate your sentences correctly.

1. They were panic-stricken by the appearance of a troop of English soldiers. These were rapidly advancing. They fled in breathless terror.

2. His coat was of dark-green cloth. It was trimmed with silver buttons. He wore this coat on state occasions.

√3. The wharf was at the end of the street. It was within a stone's throw of the warehouse. It was two doors away from the shipping company's office.

4. On this occasion a banquet was given Judge Wentworth. He was a brother of the commandant. Judge Wentworth had recently retired from practice.

5. They were returning home. They had been away twelve years. They looked in vain for the familiar landmarks.

6. Opposite her stood a young man. He had been her brother's college chum. She recognized him from his picture. She introduced herself.

7. Last night we saw a good play. It was written by Franz Molnar. The title of the play is "Liliom."

8. Yesterday I received a letter. In it was a check. The check was from my uncle.

9. His father was dead. For five generations his ancestors had inhabited this inn. He had inherited with the inn a large stock of jokes and stories.

10. The night was bitterly cold. There was a loud knock at the door downstairs. The knock woke me out of a sound sleep.

106. The Compound Sentence

A compound sentence consists of two or more simple sentences related to each other in thought. As a member of a compound sentence, each simple sentence is called a *principal*, or an *independent*, clause. The relation between these clauses may be indicated by the coördinating conjunctions (*and*, *but*, *or*, *nor*, *for*) and by certain adverbs. If the relation is clearly implied, the clauses may, if rightly punctuated, be written without any connective word.

1. The house rang with laughter, and the air was filled with the fragrance of tropical fruits.
2. They uttered no cry; not a sound escaped them.

107. Relationships between Parts of a Compound Sentence

Skill in the construction of compound sentences demands clear thinking and accurate knowledge to determine (1) what relationship exists between the clauses, (2) whether a connective word is necessary, and (3) if so, what connective is required to indicate this relationship accurately.

The six principal relationships between the clauses of the compound sentence are given below.

1. Continuation of the same line of thought. Example: The doors were opened, and the audience came crowding in. Connectives: *and, besides, also, moreover, likewise, in addition, furthermore.*

NOTE. In the following sentences the connection between clauses is so clearly implied that no connective is used:

1. The house was dilapidated; the yard was overgrown with weeds and grass; the front gate hung by a single rusty hinge.
2. Last night was a wild night: the thunder roared; the wind blew a gale; the rain fell in torrents.

Observe that wherever a connective has been omitted a semicolon or a colon has been used.

2. Contrast. Example: The bridal party assembled, but no bridegroom appeared. Connectives: *but, however, yet, whereas, still, nevertheless, notwithstanding, on the other hand, on the contrary.*

3. Alternation. Example: This machine is not rightly adjusted, or else we do not know how to operate it. Connectives: *or, nor, or else, otherwise.*

4. Correlation. Example: Not only did his friends desert him, but his family also disowned him. Connectives: *both . . . and, not only . . . but also, either . . . or, neither . . . nor.*

5. Consequence or inference. Example: He has wealth and the ablest lawyers; therefore his chance of acquittai is good. Connectives: *hence, therefore, thus, consequently, accordingly, as a result, for this reason.*

6. Reason. Example : The temperature must have fallen considerably during the night ; for I see icicles on the trees. Connective: *for*.

NOTE. The second clause in the sentence above does not state the reason for the truth expressed in the first clause, but rather acquaints us with the reason for the *speaker's or writer's knowledge* of the truth that it expresses. A principal clause of reason should not be confused with a subordinate clause of cause or reason. (See adverbial clauses of cause, section 113.)

108. Cautions in the Use of the Compound Sentence

We should avoid overworking the compound sentence in our writing. This we can do by judiciously employing simple and complex sentences, each of which is more flexible than the compound sentence. Furthermore, we should not allow ourselves to adopt the careless habit of connecting the members of every compound sentence with either *and* or *but*. We should use other connectives that indicate the same respective relationships as *and* and *but*. Better still, we should try to express by means of a simple or a complex sentence the thought that we have expressed in a compound sentence.

For a discussion of faulty coördination in compound sentences see sections 120, 3, *c*, and 121, 5, *a*. For a discussion of the correct punctuation of compound sentences see section 239, rule 11, and section 240, rules 1, 2, and 3.

Exercise 221

Write compound sentences in which you use properly each of the connectives listed under the six relationships between the clauses of the compound sentence. Think clearly and choose your connectives with care. Write five other compound sentences in which the relation between the clauses is clearly implied without the use of a connective. Punctuate all your sentences correctly.

Exercise 222

A. Examine closely the pairs of clauses given in B, below. Answer the following questions:

1. What seems to be the natural thought relationship between the two clauses?

2. Are any other relationships possible? If so, name them.

3. What connective will most accurately show the thought relationship that seems to be intended?

B. Write each sentence, supplying the best connective. In parentheses after each sentence write any other connective or connectives that might be used.

1. He was sent to school, —— he did not study.

2. The clouds had disappeared, —— the day was ideal.

3. We desired good seats; —— we made our reservations early.

4. I do not wish to be a candidate, —— I will serve if I am elected.

5. She must derive an enormous income from her investments; —— she pays a large income tax.

6. I have no suitable dress to wear; —— I shall not go.

7. We tried to persuade her, —— she refused to come.

8. He studied hard for the examination; —— he failed.

9. Shall I take the package, —— will you deliver it?

10. The lights went out at ten o'clock; —— I did not have time to solve all my problems in algebra.

Exercise 223

Add to each of the following statements a principal clause that will result in a well-constructed compound sentence. Be sure that each added clause expresses a thought closely related to that of the clause given.

1. The players were not conscious of any special regard for each other.

2. The mountain-climbers had many narrow escapes.

3. Thomas A. Edison is a great inventor.

4. The table was the picture of abundance. (Give particulars.)

5. The street was picturesque. (Give details showing this.)

6. With the dawn of a new day, Boynton quickly forgot his recent experience.

7. The memory of the whole transaction flashed before him.

8. It was a bitterly cold day in January.

9. We should learn to punctuate intelligently.

10. Judge Carlton's life was an active one.

Exercise 224

In the following exercise point out in each compound sentence the principal clauses and state the relationship between them. Indicate all the connectives. Point out all phrases and classify each according to form and according to use.

1. The children had rarely ventured into the field, but now they crept stealthily across the old stone bridge.

2. Holmes was, like Lowell, a humorist; and, like Lowell, he knew how to be earnest, serious, and even pathetic.

3. The Langtons must have gone away for the summer; for we have seen no signs of life about their house for the past week.

4. My precise examination of the room had done me good, but I still found the remoter darkness of the place too stimulating for the imagination.

5. His eyes goggled with earnestness; his mouth dropped open to catch every syllable that might be uttered; he leaned his ear almost on the doctor's shoulder.

6. He observed others closely and tried to profit by their experience; hence he was spared many humiliating reprimands.

7. She will probably arrive in a few days; for a letter addressed to her was left here today by the postman.

8. The number of employers diminished; the number of employees increased.

9. Some means of preventing war must be found; otherwise the same great waste of life and property from which humanity has suffered in the past will continue to blight the world in the future.

10. The steamship companies have advertised the attractions

of America in all parts of Europe; they have kept agents at work in many countries; they have been an important factor in promoting immigration.

Exercise 225

In Chapter XX make a careful study of the rules for the use of the comma, the semicolon, and the colon in separating principal clauses. Explain the punctuation of all compound sentences in Exercise 222 and Exercise 224. Explain the punctuation of your own sentences in Exercise 221 and Exercise 223.

Exercise 226

From your reading, copy and bring to class ten compound sentences. Underscore the connective, if one is used. After each sentence state the relationship between the principal clauses. Find, if you can, examples of all six types. Explain the punctuation used in each sentence.

109. The Complex Sentence

A complex sentence consists of one principal, or independent, clause and of one or more subordinate, or dependent, clauses.

A subordinate clause, like a phrase, is used as a single part of speech; but, unlike a phrase, it contains a subject and a predicate.

1. { Where he lived.
     Whom we met.
     When the whistle sounded.

Note that, although each of these clauses contains a subject and a predicate, in no case does it express a complete thought. The mind waits for something to be added.

2. { I told her where he lived.
     The man whom we met was my uncle.
     The game began when the whistle sounded.

By joining the subordinate clauses in group 1 to principal, or independent, clauses, as in group 2, we have made three assertions and have thus completed the statement of thoughts which the original clauses left incomplete.

The construction of the complex sentence demands clear thinking to determine which part of the sentence-thought should be put in the principal clause as the main thought and which part or parts should be subordinated to it. In addition, we must choose the proper connective to denote the relationship intended. Because of the larger number of thought relationships between principal and subordinate clauses, and because of a correspondingly greater number of connective and introductory words, the complex sentence is superior to the compound in variety and flexibility.

110. Uses of Subordinate Clauses

According to their use in the complex or the compound-complex sentence, subordinate clauses are classified as *noun clauses*, *adjective clauses*, and *adverbial clauses*. In general, they have the same constructions as the part of speech whose function they perform.

111. Noun (Substantive) Clauses

A noun (substantive) clause performs the office of a noun. It may be introduced by the following words: (1) interrogative pronouns and interrogative adjectives, as *who, which, what, whoever, whichever, whatever, whose, whosoever, whichsoever, whatsoever*; (2) interrogative adverbs, as *where, when, how, why*; (3) subordinating conjunctions, as *that, whether, if, but* or *but that* (= *that not*). Often the conjunction *that* introducing a noun clause is omitted, especially in speech.

> He said [that] he would write to me.
> We feared [that] we should be late.

The sentences given below illustrate the principal constructions of noun clauses.

1. *Who the stranger is* does not interest me. (Subject of a verb)
2. I knew *that he was right*. (Direct object of a verb)
3. We had an excellent view of the stage from *where we sat*. (Object of a preposition)
4. The fact *that he had set out very early* accounted for his escape. (In apposition)
5. The report was *that he had drowned*. (Predicate nominative)
6. Honesty, good judgment, and industry made them *who they are in the financial world*. (Predicate objective)
7. We were told *that the house had been rented*. (Direct retained object after a verb in the passive voice)

Exercise 227

Point out the noun clauses in the following sentences and tell how each is used:

1. That the world is round has been proved.
2. The fact that the forests are being cut down accounts for the scarcity of water.
3. Often we judge a person by how he dresses.
4. My fear is that we shall be late.
5. Mother asked me where I had been.
6. I was asked by my mother where I had been.
7. I could not guess whom she meant.
8. Wealth alone has made him who he is.
9. It is in dispute why he did this.
10. Did you learn whether he passed in his examination?
11. Who knows but that he may recover soon?
12. She did not tell us where she was going or when she would return.

Exercise 228

Write two original sentences to illustrate each of the seven constructions of noun clauses. Underscore each noun clause and name its use.

© Wide World Photos

Fox Hounds of the Myopia Hunt Club

112. Adjective Clauses

An adjective clause performs the function of an adjective.

The man *who knocked* is a plumber.

Note that the clause in italics modifies the noun *man* and tells which man is meant. If an adjective clause limits or restricts the meaning of a noun or pronoun in this way, it is called *essential,* or *restrictive.* Such a clause cannot be omitted without changing the meaning of the entire sentence.

Aunt Mary, *who visits us each summer,* is mother's only sister.

In the sentence above, the clause in italics, though grammatically a modifier of a noun, is not an indispensable part of the sentence. It may be omitted without changing the meaning of the principal clause, though by its use we gain additional information. Such a parenthetical clause is called *nonessential,* or *nonrestrictive.*

Observe that an essential clause requires no punctuation, whereas a nonessential clause is separated by a comma or by commas from the rest of the sentence (see section 239, rule 9).

Adjective clauses are introduced by (1) relative pronouns, *who, which, that, but* (= *that not*), and (2) subordinating conjunctions, *after, before, since, while, where, when, whence, whither, why, wherein, wherewith. whereon, whereat, whereupon, whereby.*

Exercise 229

In the following sentences point out all adjective clauses. Tell what word each modifies and explain whether it is essential or nonessential. Indicate the introductory word in each and explain its use in the clause.

1. This is the house that Jack built.
2. The farmer whose horse was stolen consulted a lawyer.

3. The old chapel belfry, where generations of bats have lived, was struck by lightning.

4. Those whose names were called stepped forward.

5. The house where he was born yet stands.

6. We who went with him fared royally.

7. My older brother, whose judgment I respect, advised me to go to college.

8. There is no one born but must die.

9. The ground whereon we stood trembled.

10. Our high-school building, which was erected in 1928, is a fireproof structure.

11. He lacks the means wherewith he may clothe his family.

12. It is difficult to teach a cat, which is naturally active, any kind of athletic tricks.

13. The day when he returns will be a holiday.

14. The reason why we fail is usually that we lack a definite intention to win.

15. The foreman, whom everyone trusted, was never suspected.

Exercise 230

Bring to class ten sentences containing essential adjective clauses and ten containing nonessential adjective clauses. Underline and name the clauses. Make sure that the sentences are correctly punctuated (see section 239, rule 9). These sentences may be original ones or they may be taken from your outside reading.

113. Adverbial Clauses

An adverbial clause performs the function of an adverb. It is introduced by a subordinating conjunction. The nine adverbial relationships expressed by adverbial clauses are the following:

1. Time. Example: The audience rose and cheered *when the celebrated speaker was presented by the chairman.* Introductory words: *when, before, after, while, since, till, ere, as, whenever, now that, as soon as, as long as, so long as.*

2. Place. Example: He remained *where I left him.* Introductory words: *where, wherever, whence, whither, whencesoever, whithersoever.*

3. Manner. Example: She walked *as if she were going to a bargain sale.* Introductory words: *as, as if, as though.*

NOTE. *Like* should never be used for *as* or *as if* (see section 233).

4. Condition. Example: He would have passed in his examination *if he had studied harder.* Introductory words: (1) the subordinating conjunctions *if, unless* (= *if not*), *except*; (2) such phrases as *on condition that, in case that, but that* (= *if not*), *so that*; (3) the participles and participial phrases *supposing, provided, supposing that, provided that*; and (4) such imperatives as *suppose, let, say.* Often the introductory word is omitted, as in the sentence "*Had I another life to live,* I could not wish for greater happiness."

5. Cause. Example: We walked home *because the cars had stopped running.* Introductory words: *because, since, as, that* ("He grieved *that his friend should have failed him thus*"), and sometimes *for.*

6. Purpose. Example: We left early *in order that we might not miss the train.* Introductory words: *in order that, lest* (= *that . . . not*), *that, so that* ("He lent me his key *so that I might open the door*").

7. Result. Example: During the night it snowed so hard *that all traffic was suspended for two days.* (Notice that, in addition to expressing result, the dependent clause expresses degree: in this sentence it tells *how* hard it snowed.) Introductory words: *that, so that, but, but that.* ("It never rains *but it pours.*" In this sentence *but* is equivalent to *that not.* The sentence means "It never rains *that it does not pour.*")

8. Degree or comparison. Example : His mind is *as* sluggish *as his body is indolent.* Introductory words : *as . . . as, just as . . . as, than, so far as, by as much as . . . by so much, as far as, in proportion as.*

9. Concession. Example : *Though I regard him as honest,* I think that he should not be trusted too far. Introductory words : *though, although, whether, however, no matter, while, notwithstanding, notwithstanding that, whatever, whichever, even if* ("*Even if you disagree with his beliefs,* you will surely like him as a man").

Exercise 231

In the following sentences point out all adverbial clauses and tell what relation each expresses. Indicate the introductory words in the adverbial clauses.

1. She does as she likes, but I do as I must.
2. The apples froze because they were left out of doors.
3. Where thou goest, I will go.
4. Unless you speak distinctly, you will not be understood.
5. As we came out of the theater, father met us.
6. We study that we may learn.
7. Should you meet him, tell him that I have gone home.
8. One plays as well as the other.
9. No matter how late you may arrive, telephone me at once.
10. He slept so late that he missed his class.
11. We will deliver the package wherever you desire.
12. When she answered, she spoke as if she were angry.
13. Granted that I fail, the effort is worth while.
14. We can enjoy even unpleasant surroundings, provided we look for something interesting in them.
15. Since youth is precious, do not squander it.
16. She appeared much stronger than I had expected.
17. Suppose you had wealth, you would not be content.
18. As long as there is life, there is hope.
19. I would accompany him, but that I know that he would object.
20. We were amused that he should make such a mistake as that

Exercise 232

In Chapter XX review all the rules for the use of the comma. Explain the punctuation employed in the sentences in Exercise 231. Change the position of the adverbial clause in the sentence, wherever it is possible, and account for the use or the omission of commas.

Exercise 233

In studying the following exercise observe these directions: (1) Point out the principal and the subordinate clauses. (2) Tell how each subordinate clause is used. (3) Mention the introductory word or phrase.

1. I confess that I do not agree with you.
2. When I looked again, I saw nothing.
3. Let them wait until I am ready.
4. Then came the thought that I had left my native land.
5. The wireless telephone, which is now very expensive, may soon be within the reach of all.
6. He paced the deck as he talked.
7. Tell me where he has gone.
8. I could not enjoy the meal that the steward brought me.
9. That you can do the task has been proved.
10. I am not so stupid as you think I am.
11. The book pleased me because it aroused cherished memories.
12. Do you not see why I cannot grant your request?
13. A plain marble slab marks the spot where he lies.
14. I placed the flowers where she would see them.
15. Take the good that the gods provide thee.
16. Who knows but that he may succeed?
17. I will ask whether he has left a message for you.
18. The accident occurred at a time when we least expected it.
19. When he came does not concern me in the slightest.
20. I am interested in when he left.
21. Jason, who was devoted to his master, would not admit the reporters.
22. Whither I go you cannot follow.

23. The reason why he fled is not known.
24. Judge Clark is the man to whom they submitted the case.
25. The truth is that I forgot to mail the letter.
26. He gave a liberal reward to the boy who found his purse.
27. Mr. Arnold Bennett said that most people cannot live on twenty-four hours a day.
28. Many people do not consider why they eat.
29. He who steals my purse steals trash.
30. She waited so long to write that we became uneasy.
31. "We live," says Stevenson, "the time that a match flickers."
32. The manager, who spoke Spanish, asked him whom he wished to see.
33. He was so sleepy that he sat nodding in his chair.
34. She proclaimed herself ignorant by the questions that she asked.
35. While she was reading "Comus," she fell asleep.

Exercise 234

Expand the following statements into complex sentences, using as many phrases and subordinate clauses as you can in each sentence without losing the meaning of the principal statement:

1. The coming week will be a busy one.
2. A reception was given for their daughter, Mary Bryce.
3. The hum of an airplane attracted our attention.
4. They had come to the edge of the cliff.
5. The stranger sat by the kitchen fire.
6. They beheld a scene of disorder.
7. He would not listen to reason.
8. The guide lived in a secluded spot.
9. His father gave him excellent opportunities.
10. The officers approached the house cautiously.

Exercise 235

Combine into complex sentences the following groups of words. Decide first upon the most important statement and make this the principal clause. The other statements may be converted into subordinate clauses and phrases, according to their importance. In your completed sentences, be prepared to tell how each subordinate clause is used, to classify it, and to name the introductory word.

1. In the middle of the yard stood a man. The yard had been empty a few minutes before.

2. She was glad to be living again in the little village. She had been born there. She had been away for four years.

3. We had been camping out for a week. We hailed a man in a car. Our matches had given out. He was able to supply us with a few.

4. He lived a wanderer and a fugitive in his native land. He had heroic qualities. These would have graced a civilized warrior. These would have rendered him the theme of the poet and the historian.

5. My father failed in business. My family came to America. I was then six years old.

6. There were two or three pretty faces among the women. The keen air of a frosty morning had given them a bright-red tint.

7. The dog looked up into his master's face. The dog lay stretched at his feet. He lazily resumed his nap.

8. He found their attention gradually diverted to other subjects. He concluded his remarks in an undertone to an old gentleman. The old gentleman sat next him.

9. Everybody had his tale of engine troubles. We sat around the dull lamp in the cabin. All hoped for better roads for the rest of the journey.

10. He was accompanied by the redoubtable Bantam. He was a little rat of a pony. He had a shaggy mane. He stood dozing by the roadside. He was unmindful of his approaching fate.

Exercise 236

In Chapter XX review all the rules for the use of the comma, the semicolon, and the colon. Explain all the punctuation found in the sentences in Exercise 233. Explain the punctuation of your own sentences in Exercises 234 and 235.

114. The Compound-Complex Sentence

A compound-complex sentence consists of two or more principal clauses and at least one subordinate clause. The following is a typical compound-complex sentence:

> Our friends, who had preceded us, promised that they would meet us; but when we arrived at the station, they were nowhere to be seen.

We should not form the habit of using long and involved compound-complex sentences; for by so doing we are likely to write in a heavy, cumbersome style and fail to make our meaning altogether clear.

115. Fragments of Sentences

A sentence, as we have learned, is the expression of a *complete* thought in words. Before any group of words can express a thought it must have both a subject and a predicate. A phrase does not contain both a subject and a predicate; therefore it cannot express a thought, and for this reason cannot be used as a sentence.

A subordinate clause, though it has a subject and a predicate, cannot express a *complete* thought; for its meaning is dependent upon its relationship to the thought expressed by the principal clause with which it is used. Without this principal clause the subordinate clause has no definite meaning.

We should, therefore, at all times avoid writing a phrase or a subordinate clause as a sentence; for each is merely a fragment of a sentence.

Exercise 237

In the following exercise classify each group of words as (1) a phrase, (2) a subordinate clause, or (3) a sentence. Write a sentence in which you use correctly each phrase and each subordinate clause. Punctuate your sentences properly.

1. That we had taken him by surprise was evident.
2. When we rose the next morning.
3. Through no fault of his.
4. What a perfect day it was!
5. Since we had not heard from him for three years.
6. Whom he said he had met the year before.
7. Though the whole experience left no pleasant memory.
8. To relieve his suffering somewhat.
9. To make such a scene was not my intention.
10. While the gayety was at its height.
11. Not that he intended to act dishonestly.
12. Wherever he happened to find anyone to listen to his story.
13. When we had eaten our lunch.
14. Not failure, but low aim, is crime.
15. Having nothing else to do.
16. That a wise man may be taught by a fool.
17. Repeatedly the old guide had warned them of the danger.
18. Some of us call it autumn, and others call it God.
19. Gazing from the dizzy height as if entranced.
20. Standing on tiptoe and reaching high with both hands.
21. In much less time than it takes to tell of the weird adventure.
22. Since I had never tried to skate before.
23. In order to keep my appointment with him.
24. A book that I have greatly enjoyed reading and re-reading.
25. Whose place it will be difficult to fill.

116. The Period Fault

The period fault consists in using a period to set off a phrase or a subordinate clause as if it were a complete sentence. Usually this fault is the result of carelessness.

In our informal everyday speech we employ many incomplete sentences. In all writing, however, we should carefully avoid the period fault, which is one of the most serious errors that we can commit in composition.

> *Incorrect:* Dalton sacrificed everything. His one aim being the attainment of his purpose.
> *Correct:* Dalton sacrificed everything, his one aim being the attainment of his purpose.
> *Incorrect:* I was surprised to learn of his prejudice. Because he had heretofore been very liberal in his views.
> *Correct:* I was surprised to learn of his prejudice, because he had heretofore been very liberal in his views.

NOTE. Setting off as a sentence an elliptical expression that functions as a sentence does not constitute a period fault. In conversation we employ many sentences in which the meaning is not fully expressed in words but is clearly implied. In answering a question we may rightly use such elliptical sentences as the following: *Yes. When? By all means. Certainly. Surely not. Very well, then. Not now. Good-by.* In each of these expressions the omitted words can be accurately supplied from the question or statement that has immediately preceded it.

"Do you think that I should go to college?" I asked.
"By all means [you should go to college]," my friend replied.

117. The Comma Fault

The use of a comma in place of a period, a semicolon, a colon, or a dash is termed the *comma fault*. This error is fully as serious as the period fault. Both errors are to be carefully guarded against. The person who is guilty of either of them proves that he does not yet know what constitutes a sentence.

> *Incorrect:* I found him asleep in his bed, I had not heard him when he entered.
> *Correct:* I found him asleep in his bed. I had not heard him when he entered.
> *Incorrect:* Hanson always did his work a little better than the rest of us, that was what won him his promotion.
> *Correct:* Hanson always did his work a little better than the rest of us; that was what won him his promotion.

Exercise 238

In the following exercise point out period faults and comma faults. Write a correct version of each sentence.

1. Our guest entertained us with many interesting stories of adventure, he had been a newspaper correspondent.

2. Art museums have a great cultural value, they furnish the public an opportunity to develop a better æsthetic taste.

3. A freshman has much to learn. Never having been dependent on himself before. And not knowing how to study.

4. It was useless to argue with mother. Though Tom always tried to convince her that he was right.

5. Blair won first place in three events. Thereby enabling us to win the meet.

6. When I left, I offered to pay him for his hospitality, he refused to accept a cent.

7. Toby has excellent table manners, I began training him when he was a small kitten, not even the smell of fish makes him forget to be polite.

8. As night approached, I became uneasy. Because father had promised to return before six o'clock.

9. The manager of our ranch telephoned father that bandits had crossed the border and raided several towns. And that they had killed one of the rangers.

10. I cannot understand the luck that some people have, last year our cook held the number that won an automobile, and now her uncle has made a fortune in oil.

Exercise 239

Using one of the subjects given below, construct a good outline and then write a composition of approximately three hundred words.

1. Advice to a Freshman.
2. If I Were a Teacher.
3. How to Lose Friends.
4. Qualities of a Good Athlete.
5. The Importance of Good Manners.

6. How to Improve Our School.
7. Habits That I am Trying to Overcome.
8. Types of People That Bore Me.
9. Teaching a Girl to Drive a Car.
10. The Trials of the Youngest (Oldest) Child.

Exercise 240

Before you submit the composition that you wrote in Exercise 239, criticize and revise it by means of the following questions:

1. Have I divided my composition correctly into paragraphs?
2. In each paragraph have I stated the topic clearly in a topic sentence? (See sections 85–86.)
3. What method have I used in developing each topic sentence into a paragraph? (See sections 92–97.)
4. Have I used the right connectives to show clearly the relationship between the sentences within each paragraph and between the paragraphs themselves? (See sections 88–89.)
5. Have I set off any fragments of sentences as sentences? (See section 115.)
6. Do any of my sentences contain a *period fault*? (See section 116.)
7. Do any of my sentences contain a *comma fault*? (See section 117.)
8. Have I used any carelessly constructed compound sentences to express sentence-thoughts that could be better expressed in simple or in complex sentences? (See section 108.)
9. Are my sentences correctly punctuated? (See sections 239–249.)

Exercise 241

After you have revised your composition by means of the questions given in Exercise 240, make a final copy according to the following directions:

1. Indicate the topic sentence in each paragraph by inclosing it in parentheses.

2. State in parentheses after each paragraph the method that you used in developing the topic sentence.

3. Indicate each phrase in your sentences by underscoring it with *one* line.

4. Indicate each clause in your sentences by underscoring it with *two* lines.

5. Above each noun clause write *1*, above each adjective clause write *2*, and above each adverbial clause write *3*.

6. On a separate sheet submit your outline.

The Sentence Rhetorically Considered

Rhetorically

Test Exercise I

If you examine closely the short sentences included in each of the groups given below, you will discover that they contain only one complete sentence-thought, which could be better expressed in a single well-constructed sentence. Out of each group of short sentences select the main idea and express this in a principal, or independent, clause. Subordinate the other ideas by means of a word, a phrase, or a clause. Express the thought contained in each group in a good simple or complex sentence. State in parentheses after each of your sentences whether it is simple or complex.

SCORE: 10 points for each sentence

1. I spent last Christmas vacation with Eleanor Calkins. She is my cousin. She lives in New York City.

2. Father gave me a dog. He is a Boston terrier. I call him Barnacle Bill.

3. Last night we attended a play. The play was "Journey's End." It was given at the Booth Theater.

4. My brother and his chum bought a used car. They drove it all the summer. They sold it for fifty dollars.

5. The house next door is vacant. I discovered a fire in it. I turned in an alarm.

6. Tom Farrell was seriously injured. He was a pilot in the World War. One wing of his plane struck a tree.

7. Our school has a new phonograph. It was bought by the school board. The classes in dancing use it.

8. Miss Norcross teaches dancing. She is a graduate of this school. She studied dancing under Ruth St. Denis.

9. Our chauffeur is in the hospital. He was injured in an accident. The accident occurred last Saturday night.

10. The Camera Club will meet next Tuesday. The meeting will be held at four o'clock in Room 216. New officers will be elected at the meeting.

Test Exercise II

You will notice that each of the following sentences lacks clearness and accuracy because some word or group of words has been placed in the wrong position or the reference of some pronoun is not definite. On your test paper put the numbers 1 to 10 at the left margin. Copy the word or group of words that is misplaced or carelessly used in each sentence and write a version of the sentence that will be unmistakably clear.

SCORE: 10 points for each sentence

1. I only paid twenty-five dollars for this suit.

2. All books are not worth reading.

3. Lying on the rug before the fire I saw a beautiful collie.

4. I nearly saved a hundred dollars out of the money that I earned last summer.

5. He took a bill from his purse, which he gave to the salesman.

6. We only had to wait ten minutes for the train.

7. George told Tom that his cousin would be a member of his class.

8. I found a letter in the dictionary that was written by my grandfather.

9. Bob almost made a perfect score in his entrance examinations.

10. My uncle once tried sheep-raising, but he did not make any money out of them.

118. Kinds of Sentences

Rhetorically considered, sentences are classified as *loose*, *periodic*, and *balanced*, according to their construction.

1. Loose sentence. A loose sentence is one that may be brought to a grammatical close before the end is reached.

> He was sitting in a large armchair before the fire when we entered.

In this sentence the meaning is clear if we stop after *armchair* or after *fire*. Simple and complex sentences are loose or periodic, according to their order of arrangement. Every compound sentence, because of its form, is loose, although each of its coördinate clauses may be periodic within itself.

2. Periodic sentence. A periodic sentence is one that is not grammatically complete until the end is reached.

> Having passed the house every day for two years, and knowing that the man was a cripple, I could not believe what the next-door neighbor told me.

This sentence is so constructed that it is not grammatically complete at any point before the period. Most simple and complex loose sentences may be made periodic by transposing adverbial phrases and clauses to the beginning of the sentence. Most sentences arranged in the inverted order are periodic (see section 100).

3. Balanced sentence. A balanced sentence is one in which the parts are alike, in that they are constructed according to the same pattern.

> 1. The dangers are real, but the benefits are great.
> 2. Helen is from the country; Marian is from the city.

Here subject balances subject, and predicate balances predicate. In a balanced sentence the clauses are similar in form but are usually contrasted in meaning.

Exercise 242

Study the following paragraph as an illustration of the use of the balanced sentence to express contrast in ideas.

What kind of sentence is the first one in the paragraph? In each of the sentences that follow name the words that balance.

There are still two widely different methods of getting what you want. One is to make yourself so useful that others are glad to pay you, or to give you what you want, in return for your service or your product; the other is to make yourself so dangerous that others will be afraid to refuse what you demand. The one pursues the method of voluntary agreement among free citizens; the other pursues the method of force. The one appeals to good will; the other to fear. The one is constructive; the other is destructive. The one is the method of civilized men,— that is, of men who have learned the art of living and working peaceably together in large numbers; the other is the method of savages,— that is, of men who have not learned how to get along peaceably together.— CARVER and CARMICHAEL, "Elementary Economics"

119. Effect of Different Kinds of Sentences

Our natural tendency is to write loose sentences, which in an easy, somewhat familiar style may be wholly appropriate. The use of a large number of such sentences in formal writing, however, gives an impression of carelessness and lack of finish. Periodic sentences add strength and dignity to our writing, but if used exclusively they make the style stiff and formal. Balanced sentences are not usually suitable in narration or in description, but are well adapted to expository and argumentative writing in which persons, things, or ideas are contrasted.

Short sentences give animation to the style, but a constant use of them becomes tiresome and detracts from smoothness of expression. The chief merit of the long sentence is that it brings a large number of related particulars into view and shows their relations more clearly or more economically than would several short sentences. The mind, however, tires of any one style of construction if it is carried to excess. Variety is obtained by the judicious use of loose and periodic, long and short, sentences.

Exercise 243

Study for sentence variety "How We Earned Our Car," in Exercise 22, and "Personality and Pencils," in Exercise 189. Classify each sentence grammatically as simple, complex, compound, or compound-complex, and rhetorically as loose, periodic, or balanced. In each paragraph note the grouping of sentences as to length.

Exercise 244

Express in a well-constructed periodic or loose sentence the thought contained in each of the following groups of sentences. Note whether you have made a simple, a complex, a compound, or a compound-complex sentence.

1. The farmer's life has been made easier of late years. The telephone keeps him in touch with his neighbors. The rural delivery brings him his daily paper. The gasoline engine does a great deal of his work. The automobile carries him quickly to town.

2. Nature is economical. No particle of matter is ever destroyed, though it undergoes numerous changes in form and in combination. Animals furnish plants carbon dioxide as food. Plants, in return, supply animals with vegetable food and with oxygen to breathe.

3. Mr. Edison is one of the greatest benefactors of mankind. Consider the innumerable conveniences that we owe to him. In the Middle Ages he would doubtless have been looked upon as a magician.

4. Fishing from a kite has two advantages. The fisherman may stand on shore while his bait is dropped far out at sea. There is no shadow to frighten timid fish.

5. Modern civilization is rapidly recognizing the equal rights of men and women. Both have the same educational advantages. They are rapidly becoming politically equal. Industrially women compete successfully with men.

Exercise 245

Write a paragraph of from six to twenty sentences in which you develop one of the topic sentences given below.

1. Our school should organize a Current Events Club.
2. Most automobile accidents could easily be avoided.
3. When we criticize others adversely, we frequently injure our own reputation more than we injure theirs.
4. A little learning is sometimes a dangerous thing.
5. The origin and meaning of proper names is a fascinating study.
6. A knowledge of science helps us to discover interest in commonplace things.

When you have completed your paragraph, study your sentences carefully and revise them so that you will achieve variety in sentence structure. Use connecting words and phrases that will make the transition from one sentence to another easy, clear, and natural. Test your paragraph for sentence variety and smoothness of phrasing by reading it aloud.

120. Unity in the Sentence

Since a sentence is the expression of a single complete thought, the first essential of sentence structure is that it shall show oneness of thought by being unified.

1. Overloaded sentence. A sentence violates the principle of unity if it contains too much.

> As we were driving out into the country yesterday, we met a young man wearing a golf suit, and we passed a car that was broken down, and on our way home we stopped at Mr. Beck's to get some flowers and fresh vegetables.

Although each clause in the sentence above has the same subject, the sentence as a whole is not a unit, because it combines ideas that are not closely related. The sentence contains material for three sentences.

As we were driving out into the country yesterday, we met a young man wearing a golf suit. Later we passed a car that was broken down. On our way home we stopped at Mr. Beck's to get some flowers and fresh vegetables.

2. Incomplete sentence. A sentence violates the principle of unity if it contains too little. Such violations occur whenever a simple, a complex, or a compound sentence is written as two separate sentences. (See section 116.)

1. He walked home with me. Having met me at the door of the office.
2. We won the election. Though the opposition was strong.
3. I was late this morning. But I will be on time hereafter.

The phrase "having met me at the door of the office," and the subordinate clause "though the opposition was strong," are fragments of sentences. They have no definite meaning except in relation to their respective principal clauses. The principal clause "but I will be on time hereafter" is related by contrast to the preceding principal clause and, when combined with it, constitutes a single unified sentence. The three examples should read:

1. (Simple sentence) He walked home with me, having met me at the door of the office *or* Having met me at the door of the office, he walked home with me.
2. (Complex sentence) We won the election, though the opposition was strong *or* Though the opposition was strong, we won the election.
3. (Compound sentence) I was late this morning, but I will be on time hereafter.

3. Obscure relationship of parts. A sentence violates unity if the relation between its parts is not rightly indicated.

a. Even when related ideas are grouped together in a sentence, the relation between them is not always clearly shown.

I am not surprised that their team lost the game, they were poorly trained and were overconfident.

In this sentence a comma is used where we should expect a period or a semicolon. This is the *comma fault* or *comma splice*, explained in section 117. The unity of this sentence may be indicated in two ways:

> (Relation indicated by connective) I am not surprised that their team lost the game, because they were poorly trained and were overconfident.
>
> (Relation indicated by punctuation) I am not surprised that their team lost the game; they were poorly trained and were overconfident.

b. Unity is often obscured through the careless choice of connectives.

> Helen went to college, and Irene became a motion-picture actress.

In this compound sentence the relation between the two principal clauses seems to be contrast, not mere addition. The sentence should therefore read:

> Helen went to college, *but* Irene became a motion-picture actress.

In a complex sentence, likewise, the connective should be carefully chosen.

> The patient's condition continued to grow worse, when he was given every attention.

In this complex sentence the relation of the subordinate to the principal clause appears to be concession, not time. The unified sentence should read:

> The patient's condition continued to grow worse, though he was given every attention.

c. Unity is often violated by the form of the sentence used.

> A well-dressed man admitted us to the house, and we afterward learned that he was the thief.

The unity of this compound-complex sentence may be improved by converting it into a complex sentence, with the second member expressed as a subordinate clause.

> We afterwards learned that the well-dressed man who admitted us to the house was the thief.

Unity demands that coördinate thoughts be expressed by means of coördinate clauses.

> I employed a detective, by whose aid I recovered the ring.

The meaning of this complex sentence is made more clear if the compound form is used; the subordinate clause then becomes coördinate.

> I employed a detective, and by his aid I recovered the ring.

4. Change in point of view. A sentence frequently violates the principle of unity by a change in the point of view.

> The *vessel* made for the shore, and the *passengers* soon crowded into the boats, and the *beach* was reached in safety, and the *inhabitants* of the island received them with the utmost kindness.

Because of this frequent change of subject the mind travels in quick succession from the *vessel* to the *passengers*, and then to the *beach* and the *inhabitants*. A confusion of ideas results. Such confusion may be avoided by selecting one point of view, and by choosing one principal clause, to which the others may be subordinated as phrases and dependent clauses.

> The vessel having made for the shore, the *passengers* soon crowded into the boats and safely reached the beach, where *they* were received with the utmost kindness by the inhabitants of the island.

Now there is one point of view, that of the passengers. The first independent clause in the original sentence has been subordinated as a phrase, and the final independent clause has been made subordinate. The result is a well-unified complex sentence.

Exercise 246

Tell how unity is violated in the following sentences. Then write a unified version of each sentence.

1. Somebody had provided native fruits, and we had many other delicacies.

2. These birds fly swiftly and mostly by day, and their food consists of seeds and berries and small shellfish.

3. I asked him how I could reach the park, and he could not tell me.

4. Everybody made a rush for the small cold-drink stand, and the proprietor soon sold out his entire stock.

5. His past life was investigated, and he was allowed to become a member of the order.

6. I could hear the sound of motors humming far up in the night sky, and they made me feel uncomfortable.

7. His father was indolent, he let the boy do as he pleased.

8. The shore of this island was rocky, and after a time we found a place suitable for landing.

9. The people of this island are lazy, and they steal all they can, and the state takes no care of them whatever.

10. Correct speech is important in the routine of daily life, and everyone should try to speak well.

11. While he is insane, he appears harmless.

12. The houses were mere shanties, and rags were stuffed in the cracks and holes.

13. In the winter we live in the city. While in the summer we go to the country.

14. I read the book hurriedly, the latter part of which did not interest me at all.

15. The road was macadamized only two years ago, and now it is full of holes.

16. Grouped around him sat the fair maidens, and below in the arena all was made ready for the sport.

17. There were aircraft of all kinds round us, and I enjoyed watching them.

18. We reached home at nine o'clock. Saving three hours by making the trip in an automobile.

19. My aunt enjoys playing with children, but she is very old.

20. My uncle left home when I was three years old. But I do not remember him.

Exercise 247

Explain the punctuation of the sentences that you wrote in Exercise 244.

121. Coherence in the Sentence

A second essential of sentence structure is that the grammatical construction and the proper relationship of the words in the sentence be made unmistakably clear.

1. Careless placing of modifiers. Coherence is violated when a word, a phrase, or a clause is so placed that it appears to modify the wrong word in the sentence.

a. Such words as *nearly, not,* and *only* should be carefully placed with respect to the word that each is intended to modify. Observe the changes in meaning that result from shifting the position of these words in the following sentences:

1. I caught *nearly* a hundred fish.
2. I *nearly* caught a hundred fish.
3. All men are *not* criminals.
4. *Not* all men are criminals.
5. *Only* I saw him speak to her.
6. I *only* saw him speak to her.
7. I saw *only* him speak to her.
8. I saw him *only* speak to her.
9. I saw him speak to her *only*.

b. Modifying phrases should be placed next to the words that they modify.

I sat watching the tide go out *on the front porch.*

Transpose the phrase, and the sentence becomes coherent.

> I sat on the front porch watching the tide go out.

c. A relative clause should be placed as near as possible to the word that it modifies.

> He carried a bag of peanuts in his hat, *which he fed to the elephants.*

The sentence slightly rearranged is coherent.

> In his hat he carried a bag of peanuts, which he fed to the elephants.

d. Sometimes a phrase or a clause is, through carelessness, so placed in the sentence that it may be construed with what has preceded or with what follows. This arrangement is called the *squinting construction.*

> 1. He said *in spite of protest* he would go.
> 2. Tell my friend, *if she is at home,* I will call to see her.

To make the meaning clear, we may write these sentences in either of the following versions:

> 1. { In spite of protest he said he would go.
>   { He said he would go in spite of protest.
> 2. { If my friend is at home, tell her I will call to see her.
>   { Tell my friend I will call to see her if she is at home.

2. Careless placing of correlative connectives. Coherence is sometimes violated by the careless placing of the two members of correlative connectives, such as *both . . . and, either . . . or, neither . . . nor, not only . . . but also, on the one hand . . . on the other hand.* The correlatives should be placed immediately before the words that they join. The words connected should always be in the same construction. The sentences that follow show the connectives properly placed:

> 1. I not only saw him but heard him also.
> 2. He came neither by train nor by automobile.

3. Incorrect reference of pronouns. Coherence is frequently violated by the incorrect reference of pronouns (see section 219).

1. I may go to the lecture, for *he* is my chum's uncle.
2. We went trout-fishing, but caught only two of *them.*
3. He struck him as *he* passed *him.*
4. I saw a bird in a beautiful cage, *which* I bought.
5. Mrs. Ward told Mrs. Gray that *her* children were playing in *her* flower bed.

In the first two sentences the pronouns have no definite antecedents expressed. In the last three the pronouns may refer to two antecedents, and for this reason the reference is ambiguous. All five sentences may be made coherent by some such reconstruction as the following:

1. I may go to the lecture, for the speaker is my chum's uncle.
2. We went trout-fishing, but caught only two trout.
3. As the burglar passed, Mr. Hoyt struck him.
4. I bought a bird that I saw in a beautiful cage.
5. Mrs. Ward said to Mrs. Gray, "Your children are playing in my flower bed."

4. Incorrect reference of participles, gerunds, and infinitives. Coherence is often violated in sentences by the incorrect reference of participial phrases, gerund phrases, infinitive phrases, and elliptical clauses (see sections 228, 229, and 230).

A participial phrase, a verbal-noun phrase, an infinitive phrase, or an elliptical clause introducing a sentence must *logically* refer to the agent of the action expressed. As a rule, the word denoting the agent of the action, or the person responsible for it, is the subject of the principal verb. The reference of the italicized expression in each of the following sentences is therefore incorrect:

1. *Listening intently,* a noise was heard.
2. *Upon entering the room,* no one was seen.

3. *To catch the ghost,* a trap was devised.
4. *While setting the trap,* the door opened noiselessly.

Each sentence becomes coherent when the word denoting the agent of the action is made the subject of the principal verb.

1. *Listening intently,* my aunt heard a noise.
2. *Upon entering the room,* we saw no one.
3. *To catch the ghost,* she devised a trap.
4. *While setting the trap,* she saw the door open noiselessly.

5. Unwarranted change in grammatical construction. Coherence is violated when the grammatical construction of a sentence is changed without reason.

a. The construction following a coördinating conjunction should be identical with the construction preceding it.

1. This is a good book, *and which I advise you to read.*
2. He said that he would come if he could, *but not to look for him.*

In the first sentence *and* connects an independent clause and a subordinate clause. In the second, *but* joins a subordinate clause and an infinitive phrase. Corrected, the sentences read:

1. This is a good book, and I advise you to read it *or* This is a good book, which I advise you to read.
2. He said that he would come if he could, but that we should not look for him.

b. A sentence is more coherent if the same voice of the main verbs is used throughout.

I *wrote* to him, but my letter *was* not *answered.*

The sentence may be improved in either of two ways:

1. I wrote to him, but he did not answer my letter.
2. I wrote to him, but I received no answer to my letter.

c. The coherence of a sentence may often be improved by arranging phrases or clauses in a series in parallel construction (see section 234).   In the balanced sentence the principal clauses are thus arranged.   Phrases or subordinate clauses may sometimes be advantageously placed in parallel construction.   The following sentences are illustrations:

1. *On the land, on the sea, in the air,* and *under the water* there were engines of warfare.
2. A man *who provides well for his family, who maintains an honest public record,* and *who contributes freely to civic improvement* is an asset in any community.

Exercise 248

Explain the violation of coherence in each of the following sentences.   Write a coherent version of each sentence.

1. It was some time before he could get into the regular track of gossip, nor could the strange events be comprehended by him.
2. The children promised to be careful and that they would come home early.
3. We accepted Carter's promise in good faith and believing him to be honest.
4. Nora is a well-trained, industrious maid, and who rarely asks for an afternoon off.
5. I received your letter, but the package that you mentioned has not been received.
6. Fred is energetic, and who is very reliable.
7. We attended the game, but not expecting that our team would be defeated.
8. The engines became overheated, and after talking the matter over they decided to camp where they were.
9. All books are not worth reading.
10. Grandfather is very active for his years, and very proud of it.
11. Two persons were only saved by sliding down a conductor pipe.
12. Having shown him his bedroom, he retired.

13. Glancing out of the window of my study, an unusual sight attracted my attention.

14. Being the youngest child, mother hated to see me leave home.

15. My watch is either fast or your clock is slow.

16. You look as if you were frightened in that picture.

17. Uncle David telephoned Mr. Joyce that his sheep were in his pasture.

18. Orville nearly made a hundred dollars last summer.

19. I promised her, when leaving, I would tell her.

20. Being in a cage, I did not feel afraid of the lion.

Exercise 249

Explain the punctuation of the sentences that you wrote in Exercise 248.

Exercise 250. Extra Credit

For the next week keep your eyes and ears open for violations of coherence in your own conversation and that of others, in newspaper articles, in advertisements, on billboards, and in books and magazines. Make a list of such errors and write a correct version of each sentence. The amount of extra credit awarded you will be determined by the number of examples that you collect and by the accuracy of your corrections.

122. Emphasis in the Sentence

Emphasis, the third essential of sentence structure, requires that the words of a sentence be so arranged as to bring into prominence the central idea and to subordinate the minor details.

1. Emphatic positions in the sentence. Ideas are often made emphatic by their position in the sentence.

a. Words placed at the beginning or at the end of a sentence receive the greatest emphasis.

Many a man has sacrificed his life for wealth, it is true.

A Cowboy Taming a Wild Horse

As the sentence now stands, the end is weak. Rearrangement improves the emphasis.

> Many a man has sacrificed his life, it is true, for wealth.
> Many a man, it is true, has sacrificed his life for wealth.

By placing the unimportant clause "it is true" in an unemphatic position we make the sentence more forceful.

b. Words placed out of their natural order in a sentence become more emphatic. Note the improvement effected, in the sentence given above, by transposing the phrase "for wealth" to the beginning of the sentence.

> For wealth many a man, it is true, has sacrificed his life.

The sentence now has proper emphasis.

Transposing words and phrases from their natural order and inverting the entire sentence are both useful devices for obtaining emphasis.

> 1. *Back* surged the crowd.
> 2. *By the fire* he sat all the morning.
> 3. *Last of all* marched the clown.
> 4. "*Fire!*" he shouted.
> 5. *Great* is the influence of money.
> 6. *To him* belongs the credit for my rescue.

c. A periodic sentence is, by its very nature, more emphatic than a loose sentence. Compare the two versions of the following sentence:

> A mysterious silence reigned about the old ruin. (Loose)
> About the old ruin a mysterious silence reigned. (Periodic)
> About the old ruin reigned a mysterious silence. (Periodic)

2. Use of contrast or antithesis. Ideas are often made emphatic by contrast or antithesis.

> 1. Worth makes the man, and want of it the fellow.
> 2. Man is finite; God is infinite.

3. Education may be acquired; culture is innate.
4. The spirit is willing, but the flesh is weak.
5. I judge by actions, not by mere words.

In such expressions of contrast the balanced sentence is effective.

3. Use of climax. Emphasis may be gained by the use of climax. That is, coördinate words, phrases, and clauses are arranged in the order of their increasing importance.

> Friends, life itself, reputation, social position, had no longer any attraction for him.

In this sentence the ideas are not arranged in the order of their importance. The sentence should read:

> Social position, friends, reputation, life itself, had no longer any attraction for him.

4. Proper subordination. Emphasis, as well as unity, may be secured by putting subordinate thoughts in subordinate clauses. This leaves the principal clause for the expression of the main thought.

1. My train was late, and I missed my first class.
2. When Watt observed the power of steam, he was helping his wife prepare breakfast.

By proper subordination both of these sentences may be made emphatic.

1. Because my train was late, I missed my first class.
2. While helping his wife prepare breakfast, Watt observed the power of steam.

5. Economy in words. Emphasis is enhanced by economy in words. If words do not add to the meaning of a sentence, they make it less effective and should be omitted.

1. All was darkness, and not a ray of light could be seen.
2. He had asked him once, and he refused to repeat the question again

The first sentence is an example of *tautology*, or repetition of the thought; the second is an example of *redundancy*, or the use of words not necessary to the sense. The following sentences are more emphatic:

1. All was darkness.
2. He refused to repeat the question.

6. Use of the active voice. Sentences in the active voice are more emphatic than those in the passive.

Your invitation was received by me.

This sentence is much less forceful than the active version:

I received your invitation.

Exercise 251

In the following exercise show in what respect each sentence is lacking in emphasis, and write a more emphatic version of each:

1. In this remote and secluded town she lived apart and unknown for some time.
2. A man was killed by an automobile while crossing the street yesterday.
3. He saw before him ruin, defeat, disaster, and broken health.
4. Summer is warm, but extremely pleasant; whereas winter brings dark, gloomy days and bitter cold.
5. While the storm was raging, a tree was struck by a bolt of lightning, which was the only flash seen during the storm, and which looked like a ball of fire.
6. The book was expensive, so I could not buy it.
7. He seems to enjoy the universal esteem of all men.
8. It is a great privilege to assemble and meet together.
9. While the thief looted the house, the family slept.
10. The gate is wide and the way is broad that leads to destruction.
11. Insects, men, beasts, all are creatures of God's hand.

12. It was once believed that men reach their decisions by reasoning and that decisions are made by women through intuition.

13. We returned back home weary and exhausted.

14. Some people seem to think that civilization is a curse, which is not true at all.

15. He gazed longingly at the bowl of fruit.

16. A preposition is an unemphatic word to end a sentence with.

17. She is a poor widow woman without any money or property.

18. I was assured by the manager that the seats had been reserved.

19. Two of Mrs. Judson's friends arrived unexpectedly, and I knew she did not have room for all of us, so I made preparations to come home, but she would not let me.

20. Be that as it may, you should have refused to remain, since you knew what inconvenience you were causing.

Exercise 252

Select from a recent newspaper a news article of national or local interest. After you have read it carefully several times, write in the form of a paragraph a good summary of the principal facts. Criticize your first draft by section 24. Have you made every sentence in every way as emphatic as possible? Make a revised copy of your paragraph and hand it in.

Exercise 253

Explain the punctuation of the sentences that you wrote in Exercise 251.

123. Euphony in the Sentence

The fourth essential of sentence structure is euphony. A sentence should be constructed with due regard to its pleasing effect on the ear, though care should be taken not to sacrifice sense to sound.

Euphony is secured by the rhythmical phrasing of the sentence. That is, words, phrases, and clauses should be so skillfully arranged that the harmonious flow of sounds adds to our enjoyment of the sentence. Oral reading in standard prose and observant practice in phrasing our own thoughts will help us to cultivate a sense of rhythm. The following passages illustrate harmonious phrasing:

1. During the whole of a dark, dull, and soundless day in the autumn of the year, when the clouds hung oppressively low in the heavens, I had been passing alone, on horseback, through a singularly dreary tract of country; and at length found myself, as the shades of the evening drew on, within view of the melancholy House of Usher. — POE, "The Fall of the House of Usher"

2. O toiling hands of mortals! O unwearied feet, traveling ye know not whither! Soon, soon, it seems to you, you must come forth on some conspicuous hilltop, and but a little way further, against the setting sun, descry the spires of El Dorado. Little do ye know your own blessedness; for to travel hopefully is a better thing than to arrive, and the true success is to labor. — STEVENSON, "El Dorado"

Although perfect euphony can be attained only by constant practice both in listening to words harmoniously grouped and in working for a more pleasing arrangement of words in our own speech and writing, there are certain common faults that we should avoid.

1. The careless repetition of words. The euphony of a sentence is improved by avoiding the careless repetition of a word at brief intervals. Compare the two sentences given below, and note the improvement in the second sentence.

1. He ordered the captain to order the soldiers to preserve good order.
2. He directed the captain to see that the soldiers preserved good order.

The study of reputable English authors shows, however, that skillful repetition may be employed to good effect.

> The poet is a heroic figure, belonging to all ages; whom all ages possess, when once he is produced; whom the newest age as the oldest may produce, and will produce, always when Nature pleases.

2. The repetition of like sounds. The euphony of a sentence is enhanced by avoiding the repetition of like sounds.

> I cannot understand how a man of his standing can take such a stand on this matter.

A little care in the choice of words overcomes this monotony.

> I cannot understand how a person of his reputation can hold such views on this matter.

Rime in prose should always be avoided. Compare these two sentences:

1. He was suffering, he said, from a cold in his head.
2. He was suffering, he told me, from a cold in his head.

Exercise 254

In the following exercise (1) point out the error in each sentence and (2) write a version of each in which you improve the euphony:

1. Did you ever see such a series of sibilant sounds!
2. In India innocent infants are thrown into the Ganges.
3. Billy ran away, but he could not stay.
4. One cannot imagine what a monotonous being one becomes if one is forced to associate constantly with oneself.
5. It seemed to us that we had never seen such scenes before.
6 The superfluity and profusion of his allusions is confusing.
7. To fly through the sky at night is my delight.
8. I will sign the petition on one condition.

9. The civilization of every nation depends on education.

10. The moment the movement is mastered, the fingers take care of the rest.

Exercise 255

In the following exercise (1) point out all errors in unity, in coherence, in emphasis, and in euphony; and (2) write a version of each sentence that will be correct according to the rules and principles stated in this chapter:

1. Hated and persecuted by the people of his time, we cannot help sympathizing with Shylock.

2. Mr. Carey shot a burglar as he was entering his house.

3. You may either spend the summer at Colorado Springs or Los Angeles.

4. He was kind to his family where some fathers were not.

5. One day when camping it had been threatening rain.

6. We occasionally saw a straw hat here and there.

7. The old veteran was delighted by a visit from his two twin granddaughters.

8. He is a man of truth and veracity.

9. Brother and I feared that mother would never recover her health again.

10. When we came along the road, we came to a field where a pleasant-faced peasant was making hay.

11. The leaves of plants radiate the heat which comes to them from the sun with great rapidity.

12. They urged me to go and that I should not worry about their safety.

13. Do you suppose she would accept this rose?

14. Our team won the meet, but it was a great surprise to everybody.

15. When I found the fountain pen, I was walking along the street.

16. Snow was falling out of doors; within, warmth and cheer prevailed.

17. Being a stranger, the bank refused to pay him the money.

18. No one had heard from him since he left, which seemed strange.

19. Billy had a dollar in his bank and lost it.

20. It is true, I suppose, that he stole the money, anyway.

21. When morning came, he felt the same.

22. I not only wasted a considerable amount of time, but money also.

23. Aunt Helen saw me coming home in the mirror.

24. Having landed in New York, Mrs. Nelson went to meet her husband.

25. Mr. Nelson is a lawyer, and who has been very successful in his practice.

26. As a clerk, Sims was honest, accurate, prompt, and neat.

27. Mother wrote Aunt Eleanor that Marion was going to visit her.

28. They were advised to take a lunch with them, which they did.

29. A trout can catch a minnow while it is swimming.

30. I slept till eight o'clock and I tried to get some breakfast, and so I was late at class.

31. The physician came, relieving the patient as soon as he arrived.

32. Tom told Bob that his answer to the problem was wrong.

33. Many persons can only speak one language.

34. I will not promise, even if you insist.

35. Very bad roads were encountered, thus causing us to be a day behind our schedule.

Exercise 256

Explain the punctuation of each sentence that you wrote in Exercise 254 and Exercise 255.

Exercise 257

Using one of the subjects given below, prepare an outline and write a composition of about three hundred words.

1. My Narrowest Escape.
2. Why I Dislike the Radio.
3. The Lure of Advertisements.
4. If I Were a Traffic Officer.

5. My First Ride in an Airplane.
6. Why _ _ _ _ _ _ _ _ _ _ Is My Favorite Author (Actor).
7. What a Well-Trained Ford Can Do.
8. A Visit to a Public Market.
9. The Torture of Being Unprepared.
10. How to Recover from Love Affairs.

Exercise 258

When you have completed the first draft of the composition that you wrote in Exercise 257, criticize and revise it by the questions given in Exercise 240.

Exercise 259

Before you make the final copy of the composition that you wrote in Exercise 257, criticize and revise your sentences for rhetorical errors. The following questions will help you:

1. Are any of my sentences overloaded?
2. Does any sentence contain more than one sentence-thought?
3. Have I used two or more short sentences to express a single sentence-thought?
4. Have I used the right connective between clauses in each compound sentence and in each complex sentence?
5. Is there in any sentence an unnecessary change in point of view?
6. Are all modifiers correctly placed?
7. Are all connectives correctly placed?
8. Is the reference of each pronoun to its antecedent accurate and clear?
9. Is the reference of each participle, infinitive, and gerund (verbal noun) accurate and clear?
10. Is there in any sentence an unwarranted change in the grammatical construction?
11. Is parallel construction violated in any sentence?
12. Which sentences can be made more emphatic (1) by re-arrangement? (2) by contrast? (3) by proper subordination?

(4) by greater economy in words?   (5) by the use of the active instead of the passive voice?

13. When read aloud, are my sentences smooth, natural, and pleasing?

14. In my composition as a whole, have I avoided monotony (1) by variety in sentence order — natural and inverted? (2) by variety in the kinds of sentences?

Exercise 260

After you have thoroughly revised the composition that you wrote in Exercise 257, make a good final copy. Underscore the topic sentence of each paragraph. Punctuate each sentence in your composition correctly. Hand in your outline on a separate sheet.

CHAPTER X

Using the Correct Word

Test Exercise I

In the sentences given below, the italicized words and expressions are used incorrectly.

A. Copy each sentence, substituting a correct word or expression for the one in italics. Underscore the substituted word or expression.

SCORE: 5 points for each sentence

B. Write original sentences in which you use correctly the italicized words and expressions in the original sentences. Underscore the word or expression in each of your sentences.

SCORE: 5 points for each sentence

1. The delay in beginning the game *aggravated* our coach.

2. Carlton was unable to play *due to* a sprained ankle.

3. I *guess* you have heard the story of a certain Scotch golfer.

4. Did you get any *kick* out of the sophomore reception?

5. Marjorie looked *like* she had been ill.

6. The play given by the senior class lasted *most* three hours.

7. She seemed *real* enthusiastic about the plan.

8. The weather report says that tomorrow will be *some* cooler than today was.

9. Did you *suspicion* that there was anyone else in the room?

10. Last week twenty-three automobile accidents *transpired*.

Test Exercise II

Each sentence below contains an error in the choice of a word or a group of words.

A. At the left margin of your test paper write the numbers 1 to 10. After each number write the word or group of words incorrectly used in the corresponding sentence.

SCORE: 5 points for each error listed

B. Rewrite each sentence, using a word or a group of words that is correct.

SCORE: 5 points for each sentence

1. Joe can't seem to learn French.
2. No, those ain't my gloves.
3. This is all the far I can go with you.
4. That experience learned me to be more careful.
5. Father had cautioned us to leave the gun alone.
6. My coat and hat were laying where I had left them.
7. I asked mother if I could go to the game with Henry.
8. My chum sits in the third seat in back of me.
9. I was sure sorry to hear of your illness, Marion.
10. You ought to have heard Norma enthuse about their new car.

Test Exercise III

Write original sentences in which you use correctly the following words:

SCORE: 10 points for each sentence

affect	dumb	healthy	mad	stature
counsel	except	less	mean	stunt

Test Exercise IV

Study closely the sentences given on page 256, each of which contains either slang words or reputable words used in a slang sense.

Rewrite each sentence, expressing the same meaning in reputable words. Consult your dictionary if necessary.

SCORE: 10 points for each sentence

1. His uncle is an old tightwad who has skads of money.
2. Yesterday I met a gob and another guy on the street.
3. Several roughnecks in the audience kidded the actors.
4. After such a hectic day mother felt rotten.
5. The southpaw pitcher on the opposing team was a flop.
6. Highbrows make themselves ridiculous by their swank.
7. I was peeved when I couldn't think of a suitable comeback.
8. The customs officer was hard-boiled and frisked all of our luggage.
9. I may be a bonehead, but you can't gyp me that way.
10. She tried to vamp me and wangle a ticket out of me for the game.

124. Words and Their Ways

A word is a symbol that stands for an object, an action, or an idea. When combined with other words to form a sentence, it helps to express a thought. In each generation a number of new words are added to the English language as new things come into existence and new ideas arise; certain words already in the language acquire new and additional meanings; and some words become archaic, rare, or obsolete, as the objects, actions, or ideas for which they formerly stood cease to interest mankind. On the whole, language tends to be conservative and economical, and additions and changes in meaning are comparatively few in each generation. The fate of words is like that of living organisms: only the fittest survive.

Exercise 261

In the following list you will find words that have been coined or added to the English language during the past

thirty years, many of them in your own lifetime. Tell
the industry, science, art, invention, or sport to which
each word belongs. If you are not familiar with a word,
find its meaning under "New Words" in Webster's New
International Dictionary.

amplifier	cellophane	plumcot	submarine
barrage	cinema	pulmotor	teletype
batik	dictograph	robot	tractor
calorie	fuselage	rodeo	travelogue
camouflage	microphone	scenario	vitamin

Exercise 262

Make a list of ten new words, not included in Exercise 261, that you have recently heard or read in newspapers and magazines. Write a brief, accurate definition for each word.

Exercise 263

For each of the following words give at least one older meaning and one recently acquired specialized meaning. Tell the part of speech of each word.

ace	cowl	hood	set
broadcast	drive	nose	spiritual
carrier	fleet	pilot	stick
charger	forum	project	tank
compact	gondola	release	traffic

Exercise 264

In the list given on page 258 you will find words that were once as familiar and useful as the new words contained in Exercise 261. Why are they rarely or never used now? Give the more modern word or expression that has taken the place of each word listed. Write original sentences

that will show clearly the meaning of the words in the list.
If necessary, consult your dictionary.

arbalest	fain	nigh	swain
blithe	froward	rathe	thrice
cordwainer	gloaming	ravening	trice
craven	lief	sere	varlet
erstwhile	nether	sooth	yore

Exercise 265

Selections from early English literature are often difficult to understand because of the changes that have taken place in the language. Study the quotations given below.

A. According to Chaucer, this is the way the language was written in the fourteenth century:

1. He was a verray parfit gentil knight.
2. The Miller was a stout carl, for the nones,
   Ful big he was of braun, and eek of bones.
3. A Cook they hadde with hem for the nones,
   To boille the chiknes with the mary-bones,
   And poudre-marchant tart, and galyngale.
   Well coude he knowe a draughte of London ale.
   He coude roste, and sethe, and broille, and frye.
   Maken mortreux, and well bake a pye.
4. Now have I told you shortly, in a clause,
   Th' estat, th' array, the nombre, and eek the cause
   Why that assembled was this compaignye
   In Southwerk, at this gentil hostelrye,
   That highte the Tabard, faste by the Belle.

What modern English words do you recognize here in spite of a difference in spelling?

What words seem entirely strange to you? Can you guess at the meaning of any? For which ones do you need to consult the dictionary?

B. Sir Walter Scott, when writing of the days of Richard the Lion-Hearted, makes his characters speak like this:

"By Saint Thomas of Kent," said he, "an I buckle to my gear, I will teach thee, sir lazy lover, to mell with thine own matters, maugre thine iron case there!"

"Nay, be not wroth with me," said the Knight; "thou knowest I am thy sworn friend and comrade."

C. At the beginning of the seventeenth century Shakespeare's plays show something of the speech of that period.

1. ROSALIND.   Were it not better,
    Because that I am more than common tall,
    That I did suit me all points like a man?
2. CASSIUS.   Will you sup with me to-night, Casca?
    CASCA.   No, I am promised forth.
3. BANQUO.   The king's a-bed.
    He hath been in unusual pleasure, and
    Sent forth great largess to your offices.
4. DUKE.   O, when mine eyes did see Olivia first,
    Methought she purg'd the air of pestilence!
5. POLONIUS.   Marry, sir, here's my drift,
    And I believe it is a fetch of warrant.

Study carefully each group of quotations. Make a list of the words or expressions not used in English today. Try to express each quotation in the best modern English at your command.

Exercise 266. Extra Credit

If you have read Scott's "Ivanhoe," imagine yourself standing next to Locksley at the moment when Prince John and Locksley exchange words at the end of the first day of the Ashby tournament. Enter into conversation with Locksley and get his story of what had roused Prince John's anger against him earlier in the day. Make Locksley talk naturally. Would you always understand him? Talk naturally yourself and explain your meaning to him if necessary.

Write this conversation as a short narrative.

If some other incident or character of Scott's novel interests you more, you may take that incident as your subject instead of the one just given.

125. Sources of the English Language

Our language has acquired its store of words from many sources. Let us consider briefly some of the principal ones.

1. **Anglo-Saxon.** From the Anglo-Saxon, or Old English, have come many of the familiar words used in everyday speech. They include (1) words relating to the family, such as *brother, father, husband, mother, wife*; (2) words expressing strong feeling, such as *dread, fear, gladness, hate, love, pride, shame, sorrow*; (3) names of common things, such as *sun, moon, earth, field, hill, sand, stone, tree, cow, horse, man, woman, day, night, cold, heat, frost*; (4) many specific verbs, such as *walk, glide, run, leap, fly, swim,* as distinguished from general verbs like *move*; and (5) many of the common adjectives and adverbs, such as *pretty, rich, smooth, quickly, slowly*. Because these words of Anglo-Saxon origin are the words of the common people, they are sometimes called *popular* words.

2. **Latin and Greek.** Thousands of English words have been derived from the Latin and the Greek languages. Among the Latin words in our language are *animal, circus, contradict, describe, fact, graduate, janitor, junior, medical, recess, suburb, vaccinate, ventilation, veto, victor, vote*. From the Greek we have derived *academy, biography, diagram, enthusiasm, microbe, photograph, skeleton, tragedy, zoölogy,* and many others. Because Latin and Greek are known as the classical languages, English words derived from them are often called *classical* words.

3. The Romance languages. The modern languages of France, Italy, and Spain have contributed many words to the English tongue. From the French we have borrowed or derived thousands of words, such as *bouquet, chaperon, chauffeur, encore, journey, pleasure, touch, vaudeville.* The Italian language has given us *gondola, influenza, madonna, malaria, opera, piano, piazza, stiletto, violin, volcano,* and many others. From Spain have come words like *banana, bolero, cigar, fiesta, mosquito, mustang, poncho, sombrero, tornado.*

4. Other foreign languages. Other languages in all parts of the world have from time to time contributed words to our language, only a few of which can be named here. The German has given us *nickel* and *zinc* ; the Dutch, *knapsack, toy,* and *yacht* ; the Scandinavian languages have contributed the nouns *sister* and *geyser* and probably the verbs *give* and *get.* The American Indians gave us *moccasin, tobacco,* and *toboggan* ; *bungalow* and *calico* come from the country of India. *Bazaar* comes from the Persian ; *alcohol* and *algebra* are both Arabic in origin ; *zebra* comes from far-off Abyssinia. Other languages also, both modern and ancient, have made their contributions to the development of the English language.

5. Coined words. Scientific discoveries and modern inventions are constantly enriching our language as new words are needed to name the things discovered or invented. In this way we have gained such words as *automobile, aëroplane* (or *airplane*), *fuselage, motordrome, radiophone,* and *telescribe.* From proper names have come words like *atlas, babel, dahlia, marconigram, panic, pasteurize,* and *volt.* Now and then, after a long struggle, a word which originated as slang is admitted to legitimate use. Among words thus admitted are *banter, cab, hoax, mob,* and *Quaker.*

Exercise 267

Here are ten words each of which had its origin in a different foreign country. Find the birthplace of each.

cocoa	cherub	gong	polka	sky
coffee	crag	landscape	potato	tea

Exercise 268

Words, like people, become much more interesting when you know something of their past life and of the changes through which they have passed. Investigate in an unabridged dictionary the words given below, and write a brief biographical sketch of each.

alphabet	cereal	dilapidated	gladiolus	silhouette
assassin	curfew	dunce	indent	zinnia

Exercise 269

Select any ten words from paragraphs 2, 3, 4, or 5 of section 125 and come to class prepared to tell all you can about their origin and meaning.

Exercise 270. Extra Credit

Your teacher will assign you one or more of the following groups of words. Look up each word in the unabridged dictionary and write out a detailed account of its derivation and meaning.

1. apron	bedlam	benefactor	biscuit	bishop
bombast	bonfire	boycott	buffalo	candidate
2. candy	canoe	cargo	cavalier	chaos
cheese	churl	cotton	cyclone	disaster
3. doll	dollar	doom	echo	fiasco
focus	garage	garlic	geography	geyser
4. good-by	hector	hyacinth	kimono	kindergarten
knave	knife	lunatic	macadamize	maize
5. maudlin	meander	mercerize	mermaid	miniature
molasses	moose	nicotine	orange	ostracize

6. parasol	pyjama	salary	sandwich	shampoo
silk	silly	sincere	skate	slogan
7. soprano	sugar	tantalize	tattoo	tawdry
thug	torture	tulip	umbrella	umpire
8. vandal	vanilla	villain	venison	vulcanize
walrus	watt	welcome	Wednesday	wistaria

126. Composition of English Words

Many of our English words are of the class known as *derivatives*; that is, they have been made by adding to a word already in use a prefix or a suffix, or both. Like the original word (sometimes called the *root*), many of these additional syllables are borrowed from Latin or Greek; others are of Anglo-Saxon origin. Many coined words are derivatives.

For a list of the more common prefixes and suffixes used in the formation of English derivative words, see Chapter XXI, sections 253 and 254.

Exercise 271

Study the prefixes and suffixes given in Chapter XXI, and then explain the formation of each of the words given below. Name each prefix and suffix and tell its meaning.

disappointment	player	coeducational	television
unwelcome	unfortunate	freedom	biweekly
boyhood	servile	antedate	surface
incurable	nonsense	windward	mettlesome
claimant	misbehavior	bindery	transatlantic

Exercise 272

Select from the list in Chapter XXI any five prefixes. How many words can you name which begin with each of these prefixes?

Select five suffixes from the list in Chapter XXI. Name all the words you know which contain these suffixes

Exercise 273

The following list contains some of the **common** Latin and Greek roots from which English words have been made by adding prefixes or suffixes, or both. By combining these roots with appropriate prefixes and suffixes make at least three words from each root.

auto-: self	*grad-* (*gres-*)*:* step
bene-: well	*jac-* (*jec-*)*:* throw
cred-: believe	*manu-* (*man-*)*:* hand
dic-: say	*mon-:* alone, single
duc-: lead	*pon-* (*pos-*)*:* put, place
fac- (*fec-*, *fic-*)*:* make, do	*voc-:* call

127. Poverty in Words and Thoughts

Financially we are considered poor if we possess insufficient money — the symbol of value and the medium of commercial exchange — to live in keeping with the standards of the social group to which we belong. Intellectually and socially we are considered poor if we have insufficient words — the symbols of ideas and the medium of thought exchange — to express our thoughts clearly and effectively. And just as we cannot spend money that we do not have, so we cannot use words that are not in our vocabulary. Yet our mastery of English as a tool, as well as our mental growth, demands first of all that we have a large stock of words which we can use intelligently. The average educated person employs from three to five thousand words, whereas many of us "get along," as we say, with five hundred to a thousand. Surely we have need of a greater number.

128. Means of Enlarging Our Vocabulary

The stock of words of each of us is made up of two groups: (1) the words that we use in speaking and writing, which we may call our *active* vocabulary, and (2) the words more or less familiar to us from reading and from the speech of others, which we may term our *passive* vocabulary. For every word that we use there are, perhaps, five that we understand. This disparity between our active and passive vocabularies is due in part to the narrow range of topics to which many of us confine our thinking and speaking; in part, to the laziness which indisposes us to search for words that are accurate and fitting; and not infrequently, to a foolish self-consciousness, which keeps us from using the best that we know, for fear that we may be thought affected or bookish.

All of us need to increase our active vocabulary, for our success in speaking and writing depends to a great extent on our ability to use correctly and effectively a large number of words. The pleasure that we derive from lectures and from reading increases as our stock of words grows. The possession of a wide and varied vocabulary adds much, likewise, to our mental enjoyment, for words aid and stimulate us in thinking. Time spent in acquiring an adequate stock of words is, therefore, time well invested.

Exercise 274

Come to class prepared to take part in a discussion of the following questions:

1. Distinguish between your *active* and *passive* vocabularies. Name several words belonging to each.

2. Should you endeavor to transfer to your active vocabulary *all* words in your passive vocabulary? If not, what kind of words should you select?

3. How may you increase your vocabulary by talking with educated persons? or by listening to well-informed speakers?

4. How does extensive reading in the works of reputable authors help you to build a larger vocabulary? Name at least one stand-

ard author who employs a wide variety of words. Name several contemporary writers of good standing.

5. In what way will the writing of précis and paraphrases help you to acquire additional words?

6. How does the study of a foreign language help you to learn new English words?

7. How may a knowledge of the origin and history of words help to fix them in your memory and stimulate interest in the study of words? Illustrate your answer by giving the origin and history of two or more words.

8. In your attempt to master a new word, what essentials besides spelling and pronunciation should you stress? Explain in detail the best procedure in mastering a new word.

Exercise 275

Using some of the specimen paragraphs in Chapter VII, prepare a list of twenty words in your *passive* vocabulary that you think would make useful additions to your *active* vocabulary.

Write original sentences that will show clearly the correct use of each word in your list. If necessary, consult your dictionary.

Exercise 276

Write original sentences in which you illustrate clearly the correct use of each of the words given below. If necessary, consult an unabridged dictionary. In each sentence underscore the word whose meaning you illustrate. Place a check (√) above those words that are already in your *active* vocabulary.

accelerate	emulate	initiative	petulant	stimulate
chaos	essential	lucid	requisite	temporary
cursory	expedite	mercenary	scope	transient
deference	frugal	nominal	stamina	valid

Harvesting Cranberries on Cape Cod

129. Good Usage in Diction

By diction is meant the choice of words for the expression of our thoughts. Correct diction is based on the usage of the best speakers and writers of the present time. Good use demands that words have a present, national, and reputable standing in the language. A word is in *present* use if it is used in modern speech or is found in contemporary literature. A word is in *national* use when it is employed not merely in certain professions and trades or in particular geographical sections but by a majority of the people throughout the nation. A word is in *reputable* use if it occurs in the speech of cultured persons and in the writings of the best authors. Unless a word satisfies all three of these requirements it is not in good use.

130. The Use of Idioms

An idiom is a phrase that in its form of expression is peculiar to a given language. Usually it cannot be translated literally into another language. Many idioms cannot be justified by the strict rules of grammar, although long-continued and general usage has established them as reputable. They frequently possess a rugged, homely strength that adds greatly to the effectiveness of speech and writing. The following are a few examples of familiar English idioms:

hard put to it	*for*	in great extremity
get rid of	*for*	free oneself from
get used to	*for*	become accustomed to
get ready	*for*	prepare
in the long run	*for*	in the course of time
pull through	*for*	succeed, recover, survive
put through	*for*	accomplish
do away with	*for*	abolish, destroy

131. Violations of Good Use

The three principal violations of good use are termed *barbarisms, improprieties,* and *solecisms.*

A *barbarism* is any word or expression that is not accepted as in accord with the standards of good use, as *cute, burglarize, enthuse, humans, autoist, vulgarian, picturization, reckon* for *guess* or *suppose, favor* for *resemble, redd up* for *put in order, complected* for *complexioned,* and *anywheres* for *anywhere.*

An *impropriety* is the use of a word in an incorrect sense. It is usually the result of transferring a word from its legitimate use as one part of speech to that of another or of confusing it with some other word, as *an invite, a combine, a steal, to gesture, to suspicion, learn* for *teach, raise* for *rear, affect* for *effect,* and *expect* for *suspect.*

A *solecism* is a deviation from correct idiom or the rules of syntax; that is, it is an ungrammatical or unidiomatic combination of words in a sentence, as *between you and I* for *between you and me*; *these kind* for *this kind*; *those kind* for *that kind*; *he (she, it) don't* for *he (she, it) doesn't*; *treat on* for *treat of*; and *different than* for *different from.*

From an unabridged dictionary we may obtain accurate information as to the standing of words and certain meanings. In general, we should avoid using in our speech and writing any words or meanings that are marked in the dictionary as *Archaic, Cant, Dialectal (Dial.), Local, Provincial, Obsolete (Obs.), Rare (R.), Slang,* or *Vulgar (Vulg.).* Those designated as *Colloquial (Colloq.)* we may use in familiar conversation and intimate friendly letters but not in formal speech and writing.

Exercise 277

From an unabridged dictionary ascertain the standing of each of the words listed below. Copy the word and write opposite it the word or abbreviation used to indicate its standing.

ain't	don't	peeve	redd	swale
boob	ensample	pep	snitch	swap
cove	enthuse	rathe	sooth	trek
cute	leal	razz	swag	wend

132. Slang

Although slang words are barbarisms or improprieties, they constitute such a grave offense against good use that they call for separate consideration. Such words as *fake, flivver, flunk, spoof, booster, jazzy, razz, whoopee, racketeer,* which have come to be used for their supposed humorous suggestiveness, are unauthorized popular coinages, sometimes called vulgarisms. Many words and expressions in good use, such as *graft, pinch, kick, can, jug, cooler, cinch, dumb, dumb-bell, swell, rotten, flop, racket, all in, cut out, on the side, take on,* and *up to,* have been given grotesque and incongruous, though often crudely picturesque, meanings that render them improprieties or barbarisms. Many other slang words result from the use of contractions, such as *exam, lab, gym, auto, soph,* and *ad,* derived from words in good use.

Though we may feel that slang occasionally lends vividness and life to everyday speech, we should use it very sparingly even in familiar conversation. In polite conversation, as well as in all writing, we should avoid its use altogether. Only when a slang word, such as *jazz,* expresses a meaning for which there is no reputable word are we warranted in using it. Most slang words quickly pass out of use and are entirely forgotten, and even during their lifetime they usually have but a vague, general meaning. If we desire to speak and write with clearness and accuracy, we should never allow ourselves to become dependent upon slang, for by its use we limit our vocabulary and render ourselves incapable of expressing our ideas intelligibly in words that have a definite and permanent meaning. ✓

133. Common Errors in Diction

The following list, though far from complete, contains a number of the more common barbarisms, solecisms, improprieties, slang terms, and archaic words, which we should avoid in our speech and writing. We should consult this list frequently and should make free use of an unabridged dictionary.

Above is a preposition or an adverb. Do not use it as an adjective ("The *above* sentence is wrong") or as a noun ("The *above* is a good picture of her").

Accept means *to receive*. It should not be confused with *except*, which means *to leave out* or *omit*.

Accept of. Of is superfluous.

Affect (verb) should not be confused with *effect* (verb and noun). *To affect* means *to influence* or *change*. *To effect* means *to bring about* or *accomplish*. *Effect* (noun) means *result* or *outcome*. "The war *affected* prices." "The lawyer *effected* a compromise." "The *effect* of his speech was marvelous."

Aggravate should not be misused as a synonym of such verbs as *annoy, irritate,* and *vex. To aggravate* is *to make worse*.

Ain't. A vulgarism. Use *am not, is not, isn't, are not, aren't,* according to the person and number of the subject.

All the far should not be used for *as far as*. "This is *as far as* (not *all the far*) I am going with you."

Allow means *permit*. It should not be misused for *admit, say, suppose,* or *think*.

Almost, most. Almost means *nearly. Most* is properly used to mean (1) *in the highest degree* or *to the greatest extent* and (2) *the greater portion* or *number*; as, "*Most* of the passengers were drowned." *Most* used for *almost* ("I was *most* asleep when he came") is a childish error.

Alright does not exist as a word. Use *all right*, though even this is colloquial.

Among, between. *Among* should be used in speaking of more than two persons or things; *between*, in speaking of only two.

And, to. Avoid using *and* for *to*. *Incorrect:* "Try *and* come." "Try *and* be careful." *Correct:* "Try *to* come." "Try *to* be careful."

And etc. *Etc.* (the abbreviation for *et cetera*, meaning *and other things, and so on*) should never be preceded by *and*.

Anxious is colloquial for *desirous* or *eager*.

Anybody's else. Say *anybody else's*.

Any place, every place, no place, some place. These phrases are vulgarisms when used for *anywhere, everywhere, nowhere,* and *somewhere*. Used as phrases they are correct; as, "We could not find *any place* in which to camp."

Anyways, anywheres. These are vulgarisms for *anyway, anywhere*.

As, that, whether. Avoid using *as* for *that* or *whether*. *Incorrect:* "I don't know *as* I understood him." *Correct:* "I don't know *whether* (*that*) I understood him."

Aught, naught. Do not confuse *aught* (anything) with *naught* (nothing, zero).

Autoist is a coined word that is not yet regarded as reputable.

Aviate is a coined verb not yet in good use.

Awful, awfully. Both are improprieties when used for *very, extremely*.

Back of, in back of. Say *behind*. "The garage is *behind* (not *in back of*) the house."

Bad, badly. In the expression "She feels bad" *bad* is colloquially permissible as a predicate adjective, indicating the person's state of health. (The adjective *ill*, not *bad*, is preferable usage.) In "She feels *badly* about making the error" the adverb *badly* is correctly used. (See section 222, rule 1.)

Badly is also often misused for *very much, greatly*.

Because, that, the fact that. Avoid using *because* for *that* or for *the fact that* to introduce a noun clause. *Incorrect:* "*Because* you overslept does not excuse you." "The reason I am late is *because* I overslept." *Correct:* "*The fact that* you overslept does not excuse you." "The reason I am late is *that* I overslept." (See section 236.)

Beside, besides. Do not confuse the preposition *beside* (by the side of) with the adverb *besides* (in addition to).

Blame on. Avoid using the verb *blame* with *on. Incorrect:* "He *blamed* it *on* me." *Correct:* " He *blamed* me *for* it." *Or,* "He *put* the *blame* on me."

Brainy. A vulgarism for *intelligent* or *scholarly.*

Bring, carry, fetch, take. These verbs are not synonymous. Consult a dictionary for the exact meaning of each.

Bunch. A vulgarism when used to mean *crowd, company, group, assembly,* or *party.*

Bursted. A vulgarism for the past tense and past participle *burst.*

But. Avoid using a negative with the verb when *but* means *only.* "There *are* (not *aren't*) *but* ten pupils in the class."

But that, but what. Avoid using these after the verb *doubt. That* alone should be used. *Correct:* "I do not doubt *that* he will come."

Calculate, believe, guess, reckon, think. These verbs are not synonymous. Consult a dictionary for the meanings.

Can, may. Can implies power or ability; *may* implies possibility or indicates permission.

Cannot help but. Often misused for *can but* and *cannot help* (followed by a verbal noun). *Correct:* "I *can* but pity him." *Or,* "I *cannot help* pitying them."

Can't hardly. Hardly implies negation in itself. To avoid a double negative, say *can hardly.* (See section 223.)

Can't seem, couldn't seem. Misused for *seem unable* and *seemed unable.*

Caused by. Avoid using *caused by* for the phrasal prepositions *because of, owing to, on account of. Caused* is correctly used in verb phrases and may then be followed by a prepositional phrase introduced by *by*; as, "His death *was caused by* accident." (See *Due to.*)

Claim. Avoid using *claim* as a synonym of *assert* or *maintain.*

Common, mutual. Common implies joint interest or possession; *mutual* implies a reciprocal relationship. Note the correct use of these words: "Mary's and Helen's letters contain many expressions of *mutual* admiration." "They have several tastes in *common*." "They have a *common* aversion to impressionistic art."

Complected. A vulgarism for *complexioned.*

Continual, continuous. Avoid using these as synonymous words. *Continual* implies repetition in close succession; *continuous* implies action without cessation or interruption. "The *continual* dripping of the water became monotonous." "The *continuous* flow of the mighty stream impressed him."

Could of, may of, might of, must of, should of, would of, are all vulgarisms resulting from the careless pronunciation of *could have, may have, might have, must have, should have, would have.*

Cute. A colloquial word used to avoid mental effort. Use such definite adjectives as *amusing, dainty, engaging, pretty, alert, lively vivacious,* but do not say *cunning,* which means *crafty, ingenious.*

Data, errata, phenomena, strata. All are plurals.

Date. Slang when used for *engagement* or *appointment.*

Deal. A colloquial expression when used as a noun to mean *transaction, bargain, agreement, arrangement, trade.*

Depot. Not a railway station. Consult a dictionary.

Die with, sick with. Die of and *sick of* are preferable idioms.

Differ from, differ with. One object differs *from* another in a certain respect. A person differs *from* or *with* another person concerning an opinion or a belief.

Different than. A solecism. Use *different from.*

Diner, sleeper, smoker. These words are still regarded as colloquialisms for *dining-car, sleeping-car,* and *smoking-car.*

Disremember. A vulgarism for *be unable to remember* or *fail to remember.*

Done. A solecism when used for *did.* "He *did* (not *done*) all that he could to help us."

Don't. A solecism when used for *does not* or *doesn't. Don't* is the contraction for *do not;* hence it is incorrect to say "He don't," "She don't," or "It don't." (See section 217, rule 10.)

Dope (noun and verb) and *dopey* (adjective). Slang. A substitute for mental effort.

Dove. Colloquial and illiterate past tense of *dive.* Use *dived.*

Drownded. A vulgarism for *drowned.*

Due to. Misused for *on account of, owing to, because of. Due* may be correctly used as a predicate adjective followed by a'phrase introduced by *to*; as, "His illness was *due to* exposure." (See *Caused by*.)

Each other, one another. Use *each other* when referring to two persons; use *one another* when referring to more than two. "Anne and Jane helped *each other* to dress." "Members of a large family often amuse *one another*."

Either, neither. Each requires a singular verb. Avoid using *either* for *any, neither* for *none*.

Elegant, grand, gorgeous, splendid, adorable, lovely, magnificent, exquisite, awful, horrible, terrible, etc. Such adjectives require intelligent use in order not to dull their meaning and effectiveness.

Enthuse. A vulgarism. Say *be enthusiastic, become enthusiastic, show enthusiasm, manifest enthusiasm.*

Except, without. When used for *unless, except* is archaic and *without* is a vulgarism. "The work will never be done *unless* (not *without*) I do it."

Farther, further. Farther should be used to indicate distance or actual progress; as, "He walked two miles *farther* than I." *Further* should be employed to indicate figurative progress or degree; as, "He refused to aid us *further*."

Feature. Colloquial when used as a verb to mean *make a feature of, give especial prominence to.*

Fewer, less. Fewer should be used when numbers are considered; *less*, when quantities or amounts are thought of. "There were *fewer* than fifty men in the fort, and they had *less* than a cask of water."

Fine. Often carelessly used instead of a more definite adjective.

Firstly. A vulgarism. Use *first*.

First-rate. Correct as an adjective, not as an adverb.

Fix. A colloquialism when used as a verb to mean *repair* and as a noun to mean *plight, predicament, condition*.

Flee, fly. Consult section 224 for the principal parts of these verbs.

Flivver is a slang word used in referring to a Ford automobile.

Flunk is a slang word used to mean *fail*.

Folks. A colloquialism for *family* or *relatives*. Consult a dictionary for the meaning and use of *folk*.

From hence, from thence, from whence. Omit *from.*

Gent, gentleman friend, lady friend, boy friend, girl friend. Vulgarisms.

Get. *Get,* meaning *find it possible,* is a provincialism when used with an infinitive; as, "I did not *get* to see him." "He did not *get* to prepare his lessons." Say, "I *was unable* to see him." "He *found it impossible* to prepare his lessons."

Go west. Slang for *die.* Such expressions should be avoided.

Got. Avoid the redundant use of *got* with forms of the verb *have* to denote possession. "I *have* (not *have got*) a new book."

Gotten. An obsolescent past participle. Use *got.*

Graft, grafter. Consult a dictionary for the slang and the colloquial uses of these words.

Grand is often carelessly used to mean *enjoyable, pleasant, pretty,* etc. It properly means *magnificent* or *great.*

Guess is colloquial for *think* or *suppose.* "I *suppose* (not *guess*) you have heard the news."

Had of. A vulgarism. Use *had.*

Had ought, hadn't ought. Vulgarisms. Use *ought* and *ought not.*

Hanged, hung. *Hanged* is used of persons; *hung* is used of things.

Healthy, healthful. *Healthy* means *possessing* health; *healthful* means *causing* or *producing* health. "Children are *healthy* when they have fresh air and *healthful* food."

Heap, heaps. Vulgarisms when used to mean a *large amount, very much, a great deal, a great many.*

Heathens. The collective form *heathen* should be used.

Human, humans. Avoid using these words as nouns. *Humans* is a vulgarism. Say *human being* or *human beings.*

Hustle. Not to be used intransitively as a synonym of *hasten* or *hurry* or *bestir oneself.* *Hustle* may properly be used as a transitive verb; as, "He *hustled* us off to the station."

Immediately. Do not use to mean *as soon as.* "I will come *as soon as* (not *immediately*) you call me."

In back of. A vulgarism for *behind.*

Individual, party, person. Avoid using these words indiscriminately. Consult a dictionary for the exact meanings.

Invite, invitation. *Invite* is a verb. When used as a noun to mean invitation ("I got an *invite* to the dance") it is an impropriety.

Its, it's. Its is the possessive case of *it*; *it's* is a contraction for *it is.* Fix this distinction in mind.

Kind of, sort of. Colloquialisms when used for *somewhat* or *rather.*

Kind of a, sort of a, style of a, etc. Good use requires the omission of the article. "I enjoy this *kind of* day." "What *style of* dress did she wear?"

Kind of, "kinder," sort of. Vulgarisms when used to mean *rather.* "I *rather* (not *kind of*, "*kinder*," or *sort of*) expected a letter today."

Lay, lie. Lay is a transitive verb meaning *place* or *put*; *lie* is an intransitive verb meaning *recline, rest,* or *occupy a position.* See section 224 for the principal parts of these verbs.

Learn, teach. Learn means to acquire knowledge; *teach* means to give instruction.

Leave, let. Leave means *depart, abandon*; *let* means *permit, allow.* "She would not *let* (not *leave*) me see her."

Less, fewer. See *Fewer.*

Like. A vulgarism when used in place of *as* or *as if. Like* is not a conjunction. "He looks *as if* (not *like*) he had seen a ghost." "Do *as* (not *like*) I tell you." *Like* may properly be followed by a noun or a pronoun, but not by a clause. (See section 233.)

Line. Grossly overworked in such phrases as *along this* (or *that*) *line, in the line of, in this* (or *that*) *line.* Seek a more definite and expressive word.

Listen, say. Inelegant when used as imperatives to preface or introduce a remark.

Literally. A colloquialism when used for *wholly, altogether.* Consult a dictionary for the correct use of *literally.*

Loan, lend. Lend is a verb. *Loan* should be used only as a noun.

Locate. A colloquialism when used for *settle.*

Look badly. See *Bad, badly.*

Lose, loose. Do not confuse these verbs. Consult section 224 for their principal parts.

Lot, lots. Colloquial when used to mean *a great amount of.*

Lovely. See *Elegant.*

Mad, angry, vexed, provoked. Do not use these words interchangeably. Consult a dictionary.

Mean. Properly used as an adjective meaning *common, base, low.* A vulgarism when used for *vicious, unkind, brutal.*

Mighty is colloquial when used to mean *very.* "I was *very* (not *mighty*) glad to hear the good news."

Mind, behave. Colloquialisms when used to mean *obey* or *act in accord with good manners.*

Most. See *Almost.*

Movies is colloquial for *motion pictures.*

Mutual. See *Common.*

Myself. Correctly used as a reflexive or an intensive pronoun. Avoid using it interchangeably with *I* and *me. Correct:* "I hurt *myself.*" "I *myself* saw him enter the house." *Incorrect:* "Mary and *myself* went to see Uncle Henry." "He told her and *myself* an interesting story."

Near by, near-by. Often misused as an adjective to mean *adjoining, adjacent,* or *neighboring.*

Neither. See *Either.*

Nice. Colloquially used as an indefinite synonym of at least a score of adjectives. Select adjectives that accurately express the intended meaning. Learn from a dictionary the legitimate meanings of *nice.*

None. Grammatically singular, though well-established idiom warrants its use as a plural also; as, "*None* (not one) of the family *was* injured" or "*None* of the family *were* injured."

No sooner. Correct when followed by *than*; incorrect when followed by *when.*

Nowheres, everywheres, somewheres. Vulgarisms for *nowhere, everywhere, somewhere.* See *Anyways, anywheres.*

O, oh. Do not confuse *O,* often used in direct address, with the interjection *oh. O* is correctly used in such exclamations as "O dear!" and "O my!"

Off of. Of is superfluous.

On the side. Slang when used to mean *in addition, besides, incidentally.*

Only, alone. Consult a dictionary for the distinction in meaning.

Onto. Not sanctioned by good use. Use *on, upon,* or *up on.*

The phrase *on to* may be correctly used; as, "The tourists went *on to* the next town."

Out loud. Say *aloud.*

Over with. *With* is superfluous. *Correct:* "The meeting is *over.*"

Overly, muchly. Vulgarisms. Use *over* and *much.*

Party. See *Individual.*

Peeve, peeved. Slang. Say *provoke* and *provoked, exasperate* and *exasperated.*

Pep is slang. Use a reputable noun or an expression that has a more definite meaning, as *vigor, enthusiasm,* or *energy.*

Peppy is slang. Use a reputable adjective or an expression that has a more definite meaning, as *animated, energetic, forceful,* or *full of life.*

Per cent, percentage. Avoid using these interchangeably.

Phone. A colloquial contraction for *telephone.*

Photo. A vulgarism.

Piano, violin, vocal, voice. Incorrect for *lessons on the piano, lessons on the violin, vocal culture, voice culture.*

Plan on. A solecism for *plan to.* *Incorrect:* "I *plan on* spending my vacation in Canada." *Correct:* "I *plan to* spend my vacation in Canada."

Plenty. *Plenty* (a noun) should not be used as a synonym of *plentiful* (an adjective) or as the equivalent of the phrase *plenty of.* *Incorrect:* "He has *plenty* money." *Correct:* "He has *plenty of* money."

Posted. A colloquialism for *informed.*

Present-day. *Present-day* should not be used as an adjective. Use *present, modern,* or *contemporary.*

Pretty is colloquial when used as an adverb to mean *very, extremely, rather,* or *somewhat.* "We were *very* (not *pretty*) tired when we reached home."

Proposition. Colloquialism when used to mean *task, matter,* or *affair.*

Proven. An obsolescent past participle. Use *proved.*

Providing. Do not use for *provided, if, on condition that.*

Punch. An impropriety when used as a noun to mean *point* or *force.* "The story lacks *point* (or *force,* not *punch*)."

Put in. Colloquial when used to mean *spend, employ, use.*

Put in an appearance. Colloquial. Say *appear.*

Put out. Slang when used to mean *disappointed, inconvenienced, discommoded, incommoded.*

Put over. Slang when used in such an expression as *put one over* to mean *accomplish, deceive, take advantage of.*

Put up with. Slang when used to mean *tolerate, endure, allow.*

Quite. Use *quite* only when it is properly a synonym of *entirely, wholly, altogether.* Avoid such colloquial phrases as *quite a few, quite a little, quite a lot, quite a number, quite a while.*

Quite some is a vulgarism.

Racket is slang when used to mean *business, occupation.* It is colloquial when used to mean *noise.*

Racketeer is slang for *gangster* or *criminal.*

Raise, rear. Consult a dictionary for the distinction in the use of these words.

Raise, rise. *Raise* is a transitive verb meaning *lift* or *cause to rise*; *rise* is an intransitive verb meaning *ascend* or *assume an upright posture.*

Rarely ever. A contraction of the phrase *rarely if ever.* *Ever* is superfluous.

Real. *Real* is an adjective, not an adverb. Avoid using *real* for *really* or *very.* "He seemed *very* (not *real*) glad to see me."

Reason is because. Use *that* instead of *because.* See *Because.*

Remember of. *Of* is superfluous.

Right away, right off. Colloquialisms for *at once, immediately.*

Right smart of. Provincialism for *a considerable amount of anything.*

Rise. See *Raise.*

Run. A colloquialism for *conduct, manage, operate.*

Same. *Same* is correctly used as an adjective to mean *identical.* It is incorrectly used as a pronoun. *The same* should not be used to mean *also, likewise.* *Incorrect:* "He read the book and returned *same* promptly." "I am well, and hope you are *the same.*" *Correct:* "He read the book and returned it promptly." "I am well, and hope that you also are well."

Says. Often misused by illiterate people for *said.*

Seldom ever. A contraction of the phrase *seldom if ever.* *Ever* is superfluous.

Set, sit. *Set* is a transitive verb meaning *place* or *cause to sit*; *sit* is an intransitive verb meaning *occupy a seat* or *assume a sitting posture.* For the principal parts of these verbs see section 224.

Settle. Colloquial when used to mean *pay.*

Shall, will. See section 225.

Shape. Colloquial when used as a noun to mean *condition, circumstances, situation.*

Show. Colloquial when used as a noun to mean (1) *a theatrical performance, concert, opera*; (2) *chance, opportunity.*

Show up. A vulgarism for (1) *appear, attend, be present, come*; (2) *display*; (3) *expose, make a spectacle of*; (4) *appear to advantage.*

Shut of. Do not use *shut of* to mean *rid of.* "We got *rid of* (not *shut of*) the dog at last."

Sight, sight of. Colloquial when used to mean *a great quantity of, a considerable amount of, much, many, a great deal of.* See *Heap* and *Lot.*

Sit. See *Set.*

Size up. Slang for *estimate, judge.*

Smart. Colloquial when used to mean *mentally alert, quick-witted, clever, talented.*

Snap. Slang when used as a noun to mean *an easy task, bargain.*

So. Colloquial when used to mean *so that, in order that,* and when used as a synonym of *very. Incorrect:* "We went early *so* we could get a good seat." "I am *so* weary." *Correct:* "We went early *so that* we could get a good seat." "I am *very* weary." Or, "I am *so* weary *that* I must rest."

Some. A solecism when used to mean *somewhat.* "He is *somewhat* (not *some*) wiser because of this experience."

Some. Slang when used to mean *a genuine, a real, an excellent* person or thing.

Somewheres. See *Nowheres.*

Stand for. Slang for *permit, allow, countenance, tolerate.*

Start in. Colloquial when used to mean *begin, enter upon, undertake.*

Start out. Colloquial when used to mean *set out, set off, leave.*

Stop. Though *stop* for *stay* is good usage in England, it is not so regarded in America.

Story. Colloquial when used to mean *lie, falsehood.*

Stunt. Slang when used as a noun to mean *feat* or *performance.*

Such. *Such* should not be used for *very.* Avoid also the vague and weak use of *such* without a result clause. A relative clause following *such* should be introduced by the relative pronoun *as.*

Suicide. A vulgarism when used as a verb; as, "He *suicided.*" Say, "He *committed suicide.*"

Sure. A vulgarism when used for the adverbs *surely* or *certainly.* "I was *surely* (not *sure*) glad to see him."

Suspicion. An impropriety when used as a verb; as, "I *suspicioned* that there was something wrong." Say, "I *suspected* that there was something wrong."

Swell. Slang when used as a noun to mean *a fashionable person, a fop,* or when used as an adjective to mean *stylish, fashionable, enjoyable.*

Take. Colloquial when used to mean *study.* "I am *studying* (not *taking*) Spanish."

Take and. Usually superfluous, often crude; as, "*Take and* measure the flour." Say, "*Measure* the flour."

Take in. Colloquial when used to mean *attend, go to,* or when used to mean *deceive, cheat, dupe.*

Talkies is a colloquialism for talking motion pictures.

Them, those. Do not use *them* for *those.* "Give me *those* (not *them*) gloves."

These kind, those kind. Solecisms and vulgarisms for *this kind, that kind,* or *these kinds, those kinds.*

Thing. Avoid overworking this word.

This here, these here, that there, those there. Vulgarisms. Use merely *this, these, that, those.*

Through. Colloquial when used to mean *have finished.* "I *have finished* (not *am through*) studying my lessons."

Too, very. Usually neither *too* nor *very* should come immediately before a past participle. Use *too much, too greatly, very much, very greatly, too well, very well.* *Correct:* "He was *too much* astonished to move."

Transpire. Correctly used to mean *become known*; as, "In spite of all precaution the secret *transpired.*" An impropriety when used to mean *happen, occur, take place.*

Try and. "Try *to* (not *and*) come early." See *And, to.*

Turn up. A vulgarism when used to mean *arrive, appear.*

Two first, two last. Illogical. Say *first two, last two.*

Ugly. Colloquial when used to mean *vicious, uncivil, angry.*

Unique. Unique means *alone of its kind, single, sole.* Like *round, level, perfect,* it cannot be compared (see section 221, rule 6). Avoid *very unique, most unique. Unique* is often misused for *odd, strange, unusual.*

Unless. See *Except, without.*

Up. Not to be added unnecessarily to such verbs as *end, rest, pay, polish, open, finish, divide.*

Up to date. Correctly used as an adverbial phrase. Often misused as an adjective to mean *modern, stylish.*

Up to you. Slang for *for you to do* (or *to decide*), *incumbent upon you.* "It is *for you* (not *up to you*) to decide."

Uplift. Colloquial when used as a noun meaning *betterment.*

Used to could. A vulgarism. Say *used to be able, could formerly, once could.*

Vamp, vampire. Consult a dictionary for the legitimate meanings of these words.

Very. Do not overwork this word. See *Too.*

Viewpoint. Point of view is preferable.

Want in, want out. Colloquial for *want to come in* and *want to go out.*

Want to. Colloquial for *should, ought to, had better.*

Way. Colloquial when used for *away;* as, "*Way* up on the top shelf."

Ways. A solecism when used for the singular *way.* "He lives a long *way* (not *ways*) from here."

When, where. Clauses introduced by *when* and *where* should not be used as predicate nouns. *When* and *where* are properly used to introduce adjective clauses and adverbial clauses. (See sections 112 and 113.) *Incorrect:* "A jail is *where* prisoners are confined." "Four o'clock is *when* I quit work." *Correct:* "A jail is a *place where* prisoners are confined." "Four o'clock is the *time when* I quit work." Exceptions occur when the subject of the sentence is some such noun as *question;* as, "The question is, When did he arrive?" (See section 236.)

Will, shall. See section 225.

Win out, lose out. Colloquial for *win* and *lose*.

Wire. Colloquial when used as a verb to mean *telegraph* or *cable* and when used as a noun to mean *telegram* or *cablegram*.

Worth while. Not to be used as an attributive adjective. *Incorrect:* "That was a *worth-while* concert." Say, "That concert was *worth while*."

Write up. Slang for the nouns *report* and *account*, or for the verb *write*.

You was. A solecism. *You were* is both singular and plural.

Yourself. Properly used as a reflexive and an intensive pronoun, but not as a substitute for *you*. "When did Mary and *you* (not *yourself*) arrive?" (See *Myself*.)

Exercise 278

In the following sentences (1) point out each violation of good use and name the class of violation to which each incorrect word or expression belongs; (2) express the thought of each sentence in words that are in good use; and (3) if the word or expression incorrectly used in this exercise has a correct use, make an original sentence in which you employ it correctly. Consult the list given above and an unabridged dictionary as often as it is necessary.

1. Your handwriting is awful, but your spelling is fine.

2. I shall not budge a step without you go with me.

3. She was very much put out because no one alluded to what had transpired.

4. I allowed it would aggravate her, alright.

5. Now, Helen, do try and behave like your sister does.

6. The reason I got mad was because the whole bunch claimed I told a story about phoning for an auto.

7. When they blamed it all on me, I sure got peeved; any guy would of.

8. I think it was real mean of them not to accept of my explanation, anyways.

9. During January and February I most froze, but now it is some warmer.

A Float from the Battle of Flowers, San Antonio, Texas

10. Due to the storm, they calculated that nobody would put in an appearance, but quite a few finally showed up.

11. When the officer came in the room, he suspicioned that something was up.

12. Of course we enthused over him, but we couldn't hardly keep from laughing, for he's so different to her first husband, who suicided.

13. Just as I reached the depot, I saw father get off of the sleeper.

14. I disremember whether he died with the influenza or with the pneumonia.

15. She don't never have less than five dates a week.

16. Those kind of folks are funny.

17. They are nice and have got lots of pull socially, but they will never get an invite from Mrs. Rankin.

18. According to the write-up of his latest oil deal, I expect he is a grafter.

19. In back of the stove set a funny-looking human.

20. The teacher found it kind of a hard proposition to learn Stubbs any Spanish.

21. Myrtle and myself always take in everything in the motion-picture line.

22. Just between you and I, drawing sure is a snap; you want to be sure and take it.

23. I plan on having a lot of time to put in making money on the side.

24. He was not overly rich, but he raised a large family.

25. One of his daughters took vocal quite a while, and spent a sight of money, but she rarely ever sings in public.

26. While I was stopping with my aunt in the country, I met a very unique old party.

27. I sized up the situation right away and started out for a near-by house to try and get help.

28. I hustled as fast as I could, and phoned his wife and the doctor.

29. When I got back, he was laying on the grass and looked badly.

30. His wife seemed deeply effected when the doctor told her that her husband was in a bad shape.

Exercise 279

In each blank left in the following sentences supply the right word. Use the rejected word correctly in a sentence of your own. Consult a dictionary to find the proper meaning of each word that you do not fully understand.

1. She refused to —— (except, accept) his apology.
2. Illness —— (effected, affected) his vision.
3. A mirage is an optical —— (allusion, illusion).
4. He —— (claimed, maintained) that he was right.
5. The earthquake on February 29, 1916, was an unusual —— (coincidence, occurrence).
6. I went to the lawyer for —— (council, counsel).
7. Marconi —— (discovered, invented) the wireless telegraph.
8. Twelve —— (disinterested, uninterested) men composed the jury.
9. His father —— (immigrated, emigrated) from Italy.
10. The —— (enormousness, enormity) of the task baffled him.
11. College offers —— (exceptionable, exceptional) opportunities to earnest students.
12. The prisoner was —— (hanged, hung) on Friday.
13. My mother is an —— (imaginative, imaginary) person.
14. My young cousin is a very naïve and —— (ingenious, ingenuous) girl.
15. Bronson's uncle was an upright, —— (notorious, notable) statesman.
16. He succeeded by consistent —— (observance, observation) of the golden rule.
17. Direct utilization of solar energy has not yet proved —— (practicable, practical).
18. A large —— (percentage, per cent) of the audience could not hear the speaker.
19. The house was almost concealed by a grove of —— (luxurious, luxuriant) tropical plants.
20. Our city is enlarging the —— (sewage, sewerage) system in order to dispose of the increased —— (sewage, sewerage).

21. This is a new —— (species, specie) of political dishonesty.

22. I received a letter written on blue —— (stationery, stationary).

23. The —— (statue, stature) was unveiled on Memorial Day.

24. I have been reading —— (a unique, an unusual) book.

Exercise 280

In your notebook make a list of all the slang words and expressions that you are able to recognize in your own vocabulary; list also those that your teacher has indicated in your compositions. For each of these slang expressions find one or more reputable expressions. Notice the superiority of the latter in accuracy and in elegance. By means of persistent self-cultivation and by the aid of your friends and the members of your family try to become independent of slang both in conversation and in writing.

Exercise 281

During the coming week make a list of violations of good use that you recognize in your own speech and writing and in the speech and writing of others. Opposite each violation write words and expressions in good use that should have been employed. On the day that your teacher may assign submit your list for criticism and discussion.

Exercise 282

Read again the student compositions "How We Earned Our Car," in Chapter I, and "The Making of Our School Magazine," in Chapter IV. Do you find in them any words not in good use?

CHAPTER XI

Choosing the Effective Word

134. Effectiveness of Diction

In expressing our thoughts we should select, as we have learned, words that are sanctioned by good use. But effectiveness is as important as correctness in the choice of words. If we desire to express our thoughts with accuracy, vividness, and force, we should choose those words that *best* convey our meaning. Such a choice requires that words be selected for their (1) exactness, (2) appropriateness, and (3) expressiveness. These three qualities we shall consider in the sections that follow.

135. Choosing Exact Words

If we say "A workman hurt himself with one of his tools," we state a fact ; but if we say "The carpenter smashed his left thumb with a hammer," we report accurately just what happened. In the first sentence we used the general terms *workman*, *hurt*, and *tools* ; in the second we employed the specific words *carpenter*, *smashed*, *thumb*, and *hammer*.

Specific words, since they fit precisely the objects, actions, or ideas for which they stand, enable us to say accurately and clearly what we mean. They are, therefore, important in all explanations and arguments. As they are far more suggestive than general terms, they stimulate the imagination and the memory to form vivid mental pictures. For this reason they are valuable in description and narration.

Exercise 283

A. Below are five nouns which are general terms. For each noun make a list of as many specific nouns as you can.

plant   occupation   science   sport   vehicle

B. Here are five verbs to be treated in the same way.

go   give   see   take   work

Exercise 284

Divide a sheet of paper into halves vertically. Head the left column with a general noun of your own selection and the right column with a general verb. List under each as many specific words of the same class as you can find to express the meaning of each general word.

Exercise 285

Rewrite each of the sentences given below, using specific words instead of general terms. Make each sentence as exact, concrete, and vivid as possible.

1. Several workmen were making noises with their tools.
2. She read them an interesting story out of a book.
3. After waiting a long time the crowd became impatient.
4. The room that he entered was in a state of disorder.
5. The men fled, but before they had gone very far they had to stop on account of an accident.
6. He read an account of the event in a newspaper.
7. The children were tired as a result of the holiday celebration.
8. While he was in school, he took part in several different school activities.
9. Recently a man risked his life in rescuing another person.
10. The trees were filled with birds.

Exercise 286

In the following selections list the specific nouns, verbs, adjectives, and other words that give exactness to the descriptions.

1. Never in her life had she seen anything so wonderful as the white-tiled kitchen, with its glistening porcelain sink and the aluminum pots and pans that shone like silver. — ANZIA YEZIERSKA

2. His withered cheeks were plowed by wrinkles that stretched, deep furrowed, from his red-gray hair to the corners of his mouth. — FREDERICK S. GREENE

3. He talked as if he were barking. His enormous, blue, clean-shaven face was covered all round the nose with red veins closely set together; his swollen, purple nose hung over his mustache. His lower lip was disfiguringly pendulous. In the corner of his mouth was stuck a smoking cigarette. — MAXIM GORKY

136. Using Synonyms and Antonyms for Exactness

Synonyms are words which convey the same general idea, although each word has its own particular application and force. This fact is easily illustrated by a comparison of the exact shade of meaning expressed by such synonymous nouns as *workman, laborer, artisan, artificer, craftsman, mechanic*; by such synonymous verbs as *obtain, get, achieve, secure, attain, acquire, procure, gain, win, earn*; and by such adjectives as *old, aged, ancient, venerable, antique, antiquated, archaic, obsolete*. Antonyms are words of opposite meaning, such as *laborer* and *idler, success* and *failure, earn* and *spend, advance* and *retreat, young* and *old, like* and *unlike*; they emphasize contrast in ideas.

A knowledge of synonyms and antonyms not only increases our vocabulary but also enables us to choose words that accurately fit our thoughts. So rich is the English language in synonyms and antonyms that we need never be at a loss for the exact word.

Exercise 287

A. Copy any ten of the following nouns and after each one write as many synonyms as you know. When you have done your best, correct and complete the list by consulting your dictionary.

advice	courage	implement	plan	smell
ambition	fear	loyalty	pleasure	spectacle
anger	ghost	origin	pride	trial
border	haste	part	skin	wages

B. Copy any ten of the following verbs and treat them in the same way:

adorn	cease	despise	imitate	release
allow	censure	excuse	kill	steal
banish	declare	give	pay	surprise
beg	decrease	hide	puzzle	try

C. Copy any ten of the following adjectives and treat them in the same way:

accidental	careful	honest	nice	small
afraid	clear	irksome	rash	strange
broad	costly	laughable	shy	strong
calm	eminent	lively	skillful	weak

Exercise 288

Copy the following words and after each one list as many antonyms as you know. Be sure that the antonym given is the same part of speech as the original word.

bravery	descent	few	noise	sincere
courteous	enemy	generous	obscure	superiority
create	expand	hostile	resist	truthful
deft	export	ignorance	reveal	welcome
delicate	fertile	minimize	rustic	worthless

137. Choosing Appropriate Words

Our diction is appropriate when it is properly adapted to our subject and purpose and to the understanding of our hearers and readers. In familiar conversation and in intimate social letters we naturally use, besides reputable words, many colloquial expressions. In stories and plays, the dialogue, since it is meant to represent the actual speech of the characters, will likewise include colloquial words, and even slang and other barbarisms, if the characters are illiterate or speak somewhat carelessly. In some forms of poetry and in solemn discourse, archaic words are often fitting. In discussing a technical subject for well-informed persons, we may employ whatever technical words the subject may demand, provided we define any terms that may not be readily understood. In talks and addresses and in formal writing we should, in seeking appropriate diction, restrict our choice to words that are in good use.

Exercise 289

Write a personal news letter to a relative or an intimate friend. Express yourself naturally. When you have written the letter, list those words and expressions that you would not use in a formal composition.

Exercise 290

"Why does my radio make that humming noise?"

"What made my cake fall?"

"How shall I prepare my perennial garden for the winter?"

"When is it safe for me to cross a busy street where there are traffic lights but no policeman?"

"Why did the crowd cheer that player just now?"

Imagine yourself called on to answer one of these questions at three different times to persons of different types.

For instance, the first question might be asked by a woman who knew nothing about radios, by a friend who knew as much as you do but was not so familiar with the particular radio in question, or by your ten-year-old brother, who was making his first set and who looked on you as an expert. To each one you should give a satisfactory answer in appropriate language.

Choose the question you prefer and the three situations that seem most suitable. Make each answer as brief as is consistent with clearness; the longest should not exceed one hundred and fifty words.

Exercise 291

Out of the following arts, sciences, sports, industries, and occupations select those with which you are familiar and list as many technical words as you can that are appropriate to each:

music	botany	golf	radio	printing
painting	geology	hockey	aviation	weaving
sculpture	zoölogy	bowling	mining	wood-carving
modeling	physics	fencing	fishing	domestic science
architecture	chemistry	football	farming	interior decorating

Exercise 292. Extra Credit

Prepare a talk to be given in class or in a school assembly on a technical subject that you understand thoroughly but that is not familiar to the majority of your audience. Explain any technical terms that you think your hearers will not readily understand.

138. Choosing Expressive Words

Many words have two degrees or levels of meaning. One meaning consists of what the word literally says. This we

call its *denotation*. In addition, the word may have acquired through long use an implied, or associated, meaning,
so that it *suggests* much more than it specifically says or
denotes. This we term its *connotation*. Let us take as
examples of denotation and connotation such pairs of
words as *man* and *father*, *house* and *home*, *path* and *trail*,
cowherd and *cowboy*, *thief* and *pirate*. In each pair both
words *denote* the same person or thing; but the second
word, besides its denotation, *connotes*, or suggests, far more
than it says, because it stimulates our imagination and
arouses in our minds certain associations and memories
that cluster around the person or thing designated.
Doubloons and *pieces of eight* not only denote Spanish
coins but suggest pirates' treasure and adventurous buc-
caneers. For those of us who have had a vivid hospital
experience such words as *hospital*, *anæsthetic*, and *nurse*
have doubtless acquired through association a connotative
meaning.

The expressiveness of a word or a phrase depends
upon both its denotative and its connotative meaning.
In explanations and arguments we desire specific words
that are exact and appropriate; hence we choose words
primarily for their denotation. In descriptions and narratives, on the other hand, we seek for words that, by
their power of suggestion and implication, will stimulate the imagination, the memory, and the emotions of
hearers and readers; we therefore select words that, besides being exact and appropriate, are rich in connotation.
Poetry, as we are aware, depends for its effectiveness
largely upon the suggestive power of words. *Galleon* for
sailing vessel, *palfrey* for *saddle horse*, *welkin* for *sky*,
and *grail* for *cup* possess an archaic flavor and a poetic
connotation.

Exercise 293

Give the specific meaning, or denotation, of each of the words listed below. Then state as clearly as you can what the word suggests, implies, or connotes; that is, tell what mental images, ideas, characteristics, or qualities you associate with each word.

argosy	caravan	desperado	minstrel	ravenous	tournament
aroma	carnival	drowsy	orphanage	sandwich	vagabond
bleak	castle	glean	peasant	savory	viands
brigand	crusader	gypsy	pilgrim	slave	wayfarer
brocade	dentist	Halloween	prowl	stadium	yuletide

Exercise 294

Study the poems "Etiquette" (pages 45–46), "Indian Summer" (pages 46–47), "Wind-Wolves" (page 47), and "Nature" (page 58), or any other poem which your teacher may suggest, and list all the connotative words that you find in each. List also any particularly appropriate words used by the author. Be prepared to show what the poem gains by the use of each word.

139. Vividness through the Use of Picture Words

In two sentences Rudyard Kipling thus described an elephant running through a tropical forest:

The huge limbs moved as steadily as pistons, eight feet to each stride, and the wrinkled skin of the elbow-points rustled. The undergrowth on either side of him ripped with a noise like torn canvas, and the saplings that he heaved away right and left with his shoulders sprang back again, and banged him on the flank, and great trails of creepers, all matted together, hung from his tusks as he threw his head from side to side and plowed out his pathway.

The vividness of this passage is the result of the author's skillful use of specific words and phrases to flash before our minds a series of images that afford us a clear picture. Specific words, particularly nouns, verbs, adjectives, and adverbs, appeal to our senses of sight, hearing, touch, smell, and taste; and by stimulating our imagination and memory they enable us to experience what the author experienced.

Exercise 295

In the preceding passage from Kipling point out all words and phrases that help you to form a mental picture. Then study and explain in the same manner the following sentences and passages:

1. The churned-up water frothed alongside the boat with a confused murmur.

2. The steersman dug his paddle into the stream, and held hard with stiffened muscles, his body thrown forward.

3. The forests, somber and dull, stood motionless and silent on each side of the broad stream.

4. As he opened the kitchen door, the heat struck his face, and the savory smells of soup, roast, vegetables, and spicy dessert greeted him all at once.

5. Beatrix came holding her dress with one fair rounded arm, and her taper before her, tripping down the stairs to greet Esmond.

6. The rays of the afternoon sun flooded through the west windows in long parallel shafts full of floating golden motes.

7. Where the sunshine fell warmest, a gray cat made her toilet, diligently licking the fur on the inside of her thigh, one leg, as if dislocated, thrust into the air above her head.

8. A droning bee blundered into a swarm of tiny, jigging gnats, disentangled itself and soared lazily on to a distant flower, unconscious of the excitement it had caused.

9. Pigeons strutted along the edge of the gray slate roof just above the gutter in undisputed sovereignty, and chatted with one another peaceably. Their purple and green necklaces glistened as they rambled along their chosen promenade.

10. St. Agnes' Eve — Ah, bitter chill it was!
    The owl, for all his feathers, was a-cold;
    The hare limped trembling through the frozen grass,
    And silent was the flock in woolly fold:
    Numb were the Beadsman's fingers, while he told
    His rosary, and while his frosted breath,
    Like pious incense from a censer old,
    Seemed taking flight for heaven, without a death,
Past the sweet Virgin's picture, while his prayer he saith.

140. Figures of Speech as Aids to Expressiveness

Our desire for vividness, picturesqueness, and force of expression often leads us to use figures of speech, which *suggest*, rather than state literally, what we mean. For example, we may say in matter-of-fact language: "He ate greedily," "The ship sank," and "The man had a bald head." We may greatly increase the effectiveness of these statements, however, by expressing them thus in figurative language: "He bolted his food like a dog," "The waves swallowed up the ship," and "The man's head was like a pink billiard ball." Figures of speech frequently state as true what is not wholly true, and leave the obvious interpretation to the hearer or reader. To be most effective, the comparison, contrast, emotion, or sensation suggested by the figure of speech must be instantly clear and appropriate.

In everyday speech and writing we make free use of figurative language. We say "Success turned his head," "The coach barked his directions to the players," "The motor purred contentedly," and "On Monday mornings women swarm into the bargain basement like bees into a hive." Our enjoyment of reading is greatly enhanced by figures of speech, for they appeal to our imagination and by their suggestiveness make the thought more impressive and entertaining.

141. Figures of Speech Based on Similarity

The principal figures of speech used in comparing persons, objects, actions, and ideas are (1) the simile, (2) the metaphor, and (3) personification.

1. Simile. A simile is a definitely stated comparison of persons or things that are unlike in all respects except the one in which they are compared. The comparison is generally expressed by *as* or *like*.

   a. She was just about as popular as poison ivy.
   b. In her search for gossip she was like a ferret.
   c. He enjoyed practicing on the piano as a child enjoys cod-liver oil.

2. Metaphor. A metaphor is an implied comparison or a suggested identity. As in a simile, the persons or things compared are, in general, dissimilar.

   a. John is the black sheep in the family.
   b. The motor is the heart of the automobile.
   c. He thinks himself a Romeo.

3. Personification. Personification, like metaphor, implies a comparison. By its use we attribute life and personal attributes to inanimate things and abstract ideas.

   a. Actions speak louder than words.
   b. The moon veiled her face with a cloud.
   c. A gentle breeze caressed her cheek.

Exercise 296

In each of the following sentences point out the figure of speech, and tell whether it is a simile, a metaphor, or personification. Express the same thought by means of literal language and note the loss in effectiveness.

   1. At one stride comes the dark.
   2. The nerves of our body are like electric wires.

3. The moonlight was a silver path across the lake.

4. If music be the food of love, play on.

5. To get information out of him was like pulling teeth.

6. The human mind should be like a good hotel — open the year round.

7. In the summer Nature beckons us to come out of doors and play with her.

8. The snow covered the ground like a fleecy white blanket.

9. Many women's clubs are incubators of gossip.

10. The love of money is the root of all evil.

11. Writing is like pulling the trigger of a gun: if you are not loaded, nothing happens.

12. He may know a great deal, but he is no Solomon.

13. Her voice was like the sound of a cracked bell.

14. The revenue officer was a wolf in sheep's clothing.

15. The laboring locomotive coughed despairingly.

16. The grass below them leaned up the hill, like the smoothly combed hair of a person's head.

17. Many a young baseball player pictures himself a Babe Ruth.

18. The face is an index of the mind.

19. Pleasure is like a sprained ankle, for you have it all to yourself; but happiness is like measles, for you cannot have it without giving it to someone else.

20. She was a little woman, whose faded flaxen hair looked like straw on an egg.

21. Looking for a strictly truthful person is like searching for a hill in Holland.

22. Our words should fit our thoughts like a glove.

23. A good book is the precious life-blood of a master-spirit embalmed and treasured up to a life beyond life.

24. Blue were her eyes as the fairy-flax,
     Her cheeks like the dawn of day,
   And her bosom white as the hawthorn buds
     That ope in the month of May.

25. There is a tide in the affairs of men,
     Which, taken at the flood, leads on to fortune;
   Omitted, all the voyage of their life
   Is bound in shallows and in miseries.

142. Figures of Speech Based on Contrast

The principal figures of speech used in contrasting persons, objects, actions, and ideas are (1) antithesis, (2) epigram, (3) irony, and (4) euphemism.

1. Antithesis. Antithesis is a figure of speech that results from bringing into prominence things and ideas that are unlike.

 a. To err is human; to forgive, divine.
 b. Worth makes the man; the want of it, the fellow.
 c. I come to bury Cæsar, not to praise him.

2. Epigram. An epigram is the concise statement of a truth. Often there is an apparent contradiction between what is said and what is meant.

 a. Language is the art of concealing thought.
 b. A little learning is a dangerous thing.
 c. The youth of America is its oldest tradition.

3. Irony. Irony is veiled sarcasm, or satire concealed in figurative language. What the speaker or writer means is the opposite of what he says.

 a. How kind it is of you to remind me of my error!
 b. Yes, my dear, you are always an angel.

4. Euphemism. Euphemism consists in expressing indirectly or more agreeably an unpleasant truth or fact.

 a. Patience was not one of her virtues.
 b. He is an architect who builds castles in Spain.

Exercise 297

In each of the following sentences point out the figure of speech, and tell whether it is antithesis, epigram, irony, or euphemism. Express the same thought in literal language and note the loss in effectiveness.

1. A man cannot be too careful in the choice of his enemies.
2. How fortunate you are that your conscience never troubles you!
3. Deeds show what we are; words, what we should be.
4. The fastest colors are those that will not run.
5. She has as little cause for vanity as any woman I ever met.
6. Surely you do not give away such wonderful advice as that!
7. Fools rush in where angels fear to tread.
8. He and Truth are not on very intimate terms.
9. A wise man is never less alone than when alone.
10. God made the country; man made the town.

143. Other Figures of Speech

In addition to the figures of speech that we have considered, there are a few others with which we should become familiar.

1. Metonymy. Metonymy consists in the use of the name of one thing for the name of another that it clearly suggests.

a. The press (that is, the *newspaper*) exercises a great influence.
b. He prefers a hoe (that is, *useful labor*) to a golf club (that is, *recreation*).

2. Synecdoche. Synecdoche consists in using the name of a part to designate a whole.

a. Give us this day our daily bread (*food*).
b. We counted thirty-five sails (*boats*).
c. Our neighbors have a new motor (*automobile*).

3. Hyperbole. Hyperbole is a figure of speech in which the speaker or writer employs conscious exaggeration for the sake of emphasis.

a. Curiosity consumed her.
b. His eyes became as large as saucers.
c. A million wrinkles carved his skin.

4. Apostrophe. Apostrophe consists in addressing the absent as if they were present, the dead as if they were living, and inanimate objects and abstract ideas as if they were human beings.

a. Wondrous Shakespeare, what genius was thine!
b. My country, 'tis of thee,
   Sweet land of liberty,
      Of thee I sing.

5. Exclamation. Exclamation, a figure confined almost wholly to poetry, is used to signify intense emotion.

a. O eloquent, just, and mighty Death!
b. Farewell, a long farewell, to all my greatness!
c. Oh, what a tangled web we weave
   When first we practice to deceive!

6. Interrogation. The figure of interrogation is a question the answer to which is usually self-evident. Interrogation is sometimes called a rhetorical question.

a. What is so rare as a day in June?
b. Who is not proud to be an American citizen?
c. What man among us is free from sin?

7. Onomatopœia. Onomatopœia is a device for making an action or a sound more vivid by the use of a word that imitates the action or the sound. All such words as *whiz, chug, crash, smash, cackle, meow, kiss, hiss, twitter, tinkle,* and *gurgle* are illustrations of onomatopœia. Poe's "The Bells" is a good example of the extensive use of this figurative device.

Exercise 298

In each of the sentences that follow point out the figure of speech, and tell whether it is metonymy, synecdoche, hyperbole, apostrophe, exclamation, interrogation, or onomatopœia.

1. After dinner father enjoys his pipe.
2. You should have more respect for his gray hairs.
3. Down his cheeks a briny torrent flowed.
4. How poor are they that have no patience!
5. Commit a crime, and every house is made of glass.
6. The bees buzzed and hummed angrily when he accidentally struck the hive.
7. In the sweat of thy face shalt thou eat bread.
8. Here [at Concord] once the embattled farmers stood,
    And fired the shot heard round the world.
9. God rest you, happy gentlemen,
      Who laid your good lives down,
   Who took the khaki and the gun
      Instead of cap and gown.
10. Shall mortal man be more just than God?
11. It seems impossible for labor and capital to agree.
12. Tom ran forty yards down the field with the pigskin.
13. Milton, thou shouldst be living at this hour.
14.   O Wind,
    If Winter comes, can Spring be far behind?
15. Was this the face that launched a thousand ships,
    And burned the topless towers of Ilium?

Exercise 299

Read again a piece of prose that you have lately read and enjoyed, perhaps a short story or an essay. Copy all the figures of speech that you find in it. Name each one, and then write out a literal version of the expression. Be prepared to tell whether the expression loses effectiveness by the change.

144. Violations of Effectiveness

Carelessness in our choice of words impairs the effectiveness of what we have to say. In our effort to make our diction exact, appropriate, and expressive we should do our utmost to avoid the following violations of effectiveness: (1) needless repetition, (2) exaggeration, (3) trite expressions, (4) hackneyed quotations, (5) the overuse of figurative language, and (6) "fine writing."

145. Needless Repetition

Conciseness, the use of one expressive word in place of several words, renders our diction more effective. We should therefore avoid *tautology*, which consists in the needless repetition of our meaning in other words, and *redundancy*, which consists in using superfluous words. Such expressions as *in plain sight and clearly visible, his own individuality and personality*, and *azure blue* illustrate what we mean by tautology. Phrases such as *advance forward, return back, join together, repeat again, finally at last*, and *rest up* are examples of redundancy. We should always be as concise as clearness will permit.

146. Exaggeration

Needless exaggeration of all types lessens rather than increases the effectiveness of our utterances. Many of us by overworking *very* and *most* have well-nigh destroyed the force that these words might otherwise have. Such modifying words as *adorable, awful, deadly, elegant, exquisite, fascinating, ghastly, gorgeous, grand, great, horrible, lovely, magnificent, splendid, stupendous, superb, terrible, weird, beautifully, gorgeously, horribly, magnificently, powerfully, splendidly, terribly*, and *wonderfully* should be used only when they express exactly the meaning intended. Our diction is weak and childish when we use such expressions as "I was literally scared to death," "Look at that ghastly hole in my handkerchief!" or "Oh, I had the grandest, the most perfectly splendid trip you can possibly imagine!" Such expressions usually savor of insincerity and are felt to be lacking in accuracy and force.

147. Trite Expressions

Within the limits of correct usage we should each strive to develop individuality in diction. This we cannot do if we lazily permit ourselves to continue to use trite expressions, such as *along this line, last but not least, green with envy, silence reigned supreme,* and *the handiwork of Mother Nature.* If we think clearly and choose words that say exactly and forcefully what we mean, we shall rarely find it necessary to use stale diction. Surely we can find fresher, more expressive phrases than the following:

the festive board
none the worse for wear
tired but happy
poor but honest
the fair sex
in our midst
the irony of fate
the moon in all its glory
order out of chaos

a worth-while life
the rippling waves
the velvety grass
the light fantastic
a long-felt want
consigned to earth
a few well-chosen words
an important factor
in all its phases

148. Hackneyed Quotations

Quotations and proverbs that have become hackneyed by too frequent use impair the effectiveness of our diction. We should avoid such threadbare expressions as the following:

method in his madness
he that runs may read
What's in a name?
sermons in stones
the strait and narrow way
far from the madding crowd
monarch of all I survey
where ignorance is bliss
A thing of beauty is a joy forever

the last rose of summer
There's no place like home
I could a tale unfold
Some have greatness thrust
  upon them
Absence makes the heart grow
  fonder
plain living and high thinking
Better late than never

© Charles J. Belden

An Understanding Friend

149. Overuse of Figurative Language

Figures of speech, although they are valuable in increasing the effectiveness of what we have to say, should never be far-fetched, forced, or inappropriate. They should be used instinctively, rather than as the result of meditation and invention. They should not call attention to themselves as a device consciously used, but should in a natural and unobtrusive manner contribute their share to the force, vividness, and attractiveness of our expression. They are a means, not an end in themselves. We should not abuse such figures as hyperbole, apostrophe, epigram, irony, and euphemism. We should be on our guard also against overworked figurative expressions, such as *the grim reaper, the table groaned, brave as a lion, ran like a frightened deer, raven tresses*, and *marble brow*. We should make our own figures rather than accept them ready-made.

150. "Fine Writing"

"Fine writing" is "rich diction applied to a plain subject, or lofty words to a weak idea." Since its use indicates insincerity or affectation on the part of the speaker or writer, and since it distracts the attention of the reader, "fine writing" is one of the worst enemies of effectiveness. The boy who, during his school days, had written *sumptuous repast* for *meal*, *partake of* for *eat*, and *palatial residence* for *house* or *home*, later in life, as the editor of a small newspaper, wrote the following:

The lovely and elegant home of that crown prince of hospitality, the big-hearted and noble-souled Daniel Stone, was a radiant scene of enchanting loveliness, for Cupid had brought one of his finest offerings to the court of Hymen; for the lovable Miss Julia, the beautiful and accomplished daughter of Mr. Stone and his refined and most excellent wife, who is a lady of rarest charms and sweetest graces, dedicated her life's ministry to Dr. Howard K. Wortham, the brilliant and gifted and talented son of that ripe scholar and renowned educator, the learned Professor Wortham, the very able and highly successful president of the Female College.

Exercise 300

In the following exercise point out examples of tautology, redundancy, exaggeration, trite expressions, hackneyed quotations, and affected writing. Rewrite each sentence to improve its effectiveness.

1. We all returned back home, tired but happy, and none the worse for wear.

2. I absolutely adore lobster salad.

3. Then there came a dull thud that was clearly audible to our ears.

4. The work of Mother Nature in this secluded spot beggars description.

5. I just loathe and detest chemistry.

6. The gentlemen's cleansing-establishment was entirely devoured by the consuming element in our recent disastrous conflagration.

7. The lake stretched before us like a vast mirror of silver, while all around us the feathered songsters were caroling their morning matins.

8. I am terribly sorry that I have kept you waiting for ages, but haste makes waste, you know.

9. The bride is a woman of wonderful fascination and a remarkable attractiveness, for with manner as enchanting as the wand of a siren and disposition as sweet as the odor of flowers and spirit as joyous as the caroling of birds and mind as brilliant as those glittering tresses that adorn the brow of winter and with heart as pure as the dewdrops trembling in a coronet of violets, she will make the home of her husband a paradise of enchantment, where the heaven-tuned harp of marriage shall send forth those strains of felicity that thrill the senses with the rhythmic pulsing of ecstatic rapture.

10. On Easter Sunday our esteemed former citizen, Mr. Floyd Agnew Perkins, deserted the ranks of single blessedness and became a happy benedict, being united in the bonds of matrimony with Miss Eustacia Farley, one of our most talented musicians and the paragon of her sex. The happy pair will reside in Mortonville, where Mr. Perkins is at present engaged in commercial pursuits.

Exercise 301

From your own vocabulary and from your observation of the speech of others make a list of tautologous, redundant, trite, exaggerated, and affected expressions.

Exercise 302. Extra Credit

Make a careful study of the current number of at least ten weekly or monthly magazines to be found on the news stands. In which of them do you find violations of effectiveness? Which show the most effective use of words? Divide the magazines into two groups, according as you think reading them will aid you in improving your diction or will tend to make you still more careless in your choice of words. List the magazines in each group in the order of their apparent value to you.

Prepare a carefully written report of your investigation, using passages from the magazines as illustrative material for the statements that you make.

If time permits you to make an oral report on this investigation, take to class with you the copies of the magazines you have studied and read aloud the most commendable and the weakest passages of which you speak.

PART THREE

Types of Speaking and Writing

WHETHER or not you have "made the team" in athletics, debating, dramatics, or music, you may well covet a place on the school-publication team as a contributor if not as a member of the staff. To win a place on this team through your ability to write well is an enviable distinction.

How do contributors and members of the staff "make the team"? They become contributors by writing for readers instead of merely writing compositions. Understanding the needs of their publication and the interests of their schoolmates, and ever on the alert for good material, they try to produce stories, articles, editorials, book reviews, familiar essays, short plays, poems, and anecdotes that will appeal to the editor as being something that other pupils will enjoy reading. They regard writing for their newspaper or magazine as an interesting competition. When their offerings are not accepted, they are not discouraged; they succeed by continuing to try. From those who have "made the team" as contributors members of the next staff are chosen.

Part Three will acquaint you with the principal types of speaking and writing. It will help you to utilize your knowledge of composition in doing original work. It will guide and stimulate you in your efforts to develop and improve your ability as a writer. As you are aware, the most interesting school newspaper or magazine is the one in which the greatest number of pupils are represented as contributors. In writing each assignment, therefore, do your best to "make the team."

CHAPTER XII

Narration

151. The Appeal of Action

Why do we enjoy working with our hands, playing, participating in athletic contests, risking our lives in adventurous undertakings, or acting a part on the stage? Why do we instinctively rush to the scene of a fire or an accident? Why do we find pleasure in watching a fight, a wrestling match, a race, a game between rival teams, or a play in the theater? The answer to these questions is obvious: it is the universal appeal of action, which is our greatest interest in life. In general, the more unusual the action, the greater is our interest. Our heroes and heroines, such as Julius Cæsar, Columbus, Joan of Arc, Napoleon, Florence Nightingale, Lindbergh, and Byrd, stand out from the rest of humanity because of their great deeds.

152. Our Interest in Narration

Next to taking part in and watching action, we enjoy relating what we have done and what we have seen others do. In our daily conversation and in our letters we entertain ourselves and others by giving accounts of various actions that have interested us. We enjoy, likewise, hearing and reading about what other persons have done and seen. We listen eagerly to the lectures of travelers and explorers. In our school paper and in newspapers we read with great interest reports of current happenings. The reading of histories, autobiographies, biographies, novels, short stories, narrative poems, and plays affords us much welcome entertainment. In fact, narration, which consists in recounting an event or a series of events, constitutes most of our voluntary reading. Many of the greatest names of literature, such as Homer, Chaucer, Boccaccio, Shakespeare, Scott, Hugo, and Tolstoy, are those of master story-tellers.

153. Learning to Tell a Story Well

Because narration plays such a large part in our daily intercourse with other people, we often say, "I wish I could write a story like the one Dan had published this month in our school magazine," or "How I envy Marion her ability to tell a good story!" When we make such statements as these, we should remind ourselves that Dan and Marion did not acquire their skill as narrators by wishing or by envying others, but by making the most of their opportunities. Good story-tellers, like good athletes, develop their ability through an accurate understanding of the rules of the game and through intelligent daily practice. All around us there are stories waiting to be told. Why can we not equal the achievements of Dan and Marion and win the admiration of our associates by telling some of these stories well?

154. Essentials of a Narrative

A narrative that is well told answers clearly, either by statement or by implication, the six questions *When? Where? Who? What? Why? How?* That is, in relating an event or a series of events, we must inform our hearers and readers as to the time (*When?*) and the place (*Where?*) at which the incidents occurred; we must acquaint them with the persons or animals (*Who?*) that took part in the action and relate in proper order the incidents that constitute the narrative (*What?*); and we must indicate the cause (*Why?*) of the action and tell in what way (*How?*) the outcome was brought about.

155. How to Plan and Tell a Story

1. Scope and completeness. A narrative, whether long or short, should be a unit, a single complete story. In planning a narrative, you should answer the following questions: (1) At what point in the action should the story begin? (2) At what point should it end? (3) What incidents are needed to make the story complete? Answering these questions helps you to limit your narrative and to satisfy the requirements of unity.

2. Narrative order. The incidents that make up your story should usually be told in the order in which they occurred.

3. Narrative movement. Remember that a narrative should move rapidly from beginning to end. Omit, therefore, all superfluous incidents, for they tend to retard the movement and detract from the interest of the story.

4. Interest and suspense. In telling your story, get under way as quickly as clearness will permit. Answer in a brief introductory sentence or paragraph the questions *When? Where?* and *Who?* and try to arouse curiosity as to what is to follow. See that the story proper answers the questions *What? Why?* and *How?* and stimulates increasing interest. Build up suspense by holding back the point, or outcome, as long as possible. As soon as you have revealed the point, bring the story quickly to an appropriate close.

5. Action and vividness. Bear in mind constantly the importance of *action*: that is, what the characters do and say and how they act and speak. To represent action, use specific verbs. Such verbs, for example, as *strode, glided, swaggered, sauntered,* and *plunged* picture different ways in which a person *moved.* To increase the expressiveness of action verbs, use specific adverbs and adverbial phrases, such as *laboriously, stealthily, deftly, at a bound,* or *with eyes flashing.* Concrete nouns and specific adjectives also add vividness to narration. Brief descriptive sentences, apt comparisons expressed in original similes and metaphors, and striking contrasts are all great aids in making a narrative more effective. In telling your story, try to make the action so vivid that your hearer or reader will feel that he is one of the actors or an eyewitness.

6. **Dialogue.** Give life, variety, and naturalness to your story by means of conversation wherever it can be used appropriately as a narrative device. Try to individualize the characters by what they say. Avoid the monotonous use of *said* and *replied.* Seek, instead, specific verbs that will denote the manner of speaking and suggest the mood of the speaker, as *protested, scoffed, murmured, simpered, chuckled, panted,* or *shrieked.* Occasionally no verb of saying is needed to designate the speaker or his manner of speaking. In writing conversation, be careful to paragraph and punctuate correctly what each speaker says. (See section 239, rule 12, and section 245, rule 1.)

Exercise 303

In Jack London's "The Call of the Wild" there is the following narrative of a fight between two dogs. You will enjoy reading it as an illustration of a vivid narration of action. Are the events told in the order of their occurrence? How and where is suspense created? Read the sentence that marks the highest point of interest in the action of the story. Make a list of at least ten of the best specific verbs used to picture action. Find at least three adverbial phrases that make the action vivid. What especially effective nouns and adjectives can you point out?

In vain Buck strove to sink his teeth in the neck of the big white dog. Wherever his fangs struck for the softer flesh, they were countered by the fangs of Spitz. Fang clashed fang, and lips were cut and bleeding, but Buck could not penetrate his enemy's guard. Then he warmed up and enveloped Spitz in a whirlwind of rushes. Time and time again he tried for the snow-white throat, where life bubbled near to the surface, and each time and every time Spitz slashed him and got away. Then Buck took to rushing, as though for the throat, when, suddenly drawing back his head and curving in from the side, he would drive his shoulder at the shoulder of Spitz, as a ram by which to overthrow him. But instead Buck's shoulder was slashed down each time as Spitz leaped lightly away.

Spitz was untouched, while Buck was streaming with blood and panting hard. The fight was growing desperate. And all the while the silent and wolfish circle waited to finish off whichever dog went down. As Buck grew winded, Spitz took to rushing, and he kept him staggering for footing. Once Buck went over, and the whole circle of sixty dogs started up; but he recovered himself, almost in mid-air, and the circle sank down again and waited.

But Buck possessed a quality that made for greatness — imagination. He fought by instinct, but he could fight by head as well. He rushed, as though attempting the old shoulder trick, but at the last instant swept low to the snow and in. His teeth closed on Spitz's left fore leg. There was a crunch of breaking bone, and the white dog faced him on three legs. Thrice he tried to knock him over, then repeated the trick and broke the right fore leg. Despite the pain and helplessness, Spitz struggled madly to keep up. He saw the silent circle, with gleaming eyes, lolling tongues, and silvery breaths drifting upward, closing in upon him as he had seen similar circles close in upon beaten antagonists in the past. Only this time he was the one who was beaten.

There was no hope for him. Buck was inexorable. Mercy was a thing reserved for gentler climes. He manœuvred for the final rush. The circle had tightened till he could feel the breaths of the huskies on his flanks. He could see them, beyond Spitz and to either side, half crouching for the spring, their eyes fixed upon him. A pause seemed to fall. Every animal was motionless as though turned to stone. Only Spitz quivered and bristled as he staggered back and forth, snarling with horrible menace, as though to frighten off impending death. Then Buck sprang in and out; but while he was in, shoulder had at last squarely met shoulder. The dark circle became a dot on the moon-flooded snow as Spitz disappeared from view. Buck stood and looked on, the successful champion, the dominant primordial beast who had made his kill and found it good.[1]

Exercise 304

Read one of the following selections and discuss the advantages of using conversation in it. Notice also the variety of substitutes for the verbs *said, asked,* and *replied* that the author used. List ten or more of the most expressive.

"Fathers Forget" and "Clothes Make the Man," Chapters XXIII and XXIV of Booth Tarkington's "Seventeen." They tell how William finally got the much-needed dress suit.

The scene at the Rainbow Inn, Chapter VI of "Silas Marner," by George Eliot.

"The Revolt of Mother," by Mary E. Wilkins Freeman.

"On the Track of the Minister," Chapter II of "A Window in Thrums," by James M. Barrie.

"Dolly Dialogues," by Anthony Hope.

"A Christmas Present for a Lady," by Myra Kelly.

"Aunt Cynthy Dallett," by Sarah Orne Jewett.

The conversations between Scrooge and his nephew, his two visitors who asked a subscription for the poor, and his clerk, in Stave One of "A Christmas Carol," by Charles Dickens.

Part I of "The Rime of the Ancient Mariner," by S. T. Coleridge.

156. Narratives Based on Personal Experience

Most of the stories that we relate concern "what I did, what I said, and what happened to me." Until we

[1] From Jack London's "The Call of the Wild." By permission of The Macmillan Company, publishers.

make an inventory, few of us are aware of the abundance of good narrative material that is available from our personal experience. Whether we live in the country or in the city, we have all, either by choice or by chance, taken part in scores of actions that were to some extent unusual. Interesting things have happened to us while we were working, playing, camping, or traveling. Many of us have been in accidents. On certain occasions curiosity, a quick temper, or disobedience has involved us in difficulties. Now and then we have made amusing or embarrassing mistakes. At home and at school we have had frequent conflicts with others. Many of these experiences we have often related to relatives and friends. Some of them our present associates will enjoy hearing and reading if we narrate them well.

Exercise 305

The story given below is a good example of a narrative based on personal experience. After you have read it carefully, show that it includes the essentials of a narrative mentioned in section 154. Indicate in detail the answer to each of the six questions.

A Fire[1]

One day in late September as I was plowing in the field at the back of the farm, I encountered a particularly troublesome thicket of weeds and vines in the stubble, and decided to burn the way before the coulter. We had been doing this ever since the frost had killed the vegetation, but always on lands after they had been safeguarded by strips of plowing. On this particular land no fire had been set for the reason that four large stacks of wheat still stood waiting for the thresher. In my irritation and self-

[1] From Hamlin Garland's "A Son of the Middle Border." By permission of The Macmillan Company, publishers.

confidence I decided to clear away the matted stubble on the same strip though at some distance from the stacks. This seemed safe enough at the time, for the wind was blowing gently from the opposite direction.

It was a lovely golden day, and, as I stood watching the friendly flame clearing the ground for me, I was filled with satisfaction. Suddenly I observed that the line of red was moving steadily against the wind and *toward* the stacks. My satisfaction changed to alarm. The matted weeds furnished a thick bed of fuel, and against the progress of the flame I had nothing to offer. I could only hope that the thinning stubble would permit me to trample it out. I tore at the ground in desperation, hoping to make a bare spot which the flame could not leap. I trampled the fire with my bare feet. I beat at it with my hat. I screamed for help. Too late I thought of my team and the plow, with which I might have drawn a furrow around the stacks. The flame touched the high-piled sheaves. It ran lightly, beautifully up the sides — and as I stood watching it, I thought, "It is all a dream. It can't be true."

But it was. In less than twenty minutes the towering piles had melted into four glowing heaps of ashes. Four hundred dollars had gone up in that blaze.

Slowly, painfully I hobbled to the plow and drove my team to the house. Although badly burned, my mental suffering was so much greater that I felt only part of it. Leaving the horses at the well, I hobbled into the house to my mother. She, I knew, would sympathize with me and shield me from the just wrath of my father, who was away, but was due to return in an hour or two.

Mother received me in silence, bandaged my feet, and put me to bed, where I lay in shame and terror.

At last I heard father come in. He questioned, mother's voice replied. He remained ominously silent. She went on quietly but with an eloquence unusual in her. What she said to him I never knew, but when he came up the stairs and stood looking down at me his anger had cooled. He merely asked me how I felt, uncovered my burned feet, examined them, put the sheet back, and went away, without a word either of reproof or consolation.

Exercise 306

Read again the directions for planning and telling a story given in section 155. Then criticize the story in Exercise 305 by means of the following questions:

1. Is the narrative a unit, a single complete story? How much time does the action cover?

2. Are the incidents related in the order in which they occurred? Prove your answer.

3. Does the narrative move swiftly? Do you find in it any superfluous incidents?

4. How much space is given to the introduction? Is it clear? Which of the six questions does it answer?

5. How does the author stimulate your interest? What is the point, or outcome, of the story? By what means is suspense built up?

6. What specific verbs and adverbs represent action and flash vivid pictures of movement?

7. What concrete nouns and specific adjectives help to make the characters and the details of the scene vivid?

8. Where is conversation mentioned that is not reported? Why did the author not give this conversation?

Exercise 307

Suppose that young Hamlin Garland, the unfortunate plowboy who told the story of the fire, overheard what his mother and his father said before the latter came upstairs. Write the conversation that you imagine took place. See that each speaks naturally. Show by this conversation how the mother persuaded the father to be tolerant toward the boy. Keeping in mind what was said in section 155 and the conversations that you read in Exercise 304, try to make your dialogue vivid and natural. Paragraph and punctuate it correctly. Avoid the overuse of *asked, said,* and *replied.*

Exercise 308

Come to class prepared to relate orally a memorable experience in your life. Do your best to make your narrative clear and vividly real. Practice telling your story to your family or to some friend. In this way you will discover means of improving it before you relate it to the class.

Exercise 309

An autobiography is a life history related by the person himself. It is made up of the most significant incidents in the life of the subject, and is usually narrated in the first person, in an easy, conversational style.

Select from the list of autobiographies given below one that you have not read. After reading it, prepare a five-minute talk to be given to the class. You may give a brief summary of the chief events narrated or retell one or more of the most unusual incidents or anecdotes narrated.

The Story of My Life	*Helen Keller*
A Son of the Middle Border	*Hamlin Garland*
The Making of an American	*Jacob Riis*
Far Away and Long Ago	*W. H. Hudson*
Story of My Boyhood and Youth	*John Muir*
A Far Journey	*A. M. Rihbany*
The Story of a Pioneer	*Anna Howard Shaw*
Up the Years from Bloomsbury	*George Arliss*
My Life as an Explorer	*Roald Amundsen*
Coming Up the Road	*Irving Bacheller*
The Promised Land	*Mary Antin*

Exercise 310

Using the title "Three Events that Influenced My Life," relate the three events in proper sequence. If possible, choose happenings that will give the reader the most important facts of your autobiography. In planning, writing, and revising your story, bear in mind what is said in sections 154 and 155. Read your story aloud to a member of your family or to some friend. He may be able to give you suggestions for making it more entertaining.

157. Incidents concerning Other People

Wherever we are, whether at home, at school, on the street, in a department store, in a station waiting-room, at a fire or the scene of an accident, we find pleasure in watching what other persons do and in listening to what they say. We enjoy relating what we have seen and heard. Much of what we observe we may fashion into good stories to tell our classmates.

From our reading we may likewise get material for narratives. The retelling of anecdotes, incidents from biographies, and episodes from histories, novels, and plays will afford us valuable practice in story-telling. We may often expand some dull statement of fact into a lively narrative by assuming the point of view of one of the persons concerned and employing appropriate conversation. News stories and news-reel pictures will yield us a large harvest of novel ideas for stories if we are alert in recognizing them.

Exercise 311. Extra Credit

In almost every family there is a favorite story of the doings of an adventurous relative or of the success or hardships that came to members of the family at some particular period. Other members of the family enjoy telling these stories to the children. One of the best examples of such a family story written in recent years is the one called "An Introduction to Two Persons," found at the beginning of "The Americanization of Edward Bok." Read this story and come to class prepared to retell it entertainingly.

Exercise 312

Ask your father, your mother, or one of your grandparents to tell you the story of something interesting that happened in your family before the days that you remember. Or perhaps you recall some recent event in your family that is worth telling. Practice relating your story until you can narrate it well. A story with plenty of action in it will probably interest your audience most, especially if you are careful to follow the suggestions given in sections 154 and 155. Before telling it to the class, criticize it yourself by means of the first seven questions in Exercise 306.

Exercise 313

An anecdote, which is the simplest and briefest type of narrative, relates concisely and pointedly a single event. To be successful, it must quickly arouse interest and create suspense as to the outcome, which is usually not given until the last sentence. In spite of its brevity, an anecdote tells and suggests a complete story. Most anecdotes either present a dramatic incident or record an amusing experience or observation. Jokes are, in general, brief humorous anecdotes.

Read the humorous anecdotes given in Exercise 193 and those printed below. Then find in a magazine a good anecdote, and come to class prepared to relate it orally. Be sure that you really understand the point of the anecdote, and do not spoil the point as you retell the story.

The Soul of Tact

A well-known speaker lectured to the members of a literary society, and at the end of his address the secretary approached him with a check. This he politely refused, saying that it might be devoted to some charitable purpose.

"Would you mind," asked the secretary, "if we add it to our special fund?"

"Not at all," said the speaker. "What is the special fund for?"

"To enable us to get better lecturers next year." — *Chicago News*

Mind Your Gears

An Englishman on a visit to the West decided to go horseback riding. The hostler who was to attend him asked: "Do you prefer an English saddle or a Western?"

"What's the difference?" he asked.

"The Western saddle has a horn," replied the attendant.

"I don't think I'll need the horn," said the Englishman. "I don't intend to ride in heavy traffic." — *Pathfinder*

Exercise 314

Relate orally to the class or write an anecdote based on your own experience or observation. The following suggestions may help you to find a subject:

1. Judging by Appearances.
2. An Embarrassing Mistake.
3. A Case of Absent-mindedness.
4. How I Got My Nickname.
5. My First "Date."
6. An Instance of Mistaken Identity.
7. When I Forgot My _____.
8. My First Burglar.
9. A Party-line Comedy.
10. When I Answered an Advertisement.

If you relate your anecdote orally, the class may give helpful criticism by answering these questions: Was the anecdote clearly and concisely told? Were there any unnecessary details or incidents brought in? Was suspense created? If so, how? What was the point of the story? Was it well brought out? What particularly specific, vivid words and expressions were used? Can you suggest any change in order or in the choice of words that would improve the anecdote?

158. Animal Stories

Many entertaining narratives, such as those told by John Burroughs, Henri Fabre, and William J. Long, concern animal actors. We enjoy telling of the actions of pets, domestic animals, and others that we have observed. Some of our most interesting observations of animals we may use in narratives that we relate to the class or write for our school publication.

Exercise 315

Read as an illustration of the animal story the following account of a fight between two snakes. Notice how carefully the author observed and reported the conflict.

When Bull Snake and Rattler Meet

One evening in summer several years ago, while I was on my way to look at a trawling-line that I had set for whitefish in the North Platte River, I observed a commotion among my sheep, which were grazing near by. I knew at once that a rattlesnake was among them, for I could hear the rattles; but a moment or two later near the bank of the river I heard a noise of a different kind. On hurrying toward it I found a huge bull snake that was lashing his head hither and thither in a frenzied attempt to disgorge an overgrown toad.

Just then I remembered the rather common tradition that bull snakes and rattlers are deadly enemies, and, grabbing the big fellow and thrusting him into a burlap bag I had expected to put my fish into, I ran at top speed to the place where I had heard the rattler. I found him; he was a gigantic fellow, thickset, powerful of jaw, and at least six feet long.

I dropped my bag, and out came the bull snake, free from the toad. He advanced threateningly toward me, but in a moment the rattlesnake sounded his rattles, and like a flash the bull snake turned. Raising his head a foot or more, he remained quite motionless as if he were listening. Another buzz perhaps twenty feet away, and the bull snake knew where his enemy was. With a rush as if he were dropping from a height, he started for the rattler, which turned and fled. Fearing that he would disappear into a hole, I ran to head him off; but the precaution was not necessary. The bull snake quickly gained on him. When the snakes were perhaps six feet apart, they stopped and remained perfectly still. At the end of perhaps a minute the rattlesnake suddenly drew himself into a coil, and the bull snake started to circle the quarry, keeping about six feet from it. Gradually the bull snake moved faster and decreased the size of the circle, and all the while among the coils at the center there was a humming and a buzzing of rattles such as I had never heard before. The flat triangular head of the rattler was almost hidden, and lifted only occasionally; whenever it did lift, the little eyes would blaze and scintillate.

When the bull snake had almost encircled his foe with his length, he suddenly drew himself together in a coil like that of his victim's, and from the midst of it raised and lowered his glistening, egg-shaped head. Never had I imagined so much fury, such terrible ferocity. The two writhing masses approached each other, and the hissing and the rattling ceased. The head of the rattlesnake began warily to emerge. Then the two heads lifted a foot and came together with an impact almost like that which a baseball bat makes when it strikes a baseball. For a time both snakes were so active that you could not see which had hold of the other. The two masses intertwined and lashed and tumbled and thrashed the earth too rapidly for the eye to follow.

Then the movements became almost imperceptibly less violent, and I could see that the bull snake had hold of his antagonist two inches behind the head. The rattler was vainly trying to embed his fangs in his adversary; both fangs, almost an inch long, were in plain sight. His head was almost flat; his beady eyes looked as if they would shoot out like his forked tongue.

Suddenly the bull snake made a terrific lunge, and his entire length shot to the other side of his enemy, which now lay stretched in the opposite direction. For a moment both lay outstretched; then the bull snake moved weakly away in the direction of the marsh. With his head bent back double, the rattler writhed in his last throes.

I followed the victor, but he had not gone far before he stopped and drew his whole length up into lumps almost like knots; then he turned on his back. By the fading light I could see many little pricks, dark with blood. The venomed fangs of the rattler had pierced him in many places. Before long he ceased to move. I returned to the scene of the fight, and there lay the rattler dead. The big toad, the unwitting cause of the struggle, was the sole survivor of the tragedy. — *Youth's Companion*

Now that you have read the story, study by the aid of the following questions the author's method of narration:

1. How many sentences are devoted to the beginning?
2. Is the beginning clear, appropriate, and natural?
3. Why does the author not tell us more about fishing?
4. What is the series of incidents that he has included in his story?
5. Has he omitted any necessary incidents?
6. In what order has he arranged the incidents? (Point them out in sequence to prove your answer.)
7. How has he secured interest through suspense? (Show specifically how your interest increases as you read the story.)
8. Where is the point, or outcome, revealed?
9. Is the end, or conclusion, satisfactory?
10. Why did the author not tell us what effect the fight had on his sheep, or what he did after he had witnessed the fight?

Exercise 316

The observation of any animal, from an ant to an elephant, will repay you. What animals have you watched? Relate orally to the class an original narrative based on your observations. Do your best to make your story as vivid and entertaining as the one told in Exercise 315. Several of the questions at the end of Exercise 315 will aid the class in criticizing your story.

Copyright, 1930, Life Publishing Company

Sinbad

" S-poo-ooks "

Exercise 317

Write an original animal story suggested by "When Bull Snake and Rattler Meet." You may take as your subject any animal whose actions you have watched, or any incident in which a group of animals played a part. Make the action vivid by the use of specific, picture-making words and phrases. Create suspense by working up to a definite point of interest.

159. News Stories

A news story may deal with any event that is of interest to the public. It consists, technically, of two parts, the lead and the body. The *lead* (pronounced *leed*) is the opening sentence or paragraph.

After getting the facts for his story, the news writer asks himself the question, What will be of greatest interest to the largest number of readers? Knowing that readers expect to find in the lead the most important fact and all other essential details, he almost invariably begins by giving the outcome of the event and stating the cause or motive that brought it about. In the lead he tries to answer briefly and in the order of their appeal to readers the six fundamental questions *Who? What? Why? When? Where? How?*

Since the lead gives the outcome of the event and the essence of the entire story, the construction of a news story differs from that of other types of simple narration. The details that make up the body of the story are rarely arranged in chronological order, but rather in the inverted time order and in the descending order of their importance. So well established has this procedure become that most readers feel that they have the essentials of a news story as soon as they have read the headlines and the first paragraph or two.

Exercise 318

Examine closely the leads given below. In each specimen tell which of the six fundamental questions the writer has answered and indicate definitely the order in which these answers are given.

1.

One man was instantly killed and three others were injured when an automobile containing four Lawrence men who were on their way to work at the Ford plant in Somerville swerved from the road and crashed against a tree near the State police barracks on the Reading-Andover boulevard, shortly after seven o'clock this morning.

2.

S. S. MAURETANIA, Nov. 19 (AP) — A thrilling triple dash to rescue a sinking vessel in the Atlantic culminated at noon today with the transfer of 28 passengers from the sinking Swedish freighter *Ovidia* to the famous dowager queen of the Atlantic, the liner *Mauretania*.

3.

OKLAHOMA CITY, Nov. 19 (AP) — A tornado cut a swath of death and destruction today through the little church colony of Bethany, seven miles west of here. Seventeen persons were killed, at least 100 were injured, and approximately 200 buildings were destroyed.

4.

PHILADELPHIA, Nov. 19 (AP) — Citing the dramatic last-minute drive of the Princeton football team against Yale last Saturday, William H. Roper, who retires this season as the Tiger coach, today warmly praised football as a game worthy of all the effort and enthusiasm put into it. Roper spoke at the weekly luncheon of the Rotarians.

5.

> Ten firemen and policemen who responded to a general alarm for a fire at 48 and 50 Warren Street, Lynn, yesterday risked their lives going through the blazing building with gas masks looking for the occupants, who neighbors insisted were in the house, although a check after the fire was under control proved that none of the tenants was at home during the fire.

Exercise 319

In the specimen news stories given below, point out the lead in each and indicate which of the six fundamental questions each lead answers. Examine also the body of each story and tell in what order the details are arranged. Notice the use of the direct quotation in the sixth paragraph of the second specimen.

1.

SURGEONS IN DOG SLED TREK
ARRIVE TO FIGHT BLOOD POISONING

RED RIVER HOT SPRINGS, IDAHO, JAN. 26 (AP) — Surgical skill, taken deep into the Central Idaho waste lands by dog sled, was pitted today against a week-old case of blood poisoning in the right arm of Roy Burke, Copper King miner at Green Mountain.

Dr. J. P. Weber, of Grangeville, mushed through blizzards and temperatures that ranged between 35 and 50 degrees below zero to reach Burke late Friday night. The last report from the mine, brought out by a miner on snowshoes, stated that while Burke was seriously ill he had a fighting chance for recovery, and that Dr. Weber would stay by his side.

The dash over the 15 miles of glacial terrain, through blizzards and winter conditions said to be the worst in many years, was an epic of heroism, performed in the face of predictions of those who knew the country, that it could not be accomplished.

Burke's condition was reported Tuesday, and Dr. Weber, L. E. Pettibone, a guide, and Sumner Stonebreaker, of Orofino, gathered at Elk City after Stonebreaker had trekked eight dogs and a sled from McCall, more than 100 miles south. Thursday morning the trek started from Elk City with the assertion by Dr. Weber that he would make the attempt knowing that the poison probably had advanced too far for him to save Burke's life. — *Boston Herald*

2.

AVIATOR SUFFERS
NO BROKEN BONES

Capt. Roy W. Ammel, from Hospital Bed, Describes Panama Crack-up

PANAMA, Nov. 22 (AP) — Capt. Roy W. Ammel, Chicago aviation enthusiast, was resting as comfortably as possible tonight in a hospital here while physicians announced he had not been so seriously injured as was at first feared when his plane cracked up yesterday at the start of a flight to Chicago.

He was suffering from severe shock and many contusions, but an X-ray disclosed there were no broken bones.

His doctors said, however, they would have to watch closely for a possible fracture of the neck, and that the patient would have to remain in the hospital for some time.

When interviewed tonight Captain Ammel complained of pain in his shoulders, neck and head, and although his left arm is almost useless he appeared bright and eager to be about.

The flier described his experiences yesterday in the accident at Ancon field.

"My air speed indicator read slightly more than 120 miles an hour immediately before the crack-up," he said. "The ship was just gaining buoyancy and about to lift when I felt a sickening sensation beneath me. I was halfway out of the cockpit when the plane completed its flip and crashed. I am very anxious to see the wreck and make future plans."

Ammel was visited today by Harry Burgess, governor of the Canal Zone, and Major Gen. Leroy Irwin.— *The News and Courier, Charleston, S.C.*

3.

MR. COLE'S 12-A ENGLISH CLASS
PUTS OUT NEW PAPER

Mr. Cole's English classes have recently undertaken a new project. It is the publishing of a two-page mimeographed newspaper, which is to be published every two weeks for the remainder of the semester. It is called the 12-A Journal.

This paper contains themes written of the students, by the students, and for the students. It is thought that this small publication will create a greater interest in the writing of personal experiences. It also consists of feature stories, jokes, Mr. Cole's column, and perhaps in the future will include editorials. Only the best themes will be published each time.

This paper is to be put out each time by a committee of five. These people select the best compositions and see to the printing and circulation of the paper also.

However, this journal will not compete in any way with the Blue and Gold as it is to be composed entirely of material chosen for its literary merit, whereas the Blue and Gold is not. It will also consist of more personal things than are to be found in the school publication.

In the first issue, which appeared last week, were found several themes relating to Pageant Day experiences. This issue was edited by a committee composed of Wanda Avery, chairman, Corinne Dickerson, Bertha Juell, Frances Herther, Florence Perkins, and Bob Hill.— *From "Blue and Gold," published by the Aberdeen (South Dakota) High School*

Exercise 320

Bring to class two of the best news stories that you can
find in current newspapers. Indicate the lead and explain
which of the six fundamental questions are answered in it.
Analyze the body of the story. Are the details arranged
in chronological order or in the reverse time order?
Analyze in the same way the news story printed in
Exercise 83.

If your school publishes a newspaper, select the best
news story that you can find in it and analyze the story
according to the directions given above.

Exercise 321. Extra Credit

Read again the first specimen news story given in
Exercise 319. Imagine yourself the guide who accompanied Dr. Weber. Write the story as you think he might
have told it when he returned to Elk City. Who will be
the hero? Try to introduce conversation that is vivid and
in keeping with the characters themselves.

160. Fictitious Narratives

Thus far we have been considering narratives of fact,
which are accounts of actual happenings. A great many
stories, however, are narratives of fiction; that is, they
are invented, either wholly or partially, by the imagination. In this type are included traditional stories, such
as folk tales, legends, and myths; didactic stories, such
as fables and parables; and most short stories, novels,
and plays. In later chapters we shall study the short
story and the one-act play. For the present we shall
devote our attention to a few of the other types of fictitious narrative.

Read and discuss the following legend or folk tale. Just how does it answer the six essential questions given in section 154? In what way does it differ from the family story mentioned in Exercise 311? Is it in any way similar?

The Convent Free from Care

Once when the Emperor Charles V was traveling in the country, he saw a convent, and in passing by a little door he read this strange inscription: "Here you live without a care."

The Emperor was very much surprised and could scarcely believe his eyes.

"It seems to me an impossibility," he thought; "does some one really exist on earth who is free from care? As Emperor I am overwhelmed with troubles, while here in this convent, which is a little kingdom in itself, one would have nothing to worry about. I cannot believe it."

Immediately on setting foot in the village inn, the Emperor sent the hostess to fetch the Abbot of this singular convent.

You can imagine what a state of mind the latter was in when he heard that he was summoned to the Emperor's presence.

"What have I done to displease him?" he asked himself. On the way he examined his conscience over and over again, and he could think of no fault of which he was guilty. "I am in troubled waters; I must steer my way through," he said.

When he was in the Emperor's presence, the latter expressed his astonishment at what he had read.

The Abbot now knew why he had been summoned, and smiled. "Sire," said he, "does that astonish you? However, it is very simple; we eat, we drink, we sleep, and worry over nothing."

"Well, Reverend Abbot, that state of things must come to an end," said the Emperor; "and in order that you may have your share of trouble, I command you to bring me tomorrow the answers to the three following questions:

"First, What is the depth of the sea?

"Secondly, How many cows' tails would it take to measure the distance between the earth and the sun?

"Thirdly, What am I thinking about?

"Try to please me, or I shall exact a penalty from you."

On hearing these words, the Abbot returned to his convent with a heavy heart. From that moment he knew no peace. He cudgeled his brains as to what answer he could make to the Emperor.

When the little bell of the abbey rang, summoning the monks to prayer in the chapel, the Abbot continued to pace his garden. He was so deep in thought that he was quite oblivious of what was taking place around him. Even if a thunderbolt had fallen at his feet, he would not have noticed it.

"What a horrible thing!" he thought. "Is it possible that such a misfortune has overtaken me? I cannot possibly answer. Who can save the situation? Perhaps our shepherd could; he has a very lively imagination; but talk of the devil —"

At that identical moment the shepherd appeared, leading his flock. He was very much surprised to see the Abbot, who was always without a care, meditating in solitude.

What could have happened?

Without more ado he went to him, and asked him what was troubling him so deeply.

"Yes, I deserve to be pitied," said the Abbot; and he told him what had happened.

"Why are you tormenting yourself over a little thing like that?" the shepherd laughingly replied. "Leave it to me, and all will be well. Tomorrow I will come here and dress myself in your robe, and I will turn the tables on him."

At first the Abbot demurred, but in the end he yielded, and the matter was settled.

The next day the shepherd went boldly to find the Emperor.

"Well, Reverend Abbot," the Emperor said with serenity, "have you found out the answers?"

"Yes, certainly, sire."

"Speak, I am listening."

"Sire, the sea is as deep as a stone's throw.

"To measure the distance between the earth and the sun, you need only one cow's tail, if it is long enough.

"Do you wish to know, sire, what you are thinking? Well, at this moment, you think, sire, that the Abbot of the convent is in your presence, and it is only his shepherd."

The Emperor laughed so heartily that if he has not stopped laughing he is laughing still. — BOSSCHERE's "Christmas Tales of Flanders"

Exercise 323

Do you know a legend or folk tale concerning the section of the country in which you live? If you or your parents have lived in some other country, perhaps you recall some traditional story told by the people of that country. Make yourself familiar with one entertaining legend or folk tale. Come to class prepared to tell it orally. The class will decide whether you make the story real and vivid. If it is a story of olden times, try to introduce a few words and expressions that show this.

Exercise 324

Have you ever read Hawthorne's "A Wonder Book" and "Tanglewood Tales"? Are you familiar with H. A. Guerber's "Myths of Greece and Rome" and "Myths of Northern Lands," C. M. Gayley's "Classic Myths," Bulfinch's "The Age of Fable," or Padraic Colum's "Orpheus: Myths of the World"? In these books the authors have retold stories that have been favorites for many centuries. Doubtless you will find them equally enjoyable.

A myth is a purely fictitious narrative "concerning supernatural beings and events, or natural beings and events influenced by supernatural agencies." Myths, unlike fables and parables, are stories told to explain something. They represent, in general, man's attempt to account for his origin and that of the world in which he lives, to give a plausible explanation of the phenomena of nature, and to picture a future abode. The characters are gods and goddesses, who direct the planets in their courses, control the forces of nature, and guide the actions of mankind and of all other living things upon the earth.

Read as many myths as your time will permit. Be sure to include the stories of Prometheus, Pandora, Echo, Narcissus, and Hyacinthus. Come to class prepared to relate orally the myth that you most enjoyed. Make your telling vivid by the use of specific words.

Exercise 325

When you have become thoroughly familiar with the myth as a type of narrative, try to devise an original myth. The following suggestions may help you to find a subject:

1. The Boastful Sunflower.
2. Why the Earth Rotates.
3. Why the Rose Has Thorns.
4. Why Dogs and Cats Are Enemies.
5. The Frost Giants, Guardians of the Poles.

Exercise 326. Extra Credit

Have you ever read the prose fables of Æsop or those in verse by La Fontaine? Many of Æsop's fables have been retold in verse by Oliver Herford. (See Exercise 332.) In Exercise 59 of this book there is a modern fable in verse. Perhaps you will enjoy reading others and then trying to write a fable.

A fable is a short fictitious narrative in which the characters are generally animals or inanimate things, though they are represented as acting and speaking like human beings. It is devised to convey simply and vividly a useful lesson in proper conduct. The concise story illustrates concretely some important truth or precept. In the final sentence the author usually states the moral, or lesson, taught by the fable.

Read again "Etiquette," the fable of the sparrow and the cat, given in Exercise 59. Read also several of Æsop's fables in both the prose and the verse form. When you feel certain that you understand what a fable is, choose some moral precept or rule of conduct and invent a good fable that will illustrate and emphasize it. The following suggestions may help you to find a subject:

1. Haste makes waste.
2. Two wrongs never made a right.
3. Overcome evil with good.
4. Honesty is the best policy.
5. Conscience makes cowards of us all.
6. Selfish persons are never happy.
7. Procrastination is the thief of time.
8. He who would rule others should first be master of himself.
9. Dare to be true; nothing can need a lie;
   The fault that needs it most becomes two thereby.
10. Oh, what a tangled web we weave
   When first we practice to deceive!

Perhaps one of the following titles will give you a suggestion for your fable:

1. The Bat and the Mouse.
2. The Peacock and the Guinea Hen.
3. The Beaver and the Sloth.
4. The Cat and the Canary.
5. The Cock and the Sun.
6. The Dandelion and the Lily.
7. The Swan and the Vulture.
8. The King and the Worm.
9. The Dragon Fly and the Snail.
10. The Cricket and the Spider.

ASSIGNMENTS IN WRITING NARRATIVES FOR THE
SCHOOL PUBLICATION

Exercise 327

During a recent vacation you perhaps enjoyed a trip
to some beautiful or unusual place. Where did you go?
Did you travel by water, land, or air? What things stand
out as the most memorable sights or experiences of the
trip? Write an account of your doings that is so vivid
and lifelike in style that your readers will feel that they
also have seen the places and had the experiences. If you
took pictures, use the best of them as illustrations. If you
have no pictures of your own, examine carefully the
illustrations in this book. Perhaps one of them was taken
by someone who knew the place that you visited and took
the picture that you might have taken.

If you have ever been aboard a ship when it crossed the
equator, you can probably write an entertaining narrative of the initiation ceremony by means of which a sailor
becomes a full-fledged seaman (see the picture of Neptune's
Court on page 457).

If you have ever taken part in or witnessed the storm-
ing of an ice castle (see the picture on page 397) during the
winter-sports season in Canada or elsewhere, relate what
happened.

Exercise 328

Have you ever heard how The Haunted Sentry Box,
near San Juan, Porto Rico, got its name? In the following paragraphs the story is briefly told:

At the old Spanish fort of San Cristóbal, near San Juan, Porto
Rico, there stands a deserted tower known as La Garita del
Diablo, or The Haunted Sentry Box.

The fort was built back in the days when Spain ruled Porto
Rico and the waters of the Caribbean were infested with pirates.

© E. M. Newman Publishers' Photo Service

The Haunted Sentry Box, San Juan, Porto Rico

One night the sentinel who had the first watch in the sentry box mysteriously disappeared. As his gun was found leaning against the wall, it was supposed that he had fallen into the water below; but he was never found. A few weeks later another sentinel placed on guard in the same box vanished. The soldiers became alarmed at the strange happenings in the tower.

A month passed. Then one foggy night, when the officer of the guard had groped his way to the tower and called "Centinelas! Alerta!" there came no reply of "Alerta estoy!" from the sentry box. Was the sentinel asleep? The officer climbed up into the tower to investigate. As on the two former occasions, he found that the sentinel had disappeared and that he had left his gun leaning against the wall. But on this occasion he found on the floor of the "garita" a small cross, and he thought that he smelled a faint odor of sulphur. That settled it: the devil was carrying off the sentinels.

The story spread rapidly through the fort. Thereafter not a soldier could be found who would stand guard in such a place. As a result, "La Garita del Diablo" was closed and allowed to fall into ruin.

Can you devise a story that will give a logical solution of this mystery? What do you think became of the sentinels? Did the same fate befall the three men? Notice the mention of the gun, the cross, and the smell of sulphur. Try to account for each of these in your story.

Suggest to the editor of your school paper that the solution of this mystery be run as a contest. The most plausible solutions may be printed for the school to read. A vote may later be taken to decide which is the best story.

Exercise 329

Acting as a reporter for your school newspaper or for one of the newspapers of your town or city, write a good news story dealing with some event that has recently occurred. Before you begin to write, get all the facts that you can. Give particular attention to the lead. Make your entire story accurate and clear. The following sources may furnish you material:

1. An athletic rally.
2. A victory of a school athletic team.
3. A fire in your town.
4. A runaway horse.
5. A recently discovered crime.
6. An insignificant person who has become a hero (or heroine).
7. An honor recently conferred on a citizen of the town.
8. A lecture, a concert, or a play.
9. The appearance in town of some person of international fame.
10. An automobile accident involving pupils or members of the school faculty.

Exercise 330

Whether you live in a village, a town, a city, or the country, your home community is full of material for good news stories. As a reporter, investigate one of the subjects listed below and write the best news story that you can.

1. How Our Town Got Its Name.
2. How My Street Got Its Name.
3. An Unusual Event in the Early History of Our Town.
4. The Life Story of Our Oldest Citizen.
5. The Story of Our Chief Industry.
6. The Deed (Person) Commemorated by _____ Monument.
7. The First School in Our Town (Community).
8. A Great Local Disaster of Early Days (Fire, Storm).
9. Favorite Games of Our Ancestors.
10. An Old-fashioned Barbecue (Play-party, Box Supper).

Exercise 331

The outcome of a narrative is usually the result of a single determining action. If this action had been different, the outcome would have been different. You may enjoy supposing that the determining action in a well-known story was different and then writing the story with a different outcome. Such a narrative, which may be termed an "If" story, you might write on one of the following:

1. If Jim Hawkins Had Not Hidden in the Apple Barrel.
2. If Bassanio Had Chosen a Different Casket.
3. If Portia Had Not Defended Antonio.
4. If Ichabod Crane Had Known that Brom Bones Was the Headless Hessian.
5. If the Black Knight Had Not Given the Bugle to Wamba.
6. If Madame Defarge Had Won in the Struggle with Miss Pross.
7. If Dunstan Cass Had Not Been Drowned in the Quarry Pit.
8. An "If" story of your own choice.

Assume that your readers know the original story as well as you do. Take it up at the point where the different determining action is introduced. All other conditions in the story up to this point must remain the same.

Exercise 332

Do you know the origin of the common expression "to bell the cat"? Here it is, as related in prose by Æsop and as retold in verse by Oliver Herford.

The Mice in Council

The Mice, being sadly distressed on account of their common enemy the Cat, called a council to devise means of ridding themselves of the annoyance. Many plans were proposed and rejected, till at last it was suggested by a young Mouse that a bell should be hung round the Cat's neck, that having notice of her coming, they might escape to their holes.

The proposal was hailed with applause and agreed to unanimously. Whereupon an old Mouse, who had sat in silence, got up and said, "That is well, but who will bell the Cat?" The Mice looked one at another, but no one answered.

The old Mouse said, "It is easy to advise; what is wanted is someone to act."

The Mice in Council

Once, in the absence of the Cat,
The Mice in solemn council sat,
Some plan of action to discuss
To curb her practice odious
Of prying into their affairs
And pouncing on them unawares.
After much talk the plan that met
With most approval was to get
A piece of cord and hang thereby
To Pussy's neck, upon the sly,
A bell that would not fail to ring
When Pussy was about to spring,
And so announce her fell intention.
Truly a wonderful invention!
The Mice delightedly agreed;
"Now," said the Chairman, "all we need
Is someone to attach the bell."
At this, an awful silence fell
Upon the meeting; no one spoke.
At length a voice the stillness broke,
"I move, since no one seems to yearn
To bell the Cat, that we adjourn."

Your school publication will welcome fables told in verse, whether the fables are the old ones retold or modern ones. Try retelling in verse the fable that you wrote for Exercise 326; or, if you prefer, put one of Æsop's fables into simple verse. Of course you will select one that Oliver Herford has not retold. (You may find a reference to Chapter XXV of this book helpful in planning your verse form and rime scheme.)

Exercise 333

In a series of drawings on page 329 the artist Edwina shows a Halloween episode in the life of the dog Sinbad. After studying the pictures, relate the episode in a vivid animal story. Before you begin to write, decide who is to tell the story: the boys outside, Sinbad's mistress, Sinbad himself, or an onlooker who observed all sides of the episode. Keep the same point of view throughout the story and use language appropriate to the character of the narrator. Create suspense and work up to a high point of interest.

CHAPTER XIII

Description

161. What Description Is

To add reality and vividness to a narrative, an author may use pictures; to illustrate an explanation or an argument, he may employ pictures or drawings. In all these types of writing he may use descriptions, or word-pictures, for the same purposes. Pictures and drawings appeal primarily to the sense of sight, whereas descriptions may appeal to other senses as well. All are illustrative devices, which supplement and are subordinate to the types of writing in which they appear. Rarely is description used alone for its own sake.

Description, which is the process of conveying to others by words a picture of what we have observed through one or more of our senses, is of two kinds. If we give an exact and complete word-picture, including every detail in the appearance of a place, an object, or a person, we produce a *photographic description*. Such descriptions, found in tourists' guidebooks, catalogues, textbooks of science, classified advertisements, and the record files of prisons and detective bureaus, are useful merely for purposes of explanation and identification. If, on the other hand, having chosen a certain dominant characteristic of the scene, object, or person to be described, we include only those details that will successfully convey this characteristic to the hearer or reader, we give an *impressionistic description*. By representation and suggestion it arouses in the mind of the hearer or reader appropriate memory images and stimulates his imagination. It creates for him, as he listens or reads, the same impression, and it excites in him the same emotional response, that we ourselves experienced. The impression to be conveyed must govern us in choosing and arranging the details of a description just as it governs an artist in painting a picture.

Exercise 334

How would a photograph of the scene pictured on page 359 differ from the etching? What single dominant impression do you get from the etching? What details suggest this impression? How does an impressionistic description resemble an etching or a painting?

162. Limiting the Picture

The principle of unity, as it applies to description, demands that we determine first of all the limits of the picture that we intend to present. In picturing a landscape, for example, what boundaries shall we set? In describing a building, shall we tell of the appearance of the front, the rear, one side, or the entire exterior? Shall we describe the whole interior, or only one room? In picturing a scene of activity, what persons or animals shall we include? How much of the setting, or background, is it necessary to describe? Usually the nature of the scene and our purpose in describing it will make it easy to limit the picture.

Exercise 335

Read carefully the description given below. Show how the author limited the picture. Point out the characteristic details that he used to help the reader visualize and experience the scene.

A wet Sunday in a country inn! Whoever has had the luck to experience one can alone judge of my situation. The rain pattered against the casements; the bells tolled for church with a melancholy sound. I went to the windows in quest of something to amuse the eye; but it seemed as if I had been placed completely out of the reach of all amusement. The windows of my bedroom looked out among tiled roofs and stacks of chimneys, while those of my sitting-room commanded a full view of the stable yard. I know of nothing more calculated to make a man sick of this world than a stable yard on a rainy day. The place was littered with wet straw that had been kicked about by travelers and stableboys. In one corner was a stagnant pool of water, surrounding an island of muck; there were several half-drowned fowls crowded together under a cart, among which was a miserable, crestfallen cock, drenched out of all life and spirit; his drooping tail matted, as it were, into a single feather, along which the water trickled from his back; near the cart was a half-dozing cow, chewing her cud, and standing patiently to be rained on, with wreaths of vapor rising from her reeking hide; a wall-eyed horse, tired of the loneliness of the stable, was poking his spectral head out of a window, with the rain dripping on it from the eaves; an unhappy cur, chained to a doghouse hard by, uttered something every now and then between a bark and a yelp; a drab of a kitchen wench tramped backwards and forwards through the yard in pattens, looking as sulky as the weather itself; everything, in short, was comfortless and forlorn, excepting a crew of hardened ducks, assembled like boon companions round a puddle and making a riotous noise over their liquor.— IRVING, "Bracebridge Hall"

163. Point of View

Our point of view, or angle of observation, is a great aid in limiting the picture to be given in our description. We should choose a position that will enable us to view advantageously the scene, person, or object to be described, and let the reader know our position. So long as we maintain this point of view, we should include no detail that we do not observe from the place where we are. If we find it necessary to describe our subject from more than one point of view, each position should be mentioned or clearly implied.

In many descriptions the time point of view is also important. If the time of day or night, the day of the week or month, or the season of the year affects the scene, person, or object described, the reader will get a clearer picture if the time of observation is indicated.

Such personal factors as age, mood, environment, or special interests in life are sometimes to be taken into consideration in the point of view. They often influence our observation and the description that we give.

For the guidance of our readers we should make clear early in our description our points of view. This information can be given naturally and unobtrusively. Sometimes it is necessary only to suggest or imply it.

Exercise 336

What is the place point of view used by the author of the selection in Exercise 335? What other position is mentioned from which he might have written his description? Does he change his position during the writing of the description? What words make clear his point of view in time? Is there anything that indicates a personal point of view?

After you have discussed the questions just asked, choose a subject for a written description of about the same length as the one in Exercise 335. These general topics may help you to select a subject:

1. A country landscape.
2. A busy corner in a city.
3. A harbor view.
4. A well-known building or monument.
5. A stage setting.
6. An old tree.
7. An indoor scene.
8. A person or a group of persons.
9. A family heirloom.
10. A Japanese dish garden.

Make a list of the characteristic details that you wish to include in your description. Establish the limits for the picture, and decide on the points of view in place and time. Do not write your description yet.

164. Singleness of Impression

In observing a scene, a person, or an object, we are usually impressed by some dominant characteristic or outstanding quality. The stable yard that Irving looked out upon from his sitting-room window impressed him as "comfortless and forlorn," and this impression he conveyed to the reader. When we have discovered the dominant characteristic of a scene, a person, or an object, and have determined the single impression that it makes on us, we should try to produce this same impression in the reader by means of our description. This we can do if we are careful in choosing details that emphasize the dominant characteristic and if, with equal care, we avoid bringing into the picture any details that distract the reader's attention from the single impression that we wish to give him.

If the dominant characteristic or the principal appeal of a scene, a person, or an object is shape, size, color, or arrangement, we may often give the reader an instant general impression of the physical appearance by comparing the subject of our description to a more familiar scene, person, or object, which we may call a *fundamental image*. For example, we may say "The old hermit reminded me of Santa Claus," or "Grandmother's flower garden resembled a patchwork quilt." An apt simile or metaphor will oftentimes give in a single sentence a general impression that will flash before the reader's mind a vivid outline of the picture. (See section 141, 1 and 2.)

Exercise 337

What is the single impression that you get from the description given below? Point out the specific words and phrases that emphasize the dominant characteristic of the scene. How is the picture limited? Indicate the points of view.

It was high noon, and the rays of the sun, that hung poised directly overhead in an intolerable white glory, fell straight as plummets upon the roofs and streets of Guadalajara. The adobe walls and sparse brick sidewalks of the drowsing town radiated the heat in an oily, quivering shimmer. The leaves of the eucalyptus trees around the Plaza drooped motionless, limp, and relaxed under the scorching, searching blaze. The shadows of these trees had shrunk to their smallest circumference, contracting close about the trunks. The shade had dwindled to the breadth of a mere line. The sun was everywhere. The heat exhaling from brick and plaster and metal met the heat that steadily descended, blanketwise and smothering, from the pale, scorched sky. Only the lizards — they lived in chinks of the crumbling adobe and in interstices of the sidewalk — remained without, motionless, as if stuffed, their eyes closed to mere slits, basking, stupefied with heat. At long intervals the prolonged drone of an insect developed out of the silence, vibrated a moment in a soothing, somnolent, long note, then trailed slowly into the quiet again. Somewhere in the interior of one of the 'dobe houses a guitar snored and hummed sleepily. On the roof of the hotel a group of pigeons cooed incessantly with subdued, liquid murmurs, very plaintive; a cat, perfectly white, with a pink nose and thin, pink lips, dozed complacently on a fence rail, full in the sun. In a corner of the Plaza three hens wallowed in the baking hot dust, their wings fluttering, clucking comfortably.— FRANK NORRIS, "The Octopus"

Exercise 338

In each of the following selections point out the fundamental image that conveys the dominant impression of physical appearance — shape, size, color, or arrangement.

1. The road between the trees was covered in all its length and breadth with fallen leaves — a carpet of pale gold.— GEORGE GISSING

2. The conveyor was perhaps thirty feet long and five feet wide, and seemed nothing more than an enormous roller towel such as you would find in the bathroom of any rooming-house, but with a roller in each end, and it stretched out across the room, about waist-high from the floor.

3. The upright lathes stand up straight from the floor, like iron pianos, with shelves sticking out in front, but there are no keys on the shelves.

4. Cape Cod is the bare and bended arm of Massachusetts: the shoulder is at Buzzard's Bay; the elbow, or crazy-bone, at Cape Mallebarre; the wrist at Truro; and the sandy fist at Provincetown, — behind which the State stands on her guard, with her back to the Green Mountains, and her feet planted on the floor of the ocean, like an athlete protecting her Bay, — boxing with northeast storms, and, ever and anon, heaving up her Atlantic adversary from the lap of earth, ready to thrust forward her other fist, which keeps guard the while upon her breast at Cape Ann.— HENRY DAVID THOREAU

Exercise 339

What is the outstanding impression that you wish your readers to get from the description you planned in Exercise 336? Can this impression be given to them by the use of a fundamental image? Write now one sentence to be placed near the beginning of your paragraph in which the single impression is clearly stated. Did you choose in Exercise 336 the characteristic details that will emphasize this impression?

165. Arrangement of Details in Description

All effective description depends upon the orderly arrangement of the details selected. In general, the order that we use in describing details will be the same as that followed in observing them. Of the various orders, patterns, or arrangements, the following are the principal ones:

1. From general to particular, or particular to general.
2. From far to near, or near to far.
3. From right to left, or left to right.
4. From bottom to top, or top to bottom.
5. From exterior to interior, or interior to exterior.

The important point for us to remember is that *clearness demands that we follow some definite order of arrangement.*

Exercise 340

Explain the arrangement of details in the selections in Exercises 335 and 337. In which is the order more clearly shown?

Decide on the order that you wish to follow in the paragraph that you have been planning in Exercises 336 and 339. Then write your paragraph.

After you have written your paragraph, exchange papers with another member of the class. Each of you will then study the paragraph on the paper that you have, and check it by the explanations in sections 162 to 165 and by the questions asked in preceding exercises. After you have thoroughly discussed together each paragraph, revise your own and copy it before handing it to your teacher.

166. Vividness in Description

All our knowledge of the physical world in which we live comes through our special senses: sight, hearing, touch, smell, and taste. Each bit of information that we get through any one of our senses we call a sensation. Through the eyes we get sensations of size, color, texture, light, and shade; through the ears, those of sound; through the nerves in the skin, those of touch and temperature;

through the nose, those of odors; and through the mouth, those of taste. Through the sense of touch and the muscles we gain sensations of pressure and weight. With our senses we observe, or experience, everything about us. So natural and familiar has the process become that we are rarely aware of it.

In giving descriptions we are confronted by two problems, so far as sense impressions are concerned. We must notice through what sense or senses we get our own impression of the scene, person, or object that we observe and intend to describe. We must then use words that will appeal to the same sense or senses of the reader and thus help him to form an accurate mental picture.

At least four of our five senses are employed in observing movement, or action, which is one of our principal interests in life. We observe movement with our eyes, our ears, our sense of touch, and sometimes our sense of smell; hence, in giving a description of action, we should use words that furnish the reader with concrete details appealing to the same sense or senses that the person, animal, or machine described appealed to in us.

In describing persons, animals, and machines in action, we use narration, for we tell what they do or did. Descriptions of persons are often made more lifelike if, by the use of conversation, we tell also what they said. Obviously verbs, including infinitives, participles, and gerunds, are most important in describing action; next in importance are adverbs and adverbial phrases.

We may observe closely and choose appropriate details, but unless we use exact and suggestive words to convey the picture or impression to the reader, he will not be made fully conscious of the scene, the person, or the object that we are trying to describe. Our success in giving a vivid description depends, therefore, on our skill in using words, phrases, and figures of speech. We should rely principally on specific nouns and verbs. Adjectives we should use sparingly, avoiding particularly too many superlative forms and such overworked and general adjectives as *beautiful, great, fine, nice, grand, wonderful,* and *gorgeous.* We should never accept a ready-made phrase or figure of speech if we can devise one of our own that is appropriate. In general, we should make it a rule to observe with our own senses and describe in our own words.

Exercise 341

Read attentively each of the specimens given below and notice how each causes a picture to flash before your mind. To what sense or senses does each appeal? What comparisons and figures of speech do you find? Point out the specific words that make each picture vivid. Are many adjectives used?

1. The station echoed with the iron coughing of engines. Men and women surged between waiting trains; their voices mingled in the uproar. — JOSEPH HUSBAND, "Semaphore"

2. She had dark-at-the-roots blonde hair and slender hips upon which, in moments of leisure, she wore her hands, like buckles of ivory loosely attached. — KATHERINE BRUSH, "Night Club"

3. It was nice to walk along just as slow as you wanted to, and feel your rubber boots squizzle into the mud. — DOROTHY CANFIELD, "The Brimming Cup"

4. The heat danced over the corn, and, pervading all, was a soft, insensible hum, like the murmur of bright minutes holding revel between earth and heaven. — JOHN GALSWORTHY, "The Man of Property"

5. On her knees before an oven that billowed forth hotly into her face, Mrs. Kantor, fairly fat and not yet forty, and at the immemorial task of plumbing a delicately swelling layer-cake with a broom-straw, raised her face, reddoned and faintly moist. — FANNY HURST, "Humoresque"

6. The leaves of the sassafras are full of spice, and the bark of the black-birch twigs holds a fine cordial. Crinkleroot is spicy, but you must partake of it delicately, or it will bite your tongue. ... Wild sorrel has an agreeable, sour, shivery flavour.— HENRY VAN DYKE, "Fisherman's Luck"

7. The larks sprang up in front of his feet, the air was full of butterflies, a sweet fragrance rose from the wild grasses. The sappy scent of the bracken stole forth from the wood, where, hidden in the depths, pigeons were cooing, and from afar on the warm breeze came the rhythmic chiming of church bells.— JOHN GALSWORTHY, "The Man of Property"

8. The air was strung with humming insects, poised like little black periods in the light. Occasionally a blue-bottle sailed majestically past, the tissue of its wings gathering the sun. A droning bee blundered into a swarm of tiny, jigging gnats, disentangled itself and soared lazily on to a distant flower, unconscious of the excitement it had caused. Below them, a few feet away, stood the gray, pocked cone of an ant hill; up and down its slope the ants twinkled, providently absorbed.— MARTHA OSTENSO, "Wild Geese"

Exercise 342

Concentrate your attention on each of the following as a subject for a description. Make a list of the senses that you employ in observing each. List also for each several specific nouns, adjectives, and verbs that you might use to give the reader concrete details that would help him to get a vivid impression of what you describe.

1. A pineapple.
2. A satin scarf.
3. A roasted turkey.
4. A fish peddler.
5. A girl in a raincoat.

6. A greenhouse.
7. A wet street at night.
8. A dairy at milking time.
9. A Christmas tree.
10. A public market.

Using one of the subjects given above, write a vivid description one paragraph in length. If possible, appeal to more than one of the reader's senses.

Exercise 343

In the following selection point out all the words and phrases that suggest action or movement. To what sense or senses has the author appealed?

Every night, at exactly eight minutes past nine, the limited roars through the village. I can see it coming several miles away, its powerful headlight fingering rails and telegraph-wires with a shimmer of light. Silently and slowly it seems to draw nearer; then, suddenly, it is almost above me. A wild roar of steam and driving-wheels, the wail of its hoarse whistle at the crossing, and then, looming black against the night sky, it smashes past, and in the swing of drivers and connecting-rods I think of a greyhound, or a race horse thundering the final stretch. High in the cab window a motionless figure peers ahead into the night; suddenly he is blackly silhouetted by the glare of the opened fire-door, and in the orange light I can see the fireman swing back and forth as he feeds his fire. The light burns against the flying steam and smoke above; then blackness — and now the white windows of the Pullmans flicker past, and through the swirl of dust and smoke I watch the two red lights sink down the track.— JOSEPH HUSBAND, "Semaphore"

Exercise 344

Point out all words and phrases that suggest action or movement in the account of the dog fight in Exercise 303 and in the narrative of the snake fight in Exercise 315.

Exercise 345

In your outside reading find and bring to class good illustrations of the principles of description and the descriptive devices that you have been studying. A few selections may afford you several illustrations. Do your best to find examples of each of the following:

1. Point of view.
2. Singleness of impression.

3. Fundamental image or comparison with a familiar object.
4. Simile or metaphor.
5. Orderly arrangement of details.
6. Appeal to several of the senses.
7. A picture of action.

167. Describing Places

Places include landscapes, seascapes, and other outdoor scenes, and likewise buildings, either exterior or interior. Descriptions of places picture the setting or background of actions and often help to create appropriate atmosphere in a narrative.

Exercise 346

By means of the following questions study each of the descriptions of places given below: To what extent and by what means is the scene limited? What is the point of view in space? Is there a time point of view? a mental point of view? What is the single dominant impression that you get? Point out the details used to give this impression. To what senses in addition to sight does the description appeal? What narrative details do you find? What specific words and phrases give vividness to the picture?

1. We landed on a bit of white beach. It was backed by a low cliff wooded on the brow, draped in creeper to the very foot. Below us the plain of the sea, of a serene and intense blue, stretched with a slight upward tilt to the thread-like horizon drawn at the height of our eyes. Great waves of glitter blew lightly along the pitted dark surface, as swift as feathers chased by a breeze. A chain of islands sat broken and massive facing the wide estuary, displayed in a sheet of pale glassy water reflecting faithfully the contour of the shore. High in the colourless sunshine a solitary bird, all black, hovered, dropping and soaring above the same spot with a slight rocking motion of the wings. A ragged, sooty bunch of flimsy mat hovels was perched over its own inverted

Fishing Boats

© J. M. Buckley

image upon a crooked multitude of high piles the colour of ebony. A tiny black canoe put off from amongst them with two tiny men, all black, who toiled exceedingly, striking down at the pale water: and the canoe seemed to slide painfully on a mirror. — JOSEPH CONRAD, "Lord Jim "

2. At this corner Suydam turned out of the side street, and went down a street no wider perhaps, but extending north and south in a devious and hesitating way not common in the streets of New York. The sidewalks of this sinuous street were inconveniently narrow for its crowded population, and they were made still narrower by tolerated encroachments of one kind or another. Here, for instance, from the side of a small shop projected a stand on which unshelled peas wilted under the strong rays of the young June sun. There, for example, were steps down to the low basement, and in a corner of the hollow at the foot of these stairs there might be a pail with dingy ice packed about a can of alleged

ice-cream, or else a board bore half a dozen tough brown loaves, also proffered for sale to the chance customer. Here and there, again, the dwellers in the tall tenements had brought chairs to the common door, and were seated, comfortably conversing with their neighbors, regardless of the fact that they thus blocked the sidewalk, and compelled the passer-by to go out into the street itself.— BRANDER MATTHEWS, "Mulberry Bend"

3.   A bed of ashes and a half-burned brand
        Now mark the spot where last night's campfire sprung
        And licked the dark with slender scarlet tongue;
    The sea draws back from shores of yellow sand,
    Nor speaks lest he awake the sleeping land;
        Tall trees grow out of shadows; high among
        Their somber boughs one clear, sweet song is sung;
    In deep ravine by drooping cedars spanned
    All drowned in glory, a flying pheasant's whir
        Rends morning's solemn hush; gray rabbits run
        Across the covered glade; then far away
    Upon a hill, each huge, expectant fir
        Holds open arms in welcome to the sun, —
        Great pulsing heart of bold advancing day.

                    HERBERT BASHFORD, "Morning in Camp"

4. It was beautifully clean inside, and as tidy as possible. There was a table, and a Dutch clock, and a chest of drawers; there was a tea-tray with a painting on it of a lady with a parasol, taking a walk with a military-looking child who was trundling a hoop. The tray was kept from tumbling down by a Bible; and the tray, if it had tumbled down, would have smashed a quantity of cups and saucers and a teapot that were grouped around the book. On the walls there were some common coloured pictures, framed and glazed, of Scripture subjects; such as I have never seen since in the hands of pedlars, without seeing the whole interior of Peggotty's brother's house again, at one view. Abraham in red going to sacrifice Isaac in blue, and Daniel in yellow cast into a den of green lions, were the most prominent of these. Over the little mantel-shelf was a picture of the *Sarah Jane* lugger, built at Sunderland, with a real little wooden stern stuck on to

it; a work of art, combining composition with carpentry, which I considered to be one of the most enviable possessions that the world could afford. There were some hooks in the beams of the ceiling, the use of which I did not divine then; and some lockers and boxes and conveniences of that sort, which served for seats and eked out the chairs.— CHARLES DICKENS, "David Copperfield"

Exercise 347

From your reading select and bring to class two good descriptions of places. Be prepared to analyze each of them by means of the questions given in Exercise 346.

Exercise 348

Write an accurate description of one of the pictures in this book representing a scene, or use a picture of your own choice. Give particular attention to the arrangement of details in your description. Shall you begin with the foreground and then proceed to the middle ground and the background? Shall you begin with the most prominent detail and then describe the others in relation to it? Shall you proceed from the right side of the picture to the left, or the left to the right? If you discover a dominant characteristic, do your best to give the reader a clear impression of it. Use specific words and phrases to make your description as vivid as the picture.

Exercise 349

Write a description of not more than three hundred words in which you picture clearly one of the places mentioned below.

1. Our front yard.
2. Our back yard.
3. Our barnyard.
4. Our athletic field.
5. Our summer camp.
6. Mother's garden.
7. An old wharf.
8. A swimming pool.

9. A public park.
10. The view from my window.
11. My room.
12. Our sitting room.
13. Our schoolroom.
14. A drug store.

15. A meat market.
16. A country store.
17. A bank lobby.
18. A railway station.
19. A public garage.
20. A scene of your own choice.

In writing your description you will find the following questions and suggestions helpful :

1. Am I thoroughly familiar with the place? If possible, observe the scene as you write.
2. What is the best point of view in space? in time? Is my mental point of view important?
3. To which of my senses does this place or scene appeal as I observe it? By appealing to the same senses of the reader, try to make him *experience* the place, not merely see it.
4. What dominant impression do I get? What details will help me to give the reader this same impression?
5. Will a fundamental image or some other comparison enable me to give the reader instantly an outline of the picture?
6. In what order shall I arrange the details of the scene? (See section 165.)
7. What concrete details are needed to furnish the reader a clear picture? Mention details that distinguish the place from other somewhat similar places.
8. Try to make your description vivid by the use of picture-making words and phrases and by employing appropriate similes and metaphors.

168. Describing Animals

In describing an animal we should include individualizing details of form, size, color, facial expression, manner or movement, disposition, peculiar habits, and any other details that will distinguish the animal from other members of its class. The subject of our description may be represented as still or in action, but usually details of action help to make the picture more interesting.

Exercise 350

Examine closely each of the following descriptions of animals. Point out all individualizing details. How are the disposition and the character of the animal shown?

1. The Tailless Tyke had now grown into an immense dog heavy of muscle and huge of bone: a great bull head; undershot jaw, square and lengthy and terrible; vicious, yellow, gleaming eyes; cropped ears; and an expression incomparably savage. His coat was a tawny lionlike yellow, short, harsh, dense; and his back, running up from the shoulder to the loins, ended abruptly in a knoblike tail. He looked like the devil of a dog's hell, and his reputation was as bad as his looks. He never attacked unprovoked; but a challenge was never ignored, and he was greedy of insults.— OLLIVANT, "Bob, Son of Battle"

2. El Rayo shone like burnished copper, his silver mane and tail glittering as if powdered with diamond dust. He was long and graceful of body, thin of flank, slender of leg. With arched neck and flashing eyes, he walked with the pride of one who was aware of the admiration he excited.

Vitriolo was black and powerful. His long neck fitted into well-placed shoulders. He had great depth of girth, immense length from shoulder points to hips, big cannon bones, and elastic pasterns. There was neither amiability nor pride in his mien; rather a sullen sense of brute power, such as may have belonged to the knights of the Middle Ages. Now and again he curled his lips away from the bit and laid his ears back as if he intended to eat of the elegant Beau Brummel stepping so daintily beside him. Of the antagonistic crowd he took not the slightest notice. — GERTRUDE ATHERTON, "The Splendid Idle Forties"

3. Agrippina will never make herself serviceable, yet nevertheless is she of inestimable service. How many times have I rested tired eyes on her graceful little body, curled up in a ball and wrapped round with her tail like a parcel; or stretched out luxuriously on my bed, one paw coyly covering her face, the other curved gently inwards, as though clasping an invisible treasure. Asleep or awake, in rest on in motion, grave or gay, Agrippina is

always beautiful; and it is better to be beautiful than to fetch and carry from the rising to the setting of the sun. She is droll, too, with an unconscious humor, even in her most serious and sentimental moods. She has quite the longest ears that ever were seen on so small a cat, eyes more solemn than Athene's owl blinking in the sunlight, and an air of supercilious disdain that would have made Diogenes seem young and ardent by her side. Sitting on the library table, under the evening lamp, with her head held high in the air, her tall ears as erect as chimneys, and her inscrutable gaze fixed on the darkest corner of the room, Agrippina inspires in the family sentiments of mingled mirthfulness and awe. To laugh at her in such moments, however, is to incur her supreme displeasure. I have known her to jump down from the table, and walk haughtily out of the room, because of a single half-suppressed but wholly indecorous giggle.— AGNES REPPLIER, "Agrippina"

Exercise 351

Describe each of the horses shown in the pictures on pages 243 and 307. Devote only one paragraph to the description of each horse.

Exercise 352

Write a good description of a pet or some other animal that you know well. Try to make your description as vivid and entertaining as the specimens given in Exercise 350.

169. Describing Persons

To describe a person successfully we must possess or develop the power of keen and accurate observation. We must also be able to discriminate between the general characteristics that make our subject like every other human being and those that individualize him. In our early efforts at writing personal descriptions we shall do well to select persons who are sufficiently striking in appearance to be easily differentiated from others and who are at the same time pictorially interesting.

Exercise 353

Study closely each of the descriptions of persons given below. Analyze each selection by answering the following questions: In what position or attitude is the person pictured? What is the setting or background? What specific details of form, posture, features, facial expression, dress, manner of moving and speaking, mood, and disposition do you find? In what order has each author arranged the details of his description? What is the single dominant impression that you get of each person or group of persons?

1. Lazily Ned turned over to a dry spot of sand, burrowed a nest for his shoulder, and again stretched out his six feet of black swimming suit and bronzed legs and arms and shut his eyes. The hot sand below him burned pleasantly for a moment and then felt cooler. The sunlight engulfed him, warm and dry on his skin, warm and wet on his swimming suit, and now and then lifted entirely from him as a cloud passed over the sky and a breeze fanning along him ruffled his rapidly drying black hair and sent delicious shivers of coolness down his spine. One hand played idly in the sand, letting it course along the palm and sift between the fingers. One foot dug deeper down, reaching the damp coolness underneath. Tired from an hour of swimming, with the sound of the sea pleasantly monotonous in his ears and the warmth of the sun on his body, he almost went to sleep. Then a wave rolled icily and with treacherous suddenness over his feet, up his ankles, hovered an instant about his knees, and departed for reinforcements. With an amused curse he got up, brushing and shaking the loose sand from him, and wriggling his shoulders underneath the now dry suit to dislodge some particles that had got down his neck. Then for an instant he indulged like a healthy young tiger in the sensuous luxury of a stretch which included every muscle of his body, and strolled leisurely up to the bath house.—ANONYMOUS

2. Rachel Wiletzky had the colouring and physique of a dairymaid. It was the sort of colouring that you associate in your

mind with lush green fields, and Jersey cows, and village maids in Watteau frocks, balancing brimming pails aloft in the protecting curve of one rounded upraised arm, with perhaps a Maypole dance or so in the background. Altogether, had the superintendent been given to figures of speech, he might have said that Rachel was as much out of place among the preceding one hundred and seventy-eight bloodless, hollow-chested, stoop-shouldered applicants as a sunflower would be in a patch of dank white fungi. — EDNA FERBER, "The Girl Who Went Right"

3. In the centre of the room, under the chandelier, as became a host, stood the head of the family, old Jolyon himself. Eighty years of age, with his fine, white hair, his dome-like forehead, his little, dark gray eyes, and an immense white moustache, which drooped and spread below the level of his strong jaw, he had a patriarchal look, and in spite of lean cheeks and hollows at his temples, seemed master of perennial youth. He held himself extremely upright, and his shrewd, steady eyes had lost none of their clear shining. Thus he gave an impression of superiority to the doubts and dislikes of smaller men. Having had his own way for innumerable years, he had earned a prescriptive right to it. It would never have occurred to old Jolyon that it was necessary to wear a look of doubt or of defiance. — JOHN GALSWORTHY, "The Forsyte Saga"

4.　　When Susan's work was done, she'd sit
　　　With one fat guttering candle lit,
　　　And window opened wide to win
　　　The sweet night air to enter in;
　　　There, with a thumb to keep her place,
　　　She'd read, with stern and wrinkled face.
　　　Her mild eyes gliding very slow
　　　Across the letters to and fro,
　　　While wagged the guttering candle flame
　　　In the wind that through the window came.

　　　And sometimes in the silence she
　　　Would mumble a sentence audibly,
　　　Or shake her head as if to say,
　　　"You silly souls, to act this way!"

And never a sound from night I'd hear,
Unless some far-off cock crowed clear;
Or her old shuffling thumb should turn
Another page; and rapt and stern,
Through her great glasses bent on me
She'd glance into reality;
And shake her round old silvery head,
With — "You! — I thought you was in bed!" —
Only to tilt her book again,
And rooted in Romance remain.

WALTER DE LA MARE, "Old Susan"[1]

5. The print represented fifteen sisters, all of the same height and slimness of figure, all of the same age — about twenty-five or so — and all with exactly the same haughty and bored beauty. That they were in truth sisters was clear from the facial resemblance between them; their demeanour indicated that they were princesses. . . . Those hands had never toiled, nor had those features ever relaxed from the smile of courts. The princesses moved in a landscape of marble steps and verandahs, with a bandstand and strange trees in the distance. One was in a riding habit, another in evening attire, another dressed for tea, another for the theatre; another seemed to be ready to go to bed. One held a little girl by the hand. . . . Why was one sister going to the theatre, another to tea, another to the stable, and another to bed? Why was one in a heavy mantle, and another sheltering from the sun's rays under a parasol? The picture was drenched in mystery, and the strangest thing about it was that all these highnesses were apparently content with the most ridiculous and out-moded fashions. Absurd hats, with veils flying behind; absurd bonnets, fitting close to the head, and spotted; absurd coiffures that nearly lay on the nape; absurd, clumsy sleeves; absurd waists, almost above the elbow's level; absurd scolloped jackets! And the skirts! What a sight were those skirts! They were nothing but vast decorated pyramids; on the summit of each was stuck the upper half of a princess. It was astounding that princesses should consent to be so preposterous and so uncomfortable. But Sophia

[1] From "Collected Poems," by Walter de la Mare. Henry Holt and Company, publishers.

perceived nothing uncanny in the picture, which bore the legend:
"Newest summer fashions from Paris. Gratis supplement to
Myra's Journal." Sophia had never imagined anything more
stylish, lovely, and dashing than the raiment of the fifteen princesses. — ARNOLD BENNETT, "The Old Wives' Tale"

Exercise 354

In Exercise 353 compare the verse description of "Old
Susan" with each of the three prose descriptions that
precede it. Does it give you as clear a picture of the person described as the ones written in prose do? Point out
the words and phrases that suggest pictures instead of
definitely giving them. When you are sure that you have
all the details of the picture of "Old Susan" clearly in
mind, rewrite it as a prose paragraph.

Exercise 355. Extra Credit

Consult Chapter XXV on Versification and determine
the verse form used in the poem "Old Susan." You will
find it is one of the simplest verse forms to use. Choose
the one of the three prose descriptions of persons which
seems to you best suited to the purpose, and try to write
a short descriptive poem similar in general form to "Old
Susan."

Exercise 356

Write a good prose description of a person that you know
well. You may begin by giving a general impression of the
person and then introduce individualizing details in the order
in which they impress you. Or you may first describe the
person in detail and then sum up your general impression
at the end. If setting or background is important, mention it. The following list will help you to select a subject:

1. My chum.
2. My mother (father).
3. An uncle (aunt).
4. A sister (brother).

5. A teacher.
6. Our postman.
7. A newsboy.

8. Our cook (maid).
9. Our janitor.
10. A local "character."

Exercise 357

Write a good description of a small group of persons. The following list may suggest to you a subject:

1. My family at dinner.
2. An athletic team.
3. A birthday party.
4. A country-store group.

5. A railway-station group.
6. A group found in any one of the pictures in this book.
7. A group of your own choice.

170. Narrative and Descriptive Elements in Combination

In most descriptions of animated scenes, such as we find in stories, narrative and descriptive details are deftly interwoven. Places and objects are described not for their own sake but in relation to some action in which persons, animals, or machines take part. Details of action, which are essentially narrative, always add vividness and interest to description. What persons do and say, as well as their manner of acting and speaking, helps to picture and characterize them.

Exercise 358

In the selection given below narrative and descriptive elements are admirably combined. Point out the purely descriptive details. Mention verbs, including participles, that picture action. What comparisons add vividness to the selection? To what senses has the author appealed?

The engineer, a torch in his hand, swung down, and we shook hands before I climbed the iron rungs to the cab. From the high windows I watched him oil and stroke the sinews of his monster. Behind, on the top of the tender, the fireman was filling the tanks with a torrent of water. Then they joined me, and in the torchlight I saw the black studded end of the boiler, like a giant cask-head, a tangle of pipes across its face; water-gauge and steam-dial dimly illumined by shaded bull's-eyes. The engineer blew out the torch and climbed into his seat. Opposite him, I settled into mine, the fireman behind me.

There was the thin piping of a whistle in the cab and the engineer slowly opened the throttle. We were off. Rumbling and swaying, we passed the upper windows of the station. Telegraphers in shirt-sleeves were fingering their instruments beneath shaded lights. The chill of the frosty night air penetrated the cab, and I buttoned my coat about me and looked ahead into the darkness. We were gathering headway. A string of freight-cars on a siding swept behind us; already the lights of the village were far behind. Ahead of the long body of the locomotive, extending incredibly beyond the small front windows of the cab, the track, hardly visible in the ray of the headlight, terminated suddenly in the darkness. The roar of drivers and machinery was deafening. From side to side the engine rocked like a plunging derelict. The crashing roar grew louder, loud beyond belief, and the rocking and trembling almost threw me from the seat.

The fireman slid open the jaws of the fire-box, flooding the cab with light and heat. Within, the flame, white to pale daffodil in its intensity, twisted like streams of fluid in the draft. Behind the cab the black end of the tender rose high above my line of vision, rocking and swaying in contrary motion to the engine, like a bulldog twisting on a stick. Balancing on the smooth steel floor, the fireman stoked his grate-bars, his shovel feeding spots where the coal was thinnest. Then darkness as he closed the doors with his foot. Only the two dim lights on gauge and indicator; and on each side, and above, the stars racing evenly beside us. I looked down at the roadbed: it was flooding past us like a torrent.— JOSEPH HUSBAND, "Semaphore"

Exercise 359

Write a good description of an animated scene. Combine narration and description as your subject and your purpose may demand. Decide upon the dominant impression, and

© Wallace Hutchinson

Hermit's Retreat

try to bring this out by means of carefully chosen details and the use of picture-making words. Do your best to make the reader experience what you experienced as an observer or as a participant in the action. The following suggestions may help you to find a subject:

1. A scene in a factory (packing house).
2. An automobile (motor-boat, horse) race.
3. A scene at a fair (circus, pageant).
4. My first ride in an airplane (on a surf board).
5. A threshing (round-up) scene.
6. Our kitchen at Thanksgiving (Christmas).
7. The school lunch room at noon.
8. The scene of a fight (an accident).
9. Spring house-cleaning at our house.
10. A subway comedy (tragedy).
11. A school athletic rally (play, exhibition).
12. A gymnasium (or other athletic) contest.

ASSIGNMENTS IN WRITING DESCRIPTIONS FOR THE SCHOOL PUBLICATION

Exercise 360

On the preceding page there is a picture of Hermit's Retreat, located near Echo Lake in the Sierra Nevadas of California. During a vacation trip you may have seen this oddly picturesque place and learned the story of the man who formerly lived there. If not, you have doubtless visited other unusual places either near your home or in other parts of the country. Select the most interesting place that you know and write a good description of it. Use the questions in Exercise 349 to guide you in planning and writing your description. You may combine narration and description as your subject and your purpose may demand.

Exercise 361

Write a good description of an animal or a group of animals that you have observed at your home, in a pet shop, in a park, in a circus, in a zoölogical garden, or on a nature hike or hunting trip. You may combine narration and description as your subject and your purpose may demand.

Exercise 362

Every town or community has at least one familiar character who stands out from his fellows because of some unusual characteristic. Study the list of subjects given on the following page and choose one of them, or a similar subject suggested by them. Plan a description of your character, to be written either in prose or in verse.

Description

Before beginning to write, decide on the most characteristic pose and situation for the person to be described. Set definite limits to the picture. Choose also your point of view and maintain it throughout. Do not try to include every detail, but bring out the dominant characteristics.

If you choose the verse form for your picture, study "Old Susan" as a model. This form and other types of verse are explained in Chapter XXV. Select the form that seems to make your picture most lifelike.

1. Bill Gates, our football star.
2. Old Charley, the fruit (candy) vender.
3. Tony, the hurdy-gurdy (balloon) man.
4. Sancho, the tamale (ice-cream) vender.
5. An old street beggar.
6. The leader of the school band (the cheering section).
7. The village postmistress (postmaster).
8. The one-armed gate-tender at the railroad crossing.
9. An old fortune-teller.
10. Patsy Ann, our cook (laundress).

Exercise 363

Sometimes you think that only persons who have had unusual experiences or who have seen unusual things can write poems. Yet all around you are subjects for poems, if only you see them. In this exercise are two short poems, the first by one of America's best-liked modern poets, the second by a high-school pupil. Each writer has taken a very commonplace object as her subject; yet neither poem is commonplace.

What are the concrete details in each poem that help to create the picture? To what sense or senses does each poem appeal? What are the most vivid picture-making words? How are comparison and contrast used? What single impression do you get from each poem?

The Pear Tree

In this squalid, dirty dooryard,
  Where the chickens scratch and run,
White, incredible, the pear tree
  Stands apart and takes the sun,
Mindful of the eyes upon it,
  Vain of its new holiness,
Like the waste-man's little daughter
  In her first communion dress.

EDNA ST. VINCENT MILLAY

City Trees after Snow

Desolate yesterday;
Shivering branches violet gray.

At night the stars sent down —
In pity of earth's nakedness —
A part of their own loveliness;
Tiny gleaming star-shapes
Lent each tree a crown.

Humble bushes, graceful trees,
For one brief ecstatic day
Stood in radiant array —
None so beautiful as these.

That was just for one brief day;
Now the city has turned them gray.

Written by a High-School Girl

After you have studied these poems, select and bring
to class other short descriptive poems in which very ordinary subjects are made attractive through the author's
skill in describing them.

Silver[1]

Slowly, silently, now the moon
Walks the night in her silver shoon;
This way, and that, she peers, and sees
Silver fruit upon silver trees;
One by one the casements catch
Her beams beneath the silvery thatch;
Couched in his kennel, like a log,
With paws of silver sleeps the dog;
From their shadowy cote the white breasts peep
Of doves in a silver-feathered sleep;
A harvest mouse goes scampering by,
With silver claws and a silver eye;
And moveless fish in the water gleam,
By silver reeds in a silver stream.

WALTER DE LA MARE

In this short poem Walter de la Mare, a modern English poet, has given a still more imaginative picture of familiar objects. The magic of the moonlight has transformed everything.

Study the details of the poem and try to see each picture clearly. What is the single impression that the poem gives? Count the number of times the word *silver* is used. Is this repetition justified? Point out the unusual words.

Exercise 365

Perhaps you would enjoy writing a short descriptive poem. First determine the dominant characteristic of your subject and decide what single impression you wish to give. Then do your best to picture clearly and enter-

---

[1] From "Collected Poems," by Walter de la Mare. Henry Holt and Company, publishers.

tainingly the person, scene, or object that you have chosen to describe. Include only a few essential details. Use picture-making words that suggest as well as describe.

In Chapter XXV you will find an explanation of verse forms, rhythm, and other details of poetic composition.

If you have difficulty in finding a subject, the following suggestions may help you:

1. An airplane in flight.
2. A flower garden by moonlight.
3. An April shower.
4. A tree beside a pool.
5. Fireflies on a summer night.
6. A sleeping child.
7. Skating by moonlight.
8. Frost fairies.
9. Open-fire fancies.
10. A mother hen and her brood.

Exercise 366

Describe in verse a picture in this book or a picture of your own selection that is familiar to your schoolmates.

Exposition

171. What Exposition Is

We are constantly asking and being asked such questions as How do you solve this problem? Why is there no dew on cloudy nights? What were the Crusades? Who were the Druids? How are sound motion pictures made? An adequate answer to each of these questions is an exposition, for it *explains* something.

We employ exposition daily in giving information to others. We use it in recitations, reports, class discussions, and examinations. We explain certain processes, as the making of an airplane model, a radio set, a motor ice-boat, a lamp shade, a cake, or a Japanese dish garden. With our associates we discuss topics of current interest, vacation plans, and numerous facts and ideas. We express our opinions concerning things that we have observed, heard, or read. When we apply for a position, we set forth our qualifications. In fact, whenever we explain anything, we use exposition.

Exercise 367

Out of the specimen paragraphs in Chapter VII select five that are expositions. On what basis did you make your selection? State the specific purpose of the author of each. How does exposition differ from narration? from description?

172. How to Explain a Subject Clearly

Clearness is most important in all exposition. No matter how familiar we are with a subject, unless we present it so clearly that our meaning is easily understood, we fail to give a satisfactory explanation. The suggestions and references given below will aid us in explaining our subjects clearly:

1. Choose your subject carefully and limit it properly. Be sure that you thoroughly understand it before you try to explain it to others. If you need more information, investigate the subject, talk with persons who have an accurate knowledge of it, or consult books or periodicals. (See sections 3, 4, and 31 and Chapter XXIII.)

2. Consider thoughtfully your subject and its possible interest to your audience or readers. Try to put yourself in their place. Answer accurately these questions: For what class of persons is my exposition intended? How much may I rightly assume that they already know about my subject? What points will require most explanation? To make my explanation complete, what details must be included? (See section 5.)

3. Think clearly in planning your exposition. Choose the necessary material, and arrange it properly by means of a good outline. The nature of your subject will determine whether you will follow the order of time or the order of logical sequence between topics. Test and revise your outline before you attempt to give your exposition. (See sections 6–7 and 32–36.)

4. Begin your explanation with a brief introduction of a sentence or two that will arouse the interest of your audience or readers and that will lead up to your subject as directly as clearness will permit. As you proceed, show the relation of one topic to another by the use of connective words. Keep to your subject. When you have completed your exposition, bring it quickly to an appropriate conclusion. (See sections 39–41 and 88–89.)

5. Adapt your vocabulary to the understanding of your audience or readers. Use words that are correct and that express your meaning accurately. Such words as *gadget* and *device*, and almost all slang words, are inexact. Whenever you employ an unfamiliar word, particularly a technical term, be sure to define it. (See sections 9–10, 131–133, and 135–139.)

6. Do your best by your choice of a subject, by your treatment of it, and by your oral delivery or the form of your manuscript to make your exposition attractive and entertaining. And most important of all, make your explanations clear. (See sections 8, 42–44, and 267.)

173. Giving Reports

Oral and written reports, in which we tell how something is done or explain something that we have seen, heard, or read, constitute the most common type of exposition. Our knowledge of the process we may have obtained through experience, observation, investigation, or reading. A satisfactory report explains *How?* and *What?* Oftentimes it answers also one or more of the questions *When? Where? Who?* and *Why?* In giving a report we usually follow the order of time, though sometimes the nature of our subject necessitates the arrangement of topics in their logical order. Occasionally the two orders are combined. Since most processes involve action, persons, and machines, we make use of narration as well as exposition in explaining them.

Exercise 368

Study as examples of exposition of a process the directions given in two of the sections of this book listed below. Is each clear and easily understood? Does it give you a complete explanation of the topic? Do you find in either of them a combination of the time order and the logical order of arrangement? Explain your answer.

1. Effectiveness of Speech, section 8.
2. General Directions for Retelling Closely What We Read, section 17.
3. Making Recitations and Giving Reports, section 21.
4. Writing Examinations, section 22.
5. Directions for Making a Précis, section 24.
6. Directions for Retelling by Expanding, section 26.

Exercise 369

The high-school pupils who wrote "How We Earned Our Car" (see Exercise 22) and "The Making of Our School Magazine" (see Exercise 111) gave reports of processes. Study these reports in connection with the outline for each. Show how the writer of each embodied most of the suggestions given in section 172. Why did he combine the time order and the logical order in explaining the steps of each process? How many of the six questions mentioned in section 173 are answered in this report?

Exercise 370

Give orally or write, as your teacher may assign, a clear and entertaining explanation of one of the processes listed below. Plan your exposition carefully by means of an outline. If you explain your subject orally, you may be able to make your explanation more vivid by the use of a model, a picture, a map, a chart, a diagram, or a rough sketch. The questions in Exercises 27, 45, and 50 will help the other members of the class to estimate your success in explaining your subject.

1. How to Perform a Card (Coin) Trick.
2. How to Make a Tailored Bow (a Patchwork Quilt).
3. How to Interpret a Weather Map (Statistical Chart).
4. How to Make a Linoleum-Block Cut (Block Print).
5. How to Cook a Meal Out-of-doors.

© Ewing Galloway

Making Cider for Halloween

6. How to Judge a Horse (Cow, Dog).
7. How to Weave an Indian Basket (a Rag Carpet).
8. How to Make Maple Syrup (Molasses, Beet Sugar).
9. How to Make Walnut Fudge (Cottage Cheese).
10. A process of your own choice.

Exercise 371

In a certain English class each pupil was asked to study some local industry and write a report of a process that he or she observed. One pupil wrote the report given below. Study it with reference to the suggestions in section 172. Which of the questions mentioned in section 173 does it answer? Is the report clear? Can you suggest any improvement?

The Casein Industry

One of the most interesting and unusual industries is the manufacture of casein, used in making buttons, billiard balls, and various other articles.

Of the comparatively few casein factories in the world, one is located near Pennellville, New York, in the heart of the dairying section. This small plant employs about twenty men. Let us view the process from the dairy barns to the refinery.

The milk is produced by tuberculin-tested herds and brought by truck to the plant, where it is received into a large modern weighing room. The milk is drawn through pipes to the steam separator. The amount of milk handled in a day ranges from 25,000 to 125,000 pounds. After being separated, the skimmed milk is put into an enormous heating and agitating tank, where it is treated with rennet. When it has been heated to a certain temperature, the yellowish curd settles, leaving a watery whey. After the whey has been drawn off, the curd is washed through several waters to remove fats, acids, and other impurities. It is then pressed under great rollers into a hard, moist, clay-like substance. Next it is run through a hot-air dryer, for if it is left damp, it will quickly spoil. After being dried, it goes into the grinders, and comes out a creamy powder.

' The whey, a by-product left from the casein, is boiled down to a thick brownish mass. It is then shoveled into draining vats and later dried. When it is dry, it resembles salt, though it is much darker in color. This, after being refined, is used in preparing food for babies and invalids and in making sugar pills.

The powdered casein goes through a secret refining process at Bainbridge, New York. It is colored many different colors or made into imitation ivory. After being rolled into sheets three-sixteenths of an inch thick by a yard square, it is sold to manufacturers of novelties. In these various factories it is made into billiard balls, umbrella handles, lamp bases and shades, trays, pen holders, cigar and cigarette holders, combs, beads, 'and many kinds of buttons.—*Written by a High-School Boy*

Exercise 372

Lectures, field trips, school assemblies, club meetings, and various public entertainments will provide material for reports. The pupil's report given below is a good illustration of expositions of this type. What order of arrangement did she follow? Which of the six fundamental questions does the report answer? What is the effect of using a few brief quotations from the lecture?

Lorado Taft's Clay Talk

If he had never in his life "sculped" anything more artistic than a mud pie, Lorado Taft might easily have made his fortune just talking. Armed with a thousand witticisms, a mass of modeler's clay, several green trunks, and one student helper, the sculptor appeared at Randolph-Macon College last Monday evening and completely captivated an audience of over five hundred students and townspeople.

Before he had talked many minutes, the speaker divested himself of his Tux coat, which he confessed that he wasn't used to, and "only wore in the first place so you'd know I had one."

He got to work all right. Omitting all explanations except those necessary to make his demonstration clear, Mr. Taft donned a ragged smock and showed how and where and why.

"I always use a lead pipe inside my figures, so that I can bend 'em any way I want to," he observed, giving the illustrative figure a friendly pat that bent him double.

"Painters can't do that," he remarked. "If they put the head in the wrong position they have to scrape it off and begin all over again. And what becomes of the paint? It's wasted. Now when I get an ear too large as I did just then, all I do is pinch off a little, and use it somewhere else. Just like this, see?" Here the artist removed half an ear, which he used as a curl to decorate the forehead.

Having finished modeling the head of a man, Mr. Taft uncovered a large preconstructed head of Marie Antoinette. He introduced the lady, and immediately put her through the most astonishing of antics known to clay heads.

A few deft twists of his wrist, and he produced a smiling queen. Fear followed with a few more lightning touches of his clever hands. He made her majesty laugh, cry, grow old, lose her teeth, grow a pug nose, Romanize it, and turn to a man, in the course of fifteen minutes; and then after letting her make "an expression of horror as an encore," he covered her tenderly with a wet blanket and "put her to bed."

Marie had a score of successors — too many to enumerate — yet not enough for his audience, who felt a "thrill that comes once in a lifetime." — *Written by a High-School Girl*

Exercise 373

Write a clear and accurate report of one of the following:

1. A public lecture.
2. A school assembly.
3. A class or club election.
4. An athletic meet.
5. A local celebration.
6. A school entertainment.
7. A field trip in science or history.

Exercise 374

Write a "promotive" report of about fifty words on some book that you have recently read and enjoyed. In your brief report, which should be written on a single card of convenient size for filing, show that you have read the book carefully, and try to interest others in reading it by mentioning some of its most attractive points. The cards may be filed alphabetically in a case and be used by members of the class as a guide to further outside reading. The two specimen reports given below were written by high-school pupils.

GLORIOUS ADVENTURE. By RICHARD HALLIBURTON. Bobbs Merrill Company. $5.

Have you ever had a burning desire to swim the Hellespont, climb Mt. Olympus, visit the island of the Sirens, or any other of the interesting places that Ulysses visited? If so, why not follow "Dick" Halliburton on his Glorious Adventure? The book is humorously written, and is full of banter.

BOY'S LIFE OF THE WRIGHT BROTHERS. By M. V. CHARNLEY. Harper and Brothers. $2.

Handicapped by meager education, the Wright brothers studied heavier-than-air flights in spare moments. Experiments were made in this unknown field. Difficulties that baffled the leading scientists of the world these men surmounted. They came out on top, "The Fathers of Aviation," and gave the world the fastest mode of transportation known. In this easily read volume one may watch the Wrights develop into the foremost aeronautical scientists of the age.

Exercise 375

After making yourself thoroughly familiar with one of the following subjects through investigation and research, write an accurate and entertaining report. Supplement your knowledge by interviewing well-informed persons and by reading articles in books and magazines relating to your subject. From the school and public libraries you can get much helpful information. In your report be sure to give due credit to your sources. (See Chapter XXIII.)

1. How a Chamber of Commerce Helps a Town.
2. The Court Procedure in a Trial before a Jury.
3. The Making of Sound Motion Pictures (Phonograph Records).
4. How a Telephoto (Teletype) Machine Works.

5. The Organization of Labor in a Federal Penitentiary.
6. How the Grapefruit (Seedless Orange) Was Developed.
7. Home Life of the Ancient Greeks (Romans, Hebrews).
8. The History of the Alphabet (Metric System).
9. The Work of the Spanish Missions in the Southwest.
10. A research topic suggested by your teacher.

Exercise 376

At the beginning of each major division of this book you will find a sketch representing one stage in the development of the art of writing. Study these pictures, and then get from your library all the information that you can on this subject. Prepare a report, to be given orally or written, as your teacher may assign. In your report refer to the sketches as illustrations.

174. Defining Words

A definition, which is the simplest form of exposition, is an explanation of what a word means. Defining a word consists in limiting its meaning and explaining it as clearly as possible in more familiar words. A definition should be stated as concisely as clearness will permit.

The procedure in defining nouns and verbs is illustrated in the examples given below.

Word	Genus or Class	Differentiæ or Distinguishing Details
A *pen* is	an *instrument*	used in writing with ink.
A *square* is	a *rectangle*	having equal sides.
A *sentence* is	a *group of words*	expressing a complete thought.
To *speak* is	*to utter vocal sounds*	for the purpose of communication.
To *sing* is	*to utter vocal sounds*	with musical inflections or melodious modulations.
To *relate* is	*to narrate, tell,* or *recount.*	
To *remember* is	*to hold in mind* or *retain in memory.*	

In defining each of the first five words just given, there are two steps: (1) identifying the word and limiting its meaning by stating that it is a member of a certain genus or class designated by the general word or phrase in the second column; (2) limiting its meaning still more narrowly by giving in the third column those specific details that distinguish it from other words included in the same class. In the last two definitions the meaning of each verb is adequately limited and explained by the word or phrase denoting the class and serving as a synonym for the verb defined.

Adjectives, adverbs, prepositions, and conjunctions, as well as many verbs, are defined by the use of synonyms — words or phrases — designating the class to which the word defined belongs. The following examples illustrate the process:

> *To desert* is to leave or abandon.
> *To malign* is to slander or traduce.
> *Curious* means habitually inquisitive or prying.
> *Precious* means of great worth or value.
> *Bravely* means courageously or valiantly.
> *Then* means at that time, immediately, or next.
> *Into* means to the inside of or within.
> *But* means however, still, nevertheless, yet.

In making definitions we should bear in mind the following points:

1. The word or phrase denoting the class should limit the word to be defined as narrowly and as accurately as possible.
2. The word or phrase denoting the class should be of the same part of speech as the word defined.
3. Choose the necessary distinguishing details with care. Be sure that they are accurate and complete.
4. Use words more familiar than the word defined.

5. Avoid using in the definition of a word the word defined or a word derived from it.

Incorrect: *Narration* is something that is *narrated.*
Correct: *Narration* is the recounting of an event or a series of events.

6. Do not attempt to define a word by the use of a *when*-clause, a *where*-clause, or a *what*-clause.

Incorrect: A *lie* is *when* a person tells a falsehood.
Correct: A *lie* is a falsehood.
Incorrect: A *park* is *where* people go for recreation.
Correct: A *park* is a tract of ground used for recreation.
Incorrect: *Clothes* are *what* people wear.
Correct: *Clothes* are a covering for the body of a human being.

7. Express each definition in a complete sentence.

Exercise 377

Test the first two groups of definitions in section 174 by applying to the definition of each word the seven points given at the end of the section.

In each of the following definitions point out the error or errors and write the definition correctly:

1. Education is the process of educating someone. .
2. A square is a geometrical figure having four sides.
3. Recreation means to take some kind of exercise.
4. A prison is where prisoners are confined.
5. To vulcanize is when you repair a tire.
6. Destitute means poverty, need, or want.
7. Pasteurization is to destroy harmful bacteria.
8. An eclipse is what happens when the moon obscures the sun.
9. A sentence is a group of words containing a subject and a predicate.
10. To define a word is an explanation of its meaning.
11. An automobile is a vehicle that runs on four wheels.
12. A noun is a word used as the subject of a sentence.

Without the aid of your dictionary write an accurate definition of each of the following words. State in parentheses after each definition the name of the part of speech that you defined. Test each definition by means of the seven points given in section 174.

elude	triangle	tranquil	dairy	among
salary	renovate	stadium	swim	release
vacant	reliable	postpone	polite	soon
circle	quietly	expensive	almost	garage
verify	cyclone	rashly	botany	profitable

Exercise 379

Many terms require a paragraph or several paragraphs to explain their meaning clearly. Study as examples of such longer definitions the two paragraphs in section 23 and the first paragraph in section 83. Note the use of contrast in the first two paragraphs. In the third paragraph both contrast and comparison are used.

Find in one of your other textbooks and bring to class a definition requiring a paragraph or more. Did the author use illustrations, comparison, or contrast?

Exercise 380

Write a good paragraph in which you explain clearly the meaning of one of the terms given below. Use illustrations, comparison, or contrast as your subject and your purpose may demand.

rayon	school spirit	free verse	vocational guidance
cellophane	open shop	social science	student government
probation	income tax	self-reliance	juvenile court
courtesy	sportsmanship	sound pictures	intelligence tests

175. Discussions and Editorials

Discussion, both oral and written, plays an important part in our education and social intercourse. In our classes and clubs we explain facts, theories, and principles. With our associates we discuss numerous topics connected with our home, school, and community life. We give our opinion of assembly speakers and programs, school activities, and various social affairs. Almost every day we acquaint others with certain of our plans, our ambitions, and our likes and dislikes.

Expository editorials constitute one of the commonest types of discussion. Editorials usually deal with the more important current events, though they may deal with any other topic possessing timely interest. The purpose of editorials of this kind is to explain facts and events, to point out their significance, and to guide readers in forming intelligent opinions.

As high-school pupils, we have the opportunity to write for our school publication editorials on a great variety of subjects. In writing an editorial we should get an accurate knowledge of the facts, consider them thoughtfully, and then explain them clearly. "The language of the editorial," as one editor has said, "should be crystal clear, the diction so simple that every reader may understand, and yet the editorial should show a fine choice of words to express exactly the editor's thought." In the opinions that we express and in the criticisms that we make, we should at all times be fair and honest.

Exercise 381

In the specimen printed below, the writer comments on an interesting fact that many of you have observed. Notice how clearly and simply the subject is explained. Point out the topic sentence in each paragraph.

Grocery Windows

The chain grocers are showing independent proprietors how to dress windows and shelves and to make goods advertise themselves. The typical old-time grocer made no visual appeal with merchandise either to the passerby or to the customer. Windows were considered simply sources of light. Shelves were regarded merely as depositories of cans and packages. Counters were devices to place bundles on. The middle of the floor was occupied by flour and sugar barrels, baskets of potatoes, the coffee mill, etc.

The chain grocers have so dressed their windows that they are almost as attractive as those of the department stores. By so arranging the foods and packages that colors blend or contrast, and by giving each window a definite scheme, the chain grocers often stop the pedestrian or motorist and persuade him to drop in. It has remained for these window artists to show the beauties of common articles of food.

It is about the same inside the shops. The chain grocers are utilizing all available space far more cleverly than the corner grocer of a decade or two ago. Goods are displayed attractively between the aisles. Wares are placed invitingly on shelves. Counters are likely to be of glass, with groceries constantly under the eye of the buyer. The chain grocers have discovered the value of silent salesmen. — *Boston Herald*

Exercise 382

Study as discussions of facts the selections listed below. Analyze each specimen to show the logical order in which the material is arranged.

1. "Carving Your Speech," Exercise 31.
2. "The Value of Précis Writing," Exercise 67.
3. "Mental-Health Conditions," Exercise 71.

Exercise 383

Give orally or write, as your teacher may assign, a discussion of one of the topics listed below. Make a good outline to guide you. Use illustrations, comparison, or contrast as your subject and your purpose may demand.

1. My Favorite Novelist (Poet, Artist, Actor).
2. Five Qualities Necessary for Success in Life.
3. My Idea of a True Sportsman (Good Student).
4. A Balanced Diet in Reading (Recreation).
5. The Meaning of Agricultural Conservation.
6. The Importance of the Gasoline Engine on the Farm.
7. Why People Leave the Country to Live in the City.
8. Some Advantages (Disadvantages) of Coeducation.
9. Why I Have Chosen _____ as My Profession.
10. A topic of your own choice or one suggested by your teacher.

Exercise 384

Study the expository editorial given below. Do you get the meaning easily from one reading? What did the editor do in addition to explaining his subject?

The Boy Scouts Come of Age

Forever young in membership and ideals, tomorrow a great organization comes to manhood in its corporate history. On February 8, 1910, the Boy Scouts of America received a charter under District of Columbia laws and opened national headquarters. February 8, 1931, constitutes, therefore, its twenty-first birthday. A robust and manly element for the nation's good it surely has made itself! Nearly 5,000,000 boys have been enrolled in it through the years. More impressive still, as an evidence of the American spirit of willing interest, 964,982 men have offered themselves and been registered as volunteer assistants of the Boy Scouts during this period. Despite business difficulties of the past year, new records were set in the organization's activities and current membership. On December 31, 1930, more than 865,000 boys were enrolled. Thanks to an increase of five per cent in the work of the Scout camps, nearly 400,000 American boys had actual camping experience during the year. More than 160 colleges conducted scouting courses and some 50,000 Scout leaders enlisted for study of a five-years training program.

In this metropolitan district, the Boston Council of the Boy Scouts of America has 4000 boys enrolled. It operates a summer camp at Loon Pond in Middleboro, accommodating 300 boys during each week of the season. All in all, there is no better or more serviceable single organization devoted to the happiness and the upbuilding of the male youth of this nation. As the Boy Scouts attain their twenty-first birthday, we salute and wish them long life. — *Boston Transcript*

Exercise 385

What is the source of the title of the following editorial? Why is it appropriate? What is the purpose of the editorial? Show that the diction is clear, simple, and exact.

It is for Us, the Living —

The great war began sixteen years ago, before some of the present high-school students were born; it ended twelve years ago, before most of them entered the primary grades. We of high-school age can now observe certain effects that the war has had on nations and people. More particularly, and more personally, we note its effect upon the people of this nation. If certain of these effects are politically and socially unhealthy, is it not well for us who are now maturing to recognize them? If these effects are evils, shall not we in our generation be the sufferers unless we combat them? We are conscious of restlessness under authority, of the rise of philosophic codes to replace the old moralities, of contempt and distaste for thrift, of the demand for the enjoyment of luxuries not earned or not deserved, of calling "old-fashioned" the habits and ideals that were accepted as a matter of course before the war, of no sense of shame in placing our responsibilities upon the shoulders of others, of the lessening of the old virtues of chivalry and respect. We have forgotten the fundamental law of compensation. Nor do we realize that we, individuals, peoples, and nations, get from the world only what we give. We must sow, and then patiently await the harvest. In a very few years we must make our decisions. — *Written by a High-School Pupil*

Exercise 386

Read several editorials in current newspapers, and bring to class the one that you consider the best. Does it deal with a current event narrated in a news story elsewhere in the paper or in a recent issue, or is it a discussion of some other topic of timely interest? State briefly the editor's purpose. Is the editorial clearly written in language that is simple and exact? Do the opinions expressed seem fair and honest?

If your school publishes a paper, select an editorial from a recent issue, and discuss it by means of the questions given above. Can you suggest any improvement in it?

Exercise 387

Write an editorial for your school or local newspaper. The suggestions given below may help you to find a limited subject of school or community interest.

1. A recent event.
2. A needed improvement.
3. Greater coöperation.
4. Traffic regulations.
5. Better motion pictures.
6. A commendable act.
7. Fire protection.
8. Nature study.
9. Citizenship classes.
10. Boys' (girls') camps.

176. Reviews and Criticisms

A satisfactory book review, which deals with both the author and his book, answers the following questions: (1) What is the book about? (2) What was the author's purpose in writing it? (3) To what extent did he succeed in achieving his purpose? (4) How does the book rank in comparison with other books by the same author or with similar books by other writers? In answering the first question we should give the reader sufficient information to arouse his interest and help him to decide whether or not he cares to read the book, but we should not write a complete summary of it, for to do so will lessen his interest in the book itself. Answers to the other three questions involve a critical estimate of the book and constitute the real review. To answer these questions adequately demands close study of the book, an acquaintance with the author's other works, and some familiarity with the writings of other authors on the same subject or in the same field. Obviously, our review will carry more weight if we support our statements with specific examples, comparison, and contrast.

In reviewing a book, we should give our own honest impression of it independently of what others may have said or written about it. We should write in our own style and use our own words. Imitating more experienced reviewers and critics is rarely helpful, for we are tempted to borrow their learning and to try to write in a clever, sophisticated style that is not our own. We may express enthusiasm for a book, but we should avoid the overuse of superlatives.

The procedure in estimating the value of any other work of art, whether it be a poem, an essay, a short story, a play, a picture, a piece of sculpture, or a musical composition, is much the same as that involved in reviewing and criticizing a book. We should consider the creator, what he has done, and how well he has done it. In criticizing a theatrical performance we should first deal with the play and the playwright and then with the acting, the scenic effects, and similar details of production.

Exercise 388

In what respects does the following specimen satisfy the requirements of a good book review? What evidence can you point out that the writer formed his own impression of the book? Do the style and diction seem to be the writer's own?

LITTLE AMERICA. By Rear Admiral RICHARD E. BYRD. G. P. Putnam's Sons, New York. 416 pages. $5.

Commander Richard E. Byrd, in his book "Little America," has woven an intensely interesting story out of his recent expedition into the Antarctic regions. This expedition is now recognized as one of the outstanding contributions to science in recent years. Commander Byrd has written "Little America" for the casual observer and admirer of his accomplishments; as a scientific record he has written a detailed treatise in four volumes containing the observations and the intricate calculations made by the expedition.

The first chapter of "Little America" is a reproduction of extracts from Commander Byrd's journal, through which the reader gets an intimate impression of the commander himself. With the modest hesitation characteristic of the great explorer, he explains that it was only at the urgent request of friends that he included these accounts of his own activities before and during the early part of the voyage. The great responsibility of providing for eighty-two men for two years in the far South fell to the young commander, who considered the preparation far more difficult than the actual expedition. The other chapters are devoted to the various experiences of the expedition. Although such an undertaking was naturally attended with many hardships and anxieties, the chronicle of events is replete with humorous incidents.

The book is made vastly more interesting by the numerous photographs and maps of the polar regions. The pictures, remarkable for their clarity considering the unfavorable atmospheric conditions, along with many explanatory diagrams, aid the author greatly in describing the equipment and the living conditions of the men.

As a conclusion to the book, Commander Byrd has expressed the feeling that lures so many explorers on their journeys. "Glad as we were to be back in the comparative luxury of

© Wide World Photos

A Canadian Ice Castle

Little America, it was with a feeling akin to the forlorn that we looked back at our sledge tracks disappearing into the limitless white to the south. We had had a good time and had, in some measure, known the joy of achievement."

"Little America" has been included in many lists of interesting books for boys. It contains all the thrills and adventures of an exciting boys' story, and is, at the same time, an interesting, instructive book for adults. Critics have considered it, on the whole, a very well-written book despite the fact that its aim has not been literary excellence. — *Written by a High-School Pupil*

Exercise 389

In a newspaper or a magazine find and bring to class a review of a book that you have read. Be prepared to show in what respects the review is satisfactory and to suggest improvements, if any, that might be made.

Exercise 390

Write a review of a modern novel that you and other members of your class have read. Do your best to make your review satisfy the requirements explained in section 176.

177. Character Sketches

1. Formal. A formal character sketch is an estimate of the life, qualities, and achievements of a person. In a character sketch we interpret the facts of narrative biography; that is, we try to show how the personality, ideals, ambitions, struggles, and achievements of our subject make him or her a significant figure. We may choose as our subject either a real person or a character in literature.

2. Informal. An informal character sketch is the portrayal of a person by giving those traits and habits that constitute, for the writer at least, the most interesting aspects of his personality. It is not an analysis of character; nor need it be, except for humorous purposes, a caricature or a cartoon in words. To as great an extent as possible, we should allow the subject of the sketch to reveal himself to the reader through what he does, what he says, and what effect he has on others. These we may supplement, if necessary, by giving certain characteristic mannerisms and other individualizing details. The sketch should be written in the familiar style of good conversation.

Examine carefully the formal character sketch given below. Point out the elements of character that the writer has included.

Joan of Arc

The work wrought by Joan of Arc, heroine, martyr, and saint, may fairly be regarded as ranking with any recorded in history, when one considers the conditions under which it was performed, the difficulties that lay before her, and the means at her disposal. A poor, unlettered peasant girl found her nation in the enemy's power, helpless, disheartened; because of years of oppression, its king was preparing to flee the country; and she, the peasant maid, "laid her hand upon that nation, that corpse, and it rose and followed her." The greatness of Joan of Arc lies not in her victories in war but in the greater victories over self. She, who saved one of the proudest of nations, and restored the crown to its monarch, remained always the pure, sweet maid who had listened to the "voices" and obeyed their divine summons. For her great service she was offered rewards and honors, but she would have none of them. All she desired was leave to return home to tend her sheep again and be her mother's handmaid. The nation she had saved allowed her in reward to be burned at the stake. But justice prevailed, tardy though it was. The world today salutes her as a saint, and youth and age alike find inspiration in her noble example. — *Written by a High-School Pupil*

Exercise 392

Write a brief character sketch of a relative, a friend, or some other person whom you know well. Or, if you prefer, you may take as your subject a well-known character in a novel, a play, or a poem. Try to discover through a close study of your subject the fundamental elements in his or her character. Illustrate and support your statements by referring to incidents in the person's life.

In what respects do the specimens given below satisfy the requirements of an informal personal sketch? Do you find them entertaining? Is the style formal or informal? Brief though they are, does each give you a satisfactory understanding of the subject?

Swan

Every small town has its "character" — a person who knows everybody else's business as well as his own. In this respect, Lone Oak is not behind the rest. In fact, Lone Oak possesses a very original one. He is known by the entire population of thirty-six as "Swan," though he insists that his correct name is Mr. Swan Holm.

Swan was born in Sweden in 1864, and there he lived until he was eighteen years old. It was then that his eyes turned towards the ocean, and he sought America as his new home. After wandering about for several years, seeing life in the large cities, Swan decided that he himself was his best friend. Those wild city ways were too much for him; accordingly, he secluded himself in the wilderness of Lone Oak, which had not at that time attained its name. There he purchased an acre of land, constructed for himself a tiny concrete house, and was at peace with the world. His house is only a three-room affair, but no house could be neater, cleaner, and daintier than his. Every day he cleans it and sets it in order. He rises at six o'clock, sweeps, scrubs, and dusts. He washes his clothes; he shines his silverware and plates; in fact, he cleans everything, although nothing ever becomes dirty.

By profession Swan is a cook. He delights in casting reflections on the pastries of the neighboring women. He greatly enjoys giving them "pointers" on the art of salad-making. It is no wonder that he is often referred to as "the old maid," for he has two beautiful hobbies, very suitable to any spinster. One is collecting pretty dishes; the other is making paper roses.

There is hardly anything in the history of Lone Oak that Swan does not remember. Whether he writes everything in his diary or just remembers it is a mystery to me. He can tell, for instance, the day that Will got his first long trousers, when each of the Mooney children got his first tooth, and the birth date of everyone in town. He likes to ask questions, and then respond to them himself. Every Sunday night he visits around at the neighboring houses. During these visits he relates everything that he saw and heard the Sunday before, asks numerous questions, and comments on the methods of modern housekeeping. He comes into Mrs. McCarthy's, shakes hands with all the family, and then begins, "Now, you must be nearly forty. Yes, you're thirty-nine, because you were married the same year that the big storm occurred in Minneapolis, and that was in 1905."

Swan is a man of affairs. In the summer he takes care of his flower beds in the afternoon, after he has finished cleaning house. He reads the newspaper from beginning to end, nor does he forget a thing in it.

Swan is content. His life is simple and happy. His only fear is that someone with muddy shoes will walk into his house and leave tracks on his spotless kitchen floor. — *Written by a High-School Girl*

My Alarm Clock

In one respect I am a very fortunate person, and, needless to say, I am perfectly aware of the fact. Indeed, it is brought to my attention so often that I cannot help being conscious of it. I need no alarm clock to awaken me every morning. Now, do not attribute this to my superior will-power, but give all the credit to my neighbor.

Mrs. Noyes lives opposite me. My back yard, but nothing else, joins us. Sleep, I think, she does not, for then she could not talk. Moreover, one may hear her bustling about the house late at night and early in the morning.

About six-thirty she announces to the neighborhood that she is awake. "Bill, it's time to get up," she calls. "Don't you dare sleep another minute."

Then she proceeds to beat up an egg (I think it's an egg) with great vigor. I often wonder why the bowl doesn't break, for bowls break by merely being dropped. While she prepares her son's breakfast, she holds discourse with her husband, a most unfortunate man. In a voice that may be heard for blocks, and speaking as a commander to his army, she gives him his instructions for the day. He utters not a word.

Next she calls her daughter Myrtle, though I cannot understand why Myrtle must be awakened, for by this time there is no sleep for anyone in the vicinity. Generally Bill and Myrtle appear for breakfast at about the same time, whereupon their mother proceeds to admonish them liberally and to give them their orders for the day.

She is usually at her best when her husband and two children are about to leave for their work. "Myrtle, wear your coat. Bill, you be home on time. Father, do just as I say." Such are the orders that ring through the house and follow them down the street.

For five days of the week I don't mind being thus awakened, but on the sixth and the seventh I suffer. On these two mornings I find it very hard to understand how one can be expected to love his neighbor as himself. — *Written by a High-School Girl*

Exercise 394

In your own community there is doubtless a "character" or some other person fully as interesting as the two about whom you have just read. Choose someone who is well known to you, and write an entertaining informal character sketch of him or her. (It will probably be best to use a fictitious name for your subject.) If you wish, you may select a person familiar to other members of the class and, without mentioning his or her name, identify the person for your classmates by means of your sketch.

178. Familiar Essays

A familiar essay is expository in nature, informal in style, and personal in treatment. In subject matter and style it resembles intimate social letters in which we comment on what we have experienced, observed, thought, or felt. Like such letters, it is written as a means of self-expression and for the entertainment of our reader. Like such letters, too, it reveals our personality both by what we say and how we say it, and gives the impression that we have enjoyed writing it.

We may take as our subject ourselves, other people, animals, nature, or any of the thousand and one things, serious, commonplace, or trivial, connected with the business and pleasure of living. The chief requirement of the familiar essay is that it be made entertaining to the reader. This we can best do by selecting a subject that greatly interests us and then treating it in an animated, natural, personal style. Our finished essay should be so well written that it makes easy and enjoyable reading for others.

Exercise 395

Examine closely each of the familiar essays given below. Notice the informal, personal style in which each is written. Do you find the essays entertaining? Do you get the impression that the authors enjoyed writing them?

"My Garden in Winter" in Exercise 186 is a good essay on a nature subject. "Personality and Pencils" in Exercise 189 is a familiar essay that you will doubtless enjoy reading again.

A Job for Job

The job I detest most is teaching a girl to drive a car. Not only does it require a great deal of courage and diplomacy, but one must have the patience of a school-teacher as well.

From the moment she enters the car, attired as if she were going to a party, until she leaves it, I am in a state of nervous suspense. I head the car toward the country, and on the way I explain every operation in detail; but she hears nothing, for she is fixing her hair. I politely call her attention to the fact that she is not listening to me, but the only answer I get is "I've just washed it and it simply won't stay up." As if I cared!

Upon reaching a wide level road, we change seats. I caution her about feeding too much gas and about letting the clutch out too quickly. With one hand on the emergency brake and the other on the door, I say as calmly as I can, "Let's go."

She never fails to step on the gas and let the clutch out with a jerk. After much grinding and racking she shifts gears, and we go zigzagging along as if she had just come from Cuba. She invariably selects without effort the roughest part of the road and never misses a chuck hole. When turning a corner, she steps on the gas instead of the brake, and while we are bumping along she proceeds to search through her pockets. Finally she brings it forth, that never-absent badge of femininity, a powder puff, and with the aid of the rear-view mirror, she calmly primps and powders, while the car careens worse than ever under the guidance of one hand.

This caps the climax. I bring the car to a sudden stop. She pauses in the act of banishing an imaginary shiny spot on her nose and asks, "What's the matter?"

"That's all for today," I reply, as we change seats.

When I am once more behind the wheel, my heart resumes its normal beating. I am more fully convinced than ever that girls were made to run sewing machines, not automobiles. — *Written by a High-School Boy*

On Being a Girl

A girl has a hard time of it, especially if her chief ambition is to be a boy. I shall never become resigned to being a girl, for really I don't believe that I was intended to be one. There must have been a mix-up somewhere.

When I was younger, I used to split kindling, bring in wood and coal, build fires, rake yards, and otherwise do boys' work. That always seemed proper enough; but when I wanted to go out and climb trees, chase dogs, throw rocks, or play football, I was considered a little "rowdy."

Boys have always treated me with a degree of awe and contempt. I am strong and can hold my own in wrestling, running, or swimming, but alas, I am — a girl. Now that I'm in high school, it is worse, much worse. If I go out and "chunk" horse-shots, play "fox and hound," or go skating with the younger members of the vicinity, the neighborhood is shocked, but not beyond words. No, I should sit at home with my feet placed just so — never crossed — my hands folded in my lap, and, with a smile on my face, listen to stupid comments from the opposite sex. Think of listening and smiling politely when I'd much rather be tinkering around with a saw, a hammer and nails, and a screw-driver!

Because I'm a girl, I must go through life bored to death. I cannot be a carpenter. Never shall I be able to take a course in architecture, mechanical engineering, or textiles over at Tech. My highest ambition, to be an electrical engineer, can never be realized because I was so unfortunate as to be born a girl. Never shall I be able to be in a night-shirt parade, or take a girl to a fraternity dance, or have some "dame" madly in love with me, — I'd like to spurn the silly thing, — or be on a football team, or yell "Rah for Tech! Down with Georgia!"

Oh, the unfairness of this world! Would I had been born a boy! — *Written by a High-School Girl*

Exercise 396

If possible, read several other familiar essays as a means of becoming better acquainted with this enjoyable type of writing.[1] Then select a good subject — one that interests you greatly and on which you have some original thoughts — and write an entertaining familiar essay. Perhaps the following suggestions may help you to find a subject:

1. Teaching a Boy to Cook.
2. On Keeping a Secret.
3. Vacation Discomforts.
4. My Two Selves (Natures).
5. On Being Misunderstood.
6. Personality in the Handshake.
7. Curiosity in Animals.
8. If I Could Choose My Name.
9. On Answering Advertisements.
10. The Attraction of Fresh Paint.

[1] Tanner's "Essays and Essay-Writing" (Little, Brown and Company, Boston) contains sixty-nine brief familiar essays and two hundred and fifty subjects for familiar essays.

ASSIGNMENTS IN WRITING EXPOSITIONS FOR
THE SCHOOL PUBLICATION

Exercise 397

What are the chief industries of your city, town, or
community? Is there one that is unusual? Select an industry that your classmates will enjoy learning about, and
when you have made yourself thoroughly familiar with
it or one of the processes involved, write an accurate and
entertaining report. It will probably be necessary for
you to visit the factory, observe the process, and get
information from some of the workers.

Exercise 398

Write for your school publication a good editorial on
some recent event or other topic that is of school interest.
You may find the following list of suggested subjects
helpful:

1. What We May Learn from the Last Athletic Meet.
2. Personal Assets and Liabilities in School.
3. How Our Assembly Programs Might Be Improved.
4. How We Waste Time in School.
5. What It Means to Think for Oneself.
6. The Value of Vocational Guidance (Military Training).
7. Advantages of Membership in the Interscholastic League.
8. Setting the Freshmen a Good Example.
9. The Obligation of Our School to the Community.
10. Every Week a " Better-English Week."
11. What It Means to Be a Camp Fire Girl.
12. A Balanced Diet in Reading.
13. How to Decrease Traffic Accidents.
14. The Advantages of a School Bank.
15. A subject of your own choice or one suggested by your
teacher.

Exercise 399

Write for your school newspaper or magazine a review or a criticism of one of the following:

1. A recent novel.
2. A book of poems.
3. A short story.
4. A single poem.
5. A painting (statue).

6. A play that you have read.
7. A play that you have seen.
8. A radio play.
9. A motion-picture play.
10. A marionette (puppet) play.

Exercise 400

Profiting by the experience that you gained in Exercise 394, write a better informal character sketch for your school publication. The list of subjects below may suggest a local "character" or some other person whom you know well and in whom your classmates will be interested. You may consult the list of subjects in Exercise 362 also for suggestions, but in writing this assignment do not rest content with a mere description. Try to make your subject reveal himself, as did the persons in the specimen sketches that you read in Exercise 393, by means of what he does, what he says, and what effect he has on others.

1. The village censor.
2. A country doctor.
3. Our postman (ice man).
4. A fish peddler.
5. A junk dealer.

6. An old-maid aunt.
7. Our wild uncle.
8. Our Beau Brummel.
9. An old soldier (sailor).
10. An amateur detective.

Exercise 401

Are you thoroughly familiar with the individual traits and habits of some pet or other animal? If so, you may enjoy writing an informal character sketch of the animal. The third specimen in Exercise 350 is taken from an entertaining sketch of a cat.

Exercise 402

Now that you have learned more about the familiar essay from your experience in Exercise 396, write the best familiar essay that you can for your school paper. One of the titles listed below, or one of those given in Exercise 396, may suggest to you a good subject.

1. How to Lose Friends.
2. The Art of Bluffing.
3. Convenient Deafness.
4. Dog (Horse) Language.
5. My Forgetting System.
6. Family Superstitions.
7. Fashions in Suicide.
8. My Book of Bores.
9. How to Become a Genius.
10. Personality in Hats.
11. On Playing a Saxophone.
12. The Monotony of Being Good.
13. The Pleasures of Loafing.
14. The Proper Training of Parents.
15. "Thoughts that Arise in Me."
16. The Magic of Seed Catalogues.
17. On Choosing a Necktie.
18. The Humor of Being Serious.
19. How to Keep Awake in School.
20. A subject of your own choice.

CHAPTER XV

Informal Argument

179. What Argument Is

In our association with people disagreements frequently arise. On such occasions we usually try to influence our opponent to agree with us. If we disagree with a friend regarding some opinion or belief, we try to induce him to accept our way of thinking. If he criticizes a certain action of ours, we seek to justify it. If he desires to study for an examination and we want to play tennis, we endeavor to persuade him to do as we wish. Often, anticipating disagreement, we defend our belief or conduct against possible opposition. Whenever we attempt, by giving reasons or evidence, to get another person to think as we do, to approve a policy or a course of action that we propose, or to do something that we desire done, we make use of argument.

Argument involves two important processes: convincing and persuading. We *convince* a person when we induce him by logical reasoning to give up his belief and accept our own. We *persuade* him when we lead him, through appeal to his emotions or motives of self-interest or altruism, to act in accord with what we have led him to believe. When Antony, in Shakespeare's "Julius Cæsar," proved to the people that Cæsar was their friend and had not deserved death, he convinced them. When he went a step further and by appealing to their emotions and passions aroused the mob to drive the murderers of Cæsar from the city, he persuaded them to act.

180. Exposition and Informal Argument

All arguments contain a certain amount of exposition, for we must make our hearers and readers understand before we can convince and persuade them. Sometimes a clear and logical explanation is all that is needed to lead people to accept our belief and to act as we wish, but more often they must be won over by argument. An informal argument is a logical discussion in which we support each important point with a sound reason. We give evidence in the form of concrete details, specific examples, or the opinions of reliable authorities to show why our statements are true, or why a policy that we propose should be accepted or a course of action should be adopted.

Exercise 403

Study as examples of brief informal arguments the specimen paragraphs in Exercises 187, 190, 202, and 207. Study also as informal argument the explanation given in section 115 and the sixth specimen paragraph in Exercise 209. State what the author of each selection is trying to prove. What reason or reasons does he give to show that what he says is true?

Exercise 404

Examine closely the informal argument given below. What is the author trying to prove? What are the three main points of his argument? Make an outline showing the topic of each paragraph.

Industries of the United States Should Adopt a Five-Day Week

For some time the people of the United States have been confronted by two very important questions: How can the greatest number of workers be assured of employment adequate to render them economically secure? and How can waste resulting from overproduction be avoided? Of the many plans that have been proposed as answers to these questions the adoption of a five-day week, which provides for five consecutive days of work and six days' pay, seems to promise the most satisfactory solution. The fact that the number of industrial plants operating on this plan has steadily increased during the past five years recommends it for serious consideration. Since the adoption of such a plan concerns workers, employers, and the general public, let us see how it affects each of these classes.

The five-day week benefits workers in many ways. The two-day period of relaxation from the strain of routine work answers the need expressed by William Green, President of the American Federation of Labor: "There must be a progressive reduction in the hours of labor so that men may have time to rebuild exhausted physical energies." It also gives them more time and incentive to improve living conditions in their homes. They have more time for family and social life and for recreation and amusement. They have likewise greater opportunity for educational improvement through wider association, reading, and visiting museums. Assured of an extra day of their own, many workers are encouraged to enjoy Sunday as a day of rest and spiritual refreshment. Finally, shortening the week by one day gives employment to a larger number of workers.

The five-day week benefits most employers. Workers, given an extra day of their own and having six days' wages, buy more manufactured articles to supply their increased needs. Henry Ford, who adopted the five-day week for all his plants in 1926, said: "A workman would have no time for an automobile if he had to labor from dawn until dusk. If, on the other hand, he enjoys a five-day week, his wants increase on the sixth day. He needs an automobile, more food, more music, more books — more happiness." Commenting on the advantage of the five-day week to both employer and worker, the manager of the Pelican Paper Company, of San Francisco, says: "Besides showing an increase in profits under the five-day week plan, we have given every employee his regular six-day salary with two weeks' vacation with pay. . . . Sales are showing an increase of eighteen per cent over last year, when we had a six-day week. With many workers enjoying the five-day week in San Francisco, there arose a greater demand for books. The Pelican Paper Company received eighteen per cent more orders. Then, in order to take care of this increase in orders, many unemployed men were given positions." The greater demand for commodities resulting from the increased needs of workers not only gives jobs to more men and women but helps to avoid waste from overproduction. To stimulate buying and selling, factories and trades might adopt a Monday-to-Friday week and merchants and owners of service and recreational institutions might agree on a Tuesday-to-Saturday week.

The five-day week is of great benefit to the general public. It insures a healthier and happier citizenship. In the opinion of many ministers and sociologists it tends to decrease crime. By providing jobs for more people it brings about better living conditions, and by lightening the burden of caring for the unemployed it helps to lower taxes. Edward A. Filene, a prominent merchant of Boston, said, "I consider the five-day week as a force that will bring about a reduction of waste in industry." Freer spending by workers results in establishing a more reliable economic balance, which tends to stabilize wages and prices and lessen the probability of overproduction.

Since the five-day week has thus far proved the best means of assuring the greatest number of workers employment that will render them economically secure, and since it benefits employers and the general public by helping to avoid waste through overproduction, it should be adopted by the industries of the United States.

Exercise 405

With a classmate select for an informal argument a good subject relating to your school life. State your subject clearly in a sentence. Then, after choosing the side — affirmative or negative — that you will argue, prepare an informal argument to be given at the next meeting of the class.

Exercise 406

The subject of an argument is called a *proposition*. A proposition should always be stated *affirmatively* in a short simple sentence; as, "Industries of the United States should adopt the five-day week."

Formulate and state correctly three propositions that relate to your school, town, community, or state.

181. Straight Thinking

Whether we are arguing with ourselves, as in making a decision, or with someone else, the necessity for straight thinking is the same. The process involved in straight thinking includes three steps: (1) analyzing the question or proposition to discover all the reasons *why* and *why not*; (2) comparing and weighing the arguments for and against; and (3) reasoning logically from these arguments to reach a decision or conclusion. Our success in arguing will depend mainly on our ability to think clearly.

Exercise 407

Write at the top of a sheet of paper the question "Should I use the money that I have to buy a radio, or should I save it and go to a camp next summer?" Divide the remainder of the sheet vertically into two equal columns. Head the left column "Why should I use the money that I have to buy a radio?" and the right column "Why should I save my money and go to a camp next summer?" Under each of these questions list as many reasons as you can think of why you should adopt that course of action. Next, compare and weigh these arguments carefully. Then, use logical reasoning in reaching your decision. At the bottom of the sheet state your decision as a proposition in the form of a simple affirmative sentence; as, "I should use the money that I have to buy a radio" or "I should save my money and go to a camp next summer."

Exercise 408

Using the system of straight thinking that you employed in Exercise 407, make a trustworthy and satisfactory decision on one of the questions given below. State your decision in the form of a proposition.

1. Should I elect French or Spanish as my required foreign language?
2. Should I go to college or get a job upon graduating from the high school?
3. Should I buy a sports suit or a suit (dress) for more formal wear?
4. Should our state provide textbooks for high-school pupils, or should each pupil buy his own books?
5. A question of your own choice or one suggested by your teacher.

182. What is Meant by Proof

Merely *asserting* that something is true does not *prove* that it is true. Proof, which is a logical demonstration that cannot be successfully denied, requires that a proposition be adequately supported by evidence. It is the result of sound reasoning.

The chief responsibility, or *burden of proof*, in an argument rests on the person who advocates a proposition. If, for example, we favor the proposition "Buying articles of luxury on the installment plan is unwise," the burden of proof rests on us to show that the statement is true

183. What is Meant by Evidence

The material used to prove a proposition is evidence. Evidence is of two kinds : that of *fact* and that of *authority*. Evidence of fact consists of concrete details, specific instances, circumstances, records, statistics, or similar mat-

ter that supports an argument. Evidence of authority
consists of the statements of persons who, as trained observers or specialists, are capable of forming reliable opinions. This latter kind of evidence carries more weight
when the opinions that we quote have been recently given
by a person who has accurate knowledge of the subject
and who is either unprejudiced or, if prejudiced, admits
facts in favor of our side of the proposition. Both kinds of
evidence are useful in argument, but evidence of fact is
usually regarded as more convincing than evidence of
authority.

Exercise 409

In each of the following groups of sentences indicate the
proposition. Then tell whether evidence of fact or evidence
of authority is used to prove it. Do you find both kinds
of evidence employed in any group?

1. I paid this bill last month. Here is the receipt, and here is
my check for the full amount, indorsed by the payee.

2. Marion is absent from school because of illness. Dr. Rowe
says that she has the measles.

3. "The skeleton found in the Stone-pit is that of my brother
Dunstan," said Godfrey Cass. "There beside it were his watch
and seals and my gold-handled riding-whip, with my name on it.
He took the whip the day he went hunting on Wildfire, the last
time that he was seen."

4. "Dunstan is the man who robbed Silas Marner," said Godfrey
Cass. "Dunstan was badly in need of money. The gold found
near the skeleton was that stolen from the weaver."

5. Motion pictures showing the methods used by gangsters and
other criminals tempt many boys to go wrong. Such pictures
appeal to boys' love of dangerous adventure and to their desire
for money and prestige in the life of the underworld. "Seven boys
out of every ten who are brought before me," says Judge Adams,
"have confessed that motion pictures depicting crimes led them
to become criminals."

184. Methods of Proving a Proposition

Of the several methods of using evidence to prove a proposition let us consider the following:

1. Proof by direct demonstration. Direct demonstration is one of the most widely used and conclusive methods of proving the truth or falsity of a proposition. It is very generally employed by salesmen. "This chemical will put out a fire instantly," says an agent for fire extinguishers. Thereupon he kindles a fire and sprays it with the liquid. If the fire is immediately extinguished, he has proved his statement — and perhaps made a sale.

2. Proof by specific instances and examples. We can frequently prove a proposition true by giving several instances and examples. If we say "The radio has become a nuisance in many American homes," and show how, in the experience of our own family and in that of several other families, the radio causes waste of time, neglect of work, loss of sleep, and quarrels over programs, we have supported our statement with evidence. The instances that we give should be representative, not exceptional, if they are to be convincing.

3. Proof by analogy. Suppose that a farmer says: "The fertilizer that I used on my wheat last year increased the yield. Wheat and rye are similar plants. If I use the same quantity of this fertilizer on similar soil where I plant rye, it should increase the yield of rye also." In reaching his conclusion the farmer employed analogy. He assumed that, since wheat and rye are similar plants, the result of using the same fertilizer would be the same for both kinds of grain.

4. Proof by circumstantial evidence. What we assume to be true we can often show to be in all probability true by using circumstantial evidence, which consists of definite facts and concrete details that support our assumption.

©.Publisher's Photo Service

Golf Course at Greenwich Country Club

A coroner, for example, may assume that a man found dead has been dead for only a short time. If he finds that the watch in the man's pocket is still running and that there is not more than a day's growth of beard on his face, he supports his assumption with circumstantial evidence that justifies the conclusion that the man has been dead not more than twenty-four hours.

5. **Proof by testimonial evidence.** Many propositions involving the placing of responsibility for an action can be proved true or false by means of the testimony of unprejudiced eye-witnesses who accurately observed the action. If, for example, one or more persons who have seen a collision of two automobiles testify that the driver of the car coming out of a side street entered the through street at high speed and failed to look in each direction or give any

signal, this testimony proves that the driver was reckless and is, therefore, responsible for the collision.

6. Proof by citing authority. We often find it necessary to support statements intended to prove a proposition by giving the opinion or the decision of a specialist who is acknowledged to be an authority on his subject. We accept as true the statement "'Othello' is Shakespeare's best constructed tragedy" if the person who makes it supports the proposition by quoting the opinion of several recognized authorities on the drama.

7. Proof by reasoning from cause to effect. Frequently by reasoning from known causes we can foretell or account for an effect. Following the World War, for instance, steamship companies prepared to accommodate a larger number of European tourists than they had ever before transported. They reasoned thus : "Since European travel has been suspended for several years, since everyone is curious to see Europe in its post-war condition, and since more Americans than ever before have money to spend for travel, the number of tourists will be very large." As experience later showed, they reasoned accurately from causes to effect.

8. Proof by reasoning from effect to cause. From a known effect we can sometimes reason back to a cause or to several causes and thus prove our proposition. If Godfrey Cass had been a detective, he might have solved the mystery of Dunstan's disappearance and the robbery of Silas Marner sixteen years earlier than he did. He would probably have begun with the effect, the theft of the weaver's gold. Instantly there would have arisen the question, What causes may have led to the theft? Among other causes would have come a very weighty one, namely, a serious need of money. Then he would have proceeded : "Dunstan needed money. He was on his way to sell Wildfire when he accidentally killed the horse. Without this means of getting money, it seems very probable that he stole the weaver's gold." This conviction would have been confirmed by the fact that Dunstan had not been seen since the robbery. Thus, by reasoning from effect to cause, Godfrey would with considerable accuracy have identified Dunstan as the robber.

Exercise 410

From the following list select five propositions that interest you. Dramatize in your mind each proposition that you choose and try to discover the best means of proving that it is true. Come to class prepared to give your proof of each. If there seem to be two or more methods of proving a proposition, give them all and let the class decide which is the most convincing.

1. A cheap used car generally proves very expensive to the owner.

2. John Corey is innocent of the crime of which he is accused.

3. The fire seems to have been caused by an overheated furnace.

4. The desire for money is the principal cause of crime.

5. This liquid will safely remove stains from silk fabrics.

6. Cod liver oil is a food rich in vitamins.

7. The house had been deserted less than a week before.

8. The robbery was evidently committed by someone formerly employed at the factory.

9. The supply of used cars will exceed the demand next year.

10. Travel by air will never entirely supplant travel by land and water.

11. In the family that last occupied this house there must have been an invalid.

12. Americans are the most wasteful people in the world.

Exercise 411

Formulate five propositions of your own, and tell what method or methods you would use to prove each of them.

185. Fallacies in Argument

A fallacy, which is an error in reasoning, impairs or destroys the validity of an argument. To argue successfully, we must reason logically and consistently and be able to point out and answer the fallacies in the arguments of our opponents. The most common fallacies are the following:

1. **Drawing conclusions from insufficient evidence.** If we say "During the past year five public officials have been found guilty of taking bribes; therefore all public officials are dishonest," we are jumping at conclusions and making hasty generalizations; for the instances cited are but a small proportion of the total number of instances implied in our conclusion.

2. **Unreliable evidence.** Evidence of authority and testimonial evidence are trustworthy only when the person who gives the evidence has full and accurate knowledge and is unbiased and honest. When a dealer states "The car that we sell is the best on the market" or a boy's mother says "I know that John did not take the money, for he has never stolen anything," the statement of neither can be taken as reliable evidence, for each is prejudiced.

3. **False analogy.** If we say "American readers will like this novel, because it was very popular in England," we are employing false analogy; for American and English readers have tastes that differ in many respects. The man who replies to an insurance salesman "Since I have never had an accident, I see no reason for carrying accident insurance" is guilty of the same error in reasoning; for conditions in the future are not likely to be the same as in the past. We can depend on analogy only when the relation between two things is accurately understood and when the two things are in all important respects similar, or when the conditions on which we base our reasoning are the same or can be relied on to remain unchanged.

4. Mistaking the cause. In attempting to account for a certain result or effect, we should not allow ourselves to be misled or try to mislead others by jumping at a conclusion and assigning a wrong cause. "I am not going to send my son to college," says a father. "Many a man who went to college is now a failure in business." Obviously other causes are responsible for the failure of these men; hence the father's reasoning is fallacious. Belief in superstitions often leads persons to reason inaccurately. For example, a superstitious person may say: "I am not surprised that she has had a lot of bad luck. She broke a mirror two years ago. Breaking a mirror always brings seven years of bad luck."

5. Begging the question. When we assume without evidence or argument that we have proved a proposition, we are said to beg the question. If we say "The illegal contract should be broken," we are begging the question. We must prove, not assume, that the contract is illegal. We commit a similar error when we reason in a circle, thus: "Installment buying and selling should be abolished, for it is economically unwise; we know that it is economically unwise because it is a practice that should be abolished."

6. Ignoring the question. When we evade, either through intent or through ignorance, the real issue or issues of an argument and come to an irrelevant conclusion or arrive at a logical conclusion by means of illogical reasoning, we are said to ignore the question. In such cases, instead of supporting our statements with real evidence as proof, we appeal to passion, prejudice, or selfish desire in our hearers or readers; we divert their attention from the real question by humor or satire; we try to overawe our opponent by quoting from authorities opinions that may have little relevancy; or we take refuge in tradition or custom that is out of date.

Exercise 412

In each of the following sentences or groups of sentences point out and explain the fallacy or fallacies in the argument:

1. My mathematics teacher does not like me. I have never received a grade higher than C in mathematics.

2. John has gone swimming. His bathing suit is not in his room.

3. A bed is a dangerous place; for, as Mark Twain observed, most people die in bed.

4. That is certainly a becoming green dress. I am going to get one just like it.

5. The brutal practice of hazing freshmen should be prohibited in all schools and colleges.

6. Jealous people are never happy; for, if they were happy, they would not be jealous.

7. I feel much better since I had my appendix removed. You would have better health if you had your appendix taken out.

8. I know that the driver of the truck was to blame for the accident. My brother, who is a careful driver and always tells the truth, said that the truck driver was to blame.

9. The threatening letter was written on paper that had the same watermark as that found in the accused man's desk. That proves that he wrote the letter.

10. It would be absurd to require high-school girls to wear uniforms. Think of how unattractive they would look! Besides, it would mean a loss of money to merchants and dressmakers.

Exercise 413

Report to the class an instance of fallacious argument that you have recently heard or read. You can probably find an advertisement that will serve as a good example.

186. How to Prepare and Give an Argument

In preparing and giving an argument, oral or written, we should proceed according to a definite system, such as the following:

1. Be sure that you understand clearly just what it is that you are going to argue about. State the proposition accurately in a brief *affirmative* sentence. For example: "All social clubs in our school should be abolished."

2. Get all the information that you can about *both* sides of the proposition. If necessary, talk with well-informed persons, interview specialists, and read articles in magazines and books written by recognized authorities.

3. Analyze the proposition carefully by making note of all the reasons for and against it. In this way you will be able to discover the issues; that is, the points to be proved in your argument.

4. Make an outline in which you provide for a brief introduction and list the points at issue in logical order. Under each point at issue, which will form a main topic of your outline, list the reasons or evidence that you will use to prove that point. Provide for a brief conclusion, which will consist of a summary of the points that you have proved.

5. Determine the best method or methods to be used in arguing each point in your outline and in proving the proposition (see section 184).

6. Test your outline to see if you have been guilty of any fallacy in reasoning (see section 185). It is far better to discover fallacies for yourself than to have an opponent later point them out for you and thus weaken your argument.

7. Expand your outline, which is the skeleton or framework of your argument, into a coherent and forceful discussion. Provide for your hearers or readers all the information and evidence that they will need, but do not include unnecessary material.

8. Whether you speak or write, rely on evidence and logical reasoning, not on unsupported assertions and cleverness, to convince and persuade your audience or readers. Try to make it easy and enjoyable for them to follow your argument.

Exercise 414

If a classmate were to ask you "What harm is there in copying another pupil's home-work?" or "What difference does it make if I get another pupil to tell me one answer in a test?" how would you proceed in trying to convince him or her that such a practice is wrong? Suppose that, after considering the question carefully, you formulate a proposition and list the principal reasons that you will use to support your argument. You will then have a tentative outline showing the plan that you will follow.

Proposition: Cheating in school is wrong.

Reasons:

1. The pupil who cheats is stealing.
2. He deprives himself of an education.
3. He destroys his self-respect.
4. He injures his reputation.
5. He hurts the reputation of his school.
6. He is a discredit to his family.
7. He weakens his character.
8. He prepares the way for more serious crimes.

The eight reasons enumerated constitute the principal topics of the outline, but at present they are nothing more than assertions. Using the tentative outline given, expand it by listing under each main topic evidence that will support it. Provide a brief introduction, and then prepare an argument to be given orally in class. Use as your conclusion a summary of the points that you have proved.

Exercise 415

Using one of the propositions in Exercise 410, or one of your own selection, prepare a good argument to be given orally or written, as your teacher may assign. Follow the system explained in section 186.

187. Argument in Salesmanship

We think of ourselves as salesmen when we induce a person to buy a commodity; as, a book, a radio, or an automobile. By a slight extension of the meaning of the term, we are likewise salesmen when we induce others to think as we think or do what we propose; that is, we "sell" them a belief or a course of action. Whether we are making a personal sales talk, writing a selling letter, preparing an advertisement, recommending a person, or indorsing a policy, we instinctively make use of argument. Whenever we anticipate or actually encounter sales resistance, we try to break it down by convincing our "customer" that he, and perhaps others, will be benefited by what we are "selling"; then, since the purpose of salesmanship is to make a sale, we endeavor to persuade him to buy the commodity or act as we recommend.

Exercise 416

Examine the selling letter given in Exercise 150. In what respect is it an informal argument? Show how the writer makes use of persuasion. How would pictures and drawings in the booklet that the writer inclosed help to make a sale? If the booklet contained testimonial letters from satisfied users or statistics showing how the weather-strips saved fuel, what methods of argument would they represent?

Exercise 417

From magazines and newspapers select and bring to class two of the best advertisements that you can find. Explain the use of argument in each of them. Which one has the stronger "pulling power" in inducing the reader to buy the commodity advertised? Why?

Exercise 418

Come to class prepared to give a good sales talk in which you try to induce your classmates to buy some article or commodity. Use direct demonstration or support each main point in your sales argument by some other kind of appropriate evidence.

Exercise 419

Suppose that you have invented and have secured a patent for some article or device. In a letter to a manufacturer explain what the article or device is, and try to induce him to agree to manufacture and market it for you. If you have drawings and pictures of it, submit these with your letter.

Exercise 420

Suppose that the library committee of your school has agreed to buy twenty-five new books recommended by pupils. The committee requests each pupil to propose one book, either fiction or nonfiction. When you have chosen a new book that you think would make a valuable addition to the library, tell who the author is, explain clearly what the book is about, and give several good reasons why the committee should buy the book.

Exercise 421

Using one of the propositions given below, prepare an oral or a written argument, as your teacher may assign, in which you try to "sell" the idea, belief, or course of action to your hearers or readers.

1. A horse (dog, other animal) thinks.
2. The early American settlers treated the Indians unjustly.
3. Travel by air is safer than travel by land or water.

4. One assembly period each fortnight should be devoted to motion pictures that have some bearing on the work in school.

5. No pupil should be permitted to hold more than two school offices at a time.

6. We should elect _ _ _ _ _ _ _ _ _ editor of our school publication. (Nominate the pupil of your choice and state the reasons why he or she should be chosen.)

7. Our school should give a course in stenography and typewriting (advertising design, china painting, photography).

8. Students interested in photography should organize a camera club.

9. Juniors and seniors should form a Big Brother and Sister Club to help the freshmen.

10. A proposition of your own choice or one suggested by your teacher.

Exercise 422

The forum letter printed below is taken from a high-school magazine. Is it an effective informal argument? Explain your answer. Point out statements not supported by evidence. Do you discover any fallacies? Rewrite the letter, making the argument more convincing.

Dear Editor of the Forum:

During the past few weeks there has been much discussion of the status of athletics in our high school. A good many of the faculty and students are of the opinion that we should abandon all branches of sport save football and basket ball. I cannot understand such an attitude. Granted that we have not been very successful in track during the past few years, is that a reason why we should give it up? On the contrary, should we not devote more time and energy to track and field sports and try to bring them up to the high standard of other sports in the school?

In my opinion, track has been sadly neglected for some time. Let us support and encourage it as we do football and basket ball, and then it will succeed. There is enough material in school this year to develop a championship team. Therefore turn out for the team, even if you have never participated in this sport before. The trained eye of the coach may discover in you certain qualifications that may enable you to develop into a successful track star.

If everybody does his share, and then we fail, let us drop track as a scholastic activity.

Sincerely yours,
John H. Brennan

188. Argument in Editorials

Some editorials, as we noticed in the preceding chapter, are nothing more than explanations — discussions of current events or other facts, and comments on their significance. In many editorials, however, the writer argues for or against certain propositions. He may champion causes that he considers worthy of support. He may defend new ideas, beliefs, or policies against ridicule. He may favor or oppose a candidate for some office, a change of policy, or a proposed law. He may attack certain practices or denounce existing conditions and suggest remedies. Whatever proposition he may argue, the editor's purpose is to influence opinion and to lead his readers to act in accord with the policy that he recommends.

Exercise 423

Examine closely the following editorial. What proposition does the editor argue? Is his argument convincing? What support for his statements does he give? What specific improvement can you suggest?

More Work, Less Play

Are the school organizations fulfilling their original purposes? We think that they are not.

Most societies were organized originally for literary, oratorical, or other educational purposes. Nowadays, it appears that these societies are changing into mere social clubs. The time of the meetings is often taken up with initiating new members or planning for the next dance, and the program is crowded out.

Some students join school organizations to acquire knowledge, but a larger number seem to become members in order to gain popularity. After initiation, the attendance at regular meetings is usually rather small; but when the group picture is to be made, all the members are there with smiling faces.

Next comes the question, Who are the members of these various societies? In their own estimation, they are the aristocratic group of the school. How are they elected? Often a boy is voted in because "he's a good kid and I know him well," and a girl because "she's popular and dresses well." Many boys and girls who might carry out the original purposes of the societies and be benefited by being members are *not* voted in. In this way several societies have almost become fraternities and sororities.

When meetings are held, they are very loosely conducted. The rules of order are rarely observed. If a program has been announced, it is probably set aside for the discussion of plans for a reception. Often it is postponed because several members who were to take part are absent and those who are present have made no preparation. The societies, in general, are always talking about what they are going to do, but rarely do any of them carry out their plans, unless they are social.

All that has been said is the result of a study of the organizations in our high school. If they accomplish nothing more than they have this year, they might as well be disbanded, for they are a waste of time. It is to be hoped that the members of the various societies will see what a mistake they are making and arrange next session to hold interesting and profitable meetings regularly. Let us have more work, less play. — *Written by a High-School Boy*

Exercise 424

From local newspapers, your school paper, or other periodicals select three good editorials in which argument is employed. Come to class prepared to answer the following questions: What is the proposition that each editor argues? Does he favor or oppose it? Is his argument convincing? What evidence does he give to support his statements? What improvement can you suggest?

189. Informal Debates

A debate is an oral argument presenting both sides of a proposition. An informal debate is an open-forum discussion in which both designated speakers and members of the audience take part. Participation in informal debates will help us to develop skill in public speaking and the ability to think quickly and to judge an argument accurately.

The best proposition for an informal debate is one about which all members of the group have some definite knowledge and concerning which opinion is evenly divided. Ideally, the possible arguments in support of each side should be equally strong. The proposition should stimulate lively debate because of its immediate interest to the group. For this reason, it is best to choose propositions that have arisen out of our individual and group experience and that relate to school and local affairs.

Exercise 425

Organize your class into a debating society. Select a chairman and a secretary. The chairman will appoint two pupils, who, with your teacher, will constitute a committee to decide on the proposition for each debate. All other pupils in the debating society should be required to hand in one question each to the committee. From these questions the committee will select the best proposition. Your teacher will serve as a general adviser.

The chairman may call on pupils to suggest orally propositions to be considered for the first debate. The proposition finally selected should be stated in the form of a resolution; as, "*Resolved*, That one assembly program each month should be given entirely by pupils." The chairman will then appoint — from volunteers, if possible — two or three speakers to argue each side of the proposition at the next meeting of the class.

Exercise 426

Hold the informal debate for which you chose a proposition in Exercise 425. Speeches should be limited to from three to five minutes each, according to the advice of the teacher. The chairman will open the meeting by announcing the proposition and introducing the first speaker who supports the affirmative side of the proposition. When the first speaker has finished, the chairman will introduce the first speaker who supports the negative side. The order of speakers is affirmative, negative, affirmative, negative, and so on. When the speakers on both teams have completed their arguments, members of the audience may volunteer to give other arguments or answer arguments given by one or more of the speakers. Each speaker, whether he is a member of the team or of the audience, should begin his speech by addressing the chairman, the teacher, and the audience; as, "Mr. Chairman, Miss Andrews, and members of the debating society." At the end of the debate, the audience will vote to determine the winning side.

(If time permits, one or two other prepared informal debates should be held at later periods.)

Exercise 427

At the beginning of the class period a member of the committee will announce a proposition for an extemporary, or impromptu, debate. The chairman will then appoint two or three speakers to uphold each side of the proposition. The procedure thereafter will be the same as that followed in the prepared debate in Exercise 426.

(If time permits, one or two other extemporary, or impromptu, debates should be held at later periods.)

ASSIGNMENTS IN WRITING INFORMAL ARGUMENTS FOR THE SCHOOL PUBLICATION

Exercise 428

Suppose that some organization in your school has offered two tickets as a prize to the pupil who writes the best advertisement for one of the school attractions mentioned below. By your originality make pupils see and read your advertisement, and by your argument persuade them to attend.

1. A school play.
2. A benefit dance.
3. An art exhibit.
4. A glee-club concert.
5. An illustrated lecture.
6. Some other attraction.

Exercise 429

Write a feature article for your school paper in which you try to "sell" your school to prospective patrons as the best school in the city, county, or state. Or you may write a feature article for your local newspaper in which you try to "sell" your town, city, or community as a desirable place in which to live or as an advantageous manufacturing location.

Exercise 430

Write a letter to the editor of your school publication to be printed under the heading "The Forum" or "Student Opinion." In your letter call attention to a practice, an attitude, or a condition of affairs that should be changed, and propose a remedy. Do your best to "sell" your policy to your readers and to induce them to take action accordingly. The following suggestions may help you to find a subject:

1. A School Pest.
2. Fire Drills.
3. School Snobs.

4. School Sanitation.
5. Unnecessary Noise.
6. Lunch-room Manners.

Exercise 431

Write for your school publication an editorial on one of the subjects mentioned below. Try by a logical argument to lead your readers to agree with you and to adopt the policy or course of action that you propose.

1. The Menace of Slang.
2. Showing Off in Public.
3. Why Intelligence Tests?
4. What Is Wrong in This Picture?
5. Put Your English to Work.
6. Know Your School (Town, City).
7. Don't Be a Sponge (Knocker, Nuisance).
8. Protect the Reputation of Your School.
9. Larger Attendance at School Debates.
10. Student Conduct at Assemblies (in the Study Hall).
11. Should Our School Buy a Radio (Motion-picture Projector)?
12. What Are You Doing for Your School Paper?
13. Should Our School Continue to Publish a Yearbook?
14. What Shall We Do with Book Thieves (Library Pests)?
15. A subject of your own choice or one proposed by your teacher or the editor of your school publication.

◄ CHAPTER XVI ►

Debating

Preliminary Exercise I. Preparing for a Mock Trial

Conducting a mock trial in accord with the rules of court procedure is an entertaining way to begin a study of formal debating. Before attempting to hold such a trial, however, your class should make the following preparation:

1. If possible, attend an actual trial, and take notes on the way in which it is conducted. If this is not possible, obtain from a textbook of civics complete information as to the procedure in both civil and criminal cases.
2. When your class has gained accurate knowledge of the process involved in a trial, select a judge, a clerk of the court, a lawyer, or counsel, for the plaintiff, and a lawyer, or counsel, for the defendant.
3. Decide upon a fictitious case in which two members of your class are supposed to be involved as plaintiff and as defendant. State the case briefly and clearly from the point of view of the plaintiff.
4. Arrange to have witnesses in the case impersonated by two or three pupils on each side.
5. Allow the two lawyers, their clients, and the witnesses for their clients a day or two in which to prepare their side of the case. Each witness should invent and dramatize in his mind what he is supposed to have seen and what he is supposed to know. Each lawyer may devise documentary and circumstantial evidence that he thinks will help him to win the case.

434

Preliminary Exercise II. Holding a Mock Trial

Devote one class period to holding the mock trial for which you have been preparing. In conducting the trial proceed according to the following steps:

1. The clerk of the court will read the indictment, or charge.
2. Twelve pupils who have no prejudice regarding the case and who are acceptable to both lawyers will be chosen to act as jurors. The jury will take oath to decide the case fairly. The judge will appoint one member foreman of the jury.
3. The lawyer for the plaintiff will state what he intends to prove concerning the indictment brought against his client. Then he will proceed to question his client and each witness for his client. Each witness, after being placed on the stand, will take an oath, administered by the clerk of the court, to "tell the truth, the whole truth, and nothing but the truth, so help me God." Besides the testimonial evidence of witnesses, the lawyer may submit any other evidence that he may have.
4. The lawyer for the defendant will proceed in the same way to submit evidence to support his side of the case.
5. After his opponent has finished questioning his client or a witness, each lawyer may, if he desires, cross-question his opponent's client or the witness in an attempt to secure evidence that will strengthen his own side of the case. At the wish of either lawyer, a witness may be called back to the stand to testify.
6. When all evidence has been submitted, the lawyer for the defendant will make his plea for his client by summing up all the points of argument in his favor. Then the lawyer for the plaintiff will make his plea for his client by summing up all the points of argument in his favor. This speech will close the trial.
7. The judge will review the main points brought out on each side, explain the law involved, and charge the jury to give a verdict in accord with the law.

8. The jury will then retire to a private room. With the foreman as chairman, the members of the jury will discuss and weigh the evidence submitted in the trial, and then ballot to decide upon a verdict. The final vote must be unanimously in favor of either the plaintiff or the defendant.
9. The jury will return to the classroom, and the foreman will announce to the court the verdict of the jury.
10. If the verdict is in favor of the plaintiff, the judge will award a judgment or pronounce a sentence in accord with the law. If the verdict is in favor of the defendant, the judge will dismiss the case.

190. Formal Debating

The practice that we have had in holding a mock trial should help us in formal debating. A formal debate resembles a court trial in several respects. Both demand proof systematically built up by logical reasoning and supported by reliable evidence. The opposing lawyers in a court trial are represented in a formal debate by two groups of opposing speakers, called teams. In a formal debate, as in a court trial, there are fixed rules of procedure.

The preparation for a formal debate must be thorough. We must investigate fully the history of the question to be argued and discover all the principal issues, or points to be proved. We must gather from various sources evidence to support each issue for our side of the question, and we must have accurate information regarding *both* sides of the proposition. We must test all evidence carefully, and arrange it logically in the form of a complete outline, or *brief*. We must then develop our brief into a finished argument. Finally, through practice we must acquire the ability to think quickly and accurately while standing before an audience and the power to speak convincingly.

191. Joint Work of the Two Teams

Before each team attempts to prepare an argument for its own side of a debate, there are certain points to be discussed and decided upon by the two teams working together.

1. Choosing the question. The subject, or question, for debate should be satisfactory to both teams. It should be two-sided and capable of specific proof. Moreover, it should be properly limited and adapted to the ability of the debaters. The best subject is a timely one that is closely related to the experience of the debaters and that possesses decided interest for them and their audience. Furthermore, it should be a question on which debate will be profitable. Suppose that the members of two teams agree on the question "Should industries of the United States adopt the five-day week?"

2. Wording the question as a proposition. The question should be stated as an affirmative proposition in the form of a resolution. The proposition should be worded exactly and impartially, and be expressed in a simple sentence. A compound sentence should be avoided, for it will usually contain *two* propositions. The question above, stated as a proposition, will read: "*Resolved*, That industries of the United States should adopt the five-day week."

3. Deciding upon the origin and importance of the question. It is desirable that the two teams, after investigating the question, formulate a brief statement of its origin and importance. This statement will constitute the beginning of the introduction for the brief written by each team.

4. Agreeing upon the history of the question. The history of the question, which will serve as the background for the debate and give the audience necessary preparatory information, should be investigated, discussed, and agreed upon by the two teams.

5. Defining terms. It is important that the two teams agree upon the meaning of all words, or terms, used in stating the proposition. Each term that calls for more exact limitation or explanation, such as *five-day week* in the proposition mentioned above, should be accurately defined.

6. Deciding upon admitted matter. In order to save time and to focus argument on points in dispute, the two teams should decide upon those points that each is willing to admit without debate.

Exercise 432

Point out the error in each of the following propositions, and state the proposition correctly in the form of a resolution :

1. Boys and girls should not attend the same high school.
2. Capital punishment, which is morally wrong, should be abolished.
3. A pupil who fails in a subject should not be allowed to play on a school team.
4. Our school should establish a free dental clinic, and each pupil should be required to have his teeth examined twice a year.
5. Military drill, which is the best kind of physical training, should be required of all able-bodied juniors and seniors.

Exercise 433

Formulate three questions of school or local interest that you think would be good subjects for debate. Then state each question correctly in a simple sentence as an affirmative proposition and in the form of a resolution.

192. Finding the Main Issues

The members of each team, working independently, should begin the preparation of the argument for their side of the proposition by finding the main issues to be debated.

These can be found by answering the question, What are the principal points involved in the proposition on which there will be conflict of opinion? The main issues are usually not fewer than three or more than five, and each issue is stated briefly as a question. It is permissible for teams composed of inexperienced debaters to work jointly in discovering and formulating the issues for their *first* debate.

Exercise 434

Your class will be divided into teams consisting of three pupils each, and the teams will be consecutively numbered. Team 1 will debate with Team 2, Team 3 with Team 4, and so on. Teams designated by odd numbers will argue in favor of the affirmative side of the proposition, and teams designated by even numbers will support the negative side. Each pair of teams, working jointly, will begin preparing for a debate by choosing a satisfactory question — possibly one of those formulated in Exercise 433 — and stating the question affirmatively as a proposition in a simple sentence. No two pairs of teams should select the same question for debate.

193. Gathering Material for a Debate

In arguing certain questions relating to school and local affairs, we may have acquired from experience and observation all the information that we shall need; but in preparing to debate many other questions, we shall require additional information. This we may sometimes get from well-informed persons through conversation, interviews, and personal letters. More often, however, we shall find it necessary to obtain material from the library. Chapter XXIII contains directions and suggestions for using a school library. It will acquaint us with the use of the card catalogue and other aids in locating material that we need.

The list that follows contains the titles of several books, periodicals, and other publications from which we may get information on a variety of subjects for debate. We should not limit ourselves to this list, however, in our search for material, but freely investigate other sources.

1. Books for general reference. The Encyclopedia Americana, The Encyclopædia Britannica, The New International Encyclopædia, Nelson's Loose-Leaf Encyclopædia, Appleton's New Practical Cyclopedia, The Everyman Encyclopædia, The Annual Register, The Americana Annual, The New International Yearbook, The World Almanac, The American Yearbook, and The Statesman's Yearbook.

2. Documents and reports. *Congressional Record*, United States Census Reports, Statistical Abstract of the United States, United States Commerce Yearbook, United States Commerce Reports, and Congressional Digest.

3. Magazines. *Foreign Affairs, The Journal of Political Economy, The American Political Science Review, The American Journal of Sociology, The Graphic Survey, Child Welfare Magazine, Nation's Business, Journal of Farm Economics, The Educational Review, School and Society, The American Review of Reviews, The Literary Digest, Current History Magazine of the New York Times, The Forum, The Open Court, The New Republic, The Nation, The Outlook, The Atlantic Monthly*, and *Harper's Magazine*. The *Readers' Guide* and the *Education Index* are valuable in finding material from magazines.

4. Newspapers. Information relating to questions of current interest may be obtained from reliable newspapers, such as *The New York Times, The Springfield Republican, The Boston Transcript, The Chicago Tribune*, and *The Christian Science Monitor*. The *New York Times Index* is valuable in finding material from newspaper files.

5. Useful helps for debaters. Immel and Whipple's "Debating for High Schools," A. C. Baird's "Public Discussion and Debate," F. M. Phelps's "Debaters' Manual," "The Debaters' Handbook Series," "Reference Shelf," and Shurter and Taylor's "Both Sides of a Hundred Public Questions."

Reaching for It — A Debate in Action

194. Preparing a Brief for a Debate

A brief is a complete formal outline of the argument to be presented by a team in a debate. In making a brief we must not use phrases, as in an ordinary outline, but sentences. The topics must be arranged in correct logical sequence and be properly indented. The sections must be labeled to show clearly their relation one to another. A brief, which consists of *introduction, brief proper*, and *conclusion*, represents in condensed form the entire argument for one side of a proposition.

The *introduction* is expository, not argumentative. It presents a complete analysis of the proposition, and usually consists of five sections: (1) origin and importance of the question, (2) history of the question, (3) definition of terms, (4) admitted matter, and (5) main issues.

The *brief proper* presents the constructive argument supporting one side of the proposition. The principal divisions of the brief proper are the main issues contained in the final section of the introduction, but here they are expressed as affirmative or negative statements, not as questions. Under each principal division are arranged the points, evidence, and sources of evidence to be used in proof. Each topic, together with its supporting evidence, is expressed in the form of a complete sentence.

The *conclusion* consists of a one-sentence summary repeating the main issues and stating that the proposition, which is likewise repeated, has been proved or disproved.

A brief shows the outline of the argument on only one side of a proposition. The affirmative and the negative teams write their briefs independently of each other, though, when the two teams have done the joint work explained in section 191, the wording of all sections of the introduction except the *main issues* will be uniform.

Exercise 435

The groups of opposing teams formed in Exercise 434 will gather whatever material may be needed in preparing to debate the proposition chosen. Then each pair of teams will proceed to work out jointly the first four sections of the introduction in accord with directions 3, 4, 5, and 6 given in section 191. The result of this collaborative work should be written out in the form illustrated in the introduction to the specimen brief given in Exercise 436.

Exercise 436

Examine closely the specimen affirmative brief that follows. How many principal sections does the introduction contain? In the brief proper do you find as many principal topics as there are main issues in the final section of the introduction? Are they identical in expression? Observe carefully the system of indention and the use of roman numerals, capital letters, arabic numerals, and small letters, to indicate coördination and subordination of topics. Notice that each numbered or lettered main division, together with its subdivisions, is a complete sentence. Note also the use of *for* to indicate that each subordinate topic is a reason supporting the statement under which it stands. Observe, finally, the wording of the conclusion.

AFFIRMATIVE BRIEF OF THE CONSTRUCTIVE ARGUMENT FOR THE PROPOSITION

Resolved, That industries of the United States should adopt the five-day week.

INTRODUCTION

I. Origin and importance of the question

When Henry Ford adopted in the fall of 1926 the five-day week for labor in all his plants, the reform attracted much attention. A little later in the same year the American Federation of Labor announced the five-day week as its objective. Since that time interest in the plan has steadily increased among workers, employers, and the general public.

II. History of the question

A. Since 1908, when the eight-hour day and the forty-eight-hour week had been established in most industries, there has been constant agitation in favor of the five-day week.

B. During the past twenty years the five-and-one-half-day week has been generally adopted in various industries.

C. Between 1918 and 1926 several trades and industries in sixty-six cities of the United States, employing about 64,000 workers, adopted a week of five days, consisting in some industries of forty-four hours and in others of only forty hours.

D. In the fall of 1926 the Ford Motor Company, which then employed nearly 200,000 workers, placed all its plants on the five-day forty-hour week basis.

E. At the present time approximately 1,000,000 workers, employed in a wide variety of trades and industries, are enjoying the five-day forty-hour week.

III. Definition of terms

A five-day week is a forty-hour week consisting of five consecutive working days of eight hours each. All workers receive six days' pay, provided they do in five days as much work as they formerly did in five and one-half or in six days. They have two days of leisure every week throughout the year.

IV. Admitted matter

A. It is admitted that present conditions of labor demand remedy by giving employment to a larger number of workers.

B. It is admitted that it is desirable to avoid waste resulting from overproduction.

C. It is admitted that the employer has the right to reject the five-day week if, after a fair trial and coöperation on his part, there is a falling off in the normal production or in the quality of his product.

D. It is admitted that the change to the five-day week will have to be made gradually so that industrial progress will not be retarded.

E. It is admitted that the two consecutive days of leisure for workers would not of necessity be the same days of the week in all industries.

F. It is admitted that some industries are not at present in a position to adopt the five-day week.

G. It is admitted that the five-day week is less easily adopted in industries demanding continuous operation.

V. Main issues

    A. Will the adoption of the five-day week benefit workers?

    B. Will the adoption of the five-day week benefit employers?

    C. Will the adoption of the five-day week benefit the general public?

Brief Proper

Industries of the United States should adopt the five-day week, for

I. The adoption of the five-day week will benefit workers, for

    A. They will improve themselves physically, for

        1. They will have two consecutive days of leisure.

        2. They will have greater opportunity for recreation.

    B. They will improve themselves mentally, for

        1. They will have more time for reading and study.

        2. They will have the opportunity to visit museums and attend public lectures.

        3. They will learn much from wider social intercourse.

        4. They may utilize their extra time in preparing themselves for better positions.

    C. They will improve their standard of living, for

        1. They will have more time in which to enjoy greater comforts in their homes.

        2. They will have more time in which to improve their homes and living conditions.

    D. They will have a better chance of employment, for

        1. The demand for goods will be increased, for

            a. Workers will require more articles of comfort.

            b. They will have more time for buying.

    2. More women will have time for gainful employment, for

       a. They can perform their necessary home duties in the extra day.

       b. They will still have one day of rest.

II. The adoption of the five-day week will benefit employers, for

  A. The demand for manufactured goods will increase, for

    1. Workers will buy more goods, for

       a. They will develop more numerous and more discriminating wants.

       b. They will have more time for buying.

    2. The number of purchasers will be increased, for

       a. More persons will be employed.

       b. More persons will have money to spend.

  B. Employees will do better work, for

    1. They will be physically refreshed by two days of change and relaxation.

    2. They will be mentally stimulated by increased opportunities for mental improvement.

    3. They will have the incentive of earning the extra day of leisure by speeding up production.

  C. Manufacturing plants can be more economically operated, for

    1. The cost of power and of operating for half a day will be eliminated.

    2. A whole day in which to repair and overhaul machinery will help to avoid breakdowns and loss of time.

III. The adoption of the five-day week will benefit the general public, for

  A. It will insure a better and happier citizenship, for

    1. Workers will have more leisure for physical and mental improvement.

    2. They will have more time for the enjoyment of home and social life.

  B. It will establish a more reliable economic balance, for

    1. Waste from overproduction will be decreased, for

       a. The purchasing demand will be increased.

       b. The number of purchasers will be greater.

2. Wages and prices will tend to become stable, for
   a. More workers will have dependable employment.
   b. The demand for goods will be more general and uniform.
C. It will improve living conditions generally, for
   1. Crime will be lessened, for
      a. More people will be employed.
      b. Home life will be more satisfactory.
   2. A greater number of people may live in comfort.
   3. The burden of taxation for the individual will be lightened, for
      a. More people will be self-supporting.
      b. More people will pay taxes.

Conclusion

Since the adoption of the five-day week will benefit workers, since it will benefit employers, and since it will benefit the general public, therefore industries of the United States should adopt the five-day week.

References

"The Five-Day Week," Lamar T. Beman.

"The Five-Day Week," William Green. *North American Review*, Vol. CCXXIII, pages 566–574.

"The Five-Day Week," *World's Work*, Vol. LIX, page 23.

"The Five-Day Week," *Current History*, Vol. XXXIII, pages 223–227.

"The Extent of the Five-Day Week in Manufacturing Industries," *Monthly Labor Review*, Vol. XXX, pages 368–371.

"How the Five-Day Week Works," *Literary Digest*, Vol. LXXXVI, pages 10–11.

"Shorter-Hours Cure for Overproduction," *Literary Digest*, Vol. XC, page 16.

"Labor Now Out for Five-Day Week," *Literary Digest*, Vol. XCI, pages 9–11.

"Coming: A Five-Day Week," *Literary Digest*, Vol. XCVI, pages 12–13.

"Five Days Shalt Thou Labor," *Literary Digest*, Vol. CI, page 8.

"Progress of the Five-Day Week," *Literary Digest*, Vol. CIV, page 48.

"The Unemployment Challenge," *North American Review*, Vol. CCXXXI, pages 269–274.

"A New Way of Looking at the Five-Day Week," H. S. Person. *The Survey*, Vol. LXI, pages 505–507.

"Progress of the Five-Day Week," *Monthly Labor Review*, Vol. XXVIII, pages 1181–1190.

"What of the Five-Day Week?" *Factory and Industrial Management*, Vol. LXXVII, pages 993–994.

"Staggered Holidays," *Forum*, Vol. LXXXIII, pages 368–372.

Exercise 437

When the introduction prepared in Exercises 434 and 435 has been approved and returned, the members of each of the teams formed in Exercise 434 will proceed independently to find the main issues and to complete the brief for their side of the proposition.

195. Developing the Brief into an Argument

After the brief for a debate has been prepared, it must be expanded into a coherent and forceful argument. Each point in the brief must be clearly explained and adequately supported by evidence as proof. Our work in gathering material and preparing the brief has acquainted us with both sides of the question and has provided us with such detailed information and evidence as we shall need in elaborating the brief. As members of the team, we should each take a definite portion of the brief and, using it as a guide, compose the constructive argument that we shall give in our speech. For example, if the argument is based on three main issues, the first speaker for the affirmative side will take the introduction and the first issue; the second affirmative speaker, the second issue; and the third affirmative speaker, the third issue. Each speaker for the negative side will develop one issue corresponding to his place on his team. After each speaker has written his speech, he should read it or give it orally before his colleagues, and by the aid of their criticism and suggestions improve it as much as he can. Each member of the team should then practice giving his speech until he can deliver it effectively.

196. Refutation

Refutation in debating consists of arguments and evidence intended to destroy arguments and evidence given as proof by members of the opposing team. Though the constructive arguments that we present in our prepared speeches are highly important, our success in debating will largely depend on our skill in the use of destructive argument, or refutation. If we have a thorough knowledge of both sides of the proposition and possess the ability to think quickly and accurately in the presence of an audience, we may greatly weaken our opponents' case, and in turn strengthen our own, by altering our prepared speeches to meet the arguments advanced by our opponents. By showing that an opponent is guilty of one or more of the fallacies explained in section 185, we may destroy his argument. Sometimes, by asking him a question or two, we may lead him to admit a point in our favor. Occasionally we may be able to quote evidence favoring our side of the proposition from an authority that he himself has cited, or show that he has misquoted an authority. Refutation of this kind may be introduced at any point in our speech where it will be effective, but it should be limited to essential points. We must avoid weakening our side of the case by attacking a point that we cannot disprove.

When all the speakers on both teams have given their arguments, the first speaker for the negative and the first speaker for the affirmative are usually allowed to make a second speech, called the *rebuttal*. In his rebuttal speech, each debater may introduce additional evidence for his side; but usually he devotes most of his attention to giving further refutation of the most important points made by the opposing team and to summing up the arguments presented by his own team.

Exercise 438

Following the directions given in section 194, the members of each of the teams formed in Exercise 434 will develop their brief into an argument. Each team should consider the arguments that may be given by the opposing team and thus prepare for refutation and rebuttal.

197. Conducting a Debate

In conducting a debate we should observe the procedure briefly summarized below.

1. Duties of the chairman. Before the debate the chairman or a committee appointed by him should see that the hall or auditorium is put in readiness. On the platform there should be a table and chairs for the chairman and the timekeepers, and at either side a table and chairs for each team. At the time of the debate, if there is a visiting team, the chairman welcomes them. He announces the number of minutes to be allowed each speaker, mentions the judges or informs the audience of the rules to be followed in judging the debate, and states the question. He introduces the speakers, and during the debate gives them the warning and final signals. As a presiding officer, the chairman should be impartial.

2. Order of speakers. In debate the order of speakers and the character of their speeches are as follows:

> *First affirmative:* Introduction and constructive speech.
> *First negative:* Constructive speech with refutation.
> *Second affirmative:* Constructive speech with refutation.
> *Second negative:* Constructive speech with refutation.
> *Third affirmative:* Constructive speech with refutation and a summary of the argument for his side of the question.
> *Third negative:* Constructive speech with refutation and a summary of the argument for his side of the question.
> *First negative:* Rebuttal speech, concluding with the statement that the speaker and his colleagues have proved their side of the proposition.
> *First affirmative:* Rebuttal speech, concluding with the statement that the speaker and his colleagues have proved their side of the proposition.

3. Etiquette in debating. In debating we should observe the following details of etiquette:

a. Before beginning your speech be sure to address the chairman and the audience, thus: "Mr. Chairman, Ladies, and Gentlemen."

b. Try to avoid the use of the pronoun "I." Refer to yourself and your team-mates as "we," "we of the affirmative," and "my colleagues."

c. Do not refer to members of the other team by name. Say "our opponents," "the opposition," "the first speaker for the negative," and "the second speaker for the affirmative."

d. Be courteous and considerate in your attitude toward your opponents. Avoid the use of sarcasm.

e. Obey the final time signal promptly. As soon as you have completed the sentence that you are speaking, stop.

f. If necessary, you may confer in whispers with your colleagues, but do not disturb the speaker or distract the attention of the audience. Most of your time, however, should be given to listening to the speaker and taking notes on points that you intend to answer in your refutation or rebuttal.

Exercise 439

The opposing teams will hold the debates for which they have been preparing in Exercises 434, 435, 437, and 438. A chairman and two timekeepers should be appointed. The other members of the class may act as judges, or three persons outside the class may be chosen as judges. Each debate should be conducted according to the procedure explained in section 197.

Exercise 440

Your class will be divided into new teams consisting of three pupils each, and the teams will be consecutively numbered. Following the same plan and procedure used in preparing for and holding the former group of debates, each˙pair of teams will prepare for and hold a debate on one of the propositions given below. No two pairs of teams should debate the same proposition. The teacher will record the propositions chosen in the order that they are reported. The time for holding the debates will be announced by the teacher.

1. *Resolved*, That high-school pupils should be allowed to select their own courses of study.

2. *Resolved*, That our school should establish a system of student self-government (the honor system in examinations).

3. *Resolved*, That secret societies in high school should be prohibited (permitted).

4. *Resolved*, That all juniors and seniors in our high school should be required to devote at least one period a week to public speaking (debating).

5. *Resolved*, That all girls in our high school should be required to wear uniforms.

6. *Resolved*, That strikes by high-school pupils are sometimes justified.

7. *Resolved*, That half of the teachers in every high school should be men.

8. *Resolved,* That the Board of Education of our city should establish night schools for laborers.

9. *Resolved,* That our city should establish a municipal airport (market).

10. *Resolved,* That our city should own and operate the electric-light (gas, street-railway) system.

11. *Resolved,* That radios should be prohibited in apartment houses and hotels.

12. *Resolved,* That the showing of motion pictures on Sunday should be permitted (prohibited) in our city.

13. *Resolved,* That every automobile owner should be required to carry liability insurance.

14. *Resolved,* That our city should adopt the zoning system (commission form of government).

15. *Resolved,* That one United States senator from each state should be a woman.

16. *Resolved,* That the publication of detailed accounts of crimes should be prohibited.

17. *Resolved,* That the Federal Government should enact uniform traffic (child-labor, divorce) laws.

18. *Resolved,* That our state should adopt compulsory health insurance.

19. *Resolved,* That the calendar year should be divided into thirteen months.

20. A proposition of your own choice relating to school, local, state, or national affairs, to be approved by your teacher.

CHAPTER XVII

The Short Story

Preliminary Exercise

Suppose that you are a reporter sent by your newspaper to cover an assignment. On your way you happen to be the sole witness of a crime. The criminals capture you and take you with them. This act of theirs places you in a serious situation. Recognizing your danger, you study your captors and your surroundings and try to devise a plan that will enable you to escape. Several hours later by your own efforts you regain your freedom, report the story of the crime to your paper, and bring about the arrest of the criminals.

Here you have the raw material for a good short story. In the opening situation you got into trouble; in the final situation you are out of trouble and have turned the tables on your captors. How did you bring about this result? Your struggle to achieve the outcome will constitute the main interest of the story. Using your imagination, invent a series of incidents that will render your struggle vividly real and make your success seem plausible and convincing. What plan of escape did you adopt, and how did you carry it out? How did you get your story to your paper? How did you bring about the arrest of your captors? How much time did the action cover? In what places did it occur? Who and how many were the criminals? What crime did they commit? Does a full account of the crime belong in this story? Explain your answer. Choose an appropriate title, and write a synopsis of your story in not more than three hundred words. Be sure that you answer clearly the six fundamental questions *Who? When? Where? What? Why? How?* The summaries of several pupils will be read and discussed in class.

198. What a Short Story Is

A short story is a brief *invented* narrative presenting characters engaged in a conflict and struggling to bring about a definite outcome. It deals with a single dominant incident involving a crisis of some kind in the life of one or more of the characters, and is intended to produce on the reader a single impression. Unlike a simple narrative of fact, in which incidents are recorded in the order of their occurrence, the short story requires that each incident produce or be responsible for the one that follows it. In other words, the short story consists of a series of incidents logically linked together as cause and effect. More accurately defined, a short story is an artistic narrative consciously devised by an author in accord with a predetermined outcome and a single predetermined effect.

The short story is a narrative unit complete in itself. It is restricted to *one* episode, related usually in 2000 to 7500 words and requiring not more than half an hour of the reader's time. Because of this limitation, economy and compression are highly important. In most short stories the number of principal characters ranges from two to six. One scene, or place setting, generally suffices for the main action, and the time covered by it is limited to as brief a period as possible. In stories requiring more than one time setting, the author brings together the significant portions of the action by passing over unimportant intervals, and thus gives the reader the impression that the time covered is relatively short.

199. Elements of a Short Story

The essence of a short story is conflict and struggle directed toward the achievement of a desired end. Reduced to its simplest terms, the action of a short story is the result of two forces brought into opposition by a complicating incident. One of the two forces is always represented by man. His opponent, or the representative of the other force, may be another person or a group of persons; a physically stronger animal; some force of nature; society, custom, convention, or religion; his environment, Fate, or destiny; heredity, fear, disease, or moral weakness. Unless there is conflict, there can be no story.

A short story may be said to be the shortest distance between an unstable and undesirable situation that constitutes the beginning and a relatively permanent, new, and more desirable situation that constitutes the end, or outcome. In constructing a short story, an author's task, so far as the principal action is concerned, consists of three stages. First, he creates an unstable and undesirable situation by bringing his characters into conflict and thus getting them into trouble. Then, he devises a series of incidents showing their struggles to get out of trouble and attain a new and more desirable situation. Finally, he provides a plausible, if not inevitable, outcome of their struggles, which is the new situation.

Exercise 441

A close examination of the following specimen will give you a better understanding of the short story as a type of narrative. When you have read the story, answer these questions: With what single dominant incident does the story deal? What is the complicating incident that brings about the conflict? What is the unstable situation with

© Ewing Galloway

Neptune's Court on the S. S. "Samaria"

which the story opens? What is the permanent situation with which it ends? What are the incidents showing Montresor's struggle to bring about this new situation? Point out clearly the cause-and-effect relationship between the incidents. At what places in the story do you learn of the preparations that Montresor has made? How many characters are there? How much time does the action cover? How many scenes, or place settings, are there? What is the single impression that you get from the story?

The Cask of Amontillado

By Edgar Allan Poe

The thousand injuries of Fortunato I had borne as best I could, but when he ventured upon insult, I vowed revenge. You, who so well know the nature of my soul, will not suppose, however, that I gave utterance to a threat. *At length* I would be avenged; this was a point definitely settled — but the very definiteness with which it was resolved precluded the idea of risk. I must not only punish, but punish with impunity. A wrong is unredressed when retribution overtakes its redresser. It is equally unredressed when the avenger fails to make himself felt as such to him who has done the wrong.

It must be understood that neither by word nor by deed had I given Fortunato cause to doubt my good will. I continued, as was my wont, to smile in his face, and he did not perceive that my smile *now* was at the thought of his immolation.

He had a weak point — this Fortunato — although in other regards he was a man to be respected and even feared. He prided himself on his connoisseurship in wine. Few Italians have the true virtuoso spirit. For the most part their enthusiasm is adopted to suit the time and opportunity — to practice imposture upon the British and Austrian millionaires. In painting and gemmary Fortunato, like his countrymen, was a quack; but in the matter of old wines he was sincere. In this respect I did not differ from him materially: I was skillful in the Italian vintages myself and bought largely whenever I could.

It was about dusk, one evening during the supreme madness of the carnival season, that I encountered my friend. He accosted me with excessive warmth, for he had been drinking much. The man wore motley. He had on a tight-fitting party-striped dress, and his head was surmounted by the conical cap and bells. I was so pleased to see him that I thought I should never have done wringing his hand.

I said to him: "My dear Fortunato, you are luckily met. How remarkably well you are looking today! But I have received a pipe of what passes for Amontillado, and I have my doubts."

"How?" said he, "Amontillado? A pipe? Impossible! And in the middle of the carnival!"

"I have my doubts," I replied; "and I was silly enough to pay the full Amontillado price without consulting you in the matter. You were not to be found, and I was fearful of losing a bargain."

"Amontillado!"

"I have my doubts."

"Amontillado!"

"And I must satisfy them."

"Amontillado!"

"As you are engaged, I am on my way to Luchesi. If anyone has a critical turn, it is he. He will tell me —"

"Luchesi cannot tell Amontillado from Sherry."

"And yet some fools will have it that his taste is a match for your own."

"Come, let us go."

"Whither?"

"To your vaults."

"My friend, no; I will not impose upon your good nature. I perceive you have an engagement. Luchesi —"

"I have no engagement — come."

"My friend, no. It is not the engagement, but the severe cold with which I perceive you are afflicted. The vaults are insufferably damp. They are incrusted with niter."

"Let us go nevertheless. The cold is merely nothing. Amontillado! You have been imposed upon. And as for Luchesi, he cannot distinguish Sherry from Amontillado."

Thus speaking, Fortunato possessed himself of my arm. Putting on a mask of black silk, and drawing a roquelaure closely about my person, I suffered him to hurry me to my palazzo.

There were no attendants at home; they had absconded to make merry in honor of the time. I had told them that I should not return until the morning, and had given them explicit orders not to stir from the house. These orders were sufficient, I well knew, to insure their immediate disappearance, one and all, as soon as my back was turned.

I took from their sconces two flambeaux, and giving one to Fortunato, bowed him through several suites of rooms to the archway that led into the vaults. I passed down a long and winding staircase, requesting him to be cautious as he followed. We came at length to the foot of the descent and stood together on the damp ground of the catacombs of the Montresors.

The gait of my friend was unsteady, and the bells upon his cap jingled as he strode.

"The pipe," said he.

"It is farther on," said I; "but observe the white webwork which gleams from these cavern walls."

He turned towards me, and looked into my eyes with two filmy orbs that distilled the rheum of intoxication.

"Niter?" he asked at length.

"Niter," I replied. "How long have you had that cough?"

"Ugh! ugh! ugh! — ugh! ugh! ugh! — ugh! ugh! ugh! — ugh! ugh! ugh! — ugh! ugh! ugh!"

My poor friend found it impossible to reply for many minutes.

"It is nothing," he said at last.

"Come," I said, with decision, "we will go back; your health is precious. You are rich, respected, admired, beloved; you are happy, as once I was. You are a man to be missed. For me it is no matter. We will go back; you will be ill, and I cannot be responsible. Besides, there is Luchesi —"

"Enough," he said; "the cough is a mere nothing; it will not kill me. I shall not die of a cough."

"True — true," I replied; "and, indeed, I had no intention of alarming you unnecessarily — but you should use all proper caution. A draught of this Médoc will defend us from the damps."

Here I knocked off the neck of a bottle which I drew from a long row of its fellows that lay upon the mold.

"Drink," I said, presenting him the wine.

He raised it to his lips with a leer. He paused and nodded to me familiarly, while his bells jingled.

"I drink," he said, "to the buried that repose around us."

"And I to your long life."

He again took my arm, and we proceeded.

"These vaults," he said, "are extensive."

"The Montresors," I replied, "were a great and numerous family."

"I forget your arms."

"A huge human foot *d'or*, in a field azure; the foot crushes a serpent rampant whose fangs are embedded in the heel."

"And the motto?"   •

"*Nemo me impune lacessit.*"

"Good!" he said.

The wine sparkled in his eyes and the bells jingled. My own fancy grew warm with the Médoc. We had passed through walls of piled bones, with casks and puncheons intermingling, into the inmost recesses of the catacombs. I paused again, and this time I made bold to seize Fortunato by an arm above the elbow.

"The niter!" I said; "see, it increases. It hangs like moss upon the vaults. We are below the river's bed. The drops of moisture trickle among the bones. Come, we will go back ere it is too late. Your cough —"

"It is nothing," he said; "let us go on. But first, another draught of the Médoc."

I broke and reached him a flagon of De Grâve. He emptied it at a breath. His eyes flashed with a fierce light. He laughed, and threw the bottle upward with a gesticulation I did not understand.

I looked at him in surprise. He repeated the movement — a grotesque one.

"You do not comprehend?" he said.

"Not I," I replied.

"Then you are not of the brotherhood."

"How?"

"You are not of the masons."

"Yes, yes," I said; "yes, yes."

"You? Impossible! A mason?"

"A mason," I replied.

"A sign," he said.

"It is this," I answered, producing a trowel from beneath the folds of my roquelaure.

"You jest," he exclaimed, recoiling a few paces. "But let us proceed to the Amontillado."

"Be it so," I said, replacing the tool beneath the cloak and again offering him my arm. He leaned upon it heavily. We continued our route in search of the Amontillado. We passed through a range of low arches, descended, passed on, and, descending again, arrived at a deep crypt, in which the foulness of the air caused our flambeaux rather to glow than flame.

At the most remote end of the crypt there appeared another, less spacious. Its walls had been lined with human remains, piled to the vault overhead, in the fashion of the great catacombs of Paris. Three sides of this interior crypt were still ornamented in this manner. From the fourth the bones had been thrown down, and lay promiscuously upon the earth, forming at one point a mound of some size. Within the wall thus exposed by the displacing of the bones we perceived a still interior recess, in depth about four feet, in width three, in height six or seven. It seemed to have been constructed for no especial use within itself, but formed merely the interval between two of the colossal supports of the roof of the catacombs, and was backed by one of their circumscribing walls of solid granite.

It was in vain that Fortunato, uplifting his dull torch, endeavored to pry into the depth of the recess. Its termination the feeble light did not enable us to see.

"Proceed," I said; "herein is the Amontillado. As for Luchesi —"

"He is an ignoramus," interrupted my friend, as he stepped unsteadily forward, while I followed immediately at his heels. In an instant he had reached the extremity of the niche, and finding his progress arrested by the rock, stood stupidly bewildered. A moment more, and I had fettered him to the granite. In its surface were two iron staples, distant from each other about two feet, horizontally. From one of these depended a short chain, from the other a padlock. Throwing the links about his waist, it was but the work of a few seconds to secure it. He was too much astounded to resist. Withdrawing the key, I stepped back from the recess.

"Pass your hand," I said, "over the wall; you cannot help feeling the niter. Indeed it is *very* damp. Once more let me *implore* you to return. No? Then I must positively leave you. But I must first render you all the little attentions in my power."

"The Amontillado!" ejaculated my friend, not yet recovered from his astonishment.

"True," I replied; "the Amontillado."

As I said these words I busied myself among the pile of bones of which I have before spoken. Throwing them aside, I soon uncovered a quantity of building-stone and mortar. With these materials and with the aid of my trowel, I began vigorously to wall up the entrance of the niche.

I had scarcely laid the first tier of the masonry when I discovered that the intoxication of Fortunato had in a great measure worn off. The earliest indication I had of this was a low moaning cry from the depth of the recess. It was *not* the cry of a drunken man. There was then a long and obstinate silence. I laid the second tier, and the third, and the fourth; and then I heard the furious vibrations of the chain. The noise lasted for several minutes, during which, that I might hearken to it with the more satisfaction, I ceased my labors and sat down upon the bones. When at last the clanking subsided, I resumed the trowel, and finished without interruption the fifth, the sixth, and the seventh tier. The wall was now nearly upon a level with my breast. I again paused, and holding the flambeaux over the masonwork, threw a few feeble rays upon the figure within.

A succession of loud and shrill screams, bursting suddenly from the throat of the chained form, seemed to thrust me violently back. For a brief moment I hesitated — I trembled. Unsheathing my rapier, I began to grope with it about the recess; but the thought of an instant reassured me. I placed my hand upon the solid fabric of the catacombs, and felt satisfied. I reapproached the wall. I replied to the yells of him who clamored. I reëchoed —

I aided — I surpassed them in volume and in strength. I did this, and the clamorer grew still.

It was now midnight, and my task was drawing to a close. I had completed the eighth, the ninth, and the tenth tier. I had finished a portion of the last and the eleventh; there remained but a single stone to be fitted and plastered in. I struggled with its weight; I placed it partially in its destined position. But now there came from out the niche a low laugh that erected the hairs upon my head. It was succeeded by a sad voice, which I had difficulty in recognizing as that of the noble Fortunato. The voice said:

"Ha! ha! ha! — he! he! he! — a very good joke indeed — an excellent jest. We will have many a rich laugh about it at the palazzo — he! he! he! — over our wine — he! he! he!"

"The Amontillado!" I said.

"He! he! he! — he! he! he! — yes, the Amontillado. But is it not getting late? Will not they be awaiting us at the palazzo — the Lady Fortunato and the rest? Let us be gone."

"Yes," I said, "let us be gone."

"*For the love of God, Montresor!*"

"Yes," I said, "for the love of God!"

But to these words I hearkened in vain for a reply. I grew impatient. I called aloud, —

"Fortunato!"

No answer. I called again, —

"Fortunato!"

No answer still. I thrust a torch through the remaining aperture and let it fall within. There came forth in return only the jingling of the bells. My heart grew sick — on account of the dampness of the catacombs. I hastened to make an end of my labor. I forced the last stone into its position; I plastered it up. Against the new masonry I reërected the old rampart of bones. For the half of a century no mortal has disturbed them. *In pace requiescat.*

200. Five Essentials of the Short Story

All short stories, though no two are identical, are alike with respect to five essentials. Every short story that is properly constructed (1) deals with *one dominant incident*, (2) presents *one preëminent character*, (3) is devised by means of a *plot*, (4) has a definite place and time *setting*, and (5) produces on the reader a *single dominant impression*. In the following sections we will discuss these essentials briefly and illustrate each of them by referring to "The Cask of Amontillado," which we have just read.

201. One Dominant Incident

By dominant incident is meant the main action that constitutes the story. Unity of contents in a short story demands that the writer limit his narrative to *one* dominant incident and admit only such minor incidents and details of action as are needed to heighten the effect of the main action and render the story more vivid and natural. In "The Cask of Amontillado" the dominant incident is the action of Montresor in avenging himself on Fortunato for the insult.

202. One Preëminent Character

In almost every short story one character stands out more prominently than any of the others. The person who dominates the story and but for whom the action would not take place is the preëminent, or leading, character. In "The Cask of Amontillado" Montresor dominates the story. Most short stories require at least two characters: a *protagonist*, the preëminent character, who initiates and attempts to carry out a certain course of action; and an *antagonist*, who opposes the action of the protagonist. In addition to these two, there may be one or two other principal characters and a few necessary minor characters.

203. Plot

A plot is the plan that an author devises as a means of shaping his material effectively into a story. In making his plot an author must consider both the single effect that the story is intended to produce on the reader and the outcome that he has chosen. In relation to the story, the plot serves as the skeleton, or framework. It gives the gist of the action by showing (1) the complicating incident, or cause of the conflict; (2) the series of causally related incidents constituting the struggle and leading up to the climax; and (3) the result of the struggle, or the outcome of the action.

The following analysis of the plot of "The Cask of Amontillado" will make clearer the meaning of plot:

1. *The complicating incident, or cause of the conflict:* Montresor, having been insulted by Fortunato, vows revenge.

2. *The series of causally related incidents constituting the struggle and leading up to the climax:* (1) Montresor encounters the intoxicated Fortunato on the street late one evening during the carnival season, greets him cordially, and tells him that he has just bought a cask of Amontillado, but that he doubts that it is genuine Amontillado. (2) Fortunato, whose weakness is his connoisseurship in wine, insists on going immediately to taste the Amontillado, and Montresor makes him all the more eager to go by telling him that he is then on his way to get Luchesi to taste it. (3) Having enticed Fortunato into his family burial vaults, Montresor intoxicates him still further, all the while goading him on by mention of Luchesi. (4) Having finally lured Fortunato into the niche previously prepared for him, Montresor chains him fast. (5) Fortunato, sobered by fright as he is being walled in, realizes Montresor's motive and pleads in vain to be spared.

3. *The result of the struggle, or outcome of the action:* Montresor accomplishes his revenge by walling Fortunato up in the niche and leaving him there to die.

The plot of a story consists of two principal divisions: everything that happens before the climax, or highest point of interest, is called the *complication*, or the rising action; and everything that happens after the climax is termed the

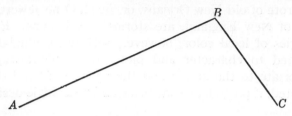

resolution, or the falling action. In the diagram, *B* stands for the climax; the line *AB* represents the complication, or rising action; and the line *BC* represents the resolution, or falling action. The climax of "The Cask of Amontillado" is Fortunato's final cry of terror and despair: *"For the love of God, Montresor!"*

204. Setting

Setting is that portion of a short story that acquaints the reader with the place where and the time when the main action occurs. In "The Cask of Amontillado" there are two place settings: an exterior one in the street, and an interior one in the burial vaults of Montresor's house. The time setting is the period from dusk to midnight. In this story the carnival going on in the streets lends atmosphere to the story and serves as an effective background of action. A larger, inclusive scene of activity, such as this, surrounding the action of the story proper is termed the *enveloping action.*

Sometimes authors find places so interesting in themselves that they devise short stories that give prominence to the peculiar characteristics or atmosphere of such places. A narrative that emphasizes a particular setting or environment is called a *local color* story. Many of the stories of such authors as Bret Harte, who wrote of the early gold-mining days of California, George W. Cable, who wrote of old New Orleans, or Sarah Orne Jewett, who wrote of New England, are stories of this type. Except in stories of local color, however, setting should be subordinated to character and plot. It should always be appropriate to the action and the characters, and should be limited, if possible, to one place and to a single occasion.

205. A Single Dominant Impression

If we ask ourselves what single impression "The Cask of Amontillado" made on us, we shall doubtless agree that it is one of *horror*. Using *revenge* as the motivating idea of his story, Poe chose *horror* as the single effect to be wrought, and then invented incidents and combined events that enabled him to produce this one dominant impression. A skillful author first determines the effect that his story is to produce, and then he fashions his story accordingly, using great care in the selection and arrangement of incidents that emphasize the predetermined effect. Singleness of impression is the principal device for securing unity and artistic completeness in the short story. We shall find that every short story that is well constructed makes one dominant impression.

Exercise 442

Examine again the short-story situation given in the Preliminary Exercise at the beginning of this chapter. Criticize with respect to the five essentials of the short story the synopsis that you wrote. Have you included only one dominant incident? Who is the preëminent character? How many other characters are needed? Write out an accurate analysis of your plot similar in form to that given in section 203. How many and what place settings will you need? Into how brief a period of time can you compress the action of your story? What single impression do you intend your story to produce on the reader?

Exercise 443

List, as possible characters for use in short stories, five of the most interesting persons whom you know or have known. Under the name of each write a paragraph in which you state what the person has done or experienced and what characteristics he or she possesses that make him or her good short-story material.

206. Angle of Narration

The point of view from which a story is related is called the *angle of narration*. If one of the characters tells the story, as in "The Cask of Amontillado" or "The Fall of the House of Usher," it is related from the first-person point of view. If a person outside the story is the narrator, as in "Tennessee's Partner," "The Necklace," or "A New England Nun," it is told from the third-person point of view. When an author relates not only what the characters do and say but also what they think and imagine, he adopts the omniscient, or all-knowing, point of view.

207. The Beginning of a Short Story

1. Where to begin. A short story should begin as near the point of climax as clearness and effectiveness will permit. The nature of his story will lead the author to adopt one of three orders of narration: (1) the chronological order, if it closely parallels the cause-and-effect order; (2) a modified chronological order, where the story opens in the midst of action, as in "The Cask of Amontillado" and Kipling's "Without Benefit of Clergy," with the necessary details of antecedent action supplied as the story progresses; and (3) the inverted order, as in detective stories, such as Poe's "The Gold-Bug" and "The Purloined Letter."

2. How to begin. Since an author must rely upon the opening of his story to induce people to read what follows, he should give special attention to the beginning. A good beginning, besides being clear, must arouse interest and excite curiosity. In addition, it should be appropriate to the particular type of story that it introduces. A story emphasizing local color or some specific mood, such as "The Fall of the House of Usher," may begin with description of the setting and its effect on the narrator. A story in which plot is of main interest, such as "The Cask of Amontillado," may open with exposition. A story of character, such as "Tennessee's Partner," may begin with general narration leading up to the story proper. Other stories, such as Jack London's "Love of Life," may begin at once with vivid narration of the main action. Often a beginning of this last type is rendered more attractive by the use of conversation, as in such stories as Mary E. Wilkins Freeman's "A Gala Dress," Stevenson's "Markheim," and Kipling's "Without Benefit of Clergy." As near the beginning as possible the writer should inform the reader as to where and when the action takes place, who the principal characters are, what the complicating incident is, and what unstable situation has been brought about as a result.

Exercise 444

Read and examine closely the beginnings of at least five short stories. Discuss their good qualities with reference to the stories themselves. Then write an appropriate and

interesting beginning for the short story that you have been
devising in the Preliminary Exercise and in Exercise 442.

208. The Title

A good title, usually expressed in a word or a brief
phrase, excites curiosity and often suggests the general
nature of the story without giving any hint as to the
outcome. Such titles as "Ethan Brand," "Markheim,"
"Tennessee's Partner," and "A New England Nun" lead
the reader to expect stories of character. Titles such as
"The Revolt of Mother," "The Sire de Malétroit's Door,"
"A Sisterly Scheme," and "The Fight That Failed" promise stories of plot. The originality or tantalizing uncer-
tainty of such titles as "The Red Mark," "The Monkey's
Paw," "Two of Them," "Our Aromatic Uncle," "A Lodg-
ing for the Night," and "The Lady, or the Tiger?" makes
the reader eager to discover what the story is about.

209. Aids in Writing a Short Story

1. **Methods of characterization.** To make the persons of
his story seem real and interesting to the reader, an author
may use several methods of characterization. He may
employ the *direct* method, giving personal descriptions,
necessary biographical details, and analyses of personality.
He may likewise explain the environment and the occupation of each of his characters. In some instances he may
resort to the *indirect* method, allowing each person to reveal himself through his actions and his reactions in dealing with other characters. Oftentimes *dialogue* — what
a person says and what others say to him and about him
— affords effective characterization. In most stories an
author will naturally employ a combination of these
methods.

2. Creating suspense. Suspense is an invaluable aid in arousing and increasing the reader's interest as the story advances. Since the climax should come as near the end of the story as possible, the skillful writer arranges the incidents in an ascending series of minor climaxes that result in rapid movement and in a growing eagerness on the part of the reader to reach the point of highest interest, or main climax, of the action. Oftentimes the author gives slight anticipatory hints that furnish the observant reader suggestive clues as to the turn that the action may take, as well as foreshadow its final outcome. In "The Cask of Amontillado," for example, we find such anticipatory hints as Montresor's reply, "True — true," to Fortunato's statement "I shall not die of a cough"; the motto on the coat of arms of the Montresors; and the trowel that Montresor draws from under his roquelaure. The experienced writer is always careful not to tell too much by such hints, for suspense is destroyed the moment that the reader feels certain of the exact nature of the outcome.

3. Use of dialogue. Dialogue, or conversation, contributes variety, naturalness, and animation to stories. Persons may be effectively characterized and individualized both by what they say and by how they speak. Besides characterizing, dialogue should be made to advance the action of the story. Conversation that does not serve one or both of these purposes, but is merely clever or attractive in itself, should be excluded. Care in the choice of synonyms of the verbs *said*, *asked*, and *replied* will aid an author in suggesting a person's manner of speaking. Unless the identity of the person who utters each speech is clearly implied, it should be accurately indicated.

4. Use of enveloping action. In "The Cask of Amontillado" the carnival celebration serves as the enveloping action, or background, of the action of the story. Life in

© 1931, by The Curtis Publishing Company

What Title Can You Suggest for This Picture?

a California mining camp during the days of forty-nine in "Tennessee's Partner" and life in Paris during the Hundred Years' War in "The Sire de Malétroit's Door" serve a similar purpose in these stories. Enveloping action helps to contribute atmosphere to a story and gives it proper perspective. Poe's use of enveloping action — the gay street scene of the carnival — intensifies by contrast the horror of the crime committed in the somber gloom of the burial vaults.

Exercise 445

Read two short stories that are related in part by means of conversation, and study closely the use of dialogue. How does it help to characterize and individualize the persons of the story? How does it help to advance the action? Is the dialogue natural and "in character" — that is, appropriate to the characters? List the verbs used as substitutes for *asked, said,* and *replied.*

210. How to Analyze a Short Story

Now that we have gained a preliminary understanding of the short story as a type of narrative, we may extend our knowledge by making a thorough study of several other specimen stories of various kinds. The groups of questions and directions given below will afford us helpful guidance in analyzing all short stories.

1. *The dominant incident.* (1) What is the single dominant incident that constitutes the main action of the story? State it clearly in one sentence. (2) Is there an enveloping action that serves as the background of the story?

2. *The plot.* (1) With what unstable situation does the story open? (2) Has it been brought about by something that happened before the story begins, or is it created by a complicating incident that occurs early in the

story? (3) What is the complicating incident that involves the principal characters in a struggle? (4) What is the new situation resulting from their struggle and forming the outcome of the story? (5) Enumerate in their proper order the incidents that constitute the struggle and bring about the new situation, and point out clearly the cause-and-effect relationship between them. (6) What is the climax? (7) How near the end of the story does it come? (8) Summarize accurately in a sentence or a brief paragraph the plot of the story. (9) To what extent has the author altered the chronological order of events in developing his plot?

3. *The characters.* (1) Who is the preëminent character? (2) How can you tell? (3) Who are the other principal characters? (4) Who are the minor characters? (5) What method or methods of characterization does the author use? (6) Are the characters clearly individualized? (7) Are they vivid and lifelike? (8) Do they act and speak at all times "in character"?

4. *The setting.* (1) What is the place setting? (2) What is the time setting? (3) Does either change in the course of the story? (4) How much time does the action of the story cover? (5) Is the setting accurately described, or is it merely implied? (6) Does the setting give atmosphere or local color to the story?

5. *The dominant impression.* (1) What is the single dominant impression that the story makes on you? (2) Show how the author has chosen and arranged details to achieve this unity of effect. (3) What is the theme, or central idea, of the story?

6. *The beginning.* (1) How near the climax in time does the action of the story begin? (2) Does the story begin with description of setting? description of a character or a group of characters? narration of the antecedent action? the main action? exposition? dialogue? (3) Explain why the author chose this kind of beginning.

7. *Use of suspense.* (1) How has the author heightened the interest in his story through the use of suspense? (2) What

anticipatory hints as to the outcome of the action do you find? (3) Is suspense successfully maintained up to the climax? (4) Is there a certain amount of suspense up to the very end of the story?

8. *Use of dialogue.* (1) To what extent is dialogue used in telling the story? (2) Does it characterize and advance the action of the story? (3) What particularly good qualities of the dialogue can you point out?

9. *The story as a whole.* (1) From what point of view is the story related? (2) What suggestion as to the character of the story do you gain from the title? (3) Does the author properly prepare the reader for the outcome? (4) Does the ending seem plausible? inevitable? Explain your answer by referring to the principal characters and the main action. (5) If the antecedent action was not related at the beginning of the story, at what points is it introduced? (6) Is it explained by the author, or is it given by means of dialogue? (7) Would you classify this as a story of plot? character? setting or local color? theme? Give reasons for your answer.

Exercise 446

Analyze by means of the questions and directions given in section 210 ten or more short stories that your teacher may recommend. During your study of these stories be on the alert for ideas, situations, plots, or characters that you may use in original stories of your own.

If a book of short stories is desired for class study, any of the collections mentioned below will afford useful material:

Short Stories of Today. Selected and edited by C. L. Hanson and W. J. Gross. Ginn and Company.

Short Stories for High Schools. Selected and edited by Rosa M. R. Mikels. Charles Scribner's Sons.

A Book of Short Stories. Selected and edited by Blanche C. Williams. D. Appleton and Company.

Representative Short Stories. Selected and edited by Hart and
Perry. The Macmillan Company.

A Book of Short Stories. Selected and edited by Stuart P.
Sherman. Henry Holt and Company.

Types of the Short Story. Selected and edited by B. A. Hey-
drick. Scott, Foresman and Company.

Modern Short Stories. Selected and edited by Frederick H.
Law. The Century Company.

Modern Short-Stories. Selected and edited by Margaret E.
Ashmun. The Macmillan Company.

Short Stories for Class Reading. Selected and edited by Ralph P.
Boas and Barbara M. Hahn. Henry Holt and Company.

Exercise 447

Using the questions and directions given in section 210,
analyze three or more short stories that you have read
aside of class in magazines or books.

Exercise 448

Now that you have learned something about the way
in which short stories are devised, you should be able to
develop the situation given in the Preliminary Exercise of
this chapter into a good short story of your own. Look
over and improve in any way that you can the work that
you did on this story in Exercises 442 and 444. Then write
a complete first draft of your story.

Exercise 449

Using the questions and directions given in section 210,
analyze the rough draft of your story. Make any changes
that seem to you advisable. When you have thoroughly
revised your story, make a final copy and submit it to your
teacher.

211. Planning and Writing Short Stories

Though no two short stories originate in the same way or involve exactly the same process in construction, we may find the following general suggestions helpful in planning and writing short stories:

1. Be on the alert for short-story suggestions, and jot down the best in your notebook. The germ, or nucleus, of your story may be an incident, a news item, an episode from history or biography, a character or a group of characters, an idea, or an imaginary situation.

2. Write of situations and conditions of life that are familiar to you. From your own experience, observation, and reading choose material that is fresh. Avoid morbid tragedies, extravagant romances, and stories dealing with social complications that are as yet beyond your experience or ability to imagine accurately.

3. Know your characters thoroughly. Choose them from life or from types of people familiar to you. Leave to more experienced writers such characters as eminent scientists, captains of industry, dowagers of society, explorers, detectives, and spies. Do not disturb hermits, pirates, and old soldiers. Let ghosts and goblins enjoy their well-earned repose.

4. Choose as settings for your stories places that are familiar to you. In general, write of your own environment. Unless you know from experience such places as Hollywood, Honolulu, Paris, Chinatown, New York City, South Africa, or the arctic regions, do not try to write about them. Mars and the moon are dangerous settings.

5. Limit yourself to telling a single complete story with a simple plot. When you have mentally planned your story, write an accurate synopsis of the main action, showing the complicating incident, the incidents that constitute the struggle of the principal characters, the climax, and the outcome.

6. Make your story as original in plot, action, and outcome as probability will permit. Have the outcome clearly in

mind from the beginning, and do your best to make your entire story seem plausible. Do not employ chance or improbable coincident as the means of bringing about the outcome. Avoid also the trite surprise ending "Just then I awoke to find it all a dream."

7. Remember that action and suspense are essential in all good stories. Get under way as quickly as possible. Arouse your reader's interest by a striking beginning, and increase his interest as your story advances. Do not hold up the action of your story by unnecessary description or by dialogue that is merely clever.

8. Make your story vivid by using specific, picture-making words. Except in stories of atmosphere or local color, limit descriptions to brief passages. Try to individualize your characters by what they do and say, and make them act and speak as real people.

9. Revise and rewrite your story until it represents your very best effort.

ASSIGNMENTS IN WRITING SHORT STORIES FOR THE SCHOOL PUBLICATION

Exercise 450

Choose an outstanding event in your own experience that will serve as the dominant incident in a short story. Devise a plot showing the opening situation, the complicating incident, the struggle, and the outcome. Decide upon the necessary characters besides yourself and choose an appropriate place and time setting. Write a good synopsis of your story. Then, after criticizing and revising it, develop it into a finished story. Use invented incidents and details as you see fit to supplement the material of your actual experience.

Exercise 451

Using as the dominant incident an experience of a relative or a friend, or an event related in a news item, devise a short story. Be sure that it has a good plot and that it satisfies the other requirements of a well-constructed short story.

Exercise 452

Devise a plot and write a short story based on one of the situations given below. Make any changes and additions that seem to you necessary.

1. Suppose that you make a wager with a friend that you will get your name on the front page of your local paper as a hero within the next month. What do you do? Do you succeed or fail? What is the result? Who are the other characters?

2. Suppose that you and your chum plan to perpetrate a practical joke on someone. Something happens, however, that gives your intended victim the advantage over you, and the two of you become the actual victims.

3. Suppose that you are cashier in some business establishment. On Saturday night preceding your month's vacation you slip away without letting anyone know of your destination, intending to give your family and friends a little thrill. On Tuesday, having reached your destination several hundred miles away, you read in the papers that the safe in the office where you worked was robbed during the week-end, though the safe was found locked. You are wholly innocent of the theft, but circumstantial evidence is against you. What do you do? What incidents constitute your struggle to get out of trouble? What is the outcome? Compress the action of your story into as brief a period of time as possible, and do not use more than two place settings. Dramatize the whole situation in your mind, and do your best to make your story seem probable.

4. Suppose that, during your freshman year at college, your roommate is invited by his wealthy aunt, whom he has never seen, to spend the week-end at her home in a neighboring city. A conflicting engagement causes him to persuade you to impersonate him and go in his stead. Limit the main action, if possible, to the scene at the home of the aunt. What happens? Does the aunt discover the deception? If so, how? What is the outcome?

5. Suppose that in a certain small town or community everyone pledges himself and herself to tell the truth, the whole truth, and nothing but the truth for one week. Think of some particular group of persons and a situation in which telling the whole truth will involve one or more of them in serious difficulty. Then devise an interesting short story in which the action is made to seem probable throughout.

6. Suppose that two burglars meet in a house from which the occupants are absent over the week-end. The first burglar tries to impersonate the owner. What happens? What will be the outcome? Will a third character be needed? Plan and write a good short story based on this situation.

7. Suppose that your desire to write short stories has led you to select for your vacation a remote little village, where you will be away from the disturbance of family and friends. You arrive in the village as a stranger, giving your name as "Mr. (Miss) Blank," and rent a room in the home of the postmaster and proprietor of the general store. You soon become acquainted with the villagers, but skillfully refrain from telling them very much about yourself. Curiosity rapidly develops as to your identity. Finally, when the postmaster, noticing that you receive no mail, asks you who you really are, you reply, "Well, if my name does not satisfy you, just call me 'The Fugitive.'" After this, there is much gossip and speculation. Soon things begin to happen. In what crisis do you become involved? How do you get out of trouble? If you wish, you may write two short stories, relating one from your point of view and the other from the point of view of the postmaster or another one of the villagers.

Exercise 453

Study closely the picture on page 473. Can you invent a short story in which this scene is an incident and the three boys are characters? To whom is the boy who is seated trying to telephone? What part might this fourth person play in your story? Does the scene in this picture represent antecedent action, or is it a part of the main action? Might it represent the outcome? Might the telephone call be in connection with some practical joke or an April-fool prank? Who will be the preëminent character? When you have decided upon the dominant incident, devise a plot and write your story.

Exercise 454

Devise a short story in which you use one or more of the characters that you listed in Exercise 443. If you select a local person, disguise him or her by at least a change of name.

Exercise 455

You may enjoy writing a story of atmosphere or local color. Using as your setting the most familiar of those listed below, write a short story in which the setting and the occupation of the characters play an important part.

1. An oil town.
2. A lumber camp.
3. A packing house.
4. A mining village.
5. A fishing village.
6. A dairy farm.
7. A truck farm.
8. A steel mill.
9. A textile mill.
10. A department store.

CHAPTER XVIII

The One-Act Play

212. What a One-Act Play Is

A one-act play is a *short* story devised for presentation by actors on a stage before an audience. In other words, it is a story related *dramatically* by means of action and dialogue, supplemented by costumes, stage setting, and lighting. Compression and economy of material are highly important. By the use of a few characters and within a brief period of time it must present a single story with *one* place setting and *one* time setting. "In exhibiting the present it should imply the past and intimate the future."

Like the short story, the one-act play deals with a single dominant incident, a crisis of some kind in the life of one or more of the characters. Both alike present, by means of a simple plot, an interesting struggle and its outcome. Both are intended to produce a single dominant impression. Effectiveness in both depends very largely upon action and suspense.

A one-act play is usually shorter than a short story dealing with the same narrative material. In a one-act play the scene is physically represented by stage setting, and the characters are impersonated by actors properly chosen for their respective parts and appropriately dressed. Almost all characterization is through action and speech. Furthermore, dramatic dialogue is much more condensed than is narrative dialogue; for many details can be suggested by the movements, gestures, facial expression, and vocal inflection of the actors.

In addition to the dialogue, a one-act play provides such information as the producer and the actors will need in presenting it before an audience. Following the title and preceding the dialogue, there are a list of the characters, the time at which the action occurs, and an adequate description of the scene, or stage setting. Accompanying the dialogue, there are indicated for the actors their various entrances and exits, their principal movements on the stage, their more important gestures, and the manner in which they should speak certain lines. All this additional information is called the *stage-business* of the play.

Exercise 456

The following one-act play was dramatized from a short story of the same title, written by H. C. Bunner and included in a volume called "Short Sixes." [1] When you have read the play, read the short story. If you cannot find the book in your school or town library, perhaps your teacher will read the story to the class. When you have become familiar with both, compare the story and the play as follows: (1) Observe how the person who dramatized the story managed to represent all the essential action in *one* scene and in a *single* brief period of time. (2) How many other place settings, or scenes, are there in the story? (3) How much time does the action of the story cover? (4) What descriptions of places, persons, and objects found in the story are omitted in the play? (5) What descriptive passages have been retained in the play? (6) What details of action in the story have been omitted? (7) What events

---

[1] The short story "A Sisterly Scheme" is found also in "The Short Story," edited by Brander Matthews and published by the American Book Company. The story is also reprinted in the "Teachers' Manual" accompanying this book.

that occurred before the beginning of the play and that are given in the story are presented in the play by means of dialogue and suggestion? (8) How much of the dialogue of the play is found in the short story? (9) Which lines appear in the play only?

A Sisterly Scheme[1]

PERSONS

MISS PAULINE BELTON
MISS FLOSSY BELTON, *her sister*
MISS REDINGTON, *their chaperon*
MR. MORPETH
MR. BROWN
MRS. MELBY

TIME: *The present.*

SCENE: *The porch of a large summer hotel in the Maine woods, on the shore of a little lake. There are several wicker chairs scattered along the wide porch. A door, center back, opens into the hallway of the hotel. At the left end of the porch, steps descend to the ground.*

[MR. MORPETH *and* FLOSSY BELTON *come up the steps together. He is a serious-looking man in his late twenties.* FLOSSY *has the face and figure of a woman, but is dressed like a child.*]

FLOSSY [*Scolding*]. Now, you mustn't get impatient, Muffets. I tell you, the game's working just perfectly.

MR. MORPETH. It seems to me she's making a great fuss over that Brown.

FLOSSY. She *has* to, you silly. Do you think she's going to let you see her moping and pining? ... But I tell you, Pauline is so jealous of me she's just hopping mad.

MR. M. Don't you think we might be carrying it too far?

[1] From "Short Plays from Great Stories," adapted by Roland E. Hartley and Caroline M. Power. Used by permission of The Macmillan Company. The acting right of this play is reserved by the authors of the adaptation. For performances of this play, either amateur or professional, arrangements must be made with the authors of the adaptation through The Macmillan Company.

FLOSSY. Well, you tried the other way, and you didn't gain much by it, did you?

MR. M. [*Gloomily*]. No.

FLOSSY. It was just a waste of time. Pauline has no use for devotion. It's a drug on the market with her.

MR. M. But Brown . . .

FLOSSY. He's coy. You were too eager. That's why you hadn't a chance in the world until Little Sister took hold of you. And now you've got Big Sister just where she'll be making up to you sweetly before very long. See if she doesn't.

MR. M. But I'm afraid . . .

FLOSSY. Now, for goodness' sake, Muffets, don't lose your nerve! I told you about those two other fellows who tried to make her jealous. They *almost* got there, but they weren't game enough to stay to the bitter end.

MR. M. [*Grimly*]. It seems to me I've been game enough! Everywhere I turn I hear whispering behind me: "Outrageous!" and "Simply scandalous!" . . . You're just a child, you know, but I'm old enough to know better.

FLOSSY. And I suppose you think it's all so easy for *me*. Don't you ever imagine the sweet sisterly talks Pauline and I have? Nights when we're fixing our hair — that's the time.

MR. M. I guess it has been hard. You've been a brick, Flossy.

FLOSSY. Oh, it's been fun! Pauline and Miss Redington are lots better company when they're mad than any other time.

MR. M. I don't quite see how you keep her from making too big a row. It seems to me she *could* put a stop to this, you know.

FLOSSY. Don't you understand, Muffets, dear? If Pauline seems to be going *too* far, I just suggest that I'm quite old enough to be courted, and that if she makes a fuss, I'm quite prepared to tell my age — and hers too.

MR. M. [*Warmly*]. Flossy, you *are* a little wonder!

FLOSSY. It hasn't been *so* bad for you, has it? — all this make-believe?

MR. M. Why, it's been — it's been — I've *enjoyed* it, Flossy! . . . But you have expected a lot of me.

FLOSSY. You mean about the candy and the flowers? I told you at the start I expected you to keep up your end. This wasn't to be any condescending encouragement from Big Sister's young man, but a *real* flirtation. . . . And it *has* been that, hasn't it?

MR. M. Judging from the talk going on here, it certainly has!

FLOSSY [*Pouting*]. You talk now as if you hadn't enjoyed it. . . . Don't you think I'm good-looking enough?

MR. M. Why, Flossy, you're good-looking enough — for *any-thing*!

FLOSSY. And you know I really *am* eighteen.

MR. M. And you have the wisdom of all the ages.

FLOSSY. I don't know just what that means. . . . But you *have* been nice to me, Muffets. It hasn't been nearly as bad as I thought it was going to be.

MR. M. [*With some dignity*]. Oh, you thought it was going to be pretty bad, did you?

FLOSSY. Well, you *were* such a stick with Pauline. . . . But you're very much better now.

MR. M. Thank you.

FLOSSY. Don't be silly now, Muffets. . . . Really, you *have* been a dear. . . . I'll always remember that you discovered me, even if I *did* have to hang out a sign, "Here I am!"

MR. M. But you seemed such a child . . .

FLOSSY. Yes, I know. I was two or three years behind the time-table. I just *had* to make that strike for liberty or die!

[MRS. MELBY *comes out of the hotel and takes a place in a chair in a corner. In the chair she is almost hidden from the young people, but* FLOSSY *has seen her come.*]

FLOSSY [*In a low voice*]. Muffets, you haven't proposed to me for the longest time!

MR. M. [*Sulkily*]. Do we have to go through all that farce again?

FLOSSY. That's a *nice* way to talk about asking me to marry you!

MR. M. But I *did* just last week.

FLOSSY. Yes, you're beautifully persistent, Muffets. . . . Come on, now; there's Mrs. Melby over there all ready to spread the news.

[*She gets up. He sits sulkily in his place.*]

FLOSSY. Don't look so frightened, Muffets. Of course I'll refuse you again.

[*He rises reluctantly, and they begin to pace the porch behind* MRS. MELBY'S *chair. When they are quite close to the lady,* FLOSSY *gives the signal.*]

FLOSSY [*Under her breath*]. Now!

MR. M. Flossy, I — I — I *love* you!

FLOSSY [*Loudly, with a ringing silvery laugh*]. Why, of course you do, Muffets, and I wish you didn't. That's what makes you so stupid half the time.

MR. M. But — but I . . .

FLOSSY. But you're a very silly boy. [*Under her breath she adds swiftly :*] You haven't asked me to marry you.

MR. M. [*Stammering*]. Will — w — will you be my wife?

FLOSSY [*Emphatically*]. No! I will not! You are ridiculous. The idea of it! . . . You are very nice as a friend, Muffets, but I certainly couldn't consider you seriously.

[*They stroll out of sight of* MRS. MELBY, *who immediately rises and darts into the hotel. The young people halt in their former place.* MORPETH *runs a hand over his brow.*]

FLOSSY. That was a little better than last time.

MR. M. I'm not used to asking women to marry me.

FLOSSY. That's quite evident. You still do it very badly.

[PAULINE BELTON *comes out of the hotel, red-cheeked and angry-eyed. She approaches* FLOSSY *and* MORPETH *threateningly.*]

PAULINE. Flossy! Will you be so good as to go up to your room at once!

FLOSSY. I was just going up for my hat.

PAULINE. You're going there to stay!

FLOSSY. No, Muffets and I are going out for a canoe ride. . . . While I get my hat, Muffets, will you go down and see if there's a canoe? — when you're through talking with Pauline, I mean. [*She moves toward the door.*]

PAULINE. I'm going to write to mama again that she's *got* to come.

FLOSSY [*Easily*]. She can't. She's got to stay home and nurse papa's gout.

[*She disappears into the hotel.* PAULINE *turns to* MORPETH.]

PAULINE. I should think, Mr. Morpeth, that you had gone far enough in playing with the feelings of a mere child. I have no words to express my contempt of you.

MR. M. But, Pauline . . . [*She gives him a cold stare.*] But, Miss Belton . . .

PAULINE. I used to think you were a *gentleman*, at least.

MR. M. You never treated me very well.

PAULINE. I suppose even then my intuition told me what an unprincipled man you were.

MR. M. If you had been — kinder to me . . .

PAULINE. Yes, I suppose you were ready to make an idiot of yourself over the very first person who encouraged you! But it's horrible that it should have to be my poor little sister!

[FLOSSY *appears in the doorway, swinging her wide straw hat gaily in her hand.*]

FLOSSY. My, what a nice long talk you two are having! . . . Muffets, *won't* you go down and see about the canoe? Just wave if it's all right.
                                    [MORPETH *goes down the steps.*]

PAULINE. It's outrageous! It's simply scandalous!

FLOSSY [*Lightly*]. What is, Pauline?

PAULINE. Why, the whole thing! To have my sister the talk of the place!

FLOSSY. It doesn't take much here to be the talk of the place. I've heard a word or two said about *you*, Pauline.

PAULINE [*Coldly*]. Certainly you've never heard that I've been proposed to in public.

FLOSSY. No, I haven't heard that. . . . *Have* you ever been proposed to, Pauline?

PAULINE [*More violently*]. And now there's Mrs. Melby running all about with the news just dripping out of her! . . . I should think the man would have *some* consideration for you.

FLOSSY. Poor Muffets! He can't help it. He's always talking to me that way. He never seems to think of anybody else. He cares so much for me, poor man!

PAULINE [*Stamping her foot*]. Oh, it's a disgrace!

FLOSSY [*Coolly*]. It isn't so bad as you might think, Pauline. It's rather fun at times.

[MR. BROWN *appears hovering in the hotel door.* FLOSSY *hails him.*]

FLOSSY. Hello, Mr. Brown. Muffets and I are just going out for a row. Why don't you and Pauline take the other canoe?

MR. BROWN. Would you care to, Miss Belton?

PAULINE. I would *not.*

[BROWN *bows sharply and withdraws.*]

FLOSSY. Poor Mr. Brown! He has to pay for all this, doesn't he?

PAULINE. He's a simpleton. *All* men are!

FLOSSY. You have to know how to handle them, Pauline.

PAULINE. Listen to little sister's wisdom!

FLOSSY. I seem to be getting along pretty well with Muffets. . . . There he is waving to me now. . . . You'd better be nice to Mr. Brown, Pauline.

[*She runs down the steps.* PAULINE *stares after her.*]

[MISS REDINGTON *comes from the hotel; she is a fluttery, ineffectual looking person of middle age.*]

MISS REDINGTON. Has she gone off with him again? . . . Oh, I have just heard from Mrs. Melby. . .

PAULINE. Mama's *got* to come!

MISS R. But she can't, Pauline, with your poor dear father so ill! If she would only *write* to Flossy!

PAULINE. She has, again and again, and Flossy pays no attention whatever.

MISS R. And I have begged her and begged her, with tears in my eyes, to remember that she's only a child.

PAULINE [*Quickly*]. We mustn't lay too much stress on that, Miss Redington. She gets so angry.

MISS R. I think we ought to go straight back home, Pauline.

PAULINE. We'll do nothing of the sort! Do you think I want to run away like that? — and acknowledge myself beaten?

[MR. BROWN *again appears in the doorway.* PAULINE *turns to him penitently.*]

PAULINE. I'm so afraid I spoke sharply to you a moment ago, Mr. Brown. You'll forgive it, won't you? That child upsets me *so*!

MR. B. [*Smiling*]. That's quite all right, Miss Belton. I'm used to harsh treatment, you know.

PAULINE [*Archly*]. Now, it seems to me you haven't much to complain of.

MR. B. Do you think you *would* like to go out on the lake?

PAULINE [*Sweetly*]. I think it would be lovely. [*She turns and looks out over the lake. Suddenly she gives a sharp cry.*] *Look* at Flossy! Standing up in the canoe! Why, the girl's crazy! ... Oh-h!

MISS R. Oh, what's happened? I can't see them! What's happened?

MR. B. [*Sharply*]. She's upset the canoe!

MISS R. Oh, oh, they'll be drowned!

[BROWN *runs down the steps, and in an instant* PAULINE *follows.*]

MISS R. [*Continuing to moan and exclaim*]. Oh, oh! They're in the water! Flossy will be drowned!

[MRS. MELBY *comes trotting out from the hotel, aware that something is taking place, and* MISS REDINGTON *breathlessly informs her what it is.*]

MISS R. Something terrible is happening! Mr. Morpeth and Flossy are drowning out there in the lake!

MRS. MELBY [*Peering out hungrily*]. I thought nothing good could come of all this!

MISS R. Can you see them? Have they gone under?

MRS. M. Somebody is swimming ashore. I can't see whether it's one or two.

MISS R. Oh, if it's only Flossy! Her mother would never for·give me if she's drowned!

MRS. M. Mr. Brown's trying to reach them. ... I think there's two of 'em swimming in. It looks too big for one.

MISS R. Surely he isn't brute enough to swim in alone and leave Flossy out there drowning!

MRS. M. Mr. Brown has got hold of him now. ... Yes, it's two of 'em, all right!

MISS R. Flossy is saved!

MRS. M. Mr. Morpeth is carrying her in his arms.

MISS R. I should think he would, after almost drowning her!

MRS. M. My, she's a sight! The water's just running off her! There, good for Pauline. She's found blankets for them.

MISS R. What presence of mind! Where did she get them?

MRS. M. Oh, probably from the boat house.

[*The two ladies have moved over to the head of the steps, and now* MR. MORPETH *appears there, with* FLOSSY *in his arms.* PAULINE *and* MR. BROWN *follow excitedly.* MR. MORPETH *deposits* FLOSSY *in a chair and stands looking down at her.*]

PAULINE. You must come right upstairs, Flossy, and get those wet things off this minute.

FLOSSY [*Rather faintly*]. Oh, let me rest here just a second, Pauline. This sun feels so good.

MISS R. Oh, I think I'm going to faint. . . Mrs. Melby! . . . Mr. Brown!

[MRS. MELBY *and* MR. BROWN *hurry to her aid and lead her into the hotel.*]

PAULINE. You'll catch your death of cold, sitting here in those wet things!

FLOSSY. I'll go up in *just* a minute, Pauline.

PAULINE. Well, I'll get your dry clothes ready for you then.

FLOSSY. All right, I'll be there.

[PAULINE *hurries into the hotel.*]

MR. M. [*Severely*]. Why *did* you do that, Flossy? It was wicked. It was cruel!

[*She lifts a hand to him and he takes it gently.*]

FLOSSY. Now, please don't say any more about it, Muffets. I don't want to be scolded.

MR. M. But it was such a dangerous thing to do!

FLOSSY. You've been awful nice to me lately, Muffets, but you'd never saved my life, and I wanted to give you the chance.

MR. M. Flossy! Suppose I hadn't been *able* to save it!

FLOSSY. Oh, I knew you could. . . . Did you see Pauline's eyes? You've got her now, Muffets. You've saved her sister's life.

MR. M. Flossy, don't you know that that is all ended? When I caught you there in the water — then I *knew*. It's you, Flossy. It's just you that I love. Don't you understand?

[FLOSSY *stretches out her arms weakly and puts them around his neck.*]

FLOSSY. You poor dear Muffets! Why do you suppose I've had you in training all summer? Did you think it was for Pauline?

CURTAIN

213. Analyzing a One-Act Play

We shall find it profitable to analyze several good one-act plays as a means of familiarizing ourselves with this type of dramatic narrative. In making such an analysis we should use the following questions and directions:

1. *The beginning.* (1) How much of the play is devoted to an explanation of the opening situation? (2) Is the opening of the play heavy and tedious because of too much exposition, or does it arouse your curiosity and stimulate interest? (3) Indicate details of antecedent action — that is, events that occurred before the action of the play begins — that are explained in the introduction by means of dialogue. (4) What principal characters, if any, take part in the opening scene? (5) What proportion of the play is devoted to the introduction?

2. *The plot.* (1) At what point in the play are you acquainted with the complicating incident — that is, the event or circumstance that brings the characters into conflict? (2) What incidents constitute the struggle? (3) What is the climax? (4) How near the end of the play does it come? (5) What is the outcome, or the new situation that serves as the ending? (6) Does it seem probable as the logical effect of the causes that lead up to it, or is it forced and mechanical? (7) Show how the author has employed suspense. (8) What anticipatory hints, or foreshadowing of the outcome, can you point out? (9) How much time does the action cover?

3. *The characters.* (1) Which character is chiefly responsible for the main action of the play? (2) Does the same character bring about the outcome? (3) Who are the other principal characters? (4) Who are the minor characters? (5) Do all the characters seem real and true to life? (6) Are they clearly individualized?

4. *The setting.* (1) What is the place setting of the action? (2) Is it realistic, suggestive, or romantic? (3) Does it help to give atmosphere to the play or serve as local color? (4) What is the time setting?

5. *The dialogue.* (1) Is the dialogue crisp and concise? (2) Does it seem fresh and spontaneous, or stilted and bookish? (3) Test the naturalness and effectiveness of the dialogue by reading a page or more of it aloud. (4) Does each person speak "in character"? (5) Show how and where dialogue is used to explain antecedent action.

6. *The stage-business.* (1) Is the stage-business adequate and clear? (2) Using the description of the stage setting, draw a floor-plan of the stage. (3) Point out details of stage-business that help you to visualize the characters and their movements. (4) Indicate stage-business that guides the actor in speaking certain lines. (5) In a printed play, how is stage-business distinguished from the dialogue?

7. *The play as a whole.* (1) Is the movement of the play rapid or slow? (2) Does it seem that the time covered by the action is longer than the time actually required to read the play or see it produced? (3) What single impression or emotional effect does the play make on you? (4) Can you point out a theme, or central idea, that helps to unify the play and to produce the single impression? (5) What is your chief interest: plot? character? theme? setting? dialogue? (6) Would you classify the play as a tragedy, a melodrama, a comedy, or a farce?

Exercise 457

Using the questions and directions given in section 213, make a careful analysis of the specimen play "A Sisterly Scheme" in Exercise 456. Come to class prepared to take part in a discussion of the play.

Exercise 458

As a means of studying the dialogue of "A Sisterly Scheme," choose from your class six pupils who read with good expression to impersonate the six characters. After

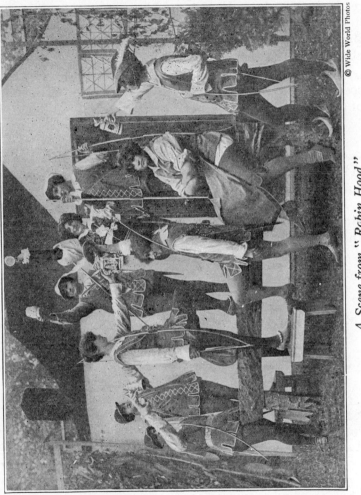

© Wide World Photos

A Scene from " Robin Hood "

reading the play at least once in rehearsal, the actors will read it to the class. Each actor should try in reading the lines to give an accurate impersonation of the character that he or she represents. As the play is read before the class, notice that dramatic dialogue is more concise and pointed than narrative dialogue. Observe also that each speech is definitely related to the action and the characters of the plays.

Exercise 459

Analyze by means of the questions and directions given in section 213 at least five one-act plays that your teacher may recommend.

Any of the following collections of one-act plays will provide entertaining reading and good material for study and discussion:

Twelve One-Act Plays. Selected and edited by S. Marion Tucker. Ginn and Company.

Types of Modern Dramatic Composition. Selected and edited by LeRoy Phillips and Theodore Johnson. Ginn and Company.

One-Act Plays. Selected and edited by Barrett H. Clark and Thomas R. Cook. D. C. Heath and Company.

One-Act Plays by Modern Authors. Selected and edited by Helen Louise Cohen. Harcourt, Brace and Company.

Contemporary One-Act Plays. Selected and edited by B. Roland Lewis. Charles Scribner's Sons.

Twelve One-Act Plays. Selected and edited by Walter Prichard Eaton. Longmans, Green and Company.

The Atlantic Book of Modern Plays. Selected and edited by Sterling Andrus Leonard. Little, Brown and Company.

The Atlantic Book of Junior Plays. Selected and edited by Charles Swain Thomas. Little, Brown and Company.

Representative One-Act Plays by American Authors. Selected and edited by Margaret G. Mayorga. Little, Brown and Company.

Representative One-Act Plays by British and Irish Authors.
Selected and edited by Barrett H. Clark. Little, Brown
and Company.

Representative One-Act Plays by Continental Authors.
Selected and edited by Montrose J. Moses. Little, Brown
and Company.

Fifty Contemporary One-Act Plays. Selected and edited by
Frank Shay and Pierre Loving. D. Appleton and Company.

Half Hours, by James Matthew Barrie. Charles Scribner's
Sons.

214. Dramatizing Stories

The comparison that we made of "A Sisterly Scheme"
and the short story from which it was adapted has given
us some understanding of the way in which such an adaptation is made. Before we attempt to devise an original one-
act play, we should gain experience in this type of narrative
composition by dramatizing at least one plot story written
by someone else. The following directions will aid us in the
process of dramatization:

1. *Choosing a suitable story.* The story that you select to
dramatize should satisfy these requirements:
    a. It should relate a single incident and possess dramatic
    interest for an audience.
    b. It should have a simple well-defined plot and only a few
    characters.
    c. It should contain a considerable amount of action.
    d. It should be told chiefly by means of conversation.
    e. The *main* action of the story should all occur in one place
    and cover a single brief period of time. (Occasionally
    it is possible, as in "A Sisterly Scheme," to dramatize
    a story that does not satisfy this requirement, pro-
    vided the main action can be satisfactorily limited to
    one place and time setting.)
2. *Writing the story in the form of a one-act play.* In making
the story into a play, proceed as follows:

a. Make a list of the characters that you will need in the play. If some characters in the story are unnecessary in the play, omit them. Rarely will an additional character be required.

b. Read the author's description of the scene of the main action. Visualize it clearly, and draw the floor-plan of the stage, showing the openings in the walls and the position of the principal furnishings or properties.

c. Write out the necessary introductory stage-business. State the time at which the action occurs. Tell where the action takes place, and give a brief description that will enable the reader to visualize the stage. Mention the style in which the characters are dressed. If the stage is occupied when the curtain rises, indicate who and where the characters are.

d. In general, follow the order of narration employed in the story. If the author of the story has explained the opening situation and related the antecedent action, invent for the right characters dialogue that will acquaint the audience with what it is necessary for them to know. Try to arouse interest in the opening scene. Get to the main action of the play as soon as clearness will permit.

e. Use as much of the author's dialogue as seems suitable for your play. Feel free to condense it or to omit portions of it if you can increase the dramatic effect by doing so. Invent dialogue of your own if it is needed, but make it appropriate and effective. Preceding each speech write the name of the character.

f. Along with the dialogue supply whatever stage directions the actors will need, such as position on the stage, posture, movements, and manner of speaking certain lines. Be sure to indicate at the right place each entrance and exit. Underscore all stage-business with one line.

g. When you have completed the first draft of the play, read it aloud, speaking the lines as you think the characters would speak them. Improve the dialogue in every way that you can. Try to make each speech natural and spontaneous and appropriate to the character and the situation. Avoid, in general, long speeches and long sentences, for they are rarely used in animated conversation. Oftentimes a single word or a brief phrase will suffice to convey the idea.

h. After you have thoroughly revised the play, make a final copy of it. Submit with your manuscript a clear drawing of the floor-plan of the stage with necessary explanation of your diagram. Give credit for the material for your play by stating the title of the story, the name of the author, and the name of the publisher.

Exercise 460

Explain to the class in what ways the short story "A Sisterly Scheme" is a suitable story for dramatization. Discuss the principal changes that the adapters made in dramatizing the story.

Exercise 461. Extra Credit

Compare the one-act play "The Kelly Kid"[1] with the short story of the same title by Kathleen Norris. Or compare the one-act play "Trifles"[2] with the short story "A Jury of Her Peers," by Susan Glaspell. Are the play and the story identical in plot, characters, setting, and dialogue? If not, what changes were made in the dramatized version? Note that each play is shorter than the corresponding story. Prepare a report dealing with these and other pertinent topics and present it to the class.

[1] This play may be found in "Types of Modern Dramatic Composition," edited by Phillips and Johnson and published by Ginn and Company. The short story from which the play is dramatized is in "The Callahans and the Murphys," by Kathleen Norris, published by the A. L. Burt Company.

[2] This play may be found in "Types of Modern Dramatic Composition," edited by Phillips and Johnson and published by Ginn and Company. The short story "A Jury of Her Peers," by Susan Glaspell, is in "Short Stories by Present-Day Authors," edited by R. W. Pence and published by The Macmillan Company.

Exercise 462

Mention a short story that you think would be suitable for dramatization, and explain to the class in what respects it satisfies the requirements given in section 214.

Exercise 463

In accord with the requirements and the directions given in section 214, choose the best plot story that you can find and dramatize it as a one-act play. In making the final copy of your play, follow the form and arrangement of material illustrated in "A Sisterly Scheme." If possible, submit with the manuscript of your play a copy of the short story that you dramatized.

Exercise 464

If your school or your community theater gives a performance of one-act plays, study the plays with reference to (1) the play itself, (2) the actors and the acting, and (3) the staging and producing. Make notes on points of special interest to be used in giving an oral report or in taking part in a class discussion.

Exercise 465

Would the short story that you wrote dealing with the situation given in the Preliminary Exercise of Chapter XVII be suitable for dramatization? Or have you written some other story that would make a better play? Select one of your stories that best satisfies the requirements stated in section 214, and develop it into a one-act play, following the directions given in section 214. Submit with your manuscript a drawing of the floor-plan of the stage.

215. Planning and Writing an Original One-Act Play

To create an original one-act play, we must first devise a good plot story that can be objectively told by means of action and dialogue, that requires only a few characters, and that can be presented in a single place and time setting. In preparing to write a play of our own, we should spend considerable time, therefore, in shaping our material into a story. Before attempting to relate the story in dramatic form, we should write out a complete synopsis of the main action that answers clearly the questions *When? Where? Who? Why? What? How?* The exercises that follow will guide us in devising and writing our first wholly original play.

Exercise 466

Using characters and a situation of your own choice, devise a story that you can relate successfully in a one-act play. When you have your story well thought out, write a complete synopsis of it in not more than three hundred words. See that your story as summarized satisfies the requirements stated in section 214. Submit with your synopsis a drawing of the floor-plan of the stage. The synopses will be read and discussed in class.

Exercise 467

When your synopsis has been approved by your teacher, develop it into a one-act play. Though you will have to invent all the dialogue, you will find many of the directions given in section 214 helpful in writing your play. In preparing the final copy of your play, follow the form and style of arrangement illustrated in "A Sisterly Scheme."

Exercise 468

Using the questions and the directions given in section 213, analyze one of the plays that you wrote in Exercises 463, 465, and 467. Which of your plays seems to you most satisfactory? Explain your answer in detail.

Exercise 469

The quality of a play and the success of the playwright can be rightly judged only when the play is presented by actors before an audience. With the aid of your teacher select the best play — adapted or original — that has been written in your class. Choose or select by competition the best actor to impersonate each character. As soon as the actors have learned their lines, conduct rehearsals under the direction of a competent adviser. Each actor should try to forget his own personality and do his best to speak and act as the character whom he impersonates would speak and act. For class production few, if any, stage furnishings and costumes will be required. When the play has been well prepared through rehearsals, it should be given before members of the class, who will serve as the audience and critics. A discussion of the play at the meeting of the class following the production will be profitable.

Exercise 470

Though plays are written primarily to be acted, they may be enjoyed by readers also. With the approval of your teacher, submit your best play to the editor of your school publication. If it is adapted from a short story written by another person, give due credit to the author and to the publisher.

PART FOUR

Aids in Using and Studying English

AS A well-bred boy or girl you do not eat with your knife, pick your teeth in the presence of others, or wear sports clothes to a dance. You take just pride in acting at all times in accord with the established rules of social etiquette, and you are quick to criticize persons who violate them.

Do you take equal pride in speaking and writing in accord with the established rules of good form and correct usage? Are you sensitive to errors in the etiquette of language that you and your associates commit? If, in commenting on the conduct of a person who has violated social etiquette, you say "Everyone should watch their manners, but he evidently don't know any better," you are guilty of two serious errors in the etiquette of English speech. When you are talking with persons who are careful of their own speech and writing, you injure your reputation for good breeding if you say "I know you will enthuse over this novel, for it sure is a good one." In your social letters you may forfeit much of the respect of your correspondents, and in your letters of application fail to get a desirable position, if you disregard good form, make mistakes in grammar or sentence structure, misspell words, use words incorrectly, or punctuate your sentences carelessly.

The first four chapters of Part Four will help you to improve in the etiquette of speaking and writing. From Chapters V, VI, VIII, and X you may also derive much aid. Do your best to make your speech and writing, as well as your social conduct, represent you as a well-bred person.

Functional Grammar: Essentials of Correct Usage

216. Purpose of This Chapter

In the present chapter many details of grammar and sentence structure that we often overlook or imperfectly understand are explained and illustrated. By studying these explanations and examples closely and by utilizing the various exercises for drill practice, we shall find help in overcoming bad habits of expression and in establishing correct habits in their stead. After we have studied the chapter, we should make regular use of it for reference.

217. Agreement of Subject and Predicate

1. A predicate verb agrees in number and person with its subject, *not* with its predicate nominative.

> *a.* They are the committee appointed.
> *b.* His chief interest in life was books.

2. A compound subject joined by *and* usually requires a plural verb.

> *a.* Constance and I are cousins.
> *b.* Tennis and rowing are my favorite forms of exercise.

If the parts of a compound subject joined by *and* are nearly synonymous, or together constitute a single unit or idea, a singular verb is required.

> *a.* The end and aim of her existence was service to others.
> *b.* Ice cream and cake was our dessert.

3. A compound subject joined by *or* or *nor* requires **a** singular verb if each portion of the subject is singular.

> *a.* Either your clock or my watch is wrong.
> *b.* Neither Tom nor Fred has returned.

If the members of a compound subject joined by *or* or *nor* differ in person or number, the verb agrees with the part of the subject nearer the verb.

> *a.* Neither you nor he has my permission.
> *Better:* Neither of you has my permission.
> *b.* Has he or I the better claim to the property?
> *Better:* Has he a better claim to the property than I have?

4. Such nouns as *measles, mumps, molasses, physics, mathematics, economics,* and *civics,* though plural in form, are singular in meaning and require a singular verb.

> *a.* Measles is often injurious to one's eyes.
> *b.* Mathematics is difficult for me.

Such nouns as *athletics, politics, means,* and *pains* (meaning *care*) are singular or plural, according to the sense.

> *a.* Athletics (the entire group of physical sports) forms an important part of school activities.
> *b.* Athletics (football, baseball, tennis, track, and basket ball) form an important part of school activities.

5. Collective nouns, such as *audience, committee, family, flock, herd, company, jury, class,* and *team,* may take either a singular or a plural verb, according to whether the group is thought of as a unit or as individuals.

> *a.* Our team has a good chance to win.
> *b.* The jury have not yet agreed on the evidence.

6. Nouns denoting quantity or amount, such as *half, part, portion, number,* may take either a singular or a plural verb, according to their meaning.

a. Half of the street has been paved.
b. Half of the audience were foreigners.
c. A number of automobile accidents occur every day.
d. The number of automobile accidents in this city is alarming.

7. A word or a group of words introduced by such connectives as *with, along with, together with, in company with, accompanied by, as well as, in addition to, besides,* and *including,* and standing between the subject and the predicate verb, does not affect the number of the subject.

a. Mrs. Ames, accompanied by her husband, has gone abroad.
b. The house, together with the furnishings, was sold.

8. The person and number of a verb having a relative pronoun as its subject must be the same as the person and number of the antecedent of the relative pronoun.

a. I, who am your friend, wish to help you.
b. She is one of the noblest women who have ever lived.

9. Such indefinite words as *each, every, either, neither, someone, anyone, everyone, anybody, everybody, one, no one,* and *a person* are singular and therefore require singular verbs and pronouns.

a. Each of us has his faults.   *c.* Everybody was excited.
b. Does everyone know his part?   *d.* Neither of us is guilty.

All, none, and *some* may take either a singular or a plural verb, according to their meaning.

a. All has been lost.   *d.* None of them were injured.
b. All were present.   *e.* Some of the fruit has spoiled.
c. None of it was found.   *f.* Some were late in arriving.

10. *Don't* (the contraction of *do not*) should never be used with a third-person *singular* subject. Always use *doesn't.*

a. She doesn't (*not* don't) enjoy reading poetry.
b. Doesn't (*not* don't) that surprise you?

11. *Was* should never be used with a second-person subject.

    a. You were (*not* was) mistaken in your guess.

    b. Were (*not* was) you at the dance last night?

12. *There is* (*was, has been*) should be used when the subject that follows it is singular; *There are* (*were, have been*), when the subject is plural.

    a. There is (was) no gasoline in the tank.

    b. There are (were) several canoes on the lake.

Exercise 471

In the following sentences point out, explain, and correct all errors in the agreement of subject and predicate ·

1. Each of the boys have been absent twice.
2. There was twelve people injured in the wreck.
3. A number of books is missing from the library.
4. For adults mumps are sometimes a dangerous disease.
5. Everybody in the audience were becoming impatient.
6. Neither his son nor his wife know when he will return.
7. Wasn't you surprised at the result of the game Saturday?
8. Father is a man who don't take any interest in politics.
9. Have either of you solved the last problem?
10. On the first Monday in October each class elect officers.

Exercise 472

In each of the following sentences supply *is* or *are*, *was* or *were*, *has* or *have*, as the meaning of the sentence demands, and explain why the verb supplied is correct:

1. There —— a large crowd at the game.
2. —— you a member of the Camera Club last year?
3. Measles —— kept several pupils out of school lately.
4. —— either of your parents at home?
5. The mob —— finally dispersed with tear bombs.
6. Rest, in addition to good food, —— improved her health.

7. It is evident that neither of us —— the right answer.

8. —— everybody in the class prepared the assignment?

9. Mother belongs to that large class of women who —— continually sharing other people's troubles.

10. The sum and substance of my decision —— that I cannot afford the trip.

218. Case of Nouns and Pronouns

1. A noun or a pronoun used as the subject of a predicate verb is in the nominative case.

a. She and I have many friends in common.
b. Who has been invited to the reception?

2. A noun or a pronoun used to complete the meaning of a predicate verb and denoting the same person or thing as the subject is in the nominative case. It is called a predicate nominative.

a. This is I.   *c.* The winners were we (they).
b. That is he (she).   *d.* Her guests were Anne and I.

3. A noun or a pronoun following *than* or *as* in a statement of comparison is in the nominative or the objective case, according to its construction in the elliptical clause in which it stands.

a. He is a better player than I [am].
b. I like him better than [I like] her.
c. Tom studies just as hard as I [study].

4. A noun or a pronoun used as the object of a verb or of a preposition is in the objective case.

a. Whom did you meet at the party?
b. Between you and me, I doubt the story.

5. A noun or a pronoun used as the subject of an infinitive is in the objective case.

a. I asked him to go with me.   *b.* He ordered us to leave.

6. When the infinitive *to be* has no subject, the predicate pronoun following it is in the nominative case to agree with the subject of the sentence; but when *to be* has a subject, the predicate pronoun is in the objective case to agree with the subject of the infinitive.

a. Were we thought to be they?   *c.* She believed me to be him.
b. Who am I supposed to be?   *d.* He suspected us to be them.

7. Appositive nouns and pronouns are in the same case as the word with which they are in apposition.

a. The culprits, he and I, were punished.
b. She put us, him and me, on probation for a month.

8. In general, the possessive case of nouns should be used only for nouns denoting persons or animals. Use an *of-*phrase in referring to plants and inanimate objects.

a. My friend's hair is brown.   *b.* The dog's collar is too small.
c. The stem of the flower (*not* the flower's stem) is broken.

There are recognized exceptions to this rule, such as *a day's outing, a stone's throw, a hair's breadth.*

9. The possessive case of a noun denoting the object of an action should be avoided. Use an *of-*phrase instead.

The inauguration of the president (*not* the president's inauguration) occurs tomorrow.

10. A noun in the possessive case or a possessive adjective should be used to modify a gerund.

a. I recall John's lending him the money.
b. Mother, do you object to my going home with Marion?

11. Personal, relative, and interrogative pronouns require no possessive sign to indicate the possessive case: *ours, yours, his, hers, its, theirs,* and *whose.*

Caution. *Remember that* **it's** *is a contraction of* **it is,** *and that* **who's** *is a contraction of* **who is.**

The possessives one's, anyone's, someone's, no one's, another's, one another's, each other's, and others' are correctly written with the possessive sign.

12. The case-form of the relative pronouns *who* and *whoever* must be determined by the construction of the pronoun in its own clause.

a. George is a boy who I believe is honest.
b. Nora is a maid whom mother says she can trust.
c. Mrs. Joyce helps whoever is in distress.
d. Be courteous to whomever you may meet.

13. The case-form of the interrogative pronoun *who* must be determined by its construction in the sentence.

a. Who shall I say you are?   b. Whom do you wish to see?

Exercise 473

In the following sentences point out, explain, and correct all errors in the case of nouns and pronouns:

1. Who, may I ask, do you wish to see?
2. Marjorie is two years younger than me.
3. America's discovery by Columbus occurred in 1492.
4. To her nieces, Alta and I, Aunt Jane gave her rings.
5. The missionary whom we thought had died came to visit us.
6. During her illness she allowed no one but I to see her.
7. Do you approve of Julia receiving company at her age?
8. When you answered the telephone, I thought you to be she.
9. Mother sat between Fred and I at the theater.
10. I once had just as many freckles as him.

Exercise 474

In each of the following sentences supply a pronoun in the proper case-form:

1. Yes, Helen, this is ――.
2. ―― do you suppose will be our next principal?
3. She appointed Gordon, Edith, and ―― as a committee.

4. Gordon, Edith, and —— were appointed as a committee.
5. No one except —— had heard the news.
6. The only pupils excused from the test were Olga and ——.
7. You cannot guess —— I saw at the circus yesterday.
8. In this picture, this is —— and that is ——.
9. —— is this boy in the back row supposed to be?
10. That is Fred Allen, —— you met last summer at camp.

219. Reference of Pronouns

The substantive (noun or pronoun) for which a pronoun stands and to which it refers is called its antecedent.

1. The reference of a pronoun to its antecedent should be unmistakably clear.

> *Correct:* Helen said, "Julia, you are mistaken." *Or* Helen said, "Julia, I am mistaken."
> *Incorrect:* Helen told Julia that she was mistaken.

2. The antecedent of a pronoun should be definitely expressed.

> *Correct:* I offered my assistance, but he refused it.
> *Incorrect:* I tried to assist him, but he refused it.
> *Correct:* We went to pick berries, but found only four quarts of them.
> *Incorrect:* We went berrying, but found only four quarts of them.

3. The relative pronoun *which* should not be used to refer to an entire clause as its antecedent.

> *Correct:* I was surprised that he was late. *Or* The fact that he was late surprised me.
> *Incorrect:* He was late, which surprised me.

4. Except in such expressions as *it rains, it is cold, it seems,* the use of *it* without an antecedent should be avoided.

> *Correct:* The author of this book (*or* This book) says that the castle was built in 1580.
> *Incorrect:* In this book it says that the castle was built in 1580.

5. Except in the colloquial expression *they say*, the use of *they* without an antecedent should be avoided.

Correct: The Japanese have many interesting customs.
Incorrect: They have many interesting customs in Japan.

Exercise 475

In the following sentences point out, explain, and correct all errors in the reference of pronouns:

1. Mother told Catherine that she was going to be late.
2. In some schools they have student self-government.
3. I was excused from the test, which pleased me greatly.
4. It says in the paper that the prices of food will be lower.
5. Father advised him to go to college, but he disregarded it.
6. They went clam-digging, but found only a few of them.
7. Marion wrote Vera that her cousin was coming to see her.
8. The building was insured, which was very fortunate.
9. They have recently established a republic in Spain.
10. Everyone awaited their turn at the cashier's window.

220. Uses of *This* and *That*

1. The demonstrative adjectives *this*, *that*, *these*, and *those* should not be used indefinitely. Either omit the adjective or supply a relative clause modifying the same noun that the adjective modifies.

Correct: My sister is a reckless driver. *Or* My sister is one of those reckless drivers who constantly take chances.
Incorrect: My sister is one of those reckless drivers.

2. The plural demonstrative adjectives *these* and *those* should not be used with such singular nouns as *kind*, *sort*, and *species*. Use *this* or *that*.

a. I like this (*not* these) kind of flowers.
b. That (*not* those) sort of people can never be happy.

The plural adjectives *these* and *those* are correctly used with the plural nouns *kinds* and *sorts*.

    a. My father grows these kinds of apples.
    b. Those sorts of books should be suppressed.

221. Adjectives and Adverbs in Expressions of Comparison

1. In comparing two persons, places, or things, use the comparative degree of the adjective or adverb.

    a. Ethel is the prettier (*not* prettiest) of the twins.
    b. Of the two books, this is the better (*not* the best).

2. In comparing a person, place, or thing with the rest of its class, use *other* or *else*, as the meaning may require, with the comparative degree of the adjective or adverb.

    a. Dorothy is prettier than any other girl in school.
    b. He studies harder than anyone else in the class.

3. With the superlative degree of an adjective or an adverb expressing a comparison of a person, place, or thing with the rest of its class, use *all*, if necessary, but not *any*, before the noun designating the entire class to which the person, place, or thing belongs.

    Correct: She is the youngest pupil in the class. *Or* She is the youngest of all the pupils in the class.
    Incorrect: She is the youngest of any of the pupils in the class.

4. In expressions of comparison do not confuse *as* and *than*. To avoid this error, always state the comparison fully before adding the qualifying expression. After a negative, such as *not*, use *so* instead of *as*.

    Correct: I am as old as you are, if not older [than you are].
    Incorrect: I am as old, if not older, than you are.
    Correct: John is brighter than his brother, but not so reliable.
    Incorrect: John is brighter but not so reliable as his brother.

5. In expressions of comparison do not use a singular noun to serve at the same time as both singular and plural.

> *Correct:* That is one of the best plays that I have ever seen, if not the best play.
> *Incorrect:* That is one of the best, if not the best, play that I have ever seen.

6. Avoid the use of the comparative and the superlative degrees of such adjectives and adverbs as *level, round, square, perfect, faultless, absolute, unique, perfectly, absolutely,* and *uniquely,* for they cannot logically be compared.

> *a.* His defeat was absolute (*not* most absolute).
> *b.* The dress fitted her perfectly (*not* most perfectly).

Exercise 476

In the following sentences point out, explain, and correct all errors in the use of adjectives and adverbs in expressions of comparison:

1. Frank is the tallest of any of my brothers.
2. Texas is larger than any state in the United States.
3. This is one of the coldest, if not the coldest, day that we have had this winter.
4. Of all my relatives, she is the most unique.
5. This hat is more expensive but not so becoming as that one.
6. I write to you as often, if not oftener, than you write to me.
7. My father is the most patient of my parents.
8. Today is the shortest of any day in the year.
9. His second novel is as good, if not better, than his first.
10. I write more rapidly but not so legibly as you do.

222. Adjectives and Adverbs Not to be Confused in Use

1. After such verbs as *appear, remain, grow, prove, feel, taste, smell, look, sound, stand,* and *turn,* use an adjective to denote the quality or the condition of the subject; but

use an adverb to signify the manner in which the action expressed by the verb is performed.

ADJECTIVE	ADVERB
a. He looked shy.	a. He looked shyly at her.
b. Charles turned red.	b. Charles turned instantly.
c. He grew strong.	c. The tree grew rapidly.
d. He appeared happy.	d. He appeared unexpectedly.

2. After such verbs as *make, fasten, keep, sweep,* and *hold,* use an adjective to denote the quality or the condition of the object, resulting from the action of the verb; but use an adverb to signify the manner in which the action expressed by the verb is performed.

ADJECTIVE	ADVERB
a. The news made me happy.	a. He made the change quickly.
b. She swept the floor clean.	b. She swept the floor briskly.
c. The coat kept me warm.	c. He kept his promise faithfully.

3. Do not use *sure* for *surely, real* for *really* or *very, mighty* for *very, some* for *somewhat,* or *awful* for *very.*

    a. I was surely (*not* sure) glad to see him.
    b. Mother woke me very (*not* real) early.
    c. The patient feels somewhat (*not* some) better.
    d. I was very (*not* awful) sorry to hear the bad news.

223. Double Negatives

Do not use in the same sentence two or more negative words unless they are coördinate. Avoid using *hardly, scarcely, only, but* (*only*), *neither, no one, none, nobody, nothing, no,* and *not* with another negative word.

    a. He could (*not* couldn't) hardly speak above a whisper.
    b. I had (*not* hadn't) never heard the story before.
    c. I cannot help pitying (*not* cannot help but pity) him.
    d. Who I am is (*not* isn't) nobody's business but my own.

Functional Grammar

Exercise 477

In the following sentences point out, explain, and correct all errors in the use of adjectives and adverbs:

1. I have always disliked flatterers and those kind of people.
2. This dessert tastes deliciously.
3. Of the two suits, I bought the least expensive.
4. I couldn't hardly hear what she said over the telephone.
5. It will probably rain tonight and be some colder tomorrow.
6. Every pupil should try to write legible.
7. I never gave him no cause to doubt my honesty.
8. His voice sounded loudly over the radio.
9. These sort of plays should be prohibited.
10. Agnes made one of the highest, if not the highest, grade.
11. How sweetly this flower smells!

Exercise 478

Write sentences in which you use appropriate predicate adjectives after the following verbs: *be, appear, seem, become, grow, prove, remain, feel, taste,* and *smell.* In each sentence explain why an adjective, not an adverb, should be used.

Exercise 479

Write sentences in which you use appropriate adjectives as modifiers of the objects of the following verbs: *make, fasten, wrap, fill, bind, paint, nail, hold, wash,* and *iron.* Write sentences in which you use these same verbs modified by appropriate adverbs of manner.

224. Principal Parts of Difficult Verbs

The principal parts of the following difficult verbs should be memorized, and should be used in short model sentences in order to fix in the mind the right tense-form of each.

PRESENT TENSE	PAST TENSE	PAST PARTICIPLE	PRESENT TENSE	PAST TENSE	PAST PARTICIPLE
am (be)	was	been	lie	lay	lain
awake	awoke	awaked	loose	loosed	loosed
bear	bore	borne	lose	lost	lost
		born	pay	paid	paid
begin	began	begun	prove	proved	proved
bend	bent	bent	read	read	read
bid	bade	bidden	ride	rode	ridden
	bid	bid	ring	rang	rung
bite	bit	bit	rise	rose	risen
		bitten	run	ran	run
bleed	bled	bled	see	saw	seen
blow	blew	blown	set	set	set
break	broke	broken	shake	shook	shaken
bring	brought	brought	shed	shed	shed
burst	burst	burst	shine	shone	shone
choose	chose	chosen	shrink	shrank	shrunk
come	came	come	sing	sang	sung
deal	dealt	dealt	sit	sat	sat
dive	dived	dived	slay	slew	slain
do	did	done	slide	slid	slid
drag	dragged	dragged	speak	spoke	spoken
draw	drew	drawn	steal	stole	stolen
drink	drank	drunk	swear	swore	sworn
drive	drove	driven	sweep	swept	swept
drown	drowned	drowned	swim	swam	swum
eat	ate	eaten	take	took	taken
fall	fell	fallen	tear	tore	torn
flee	fled	fled	throw	threw	thrown
fly	flew	flown	thrust	thrust	thrust
freeze	froze	frozen	tread	trod	trod
get	got	got			trodden
go	went	gone	wake	waked	waked
grow	grew	grown		woke	
kneel	knelt	knelt	wear	wore	worn
know	knew	known	weave	wove	woven
lay	laid	laid	weep	wept	wept
lead	led	led	write	wrote	written

Exercise 480

Following the plan given below, make short sentences in which you use the correct tense-forms of at least ten verbs that you have found difficult heretofore. Be sure that you can use correctly the verbs *see, do, come, ring,* and *go.*

PRESENT TENSE	PAST TENSE	PRESENT PERFECT TENSE
I *eat.*	I *ate.*	I have *eaten.*
We *begin.*	We *began.*	We have *begun.*
He *lies* in bed.	He *lay* in bed.	He has *lain* in bed.

Exercise 481

From the verbs given in parentheses after each of the following sentences choose the right verb and supply the correct tense-form in each blank:

1. I have —— still so long that I need exercise. (*sit, set*)

2. She has —— in that position for two days. (*lie, lay*)

3. As soon as we had —— the house in order, we —— down to rest. (*sit, set*)

4. The man across the aisle ——, —— his hat, and offered to —— the window for me. (*raise, rise*)

5. I enjoy —— down after —— out plants all the afternoon. (*sitting, setting*)

6. His uncle was —— in a room where he had —— for three years. (*lie, lay*)

7. —— the book on the table, and let it —— there. (*lie, lay*)

8. Do you think that this coat —— well? (*sit, set*)

9. Last week mother —— the old blue hen on fifteen eggs out in the woodshed, and there she has —— ever since. (*sit, set*)

10. All night my book had —— on the front step, where I had —— it when I went to play ball. (*lie, lay*)

225. Uses of *Shall* and *Will, Should* and *Would*

The following rules for the correct use of *shall* and *will, should* and *would* should be accurately learned:

1. To represent simple futurity, use *shall* or *should* in the first person and *will* or *would* in the second and third persons, both singular and plural.

> *a.* I shall be seventeen years old in November.
> *b.* If I had been invited, I should have gone.
> *c.* You will reach your destination Friday, I suppose.
> *d.* I have recently read a novel that you would enjoy reading.
> *e.* They will call for us at eight o'clock.

NOTE. *Will* is used in the second and third persons to express polite commands.

> *a.* You will report to me as soon as you have returned.
> *b.* He will deliver this letter to the general at once.

2. To express determination, resolution, desire, or promise on the part of the speaker, use *will* or *would* in the first person and *shall* or *should* in the second and third persons, both singular and plural.

> *a.* I will refuse every offer of compromise.
> *b.* We will accompany you to the boat if you wish.
> *c.* You shall not leave this house tonight.
> *d.* Were you my child, you should obey me.
> *e.* He shall pay me every cent he owes.

NOTE. *Shall* is used in the second and third persons to express prophecy.

> *a.* Thou shalt lower to his level day by day.
> *b.* Your young men shall see visions, and your old men shall dream dreams.

3. If the subject of a direct question is in the first person, use *shall* and *should*, except in repeating a question addressed to the speaker.

> *a.* Shall I see you at the game? (*Answer:* Yes, you will see me.)
> *b.* Shall we walk or ride? (*Answer:* We shall walk.)
> *c.* Will you lend me the book? (*Answer:* Will I lend you the book? Indeed, I will.)

4. If the subject of a direct question is in the second or third person, use the auxiliary that you anticipate in the

answer. The auxiliary used in the answer should be chosen according to rules 1 and 2 applying to statements.

a. Shall you attend the reception? (*Answer:* I shall . . .)
b. Will you meet me promptly at seven? (*Answer:* I will . . .)
c. Would you go if you were invited? (*Answer:* I would . . .)
d. Will she recover? (*Answer:* She will . . .)
e. Shall he be punished? (*Answer:* He shall . . .)

5. In indirect quotations retain, in general, the auxiliary *shall, will, should,* or *would* used in the direct quotation, unless a change of tense (*shall* to *should, will* to *would*) is required for proper sequence of tenses.

a. Agnes says, "I shall be late." (Direct statement)
 Agnes said that she should be late. (Indirect statement)
b. Fred says, "I will go with you." (Direct statement)
 Fred said that he would go with me. (Indirect statement)
c. "What shall I tell her?" he asked. (Direct question)
 He asked me what he should tell her. (Indirect question)
d. "Will you go with me?" Fred asked. (Direct question)
 Fred asked me if I would go with him. (Indirect question)

When the second person with *will* and *would* in a direct statement becomes the first person in the indirect statement, *will* and *would* are changed to *shall* and *should*.

Mother says, "You will be late." (Direct statement)
Mother says that I shall be late. (Indirect statement)
Mother said that I should be late. (Indirect statement)

6. *Would* is often used to express a wish.

a. Would that I were there!
b. Would that he had told us earlier!

7. *Would* is frequently used in all three persons to indicate customary or habitual action.

a. Every day we would go swimming.
b. At six o'clock each morning you would hear the gong.
c. He would often read a new novel through at one sitting.

8. *Should* is frequently used in all three persons as a synonym of *ought* to express duty, obligation, propriety, or expectation.

    a. You should be more considerate.
    b. He should have written us that he was coming.
    c. We should arrive at camp before sunset.

Caution. Avoid such vulgarisms as should ought and had ought.

9. *Shall* and *should* are used in all three persons in subordinate clauses that make provisional statements.

    a. If I should change my mind, I would notify you.
    b. Should you meet her, would you speak to her?
    c. An official who should betray such a trust would be dismissed.

Exercise 482

Supply in each of the following sentences either *shall* or *will*, according to the rules given above, and state the reason for the use of each auxiliary:

1. They —— not impose on my generosity any longer.
2. —— I tell the doctor that you are waiting?
3. —— you inform the postman of my change of address?
4. I —— drown; no one —— rescue me.
5. Before you die you —— see that I am right.
6. —— I protect you? Why, certainly I ——.
7. You —— not punish an innocent man.
8. —— I see you again before you sail?
9. When —— we three meet again?
10. Our friends —— be surprised to hear the news.
11. Generations as yet unborn —— cherish this spot.
12. We —— never have a truer friend than Cranston.
13. You —— now prepare to hand in your papers.
14. I —— not attempt to excuse myself.
15. If you —— give me the letter, I —— mail it.

© Wide World

Norman Rockwell Instructing a Class in Drawing

Exercise 483

Supply in each of the following sentences either *should* or *would*, according to the rules given above, and state the reason for the use of each auxiliary:

1. I —— ask for more time if I were you.
2. —— I tell him the whole wretched story?
3. Do you suppose that he —— believe me?
4. What —— you do if you were in my place?
5. If I had the book, you —— have it.
6. —— you be disappointed if I were not to come?
7. —— you accept a position as stenographer in our firm?
8. They —— willingly help us if they could.
9. They —— be thankful for their good health.
10. —— that I had never taken the risk!
11. If I —— tell you the truth, —— you believe me?
12. On summer evenings we —— watch the fireflies.
13. They —— not listen to our warning.
14. He promised his mother that he —— not go swimming.
15. She reminded him that he —— come home early.

Exercise 484

Write twenty sentences illustrating the various proper uses of *shall*, *will*, *should*, and *would*. In each sentence be sure to use the correct auxiliary. Place in parentheses after each sentence the number of the rule that applies.

226. Cautions Regarding Tense

1. In stating a fact that is permanently true use the present tense.

   a. At a very early age I learned that honesty is the best policy.
   b. Though ancient peoples believed that the earth was flat, Magellan proved that it is round.

2. Avoid using the past tense where the past perfect tense is required.

a. We had lived (*not* lived) in the house only six months before it burned.

b. I had gone (*not* went) without food two days before the check arrived.

3. Do not use the past participle for the past tense.

a. Then snow began (*not* begun) to fall.

b. We sang (*not* sung) several of our school songs.

4. Do not use the past-tense form of a verb for the past participle in forming the perfect tenses.

a. The first bell has rung (*not* has rang).

b. It had begun (*not* had began) to rain before we started.

5. Avoid using a perfect infinitive unless it designates an action completed at the time indicated by the principal verb.

a. I intended to write (*not* to have written) to you.

b. I should have liked to meet (*not* to have met) him.

NOTE. With the verb *ought* the perfect infinitive is properly used. *Example:* He ought to have left us his address.

6. Avoid using a present participle unless it designates an action going on at the same time as the action indicated by the principal verb.

a. Having missed (*not* missing) our train, we could do nothing but wait for the next one.

b. While waiting for the train, we read the newspaper. (The two actions were simultaneous.)

Exercise 485 √

In the following sentences point out, explain, and correct all errors in the tense of verbs:

1. Fred and I swum two miles yesterday.
2. He assured me that youth was the best period in life.

3. I should have liked to have attended the circus with you.
4. Father told us how he earned his expenses at college.
5. I had sank for the second time before I was rescued.
6. Losing his fortune at the age of fifty, he begun life anew.
7. She would have preferred to have remained at home.
8. My alarm clock rung at three and woke me.
9. I had planned to have gone to the theater tonight.
10. Astronomers long ago proved that the sun was the center of our planetary system.

Exercise 486

Write sentences using the past tense and the past perfect tense of the following verbs: *break, burst, come, do, drink, fall, freeze, go, prove, ride, ring, run, see, sing, sink, speak, swim, take, tear,* and *wear.*

227. Cautions Regarding Mood

1. To express a condition contrary to fact use the subjunctive, not the indicative, mood of the verb.

a. I wish that I were (*not* was) at home.
b. If it were (*not* was) Saturday, I would go with you.
c. If that car were (*not* was) mine, I would sell it.
d. If I were (*not* was) in his condition, I would see a doctor.
e. Were (*not* was) I in need, I would accept your offer.

2. In clauses introduced by *as if* and *as though* use the subjunctive, not the indicative, mood of the verb.

a. She looked as if she were (*not* was) ill.
b. He advised me as though he were (*not* was) my guardian.
c. The dog barked as if there were (*not* was) someone coming.

Exercise 487

In each of the following sentences supply *was* or *were,* according to the mood of the verb demanded, and explain why the verb that you supplied is correct:

1. I would not give the matter another thought if I —— you.
2. If he —— not my guardian, I might ask his advice.
3. She spoke to him as though he —— a servant.
4. I wish that this car —— mine.
5. If I —— you, I would demand an apology.
6. —— it possible, I would accompany you on the trip.
7. She would have more friends if she —— more generous.
8. He drove the car as if he —— going to a fire.
9. Yes, if I —— you, I would send her an invitation.
10. He spends money as though he —— a millionaire.

228. Reference of Participles

1. In using a participial phrase, be sure to make the participle modify the right word. An introductory participial phrase modifies the subject of the sentence.

> *Correct:* The lion, being in a cage, did not frighten me.
> *Incorrect:* Being in a cage, I was not afraid of the lion.
> *Correct:* Having returned from a visit to my aunt, I was welcomed home by my parents. *Or* When I returned from a visit to my aunt, my parents welcomed me home.
> *Incorrect:* Having returned from a visit to my aunt, my parents welcomed me home.

2. Do not end a sentence with a participial phrase in which the participle is made to refer to a vaguely implied substantive or to the entire thought of the preceding sentence or clause.

> *Correct:* The impurity of the water was caused by bad drainage. *Or* The water was impure as the result of bad drainage.
> *Incorrect:* The water was impure, caused by bad drainage.
> *Correct:* His ability to speak several languages aids him in his travels. *Or* He speaks several languages, and this ability aids him in his travels.
> *Incorrect:* He speaks several languages, thus aiding him in his travels.

229. Reference of Gerunds

Avoid using a gerund phrase to introduce a sentence unless the gerund properly refers to the subject of the sentence.

> *Correct:* In alighting from the car, I turned my ankle. *Or* As I alighted from the car, I turned my ankle.
> *Incorrect:* In alighting from the car, my ankle was turned.

230. Reference of Infinitives

Avoid using an infinitive or an infinitive phrase to introduce a sentence unless the infinitive properly refers to the subject of the sentence.

> *Correct:* To succeed, you must understand the process.
> *Incorrect:* To succeed, the process must be understood.

231. Split Infinitives

Do not split an infinitive by placing an adverbial modifier between the sign *to* and the infinitive or within the infinitive.

> *Correct:* The boat seemed hardly to move.
> *Incorrect:* The boat seemed to hardly move.
> *Correct:* He was said to have bought the house recently.
> *Incorrect:* He was said to have recently bought the house.

Exercise 488

In the following sentences point out, explain, and correct all errors in the reference of participles, gerunds, and infinitives:

1. To obtain good seats, reservations should be made early.
2. Coming out of the door, Forbes met a man as he entered.
3. After giving me a prescription, I paid the doctor and left.
4. To play on your team, the scholastic record must be good.
5. Having met her once before, she easily recognized me.
6. He is blind, caused by an automobile accident.

7. Upon entering the hall, loud applause greeted the speaker.

8. To be sure that the dress will fit, a form should be used.

9. Having recovered from his illness, the firm took him back.

10. In studying for his examinations his eyes were strained.

11. He takes exercise, thus assuring himself of good health.

12. Coming unexpectedly as it did, she was shocked by the news.

13. The price of cotton declined, caused by overproduction.

14. Being a guest, we were greatly surprised at his rudeness.

15. To save time, the package was sent by special delivery.

232. Use of Prepositions

1. Fix in mind the correct use of the prepositions printed in italics in the sentences that follow:

    a. She divided the money *between* John and me. (Two persons)

    b. The property was distributed *among* his three heirs.

    c. They live *in* a large white house. (Position)

    d. We went *into* the reception hall. (Motion)

    e. Joe sat *beside* (by the side of, next to) me.

    f. He has no relatives *besides* (in addition to) his brother.

    g. I borrowed this book *from* (*not* off) my chum.

    h. We buy eggs *of* (*not* off) a neighbor.

    i. The puppy climbed up *on* (*not* onto) the porch.

    j. The garage stands *behind* (*not* in back of) the house.

    k. Our car is different *from* (*not* than *or* to) yours.

    l. She blamed me *for* it. (*Not* She blamed it *on* me.)

2. Avoid using prepositions that are unnecessary. Study the following sentences as examples:

    a. He would not accept (*not* accept *of*) my excuse.

    b. He covered (*not* covered *over*) the flower bed.

    c. I continued (*not* continued *on with*) my work.

    d. She stepped off (*not* off *of*) the porch.

    e. I am glad that the examination is over (*not* over *with*).

    f. Do you plan to go (*not* plan *on* going) to the circus?

    g. She did not remember (*not* remember *of*) meeting me.

    h. Where does he live now? (*Not* Where does he live *at* now?)

    i. Where were they going? (*Not* Where were they going *to*?)

3. Except in colloquial speech, avoid ending a sentence with a preposition, unless the preposition is an emphatic word.

> *a.* Whom did you give the letter to? (Colloquial)
> *b.* To whom did you give the letter? (More formal)
> *c.* The prize is worth working for. (Emphatic word)

Exercise 489

In the following sentences point out, explain, and correct all errors in the use of prepositions:

1. I found my cap in back of the couch.
2. Where do you plan on spending your vacation?
3. The little boy climbed onto the porch and went in the house.
4. The officers blamed the accident on the driver of the car.
5. Your answer to this problem is different than mine.
6. I bought these toys off a sidewalk vender.
7. Where were you going to when you met him?
8. The debate was not over with until ten o'clock.
9. She slipped as she stepped off of the last step.
10. There were tennis courts in back of the hotel.

233. Use of Conjunctions

1. Do not use the coördinating conjunctions (*and, but, or, nor,* and *for*) to connect words, phrases, or clauses that are not in the same grammatical construction.

> *Correct:* I was late because I overslept and missed my car.
> *Incorrect:* I was late because I overslept and missing my car.
> *Correct:* The play was excellent, but you might not enjoy it.
> *Incorrect:* The play was excellent, but which you might not enjoy.

2. Avoid using *like* as a conjunction to connect two clauses. Use *as* or *as if.*

> *a.* I came home early as (*not* like) you told me to do.
> *b.* She cared for the child as if it were (*not* like it was) her own.

3. Avoid such errors in the use of conjunctions as those illustrated in the following sentences:

    a. I answered the telephone as soon as (*not* directly *or* immediately) it rang.
    b. You will fail unless (*not* without *or* except) you study more.
    c. She never visits us that she does not bring (*not* without she brings) her pet dog with her.

Exercise 490

In the following sentences point out, explain, and correct all errors in the use of conjunctions:

    1. The nurse cared for the patient like the doctor had directed.
    2. We will fill your order directly a new shipment arrives.
    3. I never see him without he asks me to lend him money.
    4. I met his cousin, and whom he had often mentioned.
    5. You look like you had not been taking enough exercise.
    6. He sounded the alarm immediately he discovered the fire.
    7. They bought a car, but which they soon sold.
    8. The plants were set out directly they were received.
    9. You will succeed if you make the cake like I showed you.
    10. He acted like he had some trouble on his mind.

234. Parallel Construction

Ideas that are parallel in thought should likewise be parallel in grammatical expression (see section 121, 5, *c.*).

1. Do not attempt to make a word and a phrase, a word and a clause, or a phrase and a clause parallel in construction.

    Correct: He promised me the position and twenty dollars a week as pay. *Or* He promised me the position at twenty dollars a week. *Or* He promised to give me the position and to pay me twenty dollars a week.
    Incorrect: He promised me the position and to pay me twenty dollars a week.

Correct: He promised to give me the position and to pay me twenty dollars a week. *Or* He promised that he would give me the position and that he would pay me twenty dollars a week.

Incorrect: He promised me the position and that he would pay me twenty dollars a week.

Correct: I agreed to accept the position and to begin work on Monday. *Or* I agreed that I would accept the position and that I would begin work on Monday.

Incorrect: I agreed to accept the position and that I would begin work on Monday.

2. Do not attempt to make an infinitive and a participle, or an infinitive and a gerund, parallel in construction.

Correct: Father agreed to let me go to college and to pay a part of my expenses.

Incorrect: Father agreed to let me go to college and paying a part of my expenses.

3. Do not attempt to make an infinitive and a predicate verb, or a gerund and a predicate verb, parallel in construction.

Correct: I had the choice of two trips: to accompany my parents to Maine, or to go with my chum to California. *Or* I had the choice of two trips: accompanying my parents to Maine, or going with my chum to California. *Or* I had the choice of two trips: I could accompany my parents to Maine, or I could go with my chum to California.

Incorrect: I had the choice of two trips: to accompany my parents to Maine, or I could go with my chum to California.

Exercise 491

Correct the following sentences by using parallel construction:

1. I expected her to be uneasy and that she would scold me.
2. To find the key and getting into the house required some time.
3. Father has promised me a trip and to give me a car.

4. I agreed to use my car and that he would buy the gasoline.

5. I told them that I would go if I could but not to wait for me.

235. Shift in Point of View

For the sake of clearness and emphasis, try to avoid shifting the point of view in a sentence. It is desirable to employ the same subject and the same voice throughout.

> *Undesirable:* When you have selected a satisfactory pattern, the material may then be bought.
>
> *Better:* When you have selected a satisfactory pattern, you may then buy the material.

236. Misuse of Clauses

1. Avoid using a clause introduced by *when, where,* or *what* as a predicate nominative. Use a noun instead.

> *Correct:* Narration is the relating of an experience or an event.
>
> *Incorrect:* Narration is when you relate an experience or an event.
>
> *Correct:* Inflection is a change in the form of a word to indicate a change in its meaning.
>
> *Incorrect:* Inflection is where you change the form of a word to indicate a change in its meaning.

2. Avoid using an adverbial clause introduced by *because* to perform the function of a noun clause either as the subject of a sentence or as a predicate nominative.

> *Correct:* The fact that your intentions were good does not excuse you.
>
> *Incorrect:* Because your intentions were good does not excuse you.
>
> *Correct:* The reason he failed in his examinations was that he did not study.
>
> *Incorrect:* The reason he failed in his examinations was because he did not study.

Caution. *Never say " The reason is because." Say " The reason is that."*

Exercise 492

In the following sentences point out, explain, and correct all errors resulting from the misuse of clauses :

1. A pulmotor is what doctors use to restore normal activity in the lungs of a patient who has been asphyxiated.
2. Perjury is when a person under oath to tell the truth tells a lie.
3. Because they have no money does not keep some people from buying cars and radios.
4. An abattoir is where sheep, cattle, and hogs are slaughtered.
5. The reason I cannot attend the party is because I do not have a suitable dress.
6. A mortgage is what a bank takes when property is given as security for a loan.
7. Madison, Wisconsin, is where my oldest sister lives.
8. Because I had failed on the test humiliated me greatly.
9. The Fourth of July is when the celebration will be held.
10. The reason some pupils fail is because they do not study.

237. Cautions Regarding Compound Sentences

1. Avoid overworking the compound sentence. A thought imperfectly expressed in a loosely constructed compound sentence can often be better expressed in a simple or a complex sentence.

> *Poor:* We are going to the country this summer, and we intend to visit my grandmother there.
> *Better:* We are going to the country this summer to visit my grandmother. (A simple sentence)
> *Poor:* My chum told me that I had won the scholarship, and I was overjoyed.
> *Better:* When my chum told me that I had won the scholarship, I was overjoyed. (A complex sentence)

2. Unless the second clause of a compound sentence expresses consequence, do not connect the clauses by *so*.

Usually the clause preceding *so* should be subordinated and the *so* omitted. Avoid the careless use of *and so* as a connective. A complex sentence is almost always to be preferred.

Poor: It was Saturday morning, and so I slept late.
Better: Since it was Saturday morning, I slept late.

3. Do not allow yourself to write loosely constructed, or stringy, compound sentences. Either express the subordinate portions of the sentence-thought by means of phrases or clauses, or devote a separate sentence to each sentence-thought.

Poor: The old storekeeper had queer ways, but everyone was fond of him, and he certainly was a real friend to everyone, and I never knew a man who had a kinder heart.
Better: Though the old storekeeper had queer ways, I never knew a man who had a kinder heart. Everyone was fond of him, because each recognized in him a real friend.

238. Improper Omission of Words

1. Do not omit a principal verb or a portion of a verb phrase in any part of a sentence unless the form expressed elsewhere in the sentence is grammatically correct and clearly implied at the point where it is omitted.

Correct: She has not recovered and never will recover.
Incorrect: She has not and never will recover.
Correct: I have not written, nor am I going to write.
Incorrect: I have not written, nor am I going to.
Correct: The house was painted and the rooms were papered again.
Incorrect: The house was painted and the rooms papered again.
Correct: She was a successful teacher and was loved by all her pupils.
Incorrect: She was a successful teacher and loved by all her pupils.

2. Do not omit an article or a demonstrative or possessive adjective before any noun in a series unless the nouns designate the same person or thing or are self-distinguishing.

> *Correct:* The three officers of our class are the president, the vice president, and the secretary and treasurer.
>
> *Incorrect:* The three officers of our class are the president, vice president, and secretary and treasurer.
>
> *Correct:* Last week I was the maid, cook, and nurse for our family.
>
> *Correct:* His father and mother were born in Scotland.

3. Do not omit a preposition that is either grammatically or idiomatically necessary in the sentence.

> *Incorrect:* I have no understanding or interest in golf.
>
> *Correct:* I have no understanding of, or interest in, golf.
>
> *Better:* I have no understanding of golf and no interest in it.

NOTE. In formal composition many adverbial phrases of time, place, and manner regularly require a preposition.

> I will help you at any time (*not* any time).
>
> I can be content in any place (*not* any place).
>
> I never saw him act in that way (*not* that way) before.

4. In formal composition do not omit the subordinating conjunction *that* at the beginning of a noun clause that follows a verb of *saying, knowing, thinking, feeling, perceiving,* etc.

> *Correct:* Do you realize *that* by neglecting your present opportunities you are handicapping yourself for life?
>
> *Incorrect:* Do you realize by neglecting your present opportunities you are handicapping yourself for life?

5. In formal writing do not omit *that* after *so* in the connective *so that* introducing a clause of purpose or of result.

> *Correct:* The storm raged so violently *that* no one slept.

6. Before an introductory participial or gerund phrase that is the equivalent of a subordinate clause use a subordinating conjunction.

Correct: While studying my lessons, I went to sleep.
Incorrect: Studying my lessons, I went to sleep.
Correct: Though discouraged by his failure, he did not give up.
Incorrect: Discouraged by his failure, he did not give up.

7. Do not omit the subject of a subordinate clause unless the same word serves properly as the subject of both the subordinate and the principal clause.

Correct: When I was a small boy, my father married again.
Incorrect: When a small boy my father married again.

Exercise 493

In the following sentences supply all words that have been improperly omitted and explain why the words that you have added are necessary:

1. We loved Aunt Clara better than anybody.
2. Traveling is so expensive nowadays.
3. The room was swept and the rugs placed in order.
4. Conroy had been treasurer and trusted by everybody.
5. He has acted just as anyone would.
6. I have no respect or confidence in such a man.
7. We applied early so we might secure desirable seats.
8. Waiting for the train, I read a magazine.
9. He knew in his condition he could not live very long.
10. The doctor, interne, and nurse stood by my bed.
11. While I was home I looked every place for my fountain pen.
12. A new constitution has been drawn up and new by-laws prepared.

Exercise 494

Review carefully sections 115, 116, and 117, and Exercises 237 and 238.

Achievement Test 1

Write a correct version of each of the sentences given below. On this test you should make a perfect score.

1. Julia is not near so attractive as Jane.
2. These kind of days make everyone feel good.
3. Fatigued by his long walk, he insisted on accompanying me.
4. I cannot help but wonder where they have gone.
5. The great event was when Faber made a touchdown.
6. Trent is a spectacular player, but who is sometimes not very dependable.
7. I spent a lonely summer. All my friends being away on their vacations.
8. We agreed to write regularly and that we would meet the next year as freshmen at Brighton College.
9. Being a harsh man, we stood in awe of my father.
10. Neither of the men have been seen since Friday.
11. Whom do you think will be elected?
12. She would not consent to me going home alone.
13. Each of them have had their picture made.
14. My two little nieces have better manners than any children I ever knew.
15. It don't seem that I have been laying in bed for ten hours.
16. I will be eighteen years old tomorrow.
17. We should have liked to have accompanied you.
18. If I was in your place, I would not answer his letter.
19. He spoke like he meant what he said.
20. Passengers should not enter or leave the car while moving.
21. In order to see the country at our leisure, a car was rented for three weeks.
22. He is a lecturer well worth hearing, and who never disappoints his audiences.
23. Naturalization is when a foreigner becomes a citizen of the country in which he intends to make his future home.
24. Where the Brents get their money is a mystery to me, they take a trip every summer.
25. The reason I am interested in your vagabond experience is because I was once a tramp.

Achievement Test 2

Write a correct version of each of the sentences given below. If you made a perfect score on the preceding test, you may, with the consent of your teacher, be excused from this test.

1. I always try to properly prepare my lessons.
2. She is prettier but not so amiable as her sister.
3. Arson is when a person maliciously sets fire to a house.
4. She cared for me like I was her own child.
5. I wish that today was Sunday.
6. I have forgotten whom she said would lecture tonight.
7. Our class begun studying Latin in September.
8. I shall allow no one to criticize my action; I shall die first.
9. I slept good last night, which is unusual for me.
10. She dances much more gracefully than him.
11. In Aunt Ellen's girlhood they did not have radios.
12. His investment made him a fortune, which surprised all the members of his family.
13. No one in our class but Tom had solved all their problems.
14. It was me who they blamed for the mistake.
15. Dan told George that his books were on his desk.
16. Neither the doctor nor the nurse were able to give him relief.
17. A person is known by the way they spend their leisure.
18. In order to enjoy good health, plenty of exercise should be taken.
19. The audience began hissing and to leave the theater.
20. There was not but one fault that he found in my drawing.
21. Having lived in the country, the city often oppresses me.
22. They intended to have left for their vacation yesterday.
23. Today is some cooler than yesterday was.
24. She is more popular than any woman in town.
25. Mother did not approve of us attending the dance. Unless we were chaperoned by Mrs. Gaston.

CHAPTER XX

Punctuation and Capitalization

239. The Comma

1. Use a comma or commas to set off from the rest of the sentence a word employed in direct address.

> *a.* Helen, where are you?   *b.* Here, John, are your books.

2. Use a comma after the salutation of an informal friendly letter and after the complimentary close of all letters.

> *a.* Dear Mother,   *b.* Dear Aunt Mary,   *c.* Sincerely yours,

3. Use a comma or commas to separate from the rest of the sentence appositive words and phrases, unless they are used restrictively.

> *a.* Mr. Carrington, our principal, gave an address.
> *b.* Salt, or sodium chloride, is an essential commodity.
> *c.* Everyone, old and young, was his friend.
> *d.* That is the book I mean, "Moby Dick."
> *e.* The words *salary* and *knave* have interesting histories.

4. Use commas to set off words, phrases, and clauses introduced parenthetically into a sentence.

> *a.* There is a possibility, however, of his refusing the offer.
> *b.* Robert Burns, for instance, was a self-educated man.
> *c.* The day, cold as it was, proved ideal for the game.

5. Use a comma to separate words, phrases, or clauses used coördinately in a series.

a. Grandmother gave me a quaint, old-fashioned, inlaid chest.

b. Stevenson wrote essays, novels, short stories, verses, and dramas.

c. Delegates to the convention are arriving by boat, by train, by automobile, and by airplane.

d. Everyone wondered why he had come, what he would do, and when he would return to Washington.

e. We found the key, I unlocked the chest, and together we opened it.

NOTE. If two or more adjectives used in a series constitute a single modifier of a noun, do not use a comma to separate them.

a. He wore an old gray hat.   *b.* He is a quiet little man.

6. Use a comma or commas to separate items of an address or of a date.

a. November 11, 1918, is a memorable date.

b. Address the letter to Mrs. Charles H. White, 1215 Bryan Avenue, Cleveland, Ohio.

7. Use a comma or commas to set off from the rest of the sentence a title following a proper name.

a. His brother-in-law is Norman Faraday, Jr.

b. Thornton Wakefield, Esq., is an attorney.

8. Use a comma or commas to set off a contrasting expression introduced by *not* or *though not.*

a. Stevenson became known, not as a lawyer, but as a writer.

b. The book was published in the United States, though not in England.

9. Use a comma or commas to set off nonessential (nonrestrictive) phrases and clauses. A nonrestrictive phrase or clause is one that, though it adds something to the meaning of a sentence and is a modifier of some word, may be omitted without affecting the meaning of the rest of the sentence.

> *a.* His father, wearied by the long journey, lay down to rest.
> *b.* Our principal introduced Judge Allison, who gave a talk.
> *c.* My chum, who is a senior, will enter college next year.
> *d.* "Where were you last night?" he asked, as he gave a knowing wink.

NOTE. Do not use a comma or commas to set off a restrictive phrase or clause, for such a phrase or clause is essential to the meaning of the sentence.

> *a.* The house standing on the hill is my home.
> *b.* The book that I am reading is a recent novel.
> *c.* He who will not work shall not eat.

10. Use a comma after a participial phrase or an adverbial clause when it introduces a sentence.

> *a.* Having arrived ahead of time, we waited for our friends.
> *b.* If you find the book, please return it to the library.

11. Use a comma to separate the clauses of a compound sentence, provided the clauses are joined by a coördinating conjunction (*and, but, or, nor,* or *for*), are reasonably short, and are not internally punctuated with commas. (For the use of the semicolon, see section 240, rule 3.)

> *a.* We asked for Laider, but he had already left home.
> *b.* The scenery was interesting, and the climate was pleasant.

NOTE. If the clauses are very short and are closely related in thought, no punctuation mark is required.

> The lightning flashed and the thunder roared.

12. Use a comma or commas to set off a direct quotation from the rest of the sentence, unless the sense requires some other mark of punctuation at the end of the quotation. Observe the punctuation of the following as models:

> *a.* "This is my car," he said. *d.* "Who is she?" I asked.
> *b.* "This," said he, "is my car." *e.* "Who," I asked, "is she?"
> *c.* He said, "This is my car." *f.* I asked, "Who is she?"

NOTE. Do not use a comma before an indirect quotation.

> *a.* He said that this was his car. *b.* I asked who she was.

13. Use a comma after *yes* and *no* and after such mild interjections as *oh, well, why,* and *now* when they stand first in a sentence.

a. Yes, this is I.   *d.* Oh, you must be mistaken.
b. No, I did not see him.   *e.* Why, when did you arrive?
c. Well, what shall we do?   *f.* Now, who do you think I am?

14. Use a comma to mark the omission of a verb or other important word that is clearly implied.

a. My mother was born in Virginia; my father, in Maryland.

15. Use a comma to insure the correct reading of a sentence, though otherwise the comma would be unnecessary.

a. The week before, I went to Los Angeles.
b. To Sybil, Bryson sent a birthday card.
c. Ever since, we have spent each summer in Bar Harbor.

Exercise 495

In the following sentences supply commas wherever they are needed, and give the rule governing the use of each comma:

1. Why this is not my bag porter.
2. Hope we are told deserts us at no period of our existence.
3. If a person cannot be happy without remaining idle idle he should remain.
4. This is a book that I believe you will enjoy reading.
5. Cream which is lighter than milk rises to the top.
6. My dog is an alert well-bred intelligent Skye terrier.
7. David Gray M. D. was born in Columbus Ohio June 5 1886.
8. The guide believing that we had money to spend freely gave our party every attention.
9. The natives regarded him with awe nor would they permit him to touch the sick child.
10. Ever since I have felt ill at ease in the old house.
11. The cook having eloped with the chauffeur we had to prepare our own breakfast.

12. When he learned that I was a graduate of Harvard he immediately took greater interest in me.

13. "But Mother" said Jean "it was not my fault."

14. Our guest who was a retired sea captain loved the lights and beacons the mist and fog bells the sleet and surge of winter.

15. She was offended not because I had accepted the position but because I had not asked her advice.

16. Some of our party fished others rowed on the lake and others tramped over the hills.

17. Lanham jealous of Warner's popularity tried to secure his dismissal from the team.

18. His old friends were not to be neglected but it seemed hardly decent to desert the new.

19. Irving was born in 1783; Longfellow in 1807; and Holmes in 1809.

20. That believe it or not is what she said my dear.

21. Marjorie had laughing blue eyes and wavy light brown hair.

22. From her position at the window she could see who each guest was what she wore and how she was received by the hostess.

23. Mother's flower garden not to mention caring for a large family kept her constantly employed and interested in life.

24. This necklace which was given me by my aunt was a birthday present.

25. My father by the way when he learned of our curious predicament merely laughed and said "Well boys you will have to get out of this affair the best way you can."

240. The Semicolon

1. Use a semicolon between the clauses of a compound sentence when they are not joined by a conjunction.

> *a.* Let them keep their past; we have our future.
>
> *b.* The blue sky now turned more softly gray; the stars gradually disappeared; the east began to kindle.

2. Use a semicolon between the clauses of a compound sentence when they are joined by the connectives *however, moreover, hence, therefore, nevertheless, notwithstanding, also, yet, still, so, then, furthermore, besides, otherwise, ac-*

cordingly, likewise, consequently. A comma is sometimes placed after the connective.

    a. I missed the first car; however, I arrived at school on time.
    b. The natives looked on us with suspicion; hence we found it difficult to secure the specimens that we desired.

3. Use a semicolon between the clauses of a compound sentence when they are joined by a coördinating conjunction (*and, but, or, nor, for*), provided the clauses are somewhat long or either clause is internally punctuated with commas. Many reputable writers use a semicolon regularly before *for*.

    a. He spoke to the dog, calling it to him; but in his voice there was a strange note of fear that frightened the animal.
    b. Marks of punctuation should be intelligently used; for otherwise they mislead the reader. (A comma may be used instead of the semicolon.)

4. Use a semicolon to separate phrases or subordinate clauses in a series, provided the phrases or the clauses are long or are broken up by commas within the phrase or clause.

    a. Youth is the time to go flashing from one end of the world to the other in mind and body; to hear the chimes ring at midnight; to see the sun rise in town and country; to write halting verses; to run a mile to see a fire.
    b. If only the others could be there also; if only there were no cold anywhere, and no nakedness, and no hunger; if only it were as well with all men as it was with him, — he could rest supremely happy.

5. Use a semicolon before such words, phrases, and abbreviations as *namely, as, for example, for instance, that is, e. g., i. e., viz.,* when they introduce an explanation or an illustration. A comma usually follows such introductory

expressions. A comma, or a comma and dash, will some-times be found instead of the semicolon.

a. While I was in college, my generous father proved to be my greatest handicap; that is, he gave too much money.
b. The Greeks invented three orders of architecture, namely, the Doric, the Ionic, and the Corinthian.
c. Both crimes, it was discovered, were committed by the same man, — namely, the interne.

241. The Colon

1. Use a colon after the salutation of a business letter or of a formal social letter.

a. My dear Sir: b. Dear Mr. Norton: c. My dear Mrs. Craig:

2. Use a colon between a general introductory state-ment and a list, an illustration, a long quotation, or a for-mal statement. Such phrases as *the following, as follows, in this way,* and *for this reason* often precede the colon.

a. Last month I read three interesting books: "Imperial Palace," "The Far-Away Bride," and "The Education of a Princess."
b. This, then, is the plastic part of literature: to embody character, thought, or emotion in some act or attitude that shall be remarkably striking to the mind's eye.
c. At the annual dinner of the Pioneer Club, Dr. Blount spoke as follows: "As I look back over the years . . ."

Exercise 496

In the following sentences supply all necessary commas, semicolons, and colons, and give the rule governing the use of each mark of punctuation that you supply:

1. Pitiful is the case of the blind who cannot read the face pitiful that of the deaf who cannot follow the changes of the voice.

2. Concord Massachusetts was the home of four men famous in American literature namely Thoreau Alcott Emerson and Hawthorne.

3. These hardy ancestors of ours were more than mere fighters and freebooters they were men like ourselves their emotions awaken instant response in our souls.

4. The water of Lethe has one excellent quality for a single draft of it makes people forget every care and sorrow.

5. Hadley was handicapped by entering college a month late furthermore he was compelled to earn a part of his expenses.

6. We hold these truths to be self-evident that all men are created equal that they are endowed by their Creator with certain inalienable rights that among these are life liberty and the pursuit of happiness.

7. The English language is composed of two elements the Saxon which includes the Danish Swedish and other related languages and the classical which includes the Latin and the Greek.

8. Cambridge was the home of three noted literary men Holmes who is known as "The Autocrat" Lowell whose quaint Yankee humor sparkles in "The Biglow Papers" and Longfellow who is greatly loved by young readers as the author of "Evangeline."

9. Benjamin Franklin was a versatile man he was a printer an inventor a writer a statesman and a public benefactor.

10. Three of the greatest periods of English literature coincide as Professor Palmer observes with the reigns of the three English queens namely Elizabeth Anne and Victoria.

242. The Dash

1. Use a dash to indicate an abrupt change in the sense or in the construction of a sentence.

> The name of the oculist is — oh, what is the man's name?

2. Use dashes to set off parenthetical, appositive, or explanatory expressions introduced informally into a sentence.

> *a.* This dash —— you may not believe it — I made myself.
> *b.* My dog —— he is a Boston terrier — won first prize.

3. Use a dash before an informal expression that summarizes or adds to the meaning of the sentence.

> *a.* Tennis, rowing, hockey — these are my favorite sports.
> *b.* His father was a successful failure — a hero in defeat.

4. Use a dash to mark a pause intended to heighten the dramatic or rhetorical effect of a sentence or to give strong emphasis to the word or expression following it.

> *a.* The king of France, with twice ten thousand men,
>   Marched up the hill, and then — marched down again.
> *b.* With your youth, health, and splendid opportunities, you should never think of failure — never!

Caution. Avoid using a dash with any other mark of punctuation, unless the mark would be required even if the dash were omitted. Do not adopt the slovenly rule: When in doubt, use a dash.

243. Parentheses

1. Inclose in parentheses nonessential words, phrases, or clauses introduced into a sentence, unless commas or dashes seem preferable.

> *a.* What changes (if any) would you suggest?
> *b.* At eleven o'clock (just when I was most interested in the novel) mother made me go to bed.

2. Use parentheses to inclose figures, letters, signs, and dates inserted in a sentence.

> *a.* A prophet is not without hono(u)r save in his own country.
> *b.* Shakespeare (1564–1616) lived during the reign of Queen Elizabeth (1558–1603).
> *c.* The four forms of discourse are (1) narration, (2) description, (3) exposition, and (4) argument.

244. Brackets

Use brackets to inclose a word or an expression inserted in a sentence or a passage by someone other than the author.

> *a.* I remember seeing him [Stevenson] for the last time in 1888.
> *b.* My uncle's home, like most of the historic old houses of New England, had much more atmosphere than fresh air. [Laughter]

In the following sentences supply dashes, parentheses, and brackets, as well as all other necessary punctuation, and give the rule governing the use of each mark of punctuation supplied:

1. At last I think it was the third night our party decided that the Wareham ghost was nothing but a myth.

2. Mrs. Paige allow me the pleasure of introducing my friend Mr. oh why can I never remember your name?

3. A Scotch collie a large black cat a raccoon and a garrulous parrot these were the members of Ward's queer household.

4. My acquaintance began with her Mrs. Eastman when I was in the hospital.

5. The genial old fellow we never dreamed that he was a private detective was a great favorite with all the hotel guests.

245. Quotation Marks

1. Use quotation marks to inclose a direct quotation.

   a. "Where did you spend your vacation?" I asked.
   b. "Were you," she inquired, "in school with my son?"
   c. "Yes, I knew Harry well," I replied. "He and I played on the same baseball team."

NOTE. Do not inclose indirect quotations in quotation marks.

She inquired whether I had been in school with her son.

2. Use single quotation marks to inclose a quotation within a quotation.

"In spite of all my efforts to restrain him," sobbed Vivian, "he leaped to his feet and shouted, 'That's a lie.'"

3. Use quotation marks to inclose the *quoted* title of a poem, a story, an essay, an article, a chapter, a lecture, a picture, a statue, or a single musical composition. The *quoted* title of a book, a play, a newspaper, or a magazine

may be inclosed in quotation marks or be printed in italic type (see section 251, rule 1).

   a. Have you read Bret Harte's "The Luck of Roaring Camp"?
   b. On the lawyer's desk was a copy of Rodin's "The Thinker."
   c. I read the short story "Preliminaries" in the *Atlantic Monthly.*

4. When two or more paragraphs or stanzas are quoted, use quotation marks at the beginning of each but at the end of the last one only.

5. Inclose in quotation marks nicknames, slang words, unusual or coined words, and words used humorously or ironically.

   a. "Diogenes" Brodie was a terror to all freshmen.
   b. I never saw the janitor so "dolled up" before.
   c. Many boys leave college "to help father in his business."

6. In using a quotation mark and some other mark of punctuation after a word, arrange them in one of the appropriate orders illustrated below:

   a. He shouted, "Can you hear me?"
   b. Did he reply, "That is preposterous!"?
   c. "Never," he declared, "have I read a better novel."
   d. Hamblen considers that, I suppose, another of his "inalienable rights"; the judge, however, may think differently.

246. The Apostrophe

1. Use an apostrophe to indicate the possessive case.

   a. Peter's wife's mother lay sick of a fever.
   b. Have you read Burns's poems and Dickens's novels?
   c. Miss Ames is in either the boys' or the girls' study hall.

NOTE. Do not use an apostrophe in writing the possessive case of the following pronouns: *ours, yours, his, hers, its, theirs,* and *whose.*

2. Use an apostrophe to form the plural of letters and figures.

a. Your *u's* and your *n's* are too much alike.

b. Your *3's* resemble your *5's*.

c. The B. P. O. E.'s gave a dance at their hall last night.

3. Use an apostrophe to mark the omission of letters or figures.

a. We didn't arrive until twelve o'clock.

b. Father is a member of the famous class of '13.

NOTE. Remember that *it's* is the contraction of *it is*, and that *who's* is the contraction of *who is*.

247. The Period

1. Use a period at the end of a declarative or an imperative sentence. (See sections 101 and 116.)

a. We arrived on time. *b.* Always speak distinctly.

2. Use a period after initials and abbreviations.

a. Mrs. Howard C. Joyce organized the S.P.C.A. in our town.

b. On the title-page was printed "Arnold Merriam, M.D."

3. Use a period after a figure or a letter denoting a division of an outline and after figures preceding items arranged consecutively in a list. (For illustrations see the outlines in this book and the exercises containing numbered sentences.)

Cautions. (1) *Do not use a period after a title standing at the head of a composition, unless it is a sentence.* (2) *Do not use a period after a figure denoting the number of a page.*

248. The Question Mark

1. Use a question mark after every sentence that asks a question.

a. When did they arrive? *c.* You have not heard the news?

b. You are not prepared? *d.* Did he say, "That's too bad"?

NOTE. Do not use a question mark after an indirect question.

She asked me if I had heard the news.

Caution. After a courteous request expressed in interrogative form use a period, not a question mark

Will you please lend me your dictionary.

2. Use a question mark inclosed in parentheses to indicate doubt as to the accuracy of some detail in a statement, but not to imply irony.

In the year 1340(?) the poet Chaucer was born.
Avoid: What an intelligent(?) person you are!

249. The Exclamation Mark

1. Use an exclamation mark after words, phrases, and sentences that express strong emotion, doubt, or irony.

a. O world, I cannot hold thee close enough!
b. That man a poet! The idea!
c. What an angelic disposition she has!
d. Oh, how my head aches!

2. Use an exclamation mark after a strong interjection or other exclamatory word.

a. Alas! What am I to do? *b.* Hold! Give the man a chance.

NOTE. In·a series of repeated interjections use a comma to separate them, and place the exclamation mark after the last one.

Ha, ha, ha! That's the best joke I ever heard.

250. Capital Letters

1. Capitalize the first word in a sentence and in a line of poetry.

a. A wise man tries not to make the same mistake twice.
b. Much have I traveled in the realms of gold,
And many goodly states and kingdoms seen.

2. Capitalize the first word in a sentence used as a direct quotation.

Mother asked me, "When did you come home last night?"

3. Capitalize the first word of a formal resolution.

Resolved, That war should be abolished.

4. Capitalize proper nouns, and adjectives derived from proper nouns, unless they have come, through long usage, to be regarded as common nouns and adjectives.

 a. The King of Spain went to Paris, France.
 b. In our school there are pupils of English, French, German, Spanish, Italian, and Jewish parentage.
 c. This book is printed in roman and italic type.

5. Capitalize such common nouns as *river, lake, street, avenue, park, county, college, university, high school, company, society, railway* when they are used as a part of a proper name, but *not* otherwise.

 a. I am a pupil of the Central High School.
 b. I entered the high school at the age of twelve.
 c. He was employed by the Grayson Construction Company.
 d. The company has recently failed in business.

6. Capitalize names of days, months, and holidays, but *not* names of the seasons.

 a. She arrived on Thanksgiving Day, Thursday, November 28.
 b. In New England, summer and autumn are very pleasant.

7. Capitalize names of the points of the compass when they denote a section of a country, but *not* otherwise.

 a. I spent last winter in the South. *b.* Our house faces east.

8. Capitalize titles of honor or office when they are used formally or in connection with a proper name, but *not* otherwise.

 a. The Secretary of State conferred with the President.
 b. We consulted Judge Malcolm Wade and Dr. Phillip Loring.
 c. The judge and the doctor gave us the same advice.

9. Capitalize words denoting family relationship only when they are used with the name of a person. When used alone as a nominative of address, they may begin either with a capital or with a small letter.

   a. I have been visiting Uncle John and Aunt Clara.
   b. My cousin has returned to her grandmother's home.
   c. Tell me, Mother (*or* mother), what father said.

10. Capitalize the first word and all other important words in literary titles.

   a. We are studying Shakespeare's "A Comedy of Errors."
   b. Have you ever read Keats's "Ode on a Grecian Urn"?

11. Capitalize words referring to the Deity and to sacred writings.

   In the Old Testament Jehovah is a name used for God.

12. In the salutation of a letter capitalize the first word, the title, and all nouns.

   a. Dear Sir: *b.* My dear Mrs. Wright: *c.* Dear Doctor Ames:

13. Capitalize the pronoun *I* and the interjection *O*, but not *oh*, unless it stands first in a sentence.

14. Capitalize words denoting personified objects or ideas.

   Care-charmer Sleep, son of the sable Night,
   Brother to Death, in silent darkness born.

251. Italics

In writing or in typewriting underscore with one line words, phrases, and other expressions that would be printed in *italic type*.

1. Italicize the title of a book, a newspaper, or a magazine, unless it is inclosed in quotation marks (see section 245, rule 3).

   a. On the table were *Romance of the Airman* and *Harper's Magazine.*

b. Have you read "The Five-Year Plan," an editorial in the *New York Times*?

2. Italicize a word or an expression intended to be strongly emphasized.

Remember this: *all marks of punctuation should be intelligently used.*

3. Italicize words, letters, and figures when they are referred to as such, without reference to their meaning in the sentence.

a. Do not confuse *lie* and *lay.*   *c.* Always cross your *t's.*
b. Your *7's* resemble your *9's.*   *d.* Mind your *p's* and *q's.*

4. Italicize the names of ships, airplanes, and airships.

a. He sailed on the *Ile de France.*   *b.* She piloted the *Pathfinder.*

5. Italicize a foreign word or phrase when it is used as part of an English sentence.

a. Many of his statements I accept *cum grano salis.*
b. There remained a certain *joie de vivre* in her manner.

Achievement Test 1

Copy the following paragraph, dividing it correctly into sentences and supplying all necessary punctuation, capital letters, and italics:

after a sojourn at a deserted mining station in the california coast range the story of which is told in the silverado squatters stevenson with his wife and stepson lloyd osbourne returned to scotland chronic lung disease had now settled upon him and he was subject to cough hemorrhage and fever for the next few years he spent the summers in scotland the winters in switzerland or southern france and then he tried to live in england it was during one of his visits to the scotch highlands in 1881 that he wrote the merry men a story of the terrors of the sea and that he began his best known book treasure island the success of this book in 1883 was but the prelude to other successes in 1886 came kidnapped and the strange case of dr jekyll and mr hyde the former which stevenson regarded as his best is a story of adventure in the highlands soon after the jacobite rebellion of 1745 its chief character alan breck stewart is drawn with greater subtlety and truth than john silver in treasure island the earlier triumph of stevensons art so close is kidnapped to the soil that in the long flight of alan and david the wind seems to turn the pages of that swift record and the smell of the heather comes with it dr jekyll and mr hyde is an allegory of the struggle between good and evil in human nature

Achievement Test 2

Copy the following passage, dividing it properly into sentences and paragraphs and supplying all necessary punctuation, capital letters, and italics:

novelists it seems are no heroes to their barbers mr thomas hardys barber recently confided to mr f hadland davis that in his opinion the novelist is a sadly overrated man the barbers comments as reported by mr davis to the bookman were these he is such a quiet little man youd never know it was thomas hardy he wears an old overcoat and carries a baggy umbrella he used to talk to me about london as it was years ago when cockfighting was all the rage ive never read any of his books nor do i care to read them americans seem to think a lot of him one of them came in here the other day have you seen thomas hardy he asked me oh yes i said he sat in the chair youre sitting in in this chair shouted the american much excited yes i replied i cut mr hardys hair did you keep the hair you cut off asked my customer putting his hand into his pocket no said i i didnt well thats a pity replied the yankee because if you had id have bought it *Youth's Companion*

Word-Composition and Spelling

252. Importance of Understanding Word-Composition

Familiarity with the composition of words is an aid not only in using them properly but also in spelling them correctly. As to their composition, or formation, words are of three kinds: simple, derivative, and compound.

A *simple* word is one that does not contain a prefix, a suffix, or an inflectional ending; as, *like, pure, ease, limit.*

A *derivative* word is one that is made by adding a prefix or a suffix, a prefix and a suffix, or an inflectional ending to a simple word or to a root; as, *likely, likable, dislike, liked, unlikely; purity, purify, impure, impurity; easy, easily, uneasy, uneasily, disease; limited, unlimited, illimitable, limiting, limitation.*

A *compound* word is one that is made by joining two or more words; as, *lifelike, pure-minded, ease-loving.*

253. Common Prefixes

One or more letters or syllables placed before a root to form a word, or before a simple word to make a new word, are called a prefix. In the list below are some of the most common prefixes used in the formation of derivative words:

a, ab (from, away)
ac, ad, af, ag, al, an, ap, ar, as, at, a (to)
ante (before)
anti (against, opposite)

bi, bis (two, twice)
circum (around, about)
com, con, col, cor, co (together, with)
contra, counter (against)

de (down, down from, away)
dis, dif, di (apart, away, not)
e, ex, ef (out of, out, from, off, beyond)
fore (in front, beforehand)
in, il, im, ir, em, en (into, in, within; on)
in, im, il, ir, un (not)
inter (between, among)
intro, intra (within)
mis (ill, wrongly)
non (not, without)

over (over, beyond, in excess)
per (through, thoroughly, very)
post (after)
pre (before)
pro (forward, before, in place of)
re (back, again)
se, sed (apart)
sub, suc, suf, sup, sus (under)
super, sur (above, over)
tele (afar, at a distance)
trans, tra, tres (across, beyond)
un, uni (one)

254. Common Suffixes

One or more letters or syllables placed after a root to form a word, or after a simple word to make a new word, are called a suffix. In the list below are some of the most common suffixes used in the formation of derivative words:

able, ible (capable of being)
ace, acy, ance, ancy (condition, state of being)
age (condition, state)
al, eal, ial (pertaining to)
an, ean, ian (pertaining to, one who)
ance, ence, ancy, ency (act of, state of)
ant, ent (relation, quality, one who)
ary, ery (pertaining to, one who, place where)
ate (state, condition, one who, place where)
dom (dominion, state)
eer, ier (one who does)
ful (full of, abounding in, characterized by)

fy, fic, ify (to make, causing)
hood (state, condition)
ic (made of, resembling, of the nature of)
ile (pertaining to)
ion, sion, tion (state of being, action, result of action)
ise, ize (to make, conform to, act in the way of)
ist, ile (one who does, or makes a practice of)
ity, ty (state, quality)
ive (pertaining to)
less (without, destitute of)
ment (state of being)
ness (state, condition, or quality of being)
or, er (one who has to do with, act of)

ory, ery (place where, pertaining to)

ose, ous (full of, abounding in)

ship (state or quality of)

some (full of, like, same)

tor, sor (one who does)

tude, ty (state, condition of being)

ure (act of, condition, state)

ward (direction to)

255. Common Roots

The following list contains some of the roots or stems derived from Latin and Greek that are most frequently used in the formation of derivative words:

ag, ac, act (do, drive, lead)

aud(i), audit (hear)

auto (self)

bene (well)

bio (life)

cap, capt, cept, ceive (take, hold)

ced, ceed, ces (give way, yield)

cred (believe)

dic, dict (say, speak)

duc, duct (lead)

fac, fec, fic, fact (make, do)

fer (bear, carry, bring)

ger, ges (carry)

grad, gress (step)

graph, gram (write)

hes, her (stick, cling)

jac, jec (throw)

leg, lig, lec (pick, gather, read)

mit, mis (send)

mov, mo (move)

pat(i), pas (bear, suffer)

pend, pond, pen (weigh, hang)

phon (voice, sound)

pon, pos (place, put)

port (bear, carry)

rup, rupt (break)

scrib, script (write)

sec, seg (cut)

sent, sen (perceive, think)

spec, spic (look)

sta (stand)

tele (at a distance, far)

ten (hold)

trac (draw, pull)

urb (city)

vad, va (go)

ven, vent (come)

vert, ver (turn)

vid, vi, vis (see)

voc (call)

Exercise 498

A. Classify each of the following words as simple, derivative, or compound:

speaker	airplane	security	enjoyable	undeniably
joyous	befriend	endless	believe	trustworthy
simplify	kinship	unfair	fearful	seasickness

B. Using the following simple words, make as many derivative and compound words as you can from each:

act	play	reason	kind	move
dear	sure	know	trust	vary
real	health	safe	please	dress

Exercise 499

Classify each of the following words as derivative or compound. In each derivative word indicate the simple word, or the root, and then give the prefix or the suffix, or the prefix and the suffix. In each compound word point out the simple words or the roots that were joined to form it. After you have analyzed a word, give its literal meaning and note carefully the spelling.

transmit	pronoun	biographer	diction
postpone	patience	stationary	subscribe
factory	contradict	digression	development
captive	telephone	foreground	autograph
audible	portable	dependent	playfulness
eruption	inspector	displeasure	trustworthy

256. Rules for Spelling

Rule 1. Words of one syllable ending in a single consonant preceded by a single vowel double the final consonant before a suffix beginning with a vowel.

stop	stopped	stopping	stopper
beg	begged	begging	beggar

Rule 2. Words of more than one syllable, accented on the last syllable, ending in a single consonant preceded by a single vowel, double the final consonant before a suffix beginning with a vowel.

occur	occurred	occurring	occurrence
propel	propelled	propelling	propeller

Exception: transferable.

Words of more than one syllable, *not* accented on the last syllable, ending in a single consonant preceded by a single vowel, do *not* double the final consonant before a suffix beginning with a vowel.

profit	profited	profiting	profitable

A few words may be spelled in either way; as, *travel, worship, revel, kidnap.*

Rule 3. Words ending in silent *e* drop the *e* before a suffix beginning with a vowel.

advise	advising	advisable
oppose	opposing	opposite

NOTE 1. Words ending in silent *e* following *c* or *g* retain the *e* before a suffix beginning with *a* or *o*, in order to preserve the soft sound of *c* and *g*.

change	changeable	advantage	advantageous
notice	noticeable	courage	courageous

NOTE 2. Words ending in *ie* drop the *e* and change the *i* to *y* before a suffix beginning with *i*.

lie	lying	die	dying	tie	tying

NOTE 3. A few words retain the final *e* before the suffix *ing*.

dye	dyeing	hoe	hoeing	shoe	shoeing

Rule 4. Words ending in silent *e* usually retain the *e* before a suffix beginning with a consonant.

arrange	arrangement	rue	rueful	safe	safety

Judgment and *acknowledgment* are preferably spelled without the final silent *e* of the primitive form.

NOTE. A few words drop the final *e* before a suffix beginning with a consonant.

argue	argument	awe	awful	true	truly

Rule 5. In words containing *ei* or *ie* put *i* before *e* when the combination is pronounced as *ee*, except after *c.*

believe	niece	wield	ceiling	deceive
brief	yield	conceive	receive	deceit
chief	grief	conceit	receipt	perceive

Exceptions: either, neither, leisure, weird, seized.

NOTE. When the combination of the two vowels has the sound of long *a*, long *i*, or short *e* or *i*, *i* generally follows *e*.

| neigh | weigh | neighbor | height | foreign |
| sleigh | freight | veil | heifer | counterfeit |

Exceptions: friend, sieve, ancient.

Rule 6. Words ending in *y* preceded by a consonant usually change *y* to *i* before a suffix.

| busy | business | pity | pitiful |
| easy | easily | envy | enviable |

NOTE. Final *y* is retained before the suffix *ing.*

| hurry | hurrying | amplify | amplifying |

Rule 7. The final letter of a word or prefix is generally retained before the same letter in the suffix or root.

| legible | illegible | satisfied | dissatisfied |
| equal | equally | sudden | suddenness |

Rule 8. A word ending in *ll* generally drops one *l* when used as a prefix or suffix.

| already | fulfill | skillful | almost | altogether |

257. Aids in Learning to Spell

1. Pronounce words accurately. Do not slur internal vowels or consonants: *separate,* not *seperate* or *sep'rate; government,* not *gover'ment.*
2. Observe each word carefully to discover the syllables and the order of the letters composing it: *pro-ceed, pro-ce-dure; re-ceive, be-lieve.*

3. Discover the difficulty that the word presents for you, and concentrate your efforts on mastering it: *occurred, judgment, arrangement, likable, changeable, already, all right.*

4. In spelling words that are similar in sound think of what each word means: *affect, effect; to, too, two; principle, principal; their, there; forth, fourth; aisle, isle.*

5. Learn the correct spelling of words both by sound and by sight. Speak difficult words aloud as you write them, and look at them closely in script and in type.

6. Employ your knowledge of simple words, roots, prefixes, and suffixes in spelling derivative words.

7. Make use of the rules for spelling in solving spelling problems.

8. Consult your dictionary when you are not certain of how to spell a word.

9. In a notebook keep a list of all the words that you misspell. Study your list at regular intervals until you have mastered each word.

258. Syllabication

In writing observe the following rules of syllabication for dividing a word at the end of a line:

1. Use a hyphen to indicate the division of a word.
2. Never divide a word of one syllable.
3. In most words containing double consonants make a syllabic division between the consonants.

oc-cur   com-ma   fol-low   pos-ses-sive   run-ning   pos-si-ble

4. In most derivative words made from a simple monosyllabic word ending in a double consonant, do not divide the double consonant if the suffix begins with a vowel.

cross-ing   fill-er   pass-a-ble   call-er   bluff-ing

5. Never divide two consonants that together constitute a single sound; as, *ch, rch, gh, gth, ph, sh, th, tch, ght.*

reach-ing   el-e-phant   straight-en   strength-en

259. Words Frequently Misspelled

abbreviate
absence
accept
accidentally
accommodate
accustom
acquainted
across
aëroplane
affects
all right
already
altogether
always
anxiety
apartment
apparatus
appearance
appropriate
arithmetic
ascend
athletic
awkward
bearing
becoming
beggar
beginning
believing
benefited
bicycle
business
calendar
can't
changeable
changing
choose
chose

chosen
column
coming
committee
compelled
competent
conceivable
conferred
conscience
conscientious
controlled
courteous
courtesy
cruelty
deceitful
deferred
definite
descend
description
desirous
despair
desperate
destroy
difference
dining-room
disappear
disappoint
discipline
disease
dissatisfied
doesn't
don't
dying
eighth
embarrass
eminent
encouraging

equipped
especially
exaggerate
exceed
excellent
except
existence
expense
experience
familiar
finally
foreigner
forty
friend
generally
goddess
government
grammar
grievous
guidance
having
height
immediately
incidentally
independence
indispensable
intelligence
irresistible
judgment
knowledge
laboratory
laid
library
loneliness
loosing
losing
lying

maintenance
mathematics
meant
messenger
minutes
mischievous
misspelled
murmur
necessary
niece
ninth
noticeable
oblige
occasion
occasionally
occurred
occurrence
omission
omitted
opponent
outrageous
parallel
peaceable
perceive
perceptible
perception
permissible
persuade
picnicking
planned
prairie
precede
precedence
precedents
preferred
prejudice
prevalent

principal	scarcely	surprise	usually
principle	schedule	syllable	vengeance
privilege	seize	they're	villain
really	sense	thief	visible
receive	separate	thorough	weather
recognize	shining	till	weird
referred	siege	together	whether
religious	similar	transferred	which
repetition	simultaneous	treacherous	wholly
ridiculous	specimen	truly	wield
righteous	statement	tyranny	writing
sacrilegious	stopping	until	written
safety	succeeds	using	yield

260. Difficult Proper Names

Apollo	Jonson, Ben	Sir Roger de Coverley
Carlyle	Macaulay	Shelley
Chesapeake	Macbeth	Spencer, Herbert
Coleridge	Massachusetts	Spenser, Edmund
De Quinccy	Mediterranean	Tennessee
Eliot, George	Odyssey	Thackeray
February	Parliament	Ulysses
Grecian	Philippines	Waverley
Johnson, Samuel	Renaissance	Wednesday

Exercise 500

Make a close study of the lists of troublesome words given in sections 259 and 260, and copy in your notebook, correctly spelled, all words that you find difficulty in spelling. Add to this list from time to time any other words that you misspell. Use your list for drill until you have mastered all the words.

CHAPTER XXII

The Use of the Dictionary

261. Unabridged Dictionaries

As high-school pupils, we should learn to make intelligent use of unabridged dictionaries. The two principal single-volume unabridged dictionaries of the English language are Webster's New International Dictionary and The New Standard Dictionary. Besides these there is The Century Dictionary and Cyclopedia, an American work published in twelve volumes. The first ten volumes contain dictionary information. Volume XI is a cyclopedia of names, and Volume XII is an atlas of the world. There is also A New English Dictionary (or Oxford Dictionary), a British work published in twenty volumes. It gives exhaustive and authoritative information on the derivation, meaning, and use of practically all words in the English language.

262. Abridged Dictionaries

Though we may not individually own an unabridged dictionary, we should possess and use a personal copy of an abridged edition. The five most satisfactory abridged dictionaries of the English language are Webster's Secondary School Dictionary, Webster's Collegiate Dictionary, High-School Standard Dictionary, College Standard Dictionary, and The Concise Oxford Dictionary.

Exercise 501

Not until you are familiar with the system of arrangement and the character of the contents of an unabridged dictionary are you capable of using it to the best advantage. Explore the unabridged dictionary in your classroom, study hall, library, or home by means of the following questions and write a brief report as an answer to each:

1. Where in the dictionary do you find a brief history of the English language? Name five languages that are akin to the English.

2. On what pages do you find a guide to pronunciation? What words are given to illustrate the sound of long *o* (ō)? Does the guide to pronunciation appear in abbreviated form elsewhere in the dictionary?

3. Where are the rules for spelling given? How many are there? Copy one of the rules and the illustrations.

4. Where do you find a list of the abbreviations used in the dictionary? What is the meaning of *Geol., ital., syn., v.t.*?

5. Is there a special section given to new words? If so, copy the definition of *cellophane* or *rodeo*, and give the page number.

6. What is meant by *guide words*, and where are they found? Give two illustrations.

7. If you are using Webster's New International Dictionary, explain how the words printed in smaller type on the lower section of each page differ as a class from those given in the section above.

8. Where do you find full-page plates illustrating the following: (1) flags? (2) chief foreign alphabets? (3) coins of the world? (4) the human skeleton? (5) plants, industrial and poisonous?

9. On what pages do you find a geographical dictionary of the world? Copy the information given about Oberammergau. Be sure that you understand the abbreviations and symbols used.

10. Where do you find a pronouncing biographical dictionary? Copy the information given about Chaucer and Selma Lagerlöf.

11. Where are the signs and symbols used in correcting printer's proofs given?

12. Where do you find a classified list of pictorial illustrations?

Exercise 502

The following exercises will help you to discover the wealth and variety of information to be obtained from a modern unabridged dictionary. Write reports on each of the topics and questions given below.

1. Explain the structure of the human eye and the function of each of its parts.

2. Who were the following: Cadmus? Dr. Faustus? Herodotus? Michelangelo? Captain Kidd?

3. What is the metric system of weights and measures?

4. What was the Trojan War? Who were Homer and Virgil?

5. Where is the Blarney stone? What practice and superstition are associated with it?

6. What is the present copyright law in the United States?

7. Who were the following: Merlin? Odin? Osiris? Don Quixote? Mother Shipton?

8. What and where are the following: Taj Mahal? Cleopatra's Needle? Pyramid of Cheops? Eiffel Tower?

9. Explain feudalism and the feudal system.

10. Give the location and other available facts about each of the following: Patagonia, Sumatra, Liberia.

11. What is meant by the magic square?

12. Give the literal meaning of each of the following words: *George, geometry, geology, geography.*

263. Information about Words

In the dictionary proper of an unabridged dictionary we have access to the following useful information about words:

1. *Spelling.* If two or more spellings are recognized, the preferable one is given first.

2. *Pronunciation.* If more than one pronunciation is permissible, the preferable one is placed first.

3. *Part of speech.* An abbreviation indicating the part of speech to which the word belongs follows the pronunciation. If a word may be used as more than one part of speech, each use is indicated by the proper abbreviation.

The Use of the Dictionary 569

4. *Grammatical information.* Usually there will be found the plural of nouns forming the plural irregularly, the case forms of pronouns, the principal parts and the present participle of verbs, and the comparative and the superlative forms of most adjectives and adverbs.

5. *Derivation and history.* An unabridged dictionary gives much fuller information about the origin, formation, and history of words than is possible in an abridged dictionary. A knowledge of the derivation of a word not only gives it added interest but also insures greater precision in its use.

6. *Various meanings.* The definitions of a word are given in the order of their historical development, and are preceded by the figures 1, 2, 3, 4, etc. The technical use of a word is indicated by an abbreviation or a word placed before the definition; as, *Math.* (Mathematics), *Geol.* (Geology), *Astron.* (Astronomy), *Law, Med.* (Medicine).

7. *Standing.* Words not in good use or restricted in use have this fact indicated by an abbreviation or word placed after the definition; as, *Obs.* (Obsolete), *Colloq.* (Colloquial), *Slang.* If the standing of a word is not given, it may be assumed to be in good use.

8. *Illustrations of use.* The uses of many words are illustrated in unabridged dictionaries by quotations from various writers.

9. *Synonyms and antonyms.* Synonyms (*Syn.*) and antonyms (*Ant.*), if any, are listed after the last definition.

10. *Reference.* Following the list of synonyms or antonyms there may be a reference to a word or an illustration in another part of the dictionary. Such references are indicated by *See, Cf.,* and *q.v.*

11. *Combinations with other words.* Last of all, there is a list of established phrases in which the word in question is used. In the New International Dictionary the word *false,* for example, is followed by such phrases as *false action, f. analogy, f. cadence, f. face, f. perspective, f. representation.*

Exercise 503

The following exercise will test your ability to find accurate information about words. Using an unabridged dictionary, write a brief report on each of the topics and questions given below.

1. Give the two recognized spellings of each of the following words, placing the preferred spelling first: *honor, gray, hearken, neighbor, installment, practice.*

2. Indicate by diacritical marks and by accent the two recognized pronunciations of each of the following words, placing the preferable pronunciation first: *lever, elegiac, gladiolus, respiratory, advertisement, contemplate.*

3. As what different parts of speech may each of the following words be used: *long? past? transfer? yesterday? before?*

4. Copy the grammatical information given about each of the following: *see, good, genius, early, she, who.*

5. Tell the language or languages from which each of the following words comes: *kiosk, frost, janitor, algebra, batik, yacht, calico, cargo, violin, fiesta.*

6. Explain the history of each of the following words: *bedlam, dahlia, hyacinth, meander, boycott, tantalize, atlas.*

7. What changes in meaning have the following words undergone: *peculiar? urbane? silly? indent? prevent? reduce? miser?*

8. From what languages do the prefixes *demi-, hemi-,* and *semi-* come? Give at least one derivative word in which each prefix is used.

9. Indicate the standing of each of the following words: *ain't, enthuse, rathe, whopper, redd, razz.*

10. List the synonyms given for each of the following words: *speak, beautiful, vanity, singular, frustrate, confuse.*

11. Read the definition of each of the following words, and then turn to the word mentioned in the reference: *convert, convince, funeral, ignore, renew.*

12. List the phrases in which each of the following words is used: *speak, cut, fly (v. i.), clear (v.t.), head (n.), hard (a.).*

CHAPTER XXIII

The Use of the Library

264. How to Find Information in a Library

Every modern school or public library has a card catalogue of all the books and periodicals that it contains. On each card designating a book there appear the call number (showing the library classification), the title of the book, the name of the author or editor, the name of the publisher, and the date of publication. Each book is represented by three different cards, as illustrated below:

```
629    Romance of the airman
 H
         Humphreys, Pauline A. and Hosey, Gertrude, editors
```

```
629    Humphreys, Pauline A. and Hosey, Gertrude, editors
 H
           Romance of the airman.  Ginn c1931 566p.
```

```
629    Aviation
 H
        Humphreys, Pauline A. and Hosey, Gertrude, editors
          Romance of the airman.  Ginn, c1931 566p.
```

The first specimen is the *title card*; the second, the *author card*; the third, the *subject card*. All cards of the catalogue are arranged in one alphabetical series in the trays of the filing cabinet. By the use of the card catalogue we are able to find a book by referring to any one of the three cards on which it is listed.

Another invaluable aid in finding information is *The Reader's Guide to Periodical Literature*, which is an index to articles in magazines. It is published monthly, and in it material is listed alphabetically under the subject, under the first word of the title, and under the last name of the author. Each entry contains most, if not all, of the following items: (1) title; (2) author, if known; (3) name of the magazine in abbreviated form; (4) volume number; (5) page numbers; (6) date.

Exercise 504

Find in the card catalogue of your library information that will enable you to answer the following questions, and copy accurately the entry listed on each card:

1. What books does your library have on Aviation? Radio?
2. Who wrote "The Making of an American"?
3. What volumes of poetry by Robert Frost are listed?

Exercise 505

A. Which of the following encyclopedias does your library have: (1) The Encyclopædia Britannica? (Tell what edition it is.) (2) The Encyclopedia Americana? (3) The New International Encyclopædia? (4) Nelson's Loose-Leaf Encyclopædia? Appleton's New Practical Cyclopedia? (5) The Everyman Encyclopædia?

B. Give the title, volume number, and page number of the encyclopedia in which you find information on the following: (1) Greek architecture. (2) Radium and its uses. (3) Louis Pasteur. (4) Aztec civilization.

Exercise 506

A. Which of the following unabridged dictionaries are in your library: (1) Webster's New International Dictionary? (2) The New Standard Dictionary? (3) The

Century Dictionary and Cyclopedia? (Tell the number of volumes, and state the nature of the contents of volumes XI and XII.) (4) A New English Dictionary?

B. Which of the following atlases does your library have: (1) Rand-McNally Modern Atlas? (2) Hammond's New Peerless Atlas of the World? (3) Library Atlas of the World? (4) The Century Atlas? Give the date of each.

Exercise 507

A. In addition to encyclopedias, which of the following reference books containing biographical information are in your library: (1) Dictionary of National Biography? (2) Dictionary of American Biography? (3) Thomas's Comprehensive Dictionary of Biography? (4) Men and Women of Our Time? (5) Who's Who? (6) Who's Who in America?

B. In which of these do you find articles about each of the following: (1) Richard E. Byrd? (2) James M. Barrie? (3) Sarah Bernhardt? (4) Robert Louis Stevenson?

Exercise 508

A. Which of the following yearbooks does your library have: (1) The Statesman's Yearbook? (2) The World Almanac? (3) The New International Yearbook? (4) The Chicago Daily News Almanac? (5) The Eagle Almanac?

B. Give the name of the yearbook, the date, and page number where you find information on the following subjects: (1) The members of the present Cabinet of the United States. (2) Your state flower. (3) The present president of China. (4) The chief exports of Chile. (5) The center of population in the United States at the last census.

Exercise 509

A. From *The Reader's Guide to Periodical Literature* list one entry given under each of the following: (1) Immigration. (2) Child labor. (3) Radio. (4) Farm relief. (5) Modern painting.

B. Which of the following books does your library have: (1) "Instruction in the Use of Books and Libraries," by L. E. Fay and A. T. Eaton? (2) "Guide to the Use of Libraries," by Margaret Hutchins and others? (3) "How to Use the Library," by M. S. and E. F. Rowse? (4) "Find It Yourself," by E. Scripture and M. R. Greer?

Exercise 510

A. Which of the following books of quotations and literary allusions are in your library: (1) Brewer's Reader's Handbook? (2) Brewer's Dictionary of Phrase and Fable? (3) Bartlett's Familiar Quotations? (4) Hoyt's New Cyclopedia of Practical Quotations? (5) Ward's Poetical Quotations: English and American Poets?

B. Which of the following books of synonyms and antonyms does your library have: (1) Crabb's English Synonyms? (2) Allen's Synonyms and Antonyms? (3) Fernald's English Synonyms and Antonyms? (4) Roget's Thesaurus of English Words and Phrases?

C. Which of the following books of mythology do you find in your library: (1) Bulfinch's Age of Fable? (2) Gayley's Classic Myths in English Literature? (3) Guerber's Myths of Greece and Rome? (4) Guerber's Myths of Northern Lands?

Exercise 511

Using as material for illustration a textbook of history or science, a history of literature, a collection of plays or short stories, or an anthology of poetry, give an oral report on the purpose of the title-page, the preface, the table of contents, the introduction, the list of maps or illustrations, the lists of readings, the index, and any other parts that precede or follow the book proper.

265. Taking Notes on What We Read

In preparing assignments and reports we often find it necessary to record in the form of notes the main points and other essential details of selections that we read. Note-taking is of so great practical importance that we should learn during our high-school career to take good notes.

To be useful and easily interpreted, notes should be accurate in content and clearly recorded in convenient form. To this end, we should adopt a definite system of note-taking. For the purpose we may use a notebook, with loose or permanently attached leaves, or cards of uniform size that may be arranged in order in a filing box or drawer.

Notes may be taken in any one of the three following forms, depending on the time that we have for making them, the subject matter, and the use that they are to serve:

1. *Running notes.* Running notes are very brief and serve to help the writer recall the most important details and illustrations used by the author of the original. Such notes usually consist of key words and phrases, though short sentences may be used. As a rule, running notes should be revised, expanded, and rewritten while the subject matter is still fresh in the mind of the person who records them.

2. *Topical notes.* Topical notes are expressed in phrases or in short sentences, and should be arranged in the form of an outline. Since they show more clearly the organization of the subject matter, they are preferable to running notes.

3. *Summarizing sentences.* In taking notes on a story, a play, or other type of narrative, you will often find it convenient to record each episode or scene in a few well-constructed sentences. These sentences, taken together, should give an accurate summary of the narrative.

266. Directions for Taking Notes

1. Read the selection through rapidly, but attentively, to get a clear general idea of its contents. In this first reading be on the alert to discover the larger topics and the plan of organization of material that the author has used.
2. Read the selection again more carefully. After you have read each paragraph or group of paragraphs dealing with the same main topic, write your notes, using as far as possible your own words. Along with each principal topic record any *essential* details.
3. If you make running notes, you may use phrases, catchwords that will represent the meaning accurately, and abbreviations of words. When you have finished making such notes, it will be well for you to rewrite them in topical order while you have the original before you.

Exercise 512

Examine closely the following running notes made on the selection given in Exercise 71. Notice the form used. Observe that the notes on each of the four paragraphs are grouped separately. What is the importance of the information given in the two lines preceding the notes?

"Mental-Health Conditions," Benjamin C. Gruenberg, "Biology and Human Life," pp. 387–388.

1. Effect of irregularity of employment on health of workers. Low income, lack of proper food, shelter, clothing, recreation. Leads to worry. Worry injures mental health: bad mental habits, irritability, nervousness, loss of sleep. Worry injures physical health: indigestion, weakening of whole system.

2. Similar effect of fear. Poor working and living conditions. Possibility of unemployment, accidents. Lack of chance to become skilled worker.

3. Bad effect of small annoyances: vexatious fellow workers, uncongenial foreman, irritating noises, monotony of work, poor working quarters. Such difficulties rarely discovered by those who could remedy them.

4. Importance of harmony among workers, between worker and manager, between worker and work.

Exercise 513

Below you will find the running notes given in Exercise 512 revised and arranged topically in the form of an outline. Observe how much easier it is to distinguish the most important topic in each paragraph from the subordinate topics.

"Mental-Health Conditions," Benjamin C. Gruenberg, "Biology and Human Life," pp. 387–388.

1. Effect of irregularity of employment
   a. Lack of the necessities of life
   b. Injury to mental health through worry
   c. Injury to physical health through worry
2. Effect of fear arising from
   a. Poor working and living conditions
   b. Possibility of unemployment
   c. Possibility of accidents
   d. Lack of chance to become skilled worker
3. Effect of small annoyances
   a. Vexatious fellow workers
   b. Uncongenial foreman
   c. Irritating noises
   d. Monotony of work
   e. Poor working quarters
4. Importance of harmony
   a. Among workers
   b. Between worker and manager
   c. Between worker and work

CHAPTER XXIV

Good Form in Writing

267. How to Prepare a Manuscript

Unless we are given different instructions, we should prepare the final copy of all our compositions in accord with the following directions:

1. Use white theme paper and black or dark-blue ink. Write with a clean pen that does not blot or scratch.
2. Write on only one side of each sheet of paper.
3. On the first line or the first two lines of page 1 write the title centrally spaced. Begin the first word and all other important words with a capital letter. If you typewrite your composition, capitalize all letters in all words of the title. Unless the title is a sentence, use no punctuation after it.
4. Leave a margin of at least one inch on each side of the page.
5. Indent the first line of each paragraph at least one inch.
6. Begin the first paragraph of your composition two line-spaces below the title.
7. Write legibly. Do not crowd words in a line or the letters of a word at the end of a line. Avoid overlapping stem letters between lines.
8. In the upper left corner of each page write your name.
9. In the upper right corner of each page after the first write the page number, using an arabic numeral and no punctuation.
10. If you discover that you have misspelled a word, erase it neatly and write it correctly spelled. Try to avoid crossing words through and writing other words above the line.

11. When you find that you have omitted a word or a brief expression, place a caret (∧) at the point of omission and write the omitted word or expression above. If time will permit, it is much better to rewrite the entire page.

12. If you typewrite your composition, use unruled white paper 8½ by 11 inches. Leave a margin of two inches above the title, and a margin of at least an inch on each side of the page. Between lines leave double space. After each mark of punctuation within a sentence skip a space, and following each mark of punctuation after a sentence skip two spaces.

13. When you have arranged the pages of your manuscript in their right order and have the edges even, fold the manuscript lengthwise down the center. Never roll it. You may fasten the pages with a paper clip.

14. Place the folded manuscript on your desk before you with the loose edges toward your right hand. Be sure that you have not carelessly turned your paper upside down. About two inches down from the top, or on the first line of ruled paper, begin the indorsement. It should include your name and class number, the name and section of the course, and the date, and should be arranged thus:

```
Helen F. Arnold, 10B

English 3, 1

October 16, 1931
```

15. If you have occasion to quote verse in your composition, arrange the lines exactly as they are printed in the original.

16. Make every composition neat and attractive in appearance. Never present a soiled or blotted manuscript. Remember that a good composition makes a better impression when it is arranged in strict accord with the demands of good form.

Exercise 514

After you have studied carefully the directions given in section 267, copy the selection given below. · Use the paper regularly prescribed for written compositions, and follow each of the directions given. Try to make your manuscript perfect in every detail.

School Spirit

After the battle of Crécy, so the story goes, there was found on the field of conflict the crest of King John of Bohemia, bearing the words *Ich dien*, "I serve." Inspired by the unselfish devotion of this blind old king who had died fighting bravely in the thickest of the fray, where his knights at his request had led him, Edward, the Black Prince, forthwith adopted the device as his own. From that day to this the phrase "I serve" has been the motto of the heir to the throne of Great Britain.

He who would get the most out of school must cherish the same ideal, for in school, as in life, the highest satisfaction is to be found in giving, not getting. The boy or the girl who thinks first of the interests of the school, who is jealous of its good name, who is eager to aid any enterprise which will be to its benefit, who is willing to sacrifice time and personal advantage for its welfare, is the one who will find school a delight and its memory a lasting satisfaction.

Such a pupil has the finest sort of school spirit, for school spirit consists not so much in cheering the team on to victory or even in supporting it in times of defeat — important as such support is — as in being loyal to its ideals and purposes. School spirit in fact is not noise: it is an attitude of mind and heart. It manifests itself in pride in the appearance of the school and its surroundings and in thoughtful care of its property. Pupils who have true school spirit are considerate of schoolmates and teachers and are enthusiastic and loyal supporters of all school activities. — HOWARD COPELAND HILL, "Community Life and Civic Problems"

Versification

268. Rhythm

A single line of poetry is called a *verse*. Each verse in poetry is characterized by a uniform, measured movement which results from the regular recurrence of accented and unaccented syllables. This characteristic, the essential quality of all verse, is called *rhythm*. Rime, which we shall consider later, often occurs in verse, but it is not a really necessary element. Let us observe the difference in the movement of the two lines that follow:

> I have camped | in the whis|pering for|est of pines.
> Up, lad, | up, 'tis | late for | lying.

Each line, we notice, is divided into four groups of syllables. In the first line there are three syllables in each group; in the second, two syllables. Each group of syllables is called a *foot*.

269. Kinds of Feet

The character, as well as the name, of a poetic foot is determined by (1) the number of syllables in the foot and (2) the position of the accented, or stressed, syllable. The four principal kinds of feet in English verse are the following:

The *iambic* foot, consisting of an unaccented syllable followed by an accented syllable, is represented thus: ◡ —.

O beau|tiful | for spa|cious skies.

The *trochaic* foot, consisting of an accented syllable followed by an unaccented syllable, is represented thus : _ ∪.

Clay lies | still but | blood's a | rover.

The *anapæstic* foot, consisting of two unaccented syllables followed by an accented syllable, is represented thus : ∪ ∪ _.

I am haunt|ed by num|berless is|lands, and ma|ny a
Da|naan shore.

The *dactylic* foot, consisting of an accented syllable followed by two unaccented syllables, is represented thus : _ ∪ ∪. The following line is composed of four dactylic feet with a trochaic foot at the end :

Hearing the | shaking of | shields and the | quiver of | bow-
strings.

In addition to the four principal feet mentioned above, there are two other types, less frequently used :

The *spondaic* foot, consisting of two accented syllables, is represented thus : _ _.

The *pyrrhic* foot, consisting of two unaccented syllables, is represented thus : ∪ ∪.

Spondaic and pyrrhic feet are comparatively rare and are practically never used alone.

270. Variations in Rhythm

Certain regular variations in rhythm are likely to be found in verse, and unless we are prepared for them the verse may seem irregular and confusing. Often a line may contain two or more kinds of feet. The following variations should be noted :

1. *Iambic* and *anapæstic* feet often occur in the same line :

And thĭs | wăs thĕ rēa | sŏn thăt, lōng | ăgō,
Ĭn thĭs kīng | dŏm bȳ | thĕ sēa.

In these lines from Poe's "Annabel Lee" the rhythm is chiefly anapæstic. Yet they contain four iambic feet.

2. *Trochaic* and *dactylic* feet often occur in the same line :

Jūst fŏr ă | hāndfŭl ŏf | sīlvĕr hĕ | lēft ŭs.

3. In an *iambic* line the first foot is often *trochaic* :

Sōmethĭng | thĕre īs | thăt dōes | n't lŏve | ă wāll.

Mūfflĕd | ănd dūmb | lĭke bāre | fŏot dēr | vĭshes.

In addition to these regular variations, verse is often written with lines ending in an additional unaccented syllable or in a foot of one accented syllable.

Ĭ hūng | mў sōul | tŏ thĕ āir | lĭke ă fāl | cŏn flȳ | ĭng.

Lĭfe hās | lōvelĭ | nĕss tŏ | sēll.

Hŏw thĕ | ōriŏle's | nĕst ĭs | hūng.

Though a line may contain different kinds of feet, one kind usually predominates and gives its name to the line.

271. Kinds of Verse

Different lines contain different numbers of feet. The number of feet in a line determines its meter, or measure. English poetry includes the following eight kinds of lines :

Monometer line (one foot) :

Ĭ trūst.

Dimeter line (two feet) :

Thĭck drāws | thĕ dārk.

Trimeter line (three feet) :

˘ ‾ ˘ ‾ ˘ ‾
I nev|er saw | a moor.

Tetrameter line (four feet) :

˘ ‾ ˘ ‾ ˘ ‾ ˘ ‾
So way|ward is | the wind | tonight.

Pentameter line (five feet) :

˘ ‾ ˘ ‾ ˘ ‾ ˘ ‾ ˘ ‾
The crim|son drag|on dies | in dusk|y gold.

Hexameter line (six feet) :

˘ ˘ ‾ ˘ ˘ ‾ ˘ ˘ ‾ ˘ ‾ ˘ ˘ ‾
It is good | to be out | on the road, | and go|ing one knows |
˘ ‾
not where.

Heptameter line (seven feet) :

˘ ˘ ‾ ˘ ˘ ‾ ˘ ˘ ‾ ˘ ˘ ‾ ˘ ˘
She is fair|er than earth, | and the sun | is not fair|er, the
‾ ˘ ˘ ˘ ˘ ‾
wind | is not blith|er than she.

Octameter line (eight feet) :

‾ ˘ ‾ ˘ ‾ ˘ ‾ ˘ ‾ ˘ ‾ ˘ ‾
We were | only | singing | seamen | from the | dirt of | Lon-
˘
don|-town.

A verse is named according to the number of feet it includes and the kind of foot that predominates. In describing a line we should first tell the rhythm, or kind of
feet, and then the meter, or the number of feet, thus:
iambic pentameter, trochaic tetrameter, dactylic hexameter.

272. Rime

When we come to consider groups of lines, we are
brought immediately to the subject of rime. Rime may
be defined as similarity of sound between words, espe-

cially words at the ends of lines. A perfect rime requires the following conditions regarding riming words:

1. The vowel sounds bearing the verse stress should be the same.

2. The consonants, if any, preceding the vowels should be different.

3. The consonant sounds following the vowels should be the same.

The following groups of words meet these conditions and constitute perfect rimes:

park	greet	play	be	make	fate
lark	meet	gay	sea	break	late

Such groups as the following are sometimes rimed, but they are not perfect rimes:

blood	wood	dove	move	pen	been

Such groups as the following are not rimes at all:

then	send	bent	bend	bless	nest

The identical sounds below are not considered rimes:

weigh	rain	break	scene
way	rein	brake	seen

273. Couplets and Stanzas

A group of two consecutive riming lines is called a *couplet*. The commonest form of couplet is the iambic pentameter, often called the *heroic* couplet, or simply the *riming* couplet. It is the prevailing form of verse in the works of Pope and several other eighteenth-century writers.

> Know then thyself, presume not God to scan;
> The proper study of mankind is man.

Another common couplet is the iambic tetrameter:

> The stag at eve had drunk his fill,
> Where danced the moon on Monan's rill.

A third familiar couplet is the trochaic tetrameter:

> Tiger, Tiger, burning bright
> In the forest of the night.

A group of more than two riming lines is called a *stanza*. There are a great variety of forms of the stanza in English verse, but we need consider only a few in this brief discussion. A common form is the *ballad stanza*, of four iambic lines, alternating tetrameter and trimeter, as follows:

> "No, Douglas," saith Earl Percy then,
> "Thy proffer I do scorn;
> I will not yield to any Scot
> That ever yet was born."

It may be well at this point for us to learn the way of indicating the arrangement of the rimes in a stanza. Such an arrangement is called the *rime scheme*. It is indicated by the first letters of the alphabet, and the same letter is used to represent rimes, or riming words. Thus the preceding ballad stanza would be represented as follows: *abcb*, the *b's* denoting the rime. Hereafter rimes will be indicated by means of the rime scheme.

A second familiar stanza is the iambic tetrameter, riming *abab*. It is illustrated by the following lines referring to Shakespeare:

> Yet 'twas the king of England's kings;   [a]
> The rest with all their pomp and trains,   [b]
> Are moldered, half-remembered things;   [a]
> 'Tis he alone that lives and reigns.   [b]

Another familiar stanza is the so-called *elegiac*:

Full many a gem of purest ray serene	[a]
The dark unfathomed caves of ocean bear:	[b]
Full many a flower is born to blush unseen,	[a]
And waste its sweetness on the desert air.	[b]

The foregoing stanzas are examples of the *quatrain*, or stanza of four lines riming alternately. Besides quatrains, there are stanzas of three, five, six, seven, eight, and nine lines. A good example of the five-line stanza is found in Shelley's "To a Skylark":

The pale purple even	[a]
Melts around thy flight;	[b]
Like a star of Heaven,	[a]
In the broad daylight	[b]
Thou art unseen, but yet I hear thy shrill delight	[b]

The stanza of six lines is used in Longfellow's "Village Blacksmith," and the seven line stanza in "America." A stanza of eight lines is illustrated by Swinburne's "The Garden of Proserpine":

I am tired of tears and laughter,	[a]
And men that laugh and weep;	[b]
Of what may come hereafter	[a]
For men that sow to reap:	[b]
I am weary of days and hours,	[c]
Blown buds of barren flowers,	[c]
Desires and dreams and powers	[c]
And everything but sleep.	[b]

The stanza of nine lines, known as the *Spenserian stanza*, Keats employed in his "Eve of St. Agnes."

274. Blank Verse

A great deal of verse does not contain any rime at all. Rhythm is essential to verse, but rime is not. Neither

"Evangeline" nor "Hiawatha" contains rime. The term *blank verse* is used loosely to designate any unrimed verse, but strictly the term should be used in reference to *iambic-pentameter* lines only. The following blank-verse lines are from Tennyson's "Morte d'Arthur":

> So all day long the noise of battle rolled
> Among the mountains by the winter sea,
> Until King Arthur's table, man by man,
> Had fallen in Lyonnesse about their lord.

275. Free Verse

Free verse may be defined as rhythmical poetry composed without regard for meter or rime. These lines from Walt Whitman illustrate free verse:

Sing on there in the swamp,
O singer bashful and tender, I hear your notes, I hear your call,
I hear, I come presently, I understand you,
But a moment I linger, for the lustrous star has detain'd me,
The star, my departing comrade, holds and detains me.

276. The Sonnet

The sonnet is a complete poem consisting of fourteen iambic-pentameter lines. It includes two distinct types: the Italian, or regular, and the English, or Shakespearean. The Italian sonnet consists of two parts: the first eight lines constitute the *octave*, which is composed of two quatrains; the last six lines form the *sestet*. The rime scheme of the regular, or Italian, sonnet is *abba abba cde cde*; or the sestet may rime *cdcdcd*. The rime scheme of the English, or Shakespearean, sonnet is *abab cdcd efef gg*. The couplet at the end is felt to emphasize the thought or the emotion expressed in the preceding lines.

The sonnet, "Nature," by Longfellow, given in Exercise 69, is a good example of the Italian, or regular, form.

The Athenæum Press

GINN AND COMPANY · PRO-
PRIETORS · BOSTON · U.S.A.

SYMBOLS USED IN MARKING COMPOSITIONS

[Numbers refer to sections and divisions of sections.]

❖ GRAMMAR ❖

Ag.	Error in agreement: subject of verb (217); pronoun and antecedent (219); *this* and *that* (220).
Cs.	Wrong case form (218).
Gr.	Unspecified error in grammar (98–117; 217–238).
M.	Wrong mood of verb (227).
Pl.	Use plural instead of singular of a word.
Sg.	Use singular instead of plural of a word.
Tn.	Wrong tense of verb (225, 5 ; 226).

❖ SENTENCE STRUCTURE ❖

C.	Lack of coherence: in sentence (121).
C.F.	Comma fault (117).
E.	Poor sentence emphasis (122).
F.S.	Fragment of a sentence (115).
Ger.	Faulty reference of gerund (229).
Inf.	Faulty reference of infinitive (230).
K.	Awkward sentence; improve it.
O.S.	Overloaded sentence (120, 1 ; 237, 3).
P.F.	Period fault (116).
Pll.	Violation of parallel construction (121, 5 c ; 234).
Ptc.	Faulty reference of participle (228).
Ref.	Faulty reference of pronoun (121, 3 ; 219).
S.	Unspecified error in sentence structure (98–123; 216–238).
Tr.	Transpose a word, phrase, or clause to a better position in the sentence.
U.	Lack of unity (120).
∧	Necessary word or words omitted (238).
δ	Omit unnecessary word or words.

❖ CAPITALIZATION AND PUNCTUATION ❖

Cap.	Use capital letter (250).
Ital.	Underscore word or words once to denote italics (251).
l.c.	Use small letter instead of capital (250).
P.	Error in punctuation (239–249).